Praise for *The Scholar Denied*

"In *The Scholar Denied,* Aldon Morris tests, and convincingly proves, the belief, too long repressed, that W. E. B. Du Bois not only played a pivotal role in the birth of modern scientific sociology in America but was its founding father, on either side of the color line. Toppling prevailing truths like the towering genius at the center of this development, Morris's account offers a fresh and crisply researched reinterpretation of Du Bois's pathbreaking Atlanta school of sociology and is sure to be a major book."

—Henry Louis Gates Jr., Alphonse Fletcher University Professor, Harvard University

"Aldon Morris's *The Scholar Denied: W. E. B. Du Bois and the Birth of Modern Sociology* is one of those landmark studies that change the way we think about a historical occurrence. This well-written book is replete with original insights that challenge conventional wisdom on the origins and development of American sociology. Morris's meticulous scholarship, based on a careful analysis of revealing primary documents as well as secondary sources, details fascinating and new information regarding Du Bois's seminal role in the development of scientific sociology and his relationships with Booker T. Washington, Robert Park, and other members of the Chicago school, and with the preeminent social scientist Max Weber. *The Scholar Denied* is a must-read for those interested in how race, power, and economics determine the fate of intellectual schools."

—William Julius Wilson, Lewis P. and Linda L. Geyser University Professor, Harvard University

The Scholar Denied

The publisher gratefully acknowledges the generous support of the African American Studies Endowment Fund of the University of California Press Foundation.

The Scholar Denied

*W. E. B. Du Bois and
the Birth of Modern Sociology*

Aldon D. Morris

UNIVERSITY OF CALIFORNIA PRESS

University of California Press, one of the most distinguished university presses in the United States, enriches lives around the world by advancing scholarship in the humanities, social sciences, and natural sciences. Its activities are supported by the UC Press Foundation and by philanthropic contributions from individuals and institutions. For more information, visit www.ucpress.edu.

University of California Press
Oakland, California

Library of Congress Cataloging-in-Publication Data

Morris, Aldon D., author.
 The scholar denied : W.E.B. Du Bois and the birth of modern sociology / Aldon D. Morris.
   p. cm.
 Includes bibliographical references and index.
 ISBN 978-0-520-27635-2 (cloth : alk. paper)
 ISBN 978-0-520-28676-4 (pbk. : alk. paper)
 ISBN 978-0-520-96048-0 (ebook)
   1. Du Bois, W. E. B. (William Edward Burghardt), 1868–1963. 2. Sociology—United States—History. 3. Sociologists—United States. I. Title.
 E185.97.D73M67 2015
   301.092—dc23

                                    2014042410

Manufactured in the United States of America

24 23 22 21 20 19 18 17
10 9 8 7 6 5 4 3 2

In keeping with a commitment to support environmentally responsible and sustainable printing practices, UC Press has printed this book on Natures Natural, a fiber that contains 30% post-consumer waste and meets the minimum requirements of ANSI/NISO Z39.48–1992 (R 1997) (Permanence of Paper).

This book is dedicated to the pioneering scholars and researchers of the Du Bois–Atlanta school of sociology and to all scholars who have been denied because of discrimination and oppression. It is also dedicated to my mother, Mary Lyles, and my grandparents, Albert and Flavelia Morris.

Contents

Plates follow page 160

Preface

The origins of this book lie in my childhood in the heartland of Jim Crow racism in rural Tutwiler, Mississippi, where I was born in 1949. As a boy, I experienced and witnessed black life in the Deep South of the 1950s, drinking from the "colored" water fountain and receiving ice cream through the small shutter in back of the segregated Dairy Queen. I attended the small, colored elementary school, where during fall terms my classmates, who had not yet reached puberty, disappeared for several months to pick cotton so their families could survive. I was aware in the early hours of fall mornings that white men drove pickup trucks to the black side of town and loaded blacks to drop off on farms. I remember in blistering hot weather how whites sat under shade trees while we worked the fields dripping sweat from sunup to sundown. Yet, with all the backbreaking work, we never had enough to eat or adequate clothes to wear. As a young child, I tried to make sense of why we had it so bad while white children seemed to have it all. As an adult I now understand that I experienced a predicament that Du Bois had conceptualized as a caste system and a new slavery of debt peonage.

There was also fear and violence, both of which I experienced through the indoctrination of Jim Crow rules early in life. Those rules dictated how blacks were to respond to whites with deference, respect, and formality. They prescribed how black males were to act toward white women, including looking downward when in their presence and crossing the street when approaching them. Violating Jim Crow rules either out of ignorance or deliberately could result in severe punishment, including death. I also sensed the presence of fear and violence through hearing adults whispering about the horrors of blacks hanging from trees. They knew exactly what Billie Holiday meant when she sadly wailed, "Southern trees bear a strange fruit, / Blood on the leaves and blood at the root, / Black bodies swinging in the southern breeze, / Strange fruit hanging from the poplar trees." One of my earliest memories was the 1955 lynching of fourteen-year-old Emmett Till, a Chicagoan visiting Money, Mississippi, located less than thirty miles from my home. I am a member of what sociologist and freedom fighter Joyce Ladner coined the "Emmett Till Generation," blacks traumatized by the lynching, which left a lasting imprint. When I was six years old his murder rudely awakened me to racism and prompted the question of why whites could commit such a terrible crime against a boy not much older than I was. Caste, peonage debt, and racial violence became an enduring emotional and intellectual obsession that I sought to understand from a young age.

As a member of the last generation migrating northward in search of the Promised Land, I arrived in Chicago at the age of thirteen with my family. Shocked that Chicago had many features associated with Mississippi, I came to realize that being north of the Mason-Dixon line meant only that discrimination was more subtle and sometimes hidden. In fact, residential segregation in Chicago was even worse than that in Mississippi. Not long after our fishtailed 1957 Plymouth pulled up to my new residence on the South Side, I recognized that our northern home was in the all-black section of the Morgan Park community east of Vincennes Avenue and that it was clearly unequal to the all-white section of the Morgan Park and Beverley communities west of Vincennes. These inequalities were stamped in my consciousness as I cut grass and shoveled snow at the home of a wealthy white family while my mother cooked and cleaned their house. As fall set in, I found myself in the all-black Shoop Elementary School, although some of our teachers were whites and my new northern classmates ridiculed and disobeyed them in ways unimaginable to a southern boy. There were stark inequities between the schools in white and black communities. Because Morgan Park High School, which I had been about to attend, was predominantly white, officials intent on preventing a "black invasion" transformed my middle school into a "Shoop Branch" of Morgan Park, forestalling my entrance into the real high school by a year. In my own family life, my brother, Freddie, and I learned to anticipate fights when we crossed the color line to shop in the Evergreen Mall, located in the all-white Evergreen Park community. Shouts of "Niggers go home" and the harassment of aggressive white gangs became all too familiar.

When I was seventeen, I secured a job in the factory and discovered that blacks tended to be restricted to manual labor while whites filled managerial positions. That setting was reminiscent of Mississippi cotton fields where blacks labored and whites supervised. I became aware that racism did not stem merely from the hate of mean white segregationists but rather was a national phenomenon. Yet I had not developed the conceptual tools to dissect racism and expose the core mechanisms on which it thrived.

In 1963 a new and encouraging development hit like a bolt of lightning. As I tuned in to television, I witnessed southern blacks confronting racial injustices head on in Birmingham, Alabama, where blacks faced down the commissioner of public safety, Bull Connor, and his deputies, who employed vicious attack dogs and high-powered water hoses against them. I saw young black men and women students, along with preachers, workers, and ordinary people, courageously protesting and confronting dangerous and hostile segregationists in the streets and segregated establishments throughout the city. I saw Martin Luther King Jr. orate boldly to his people and in front of worldwide television cameras before leading the insurgents into notoriously dangerous jails. I marveled that the black masses agreed with King that protest was not wrong because, as King declared, if it were, the Constitution and God Almighty were wrong. I identified with Fannie Lou Hammer, whose home was twenty miles from my birthplace, when, even after being viciously beaten by jail guards on June 3, 1963, in Winona, Mississippi, she refused to accept oppression because she was "sick and tired of being sick and tired." But now I had a new puzzle with which to grapple. What stirred in the souls of black people to cause them to be swept into the vortex of a powerful social movement? What changed in these people who had been taught to obey racists or face the awful consequences? Would they be able to overthrow Jim Crow? I was consumed with issues social scientists would come to conceptualize as human agency and the ways oppressed people could use it to generate change.

While I am a product of the poor, black working class, whose members labored in factories, stockyards, construction sites, and the kitchens of the well-to-do, the value of education was always supreme in my grandparents' home in Mississippi and my mother's residence in Chicago. Although none of them had the opportunity to acquire much formal education, they preached its virtues among the young as the ticket out of poverty and hopelessness. When my siblings and I returned from any one day's activities, it was time for writing, spelling, and arithmetic, backed by parental claims that at least the white man could not take away your education. Nevertheless, making ends meet superseded purely intellectual endeavors such as reading scholarly or creative works, attending lectures or seminars, or engaging in intellectual sparring. Like all members of my social class, I seemed to face a future of manual labor, obeying bosses, and possibly joining a labor union.

The Vietnam War interrupted the preordained working-class script. I was jolted from my routine when, in 1968, I received my draft notice while working as a stock boy in a Spiegel Warehouse in Chicago. Keenly aware of images of the dancing, rhyming, heavyweight boxing champion Muhammad Ali, who had refused military induction, declaring, "No Viet Cong ever called me nigger!," I was torn between two paths: being forced to enroll in the military and most likely getting sent to Vietnam, or choosing to defy the government and being sent to jail. My solution came from a white hippie coworker, who advised, "Hey, why don't you do like my buddies and attend college so you can get a 4-F deferment?" Before the hippie's advice, my mother, Mary Lyles, had pleaded that I enter college and had issued a disguised challenge by suggesting I was afraid to compete. Thus the advice of my mother, the advice of a hippie, and a war raging in East Asia together caused me to enroll in Southeast Community College on the South Side of Chicago.

Choosing college was not simple. I did not have the conventional academic background or the resources to consider a four-year college and certainly not an elite university. When I had attended my predominantly white high school, I had been informed by teachers and counselors that I was not college material. I did not challenge this message because no one in my family or friendship circles offered counterclaims; most had not attended college themselves or even completed high school. My black classmates received the same message and prepared for vocational careers as our white counterparts took college preparatory classes and selected the universities they would attend. Thus, when pursuing higher education, like members of most poor, black and working-class families, I settled on junior college. After entering Southeast, I enrolled in a course titled "The Black Man in the United States," taught by an elderly black professor from the South. On the first day, as I entered class, he sat on his desk, legs crossed, surveying students as we took seats; suddenly, leaping up, he proclaimed, "When students enter a class and see a black instructor, they wonder whether he is competent. Well, stop it right now! I know what I am doing." For the entire semester, Professor Richard Maxwell mesmerized us with his profound understanding of black people and his sociological knowledge. Under his influence, I decided I wanted to become a sociologist and be like the dazzling, brilliant Maxwell who had introduced me to the works of the activist scholar W. E. B. Du Bois.

The centerpiece of Du Bois's scholarship was an account of his historic political confrontation with Booker T. Washington regarding effective routes to black liberation. Because accounts of this ideological struggle, as well as Du Bois's *Souls of Black Folk*, were riveting, I sought additional works authored by Du Bois.[1] One black English professor focused on Du Bois's literary significance: his writings ranged from sociological works to poetry, short stories, journalism, and fiction, and the often lyrical style of even his more academic work transgressed genre boundaries. I admired Du Bois not only for his sheer brilliance but also for his championship of black liberation and his role as a major contributor to the civil rights movement sweeping the country in the 1960s. My black professors appreciated Du Bois because he rose to leadership by the power of his pen. They also understood his importance as a leader of social movements and as a believer in social protest to generate liberation for black people. To embrace Du Bois was to claim their own heritage. Looking back, I realize that Southeast had an array of excellent black (and white) teachers who were locked out of elite institutions mostly because of discrimination or lack of the requisite credentials, such as a terminal degree. Yet they devoted themselves to educating generations of black students in the hope that, in so doing, they were contributing to black liberation and improving the chances of black people.

As I neared that day when I would proudly receive the associate of arts degree from Olive Harvey College (created by a merger between Southeast and Fenger College), I did not have plans to pursue additional education. Then one afternoon I marched in a protest of the December 4, 1969, early morning assassination, by Illinois Cook County sheriffs, of Black Panthers Fred Hampton and Mark Clark while they slept. As the protest reached its highest pitch, Professor Maxwell gently tapped my shoulder, suggesting that I go on to earn a bachelor's degree because it would be needed and because I possessed the intellect to succeed at the next level. By that time I was twenty years old, a full-time worker at International Harvester making "good money" and living in my own apartment. Over the next weeks, somewhat reluctantly, I accepted

Maxwell's advice because I had grown tired of monotonous factory work and the never-ending barking orders of white bosses. So I applied to Bradley, a private, mostly middle-class white university located in Peoria, Illinois, and, much to my surprise, was accepted as a junior.

A strange thing happened as I embarked on higher education at the white university: I grew to appreciate more fully my intense, challenging community college education. Naively I had entered Bradley unaware that black scholars, even at community colleges, were far more likely than white professors at elite universities to have read Du Bois and exposed students to his scholarship. I had thought I would have vast opportunities to become a sophisticated scholar because surely those white, elite professors would be well versed in Du Bois's scholarship, but that was not the reality. At Bradley, I was never introduced to any of Du Bois's work, although the one black sociology professor, Romeo B. Garrett, assured me that Du Bois had indeed been a sociologist, and it was obvious that Garrett had been influenced by the black pioneer.

Nevertheless, my undergrad years were full of intellectual excitement as I encountered the scholarship of Karl Marx, Max Weber, and Emile Durkheim. Immediately, I embraced Marx's class analysis along with his claims that proletarians would determine human history. From Weber, I gathered how modern capitalist societies were under the sway of large bureaucracies and were marching toward becoming dictatorships of monstrously large corporations. While I appreciated Durkheim's emphasis on stubborn social facts, I was less impressed by his obsession with solidarity because I did not think *that* concept was the paramount virtue to be embraced by an oppressed people in a society deeply stratified by race. Still I felt there was an intellectual lacuna because Du Bois's scholarship and worldwide racial inequalities were not topics of analysis. Their absence from discussion seemed particularly perverse at a time when protest and revolutions were forcing white oppressors in America and around the world to confront the color line and to begin the process of dismantling the systems that produced and maintained inequality.

Several Bradley professors played key roles in pushing me forward. Professor Leonardo Salamini introduced me to the Italian theorist Antonio Gramsci, with his ideas about organic intellectuals producing change. However, it was Professor Mohamed Najmi who insisted I attend graduate school and earn a doctorate. While I argued that I wanted to help liberate my people rather than become a do-nothing intellectual, Najmi feigned empathy but painted an idyllic picture of graduate school as a place where scholars sought knowledge to feed their hunger for understanding. Through this process, he claimed, students became intellectuals who were listened to because they had important things to say that the world needed to hear. Najmi guided me through the application process, writing numerous letters of recommendation on my behalf and insisting I rework countless drafts of my personal statement. An acceptance letter arrived, and off I went to SUNY, Stony Brook, hopeful that Du Bois's scholarship would be a part of the graduate curriculum.

In a graduate department of sociology I expected to study power and inequality, sociological theory, social movements, and Du Bois. Portions of that curriculum were fulfilled, but studying Du Bois proved elusive—even with Lewis Coser, who became an adviser and mentor that I met with every two weeks to discuss readings and "talk" sociology. Professor Coser interested me deeply because he was an important conflict analyst and an expert sociological theorist. Indeed, on the walls of Coser's office were arrayed pictures of Marx, Weber, Durkheim, and Mannheim that seemed to beckon the uninitiated to the paths of sociological wisdom. Yet as I studied the images I was disappointed to see no picture of Du Bois gracing Coser's wall.

In one session, I steeled my nerve and asked Professor Coser, "Why don't you have a picture of Du Bois on your wall?" From behind a gigantic puff of cigarette smoke, he responded in his cultured European accent, "Masters of sociological thought are those rare scholars who build theoretical systems, and Du Bois did not build such a system." I straightened up and responded, "But Professor Coser, what about Du Bois's pioneering work on race where he accurately predicted that the problem of the twentieth century would be the color line?" Coser was not persuaded. In a barrage of words, I inquired, "What about *The Philadelphia Negro* and *The Souls of Black Folk?*[2] Don't they show a master at work?" Coser, always graceful and gentle when it came to students, softly replied, "Du Bois was not a master of sociological thought." In that conclusion, Coser mirrored his generation, which also excluded Du Bois from mainstream sociological canons. White scholars of the second half of the twentieth century did not purposely ignore Du Bois; rather, thanks to the marginalization of Du Bois by the white founders of sociology, they were ignorant of his work. After that exchange with Coser, I took cues familiar to first-year graduate students that it was time to move to the next topic. However, I silently made a pledge in that office as the masters gazed from the wall: insofar as Du Bois was concerned, I would, one day, set the record straight. This book is my attempt to honor that promise by demonstrating that Du Bois was, indeed, a master of sociological thought.

From my junior college years I learned enough social thought to know that Du Bois had grappled with the meaning of race in America and the world. I was aware that he had revealed some of the dire consequences of racial oppression by peering deeply into the scarred psyches of whites and blacks who lived under the system of white supremacy. I also knew that Du Bois's scholarship was not limited to the academy because it was equally relevant for activists, political actors, and others who dared to change the world. I was struck that Du Bois did not erect insurmountable walls between scholarship and activism: as he wrote, he led and participated in important movements for justice. Thus, while Professor Maxwell primed my appetite for sociology, Du Bois deepened my desire to become a sociologist because he embodied the highest standards of scholarship and the courage to employ knowledge to inform social change.

Upon receiving my PhD in 1980, I landed my first academic job as an assistant professor at the University of Michigan, where I confronted, once again, the reality that Du Bois was not part of the curriculum. The absurdity of the omission was glaring because I was writing my first book, *Origins of the Civil Rights Movement,* which argued that the movement would not have been possible were it not for the cultural and material resources of the black church.[3] That insight had been gleaned from Du Bois's scholarship, which in 1899 had argued that the black church would be key in movements for liberation. When I relocated to Northwestern University in 1988 I began teaching graduate seminars on Du Bois's scholarship; in that manner, I made sure his scholarship was represented in the department of sociology. I felt, however, that the important but buried role Du Bois played in the founding and trajectory of American sociology was a story that deserved to be shared widely. The desire to tell that story is the motivation behind writing this book.

My purpose in writing *The Scholar Denied: W. E. B. Du Bois and the Birth of American Sociology* is an ambitious one, namely, to shift our perspective on the founding, a hundred years ago, of one of the social sciences in America. As it currently stands, narratives of the founding of American scientific sociology maintain that white men, at prestigious white universities, were the sole founders and developers of American sociology. In this view, black social scientists, and black universities, were not foundational contributors to the rise and development of the discipline. It is my contention that these narratives are inaccurate because they fail to acknowledge, or even mention, the pioneering role that Du Bois and his Atlanta school of sociology have played in American social science from its beginnings up to the present. In this work I argue that if Du Bois's scholarship had been placed at the center of the founding of the discipline a century ago, it would have provided both theoretical and methodological direction to this new intellectual endeavor.

Concomitantly, I am asking why Du Bois's seminal role in the founding of the discipline has been ignored, indeed, not even acknowledged. My journey here over the last decades is one of exploring, through primary documents, the role of Du Bois's school in founding sociology as an intellectual discipline, seeking to bring to the fore an as yet unexplored facet of American intellectual and social history. I show that such intellectual schools are not merely the products of intellectual networks and original, meritorious ideas but are deeply entangled with power, ruling ideologies, and economics. In this work, I lay bare the racism and power of dominant whites responsible for suppressing a seminal body of social scientific thought. My research shows also that even in the face of such discrimination intellectual work may, under certain conditions, have great influence through back channels and may actually flourish even a century later when discrimination eases.

METHODOLOGY

The Scholar Denied is based on a plethora of primary and secondary data. Because Du Bois was a public figure for well over six decades, I was able to draw upon an astounding wealth of documents, including autobiographies, letters, and papers. I began by examining archives at the University of Massachusetts–Amherst, Yale University, and Atlanta Clark University, then moved on to the Robert Park Papers at the University of Chicago, which proved invaluable in shedding light on the multiple roles Park played in the development of American sociology. These archives suggest that Du Bois had presciently anticipated the need for future scholars to be able to use his records to reconstruct his work and the era in which it unfolded. David Levering Lewis, Du Bois's Pulitzer Prize–winning biographer, alluded to this facet of Du Bois's sensibility by revealing that he had hoped his work would be appreciated and influential for future generations of scholars. I also dug into archival materials on Booker T. Washington. The substance of

Washington's life and politics is contained in the fifteen volumes of *The Booker T. Washington Papers*, edited by Louis R. Harlan, and these volumes also contain numerous letters concerning Du Bois, Robert Park, and other figures relevant to the origins of American sociology. Additionally, conference proceedings and biographies contributed exceedingly valuable primary data for this study.

Without primary sources many of the pivotal findings presented in this book would not be possible. For example, a central finding here is that although Du Bois is usually portrayed as a great isolated genius, he actually developed the first school of scientific sociology in the company of many thinkers and researchers. This group, consisting of the sociologists Monroe Work, Richard R. Wright Jr., George Edmund Haynes, and numerous educators and community leaders, conceptualized race as socially constructed and employed rigorous empirical methodologies to support their novel ideas. By utilizing letters, autobiographies, and conference proceedings, I bring these historical actors out of obscurity and onto the academic stage so that their contributions to modern social science can be integrated into the common stock of knowledge. In this manner, I resurrect a hidden generation of black sociologists who have been erased from the collective memory of the discipline.

Through letters, correspondences, and conference proceedings, I document how Booker T. Washington and his compatriot Robert E. Park conspired to obstruct and silence Du Bois politically, and how their actions imperiled Du Bois's influence as a founder of American sociology. In essence, I contend here that two black men—Du Bois and Washington—profoundly shaped the trajectory of American sociology. Finally, on the basis of letters and documents, I present a new interpretation of the relationship between Max Weber and Du Bois, differing from the usual one that describes Du Bois as having been an acolyte of Weber while attending the University of Berlin. My data reveals that, in actuality, the two scholars were contemporaries who mutually influenced each other. Moreover, I demonstrate that Du Bois had profound intellectual and political influence on the great German sociologist. Multiple sources of primary and secondary data drive the analyses of this book, making it possible to uncover neglected intellectual contributions from which to reevaluate the emergence of American social scientific thought. My analysis also sheds light on how intellectual schools take root and become enduring enterprises of thought. In particular, I focus on power, economics, and race as potent determiners of the fates of intellectual schools.

WHAT WE KNOW ABOUT DU BOISIAN SCHOLARSHIP

We are in the age of Du Bois. Over the last two decades an explosion of works has appeared on his life and scholarship. These works have been accompanied by conferences, panels, and awards honoring Du Bois. As this book makes clear, this is a new departure because the sociological profession, including the American Sociological Association (ASA), largely ignored Du Bois's work for a century. In 2005, I organized a small group of sociologists (Michael Schwartz, Mary Pattillo, Walter Allen, Dan Clawson, Howard Winant, and Cedric Herring) to head a campaign to persuade ASA's membership to vote to rename its top award for Du Bois. As a result of that campaign, the most prestigious award of the Association was renamed the W.E.B. Du Bois Career of Distinguished Scholarship Award. Such awards and new works on Du Bois have brought this pivotal thinker from relative obscurity to the forefront of academia.

In the 1970s, a few scholars documented Du Bois's pioneering efforts in the discipline. In 1974, Blackwell and Janowitz published a volume, *Black Sociologists,* highlighting important works of pioneering black sociologists and including two articles on Du Bois's scholarship.[4] That was followed by Green and Driver's 1978 volume, *W.E.B. DuBois on Sociology and the Black Community,* which contained excellent discussions of Du Bois's scholarship and selected works.[5] While these books brought Du Bois's work before sociologists, they tended to treat him as an important black sociologist who pioneered the sociological study of blacks, especially urban blacks given that Du Bois's *Philadelphia Negro* was the first scientific study of an urban black community.[6] The historian Manning Marable was one of the first to publish a full-length volume on Du Bois in 1986, *W.E.B. Du Bois: Black Radical Democrat,* addressing various aspects of his political and intellectual contributions.[7] And David Levering Lewis's two magisterial Pulitzer Prize–winning biographies of Du Bois in 1993 and 2000 marked the beginning of an upsurge in new scholarship on Du Bois. Lewis's biographies dealt with myriad aspects of Du Bois's long life and prolific scholarship.[8] Though not a social scientist himself, Lewis established Du Bois's importance as a pioneering social scientist and signaled the need for work focusing on Du Bois's foundational social scientific contributions. These works were followed by important edited volumes on Du Bois's scholarship, including those by Eric Sundquist in 1996, Michael Katz and Thomas Sugrue in 1998, and Gerald Horne and Mary Young in 2001.[9]

In 2004 the sociologist Phil Zuckerman edited an important volume, *The Social Theory of W. E. B. Du Bois,* demonstrating, contrary to the claims of those who viewed Du Bois merely as an analyst of blacks, that he was a major social theorist.[10] Zuckerman asserted that Du Bois deserved the canonical recognition as a founder of sociology that had been conferred on Marx, Weber and Durkheim. He made this case by selecting Du Bois's writings on important sociological issues and documenting how his various studies and essays made original contributions to sociological theory. Zuckerman argued that although race had been central in the development of the modern world, the white founders of the discipline had ignored it as a major variable in their analysis. For Zuckerman, Du Bois became the great theorist of race, contributing substantially to our understanding of modernity. My analysis agrees with Zuckerman's argument and builds on and extends it.

Adolph Reed's *W. E. B. Du Bois and American Political Thought* and Robert Gooding-Williams's *In the Shadow of Du Bois* are philosophically oriented works.[11] They concentrate on Du Bois's conception of race and his elitist views toward the black masses and how these greatly affected Du Bois's intellectual and political leadership. While benefiting from the arguments of Reed and Gooding-Williams, my work breaks new ground by placing Du Bois's views in the context of the development of the discipline of sociology. All these works discussed here represent a trend that began around the turn of the twenty-first century: Du Bois has emerged as a central figure in the academy and in a variety of intellectual endeavors and approaches.

Several works contain ideas directly relevant to this book. In 1998 Lee Baker authored *From Savage to Negro,* which advanced the idea that Du Bois was a major pioneer of American anthropology.[12] Lee also argued that Du Bois and Franz Boas generated a paradigmatic shift in racial thinking in the social sciences whereby race came to be viewed as a social construct rather than a biological category. He concluded that only Boas receives credit for the shift because of the power of American racism. In 2007 Shaun Gabbidon published *W. E. B. Du Bois on Crime and Justice: Laying the Foundations of Sociological Criminology,* which argued that Du Bois was an intellectual father of American criminology and that he established the first school of social scientific research in the United States.[13] *The Segregated Scholars,* by the historian Francille Wilson, has been extremely helpful in informing this book.[14] Wilson's study is not primarily concerned with Du Bois's scholarship; it also covers numerous other black social scientists and their work during the period of racial segregation in the United States. However, Wilson devotes a great deal of attention to Du Bois's pioneering social science and his mentoring of generations of black social scientists.

This book has benefited greatly from research by the sociologist Earl Wright II on the pioneering nature of Du Bois's sociological scholarship. In a series of articles, Wright has demonstrated that Du Bois founded the first school of American sociology.[15] He has described the contours of the Sociological Laboratory established by Du Bois at the turn of the twentieth century at Atlanta University. Wright has also explored the empirical methodologies Du Bois pioneered and has shed light on some of the scholars and researchers who contributed to Du Bois's school of sociology. Although my book goes far beyond Wright's efforts and differs substantially in many respects, his work has served as a foundational resource that has been enormously valuable to this book.

In 2010 Reiland Rabaka published *Against Epistemic Apartheid,* the first full-length book to explore the sociology of Du Bois.[16] Rabaka carefully compares Du Bois's insights with those of mainstream sociology, emphasizing their profound differences. He demonstrates how Du Bois's sociology defies disciplinary boundaries because it embraces history, anthropology, political science, economics, and the humanities. Rabaka shows that even within sociology Du Bois was a master of a broad range of topics, including urban and rural sociology and the sociology of education, class, race and gender stratification, recreation, culture, methodology, religion, and crime. *Against Epistemic Apartheid* offers valuable insight for the present work in providing a comprehensive assessment of Du Bois's sociological scholarship. However, it does not explore fundamental issues discussed in this book, including an account of Du Bois's social scientific school, the role of specific elites in blocking Du Bois's work, or the important relationship between Weber and Du Bois. In 2011 Lawrence A. Scaff published *Max Weber in America*, which contains new scholarship on how American race relations influenced Weber.[17] In a section directly relevant to this book, Scaff discusses aspects of the relationship between Weber and Du Bois and points to the important ways Du Bois influenced Weber. I build upon and extend Schaff's treatment of Weber and Du Bois.

The Scholar Denied offers new interpretations of the origins and development of American sociology even as it builds on the scholarship discussed above. I present an in-depth, detailed analysis of the reasons why Du Bois's school was the founding social scientific school of sociology, tracing the historical, political, and economic factors that gave rise to Du Bois's work; further, I probe how these factors also marginalized Du Bois's approach for a century while cementing the conventional story of the development of the Chicago school of sociology. This book offers, for the first time, a comparison between the Chicago school of sociology and Du Bois's Atlanta school, clearly showing that the latter theorized the novel view that race was a social construct and supported this position with pioneering methodologies and empirical research.

The Scholar Denied details the powerful roles of philanthropists, elite white scholars, and the conservative black leader Booker T. Washington in the development of the discipline. The important relationship between Du Bois and Max Weber is uncovered as well, as are the connections between Weberian and Du Boisian sociology. Finally, this book examines the achievements of Du Bois's social scientific school and sheds light on how schools of thought may develop under the most adverse conditions.

LOOKING AHEAD

Chapters 1 and 2 explore the role of race in the development of American sociology as well as Du Bois's general theoretical framework, contrasting it with that of his white predecessors and contemporaries. The evidence shows that Du Bois diverged sharply from the ideas of those white sociologists and that his ideas have endured because of their intellectual power. Chapter 3 describes Du Bois's social scientific school, revealing its organizational structure, collaborators, theoretic frame, and methodologies, and providing an overview of some of the main scholarship it produced.

Chapters 4 and 5 concentrate directly on the relationship between the Chicago school, Robert Park, Booker T. Washington, and Du Bois, demonstrating why the Chicago school and Washington had vested interests in marginalizing Du Bois; I argue that this marginalization was not accidental but deliberate. Here the interaction between economic and political ideologies and power is at the center of the analysis. Chapter 6 examines how Max Weber made his own scholarship richer by embracing Du Bois's scholarship, while Park, and the Chicago school, ignored Du Bois's scholarship, thus relegating a unique brand of scholarly work to the sidelines of American sociology.

Chapters 7 and 8 focus on how the Atlanta school survived powerful countervailing political and economic forces and became a major intellectual influence, leaving behind an important scholarly legacy that is still relevant today. These concluding chapters examine the social forces that affect the trajectories of schools of thought. They demonstrate that the fate of such schools is influenced as much by societal forces as by purely intellectual matters. Nevertheless, I contend that under certain conditions powerful ideas can triumph, even in the face of tremendous political and economic odds.

Acknowledgments

Many colleagues and friends were crucial in shaping *The Scholar Denied*. I am fortunate to have talented, insightful scholars as friends and critics. My friends have been my most challenging critics because they sought to leave no stones unturned as they examined the manuscript at various stages. Professors Walter Allen, Michael Schwartz, who has been my teacher and mentor since graduate school, Mary Pattillo, and Cheryl Johnson Odim treated this work as if it were their own, not only critiquing early drafts but also recommending revisions. Without their stern but loving guidance, this would be a different book. Their indefatigable efforts made this a better book by far.

Numerous scholars provided searching written critiques of *The Scholar Denied*. They include Art Stinchombe, Monica Prasad, Quincy Stewart, Gary Fine, Wendy Espeland, Joe Feagin, William Gamson, Lawrence Scaff, Pierre Saint-Arnaud, William Darity Jr., Mosi Ifatunji, Damon Sajnani, Earl Wright II, and Stephen Steinberg. Among this group are four generous and brilliant scholars who deeply influenced *The Scholar Denied*. I thank Professors David Levering Lewis, Robin G. Kelley, Martin Bulmer, and Charles Camic for providing ideas for the book that only they could render. I also thank Doug Mitchell of the University of Chicago Press for his feedback on an early version of the manuscript.

This book profited greatly from feedback I received from presentations at various universities including Princeton, Harvard, Chicago, and

Northwestern and the Universities of California, Los Angeles, Wisconsin, and North Carolina, as well as the annual meeting of the Association of Black Sociologists. Among those whose responses were compelling were William J. Wilson, Lawrence Bobo, Henry Louis Gates Jr., Pamela Oliver, Howard Taylor, Darnell Hunt, Franklin Wilson, Myra Ferree, Mitchell Duneier, John Bracey, Dorothy Roberts, Cheryl Gilkes, Karolyn Tyson, Kenneth Andrews, Darnell Hunt, Robert Paynter, Elijah Anderson, Tukufu Zuberi, Darlene Clark Hine, and Professor Sandra Taylor, who also facilitated my research at the Robert W. Woodruff Library, Atlanta University Center. I thank Yunuen Rodriguez for the research she provided on important topics of *The Scholar Denied*. I thank all the students at Northwestern University who have participated in my graduate seminar on Du Bois and helped to deepen and clarify my knowledge of Du Bois and sociological theory.

The Scholar Denied is heavily based on primary sources, especially those from over a century ago. Tracking down these sources required assistance from skilled librarians and archivists. I had two of the best in the world. Kathleen Bethel, African American studies librarian, has always taken the time to find sources nobody else could. I knew when I made a request that she would not rest until she exhausted all her "search engines" and was pleased to inform me, "Here it is, Professor Morris." Michael Flug, longtime archivist at the Vivian G. Harsh Research Collection and now director of the Harsh Archival Processing Project, has supported my research over three decades, always going the extra mile to find what I need. Like Kathleen, Michael is a gifted expert when it comes to unearthing difficult sources. I commend both Kathleen and Michael because they are treasures for the community of researchers and scholars. I thank Andrea Jackson and Kayin Shabazz at the Robert W. Woodruff Library, Atlanta University Center, for facilitating my research on Du Bois and his Atlanta school of sociology. Finally, I thank Jeremy Smith, digital project manager of the W.E.B. Du Bois Digitization Project Special Collections and University Archives at University of Massachusetts–Amherst, for facilitating my research on Du Bois and making available many of the photographs used for this book.

I had the good fortune of having as my editor Naomi Schneider, executive editor at the University of California Press. From the outset, Naomi developed an intellectual vision for *The Scholar Denied*. She challenged me to keep the big picture front and center and to always strive for clarity. Naomi assigned top-notch professionals to work with me, including editorial assistant Ally Power, production editor Jessica

Moll, and expert copyeditor Elisabeth Magnus. Naomi doubled as a stand-in psychoanalyst who soothed my anxieties as I confronted the inevitable twists and turns associated with writing a book. Thanks, Naomi, for being my partner on this project.

My personal posse sustained me, offered valuable input regarding the book, and demanded I listen. They had two concerns: Will you ever finish that book, and are you secretly gathering information on us to put in that book? They include comrades associated with Beauty Solution and other venues, including Wardell Luvert, Jet Ferguson, B.J. Slay, Renee Rose, Mary Whitehead, Carla Slay, Crystal Culler, Earl Gibson, Eugene Rogers, Clarence Burke, Marietta Bailey, Sharonda Ballentine, Dorothy Averyhart, Norvel Watkins, Beverly Coley, Thomas Sumner, Toni Brown, Gary and Marcia Everett, and David and Ingrid Myles. The inspiration of Donald Brown and Terry Murphy is always present in my work, and this is true for *The Scholar Denied*.

This book could not have been completed without the help of my family. My wife, Kim Morris, has put up with me all the years I have worked on this book. Over the final weeks, she was indispensable, choosing photographs and taming those unruly endnotes and references. I know I owe you big time, Kim. My daughters Kiana, Yondi, and Kamaria have assisted on various aspects of the book and have suffered mightily from hearing me repeat the arguments of the book. I thank my sons-in law, Michael Andrews and Pierre Keys, who supported me as I researched and wrote. To my grandchildren Jaden Merritt and Jordyn and Dallas Keys, I thank you for your patience when you simply wanted to play games with Big Papa, only to discover he was unavailable because he was working on something called a manuscript.

Introduction

Race and the Birth of American Sociology

There is an intriguing, well-kept secret regarding the founding of scientific sociology in America. The first school of scientific sociology in the United States was founded by a black professor located in a historically black university in the South. This reality flatly contradicts the accepted wisdom.

A broad consensus exists among sociologists that the Chicago school, which emerged in the second decade of the twentieth century, was the first school of American empirical sociology.[1] This hegemonic narrative maintains that the school's primary leader was the premier second-generation University of Chicago sociologist Robert Ezra Park. The Chicago school of sociology, which dominated the field well into the 1930s, was housed in the University of Chicago's prestigious department of sociology, founded in 1892, which included such other pioneering first-generation sociologists as W.I. Thomas, Charles Henderson, Ernest Burgess, Ellsworth Faris, and the chairman, the innovative Albion Small. These founding faculty members were augmented by the social psychologist George Herbert Mead and the philosopher John Dewey, both housed in Chicago's philosophy department, and colleagues in the geography and political science departments. The dominant narrative claims that this faculty, and especially Park, produced the major theories, concepts, and pathbreaking textbook that guided the emerging field for decades. The Chicago department trained large numbers of graduate students who conducted empirical research, published their scholarship widely, and became leaders in the field, thus spreading the influence of the Chicago school throughout American sociology and the other social sciences. Numerous works of the faculty and students were published by the University of Chicago Press and by the first journal of American sociology, the *American Journal of Sociology*, also published by the University of Chicago Press and edited by University of Chicago sociology professors.

The architects of the Chicago school established deep organizational roots at the University of Chicago. They successfully secured the funds that allowed it to build a formidable infrastructure to support the research activities of faculty and graduate students. Additionally, the city of Chicago served as a social laboratory where empirical research was conducted on the major social processes unfolding in one of the world's great modern cities. Because of these characteristics, the Chicago school dominated the early field of sociology, thus marking the rise of American scientific sociology. This lily-white and elite conception of the origins of American sociology has long been accepted as received wisdom.

Yet although it was only occasionally articulated in the twentieth century, there is a counterview. It argues that in the first years of that century the black sociologist, scholar, and activist W. E. B. Du Bois developed the first scientific school of sociology at Atlanta University, a historically black institution of higher learning located in the heart of Atlanta's black community. This counterview is largely unknown in mainstream academia, for it flies beneath the academic radar, disconnected from the dominant narrative of the origins of American sociology. Nevertheless, it has become more visible and has been developed by a small number of innovative scholars.[2] Even before it was explicitly formulated, a number of earlier accounts documented the importance of Du Bois as a black sociologist and his enduring but usually unacknowledged influence as a pioneer in sociology.[3] This tradition regarding Du Bois's importance as a sociologist has continued in contemporary accounts.[4] Though these earlier works provide only the beginnings of a definitive counternarrative, they nevertheless represent a solid foundation on which to build a comprehensive and accurate account of the emergence of American scientific sociology. Upon this foundation, I will develop an analysis of the myriad factors that gave rise to the Du Bois–Atlanta school.[5]

Definite political, economic, cultural, and personality factors led white social scientists to suppress Du Bois's scholarship of race and his unique contributions to the developing social sciences at the dawn of the twentieth century. That scholarship stood in direct opposition to the dominant racist views held by most social scientists, especially white sociologists. During this period, the Jim Crow regime, which defined blacks as biologically and culturally inferior, was developing deep roots. Du Bois's sociological arguments stressing that races were socially constructed and blacks were not biologically inferior flew in the face of white racial beliefs. As James McKee has demonstrated, white social scientists concurred with the general white consensus that blacks were created inferior and incapable of functioning as social equals of whites.[6] For them, genetics and culture, rather than social conditions, produced racial inequality. Yet that "scientific" knowledge constituted scientific racism, for it was based on folk concepts rather than careful, systematic, empirical research. The racial analyses of white social scientists, therefore, provided ideological cover for racism.

For Du Bois, externally imposed social conditions constituted the foundations of race oppression and white supremacy. In contrast to white social scientists, Du Bois insisted that the newly emerging social sciences be built on careful, empirical research focused on human action in order to pass the test as genuine science.[7] Because he believed that an authentic social science was possible and that inferior and superior races did not exist, Du Bois was the first social scientist to establish a sociological laboratory where systematic empirical research was conducted to determine the scientific causes of racial inequality. In this manner, Du Bois treated claims of inherent race superiority as hypotheses to be accepted or rejected on the basis of data collected through the best scientific methods available. Given his approach, Du Bois decried any racial findings stemming from racial prejudice and vested interests. Therefore, as the twentieth century opened, Du Bois continued to develop a sociology whose mission was to interject science into the emerging field by relying on data and the execution of scientific research based in empirical methodologies. This book will demonstrate that Du Bois, and his collaborators, did indeed build a sociological school that challenged scientific racism by generating findings suggesting races were socially constructed and that social conditions largely determined racial inequality. From a purely scientific perspective, Du Bois's school of sociology examining race was superior to the "scientific" research of the period—and of decades to come—that was based largely on conjecture, speculation, racist assumptions, and scant empirical data.

Thus there were obvious reasons why white sociologists suppressed Du Bois's scholarship. To embrace Du Bois's sociology, they would need to acknowledge that their theories proclaiming the biological and cultural inferiority of blacks could not be supported scientifically. Such an admission would have placed white social scientists at odds with the racial views of the white majority and those of white elites in particular. That would have been too ideologically jarring for them because they shared the white racist consensus and were not willing to distance themselves from the white privileges that sustained their "science."

Additionally, there were deep personal and cultural reasons why white social scientists suppressed Du Bois's scholarship. Early in the twentieth century, whites viewed all African Americans as inferior, even black intellectuals such as Du Bois. White social scientists could not embrace black excellence in science, let alone the superiority of a black scientist. To acknowledge Du Bois's pioneering science, they would have had to admit that Du Bois was a scientific role model deserving white followership. They could not conceive such a view and definitely could not translate it into practice. Thus they suppressed Du Bois's scholarship because it concluded that there were no scientific grounds on which to justify racial oppression and because they could not view Du Bois as an exemplary scholar who pioneered scientific sociology. Because the stakes were exceedingly high for white sociologists, Du Bois's sociology was suppressed, resulting in an impoverished sociology that endured over a century.

On the basis of my findings, I will argue that the Du Bois–Atlanta school deserves credit for founding scientific sociology in America. This book documents the unique contributions that Du Bois's school made to the development of American sociology in terms of scholarship, research, and teaching.

I posit that it was Du Bois who made the most distinctive contribution to American sociology in the first half of the twentieth century. That contribution, rooted in the idea that sociology was an empirical science, consisted of producing community studies and theoretical formulations based on empirical methodology.[8] Though Du Bois's pioneering community studies utilized scientific methodology two decades before Park and his students, this distinctive contribution has nevertheless been attributed to the Chicago school. Moreover, I will provide evidence that Park knew about Du Bois's pioneering studies but failed to accord them the scholarly credit they merited. Even worse, by ignoring Du Bois's groundbreaking scientific work, the Chicago school, mainstream sociology, and social science generally were impoverished theoretically and methodologically for a century—and this is especially true regarding the study of race. Because Park and the Chicago school failed to acknowledge and engage the work of Du Bois and his students, they were able to claim Chicago's primacy. This stance prepared the way for succeeding generations of scholars to reproduce this fictitious account, thus solidifying the claim that Chicago was the first school of American scientific sociology. The influence of this inaccurate account of the origins of American sociology reflects the wisdom of W.I. Thomas's precept: If people define situations as real, they are real in their consequences.[9]

CHAPTER I

The Rise of Scientific Sociology in America

American sociology began in the last decade of the nineteenth century, less than a generation after the emancipation of American slaves. The fate of emancipated blacks, who desired rights and privileges accorded free citizens of a democracy, was a divisive issue. The majority of whites, both North and South, were squeamish about granting citizenship to blacks, whom they viewed as an inferior race. Beyond ideology lay naked economic and political interests because southern white elites needed cheap labor akin to that provided by slaves if they were to remain a ruling aristocracy. During the late nineteenth and early twentieth centuries, white northern capitalists also required cheap labor to fuel the massive industrialization rapidly developing within the factory system embedded in American cities. Northern elites addressed their vast needs for cheap labor by hiring European immigrants. Yet African Americans fleeing southern economic exploitation, political disenfranchisement, and social degradation were also utilized in the North to augment the labor force and to serve as a divisive wedge preventing the development of a working class united across racial lines.[1]

Class conflict between recent immigrants and capitalists generated protest, strikes, and violence. However, when blacks were added to the equation, social relations between all parties became explosive.[2] In the North, racial tensions were exacerbated when blacks were used as strikebreakers and when the two races competed for limited housing and desirable spaces in urban areas.[3] In the South, white elites struggled

6

with challenges stemming from exploiting both .
white working class.[4] The question concerning the t...
toward an answer at the dawn of the twentieth centu...
look shaped by two and half centuries of slavery, the
along with white scholars such as Frederick Hoffman, vie...
an inferior, criminally diseased race, unfit for intimate a...
Indeed, leading white scholars argued that blacks were so me...
physically afflicted they would soon become extinct.[6] Black s ...lars
such as Du Bois and Kelly Miller, who were appalled by these claims
and the flawed evidence on which they rested, felt compelled to dispute
the thesis by presenting evidence to the contrary.[7] Even newly arrived
poor immigrants quickly internalized the view of black inferiority and
embraced whiteness because it conferred racial privileges.[8] For most
whites, the place for blacks was at the bottom of the social order.

The formal Jim Crow regime was hammered into place throughout
the South during the last decade of the nineteenth century.[9] Its purpose
was to relegate blacks to the bottom of southern society, rendering them
vulnerable to maximum exploitation. Jim Crow laws spread rapidly
through the South, leaving in their wake racial segregation, lynching,
white terrorist organizations, widespread black economic exploitation,
and political disenfranchisement.[10] In the North, de facto racial segregation and widespread economic exploitation and political oppression differed only in degree from the southern Jim Crow regime.[11] Tensions
between blacks and white immigrants were acute, giving rise to hostile
confrontations and race riots, especially over economic competition,
housing, and racial segregation. The combination of social conditions
that came to be known as the "Negro Problem" encapsulated the struggles between whites and former slaves, who, as free persons, competed
for jobs and demanded social equality. Because of stiff white resistance
to black aspirations, Du Bois, at the beginning of the twentieth century,
concluded that the major unasked question of whites regarding blacks
was: How does it feel to be a problem?[12] Du Bois answered that "being
a problem is a strange experience,—peculiar even for one who has never
been anything else, save perhaps in babyhood and in Europe."[13] Because
American sociology rose during the period of rapid industrialization
accompanied by race and ethnic conflicts, it had little choice but to
address these realities theoretically and empirically if it was to be relevant as a newcomer to the social sciences.[14] Indeed, during this period,
huge numbers of immigrants from diverse European countries flooded
American cities.[15] By the second decade of the twentieth century, tens of

...ions of immigrants with a variety of cultural heritages and languages had settled into distinct American neighborhoods. Because of limited space, resources, and housing, as well as growing ethnic hostilities and limited cultural familiarity with the host society, immigrants faced daunting conditions. The central question they confronted was whether they could be successfully assimilated into American society.

Thus America faced serious challenges regarding social relations between immigrants, blacks, and native-born whites during the period of rapid industrialization. Should it attempt to assimilate the immigrants, and if so, what should happen regarding their native cultures, languages, politics, religions, and ethnic associations?[16] How could the various class and ethnic differences be reconciled with the needs of capital? Like race issues, these combustible immigrant issues swirled in America as the new science of sociology struggled to gain a foothold in academia. At its birth, American sociology was faced with providing explanations for racial issues as well as for challenges associated with massive immigration from various European countries.

BOOKER T. WASHINGTON AND THE NEGRO SOLUTION

The saga of the highly significant role played by the great conservative black leader Booker T. Washington in the emergence of American sociology is unfamiliar to most social scientists. Given Washington's significance, it is crucial to provide a brief history of his leadership. In 1903, Du Bois predicted that the twentieth century's major problem would be the color line.[17] Du Bois, who had written his dissertation on the slave trade and published an important book based on it, was well aware that race had been a major global issue for centuries.[18] He was also aware of the "scramble for Africa" that had consolidated European colonization of Africa during the last two decades of the nineteenth century.[19] Yet for Du Bois this global system of racial inequality that stretched throughout Africa, the Americas, and Asia would reach its zenith in the twentieth century, triggering far-flung economic, political, and racial consequences. Booker T. Washington was to become a major player in this global struggle, especially within the American context.

Racial domination was a volatile enterprise whose management and future were uncertain. As a result, in the early twentieth century dominant white regimes searched for the paths of least resistance to their rule. By 1895, the racially egalitarian practices of the Reconstruction period were being replaced by the oppressive Jim Crow regime. This brutal neo-slavery regime stripped blacks of political and social rights and segregated them at the bottom of society. Lynchings and other white terror attacks were effective tools used to achieve black subordination, ensuring that the recently freed slaves remained an available and docile workforce.[20] Meanwhile, in the North, racial discrimination, enforced by legal measures, customs, and violence, was becoming a fact of daily life.[21]

Cooperation by blacks in their own oppression was a key factor in their subordination. This cooperation was not guaranteed, given the protest tradition developed during slave revolts, the abolitionist movement, the Civil War, and the Reconstruction period. Indeed, Frederick Douglass, the militant black leader of the abolitionist movement, who died in 1895, had represented bold, ceaseless protest as the route to black freedom. The ability of southern whites to subordinate blacks without serious resistance rested significantly on the type of black leadership that would replace Douglass. Just seven months after Douglass's death, white Americans, and European powers involved in colonizing Africa received a wonderful gift of black leadership—Booker T. Washington. In September of 1895, Washington delivered an epochal speech that came to be known as the Atlanta compromise. As soon as it was uttered, whites knew they had found a black leader who did not threaten their basic interests. Indeed, rabid southern segregationists, as well as northern white elites, engaged in immediate and unprecedented praise of the new black Moses.

Born a slave on a plantation in Virginia around 1856, Washington upon his emancipation began toiling in salt furnaces and coal mines at the age of nine.[22] After completing elementary school, he attended the Hampton Normal and Agricultural Institute in Virginia, where he paid his expenses by working as the school's janitor. Hampton's guiding philosophy, and its specialized curriculum, promoted industrial education as the solution for the oppressed black race. Such education was designed to teach students to perform manual labor, which was proclaimed to be the foundation on which blacks could establish economic independence. The industrial curriculum taught that blacks were best fitted for manual labor, which required patience and discipline. Because this philosophy embraced industrial education, blacks were counseled to avoid politics and eschew notions of social equality. By the time Washington graduated from Hampton in 1875, he had thoroughly internalized the school's doctrine stressing industrial education, manual labor, and subservience as the salvation for recently emancipated blacks.

In 1881, Washington became the principal of Tuskegee Normal Institute for Industrial Education in Tuskegee, Alabama. In this setting, he quickly emerged as the most prominent black educator, spreading the doctrine throughout the nation that industrial education, rather than politics and agitation, was the route to black success and white acceptance. Tuskegee served as the operating base where Washington, his faculty, and his staff trained scores of students in industrial education and the etiquette required of civilized people. As a result, Tuskegee became the model for other schools that spread across the South preaching racial uplift through character building and industrial education. However, Washington was not destined to remain a mere educator because his racial message was sweet music to the ears of southern elites and northern capitalists seeking to nurture a docile black labor force and maintain deeply unequal race relations that would nevertheless be harmonious.[23] Washington's philosophy and its implementation did not threaten the emerging Jim Crow regime requiring racial segregation and black subordination.

Washington's opportunity to spread his message more broadly came during the 1895 Atlanta World Exposition, where he delivered a gripping speech. Standing before an audience of white elites and recently emancipated blacks, he thundered out positions addressing economics, politics, and social relations. Economically, he declared, blacks were best fitted for manual jobs like carpentry, cooking, brick masonry, housekeeping, and blacksmithing. Implicitly referring to blacks' political equality during Reconstruction as a mistake, he argued that because blacks were "ignorant and inexperienced, it is not strange that in the first years of our new life we began at the top instead of at the bottom; that a seat in Congress or the state legislature was more sought than real estate or industrial skill; that the political convention or stump speaking had more attractions than starting a dairy farm or truck garden."[24] Washington embraced racial inequality, declaring, "It is at the bottom of life we must begin, and not at the top."[25]

At the time of the speech, Jim Crow laws were sweeping the South. Washington embraced their political consequences, counseling that "in all things that are purely social we can be as separate as the fingers, yet one as the hand in all things essential to mutual progress."[26] Concerned that whites would fear black anger and rebellion nourished by oppression, Washington assured them that blacks would remain loyal and politically passive. Soothing the concerns of white elites, Washington attempted to touch their hearts, informing them: "You and your families will be surrounded by the most patient, faithful, law-abiding, and unresentful people that the world has seen. As we have proved our loyalty to you in the past, in nursing your children, watching by the sickbed of your mothers and fathers, and often following them with tear-dimmed eyes to their graves, so in the future, in our humble way, we shall stand by you with a devotion that no foreigner can approach, ready to lay down our lives, if need be, in defense of yours."[27]

Washington made clear that balmy day, as he would the rest of his career, that blacks should pursue manual labor and industrial development rather than concentrating on liberal arts. He urged blacks to learn to glorify and dignify manual labor because "no race can prosper till it learns that there is as much dignity in tilling a field as in writing a poem."[28] Because of these calculated pronouncements, the Atlanta speech catapulted Washington into leadership status over black America and made him useful to European colonizers, who elevated him as a model to be imitated by colonized people globally.

Washington did not hesitate to solidify his leadership. His overall racial philosophy meshed with that era of white supremacy, for it was rooted in a social Darwinism that divided the world into a racial hierarchy with civilized white people at the top and uncivilized people of color at the bottom.[29] In this scheme, Western whites represented the most advanced civilization the world over, while Africans represented the world's crudest, most uncivilized savages.[30] Consistent with this theory, Washington viewed recently emancipated slaves as existing in a state of semibarbarism. He argued that slavery had been a civilizing force for American blacks because, "notwithstanding the cruelty and moral wrong of slavery, the ten million Negroes inhabiting this country, who themselves or whose ancestors went through the school of American slavery, are in a stronger and more hopeful condition, materially, intellectually, morally, and religiously, than is true of an equal number of black people in any other portions of the globe."[31] For Washington, "The black man got nearly as much out of slavery as the white man did."[32] Because Washington viewed American whites as the most advanced civilization in the world, it followed that blacks needed to prove their worth to earn white respect.[33] Such recognition could be gained only through manual labor, which built character and the industrial skills that could make blacks economically independent. Washington steadfastly preached that black racial development could not be hurried by force or protest; it would emerge gradually over centuries by the efforts of patient, disciplined, blacks bearing no ill will or desire for revenge.

Washington believed that blacks, who had only recently shaken off the chains of slavery, had to engage in an all-out effort of character building if they were to become fully civilized.[34] Blacks, in his view, had to learn to use basic hygiene techniques, eat properly, speak and dress correctly, and avoid suspicious immoral activities, including crime, drinking, and carrying weapons.[35] Blacks should conduct themselves in a manner connoting dignity and self-respect. At his Tuskegee Institute, Washington constructed a social environment designed to create a modern civilized black race with a solid economic base that would garner white respect and acceptance. In Weberian terms, Washington believed that blacks needed to develop an inward asceticism that would inculcate the discipline and cultural practices necessary for a people to become successful in a capitalist world.[36] In 1904 Max Weber wrote Washington that "I was, some weeks ago, at Tuskegee, and my wife and myself were so deeply impressed by all we saw and learned there," concluding, "It was—I am sorry to say this—*only* at Tuskegee I found *enthusiasm* in the South at all."[37] According to the Weberian scholar Lawrence Scaff, Tuskegee represented for Weber an "effort aiming at the reconstitution of the moral order and the human personality."[38] Washington was as adamant about this cultural work as he was about developing black economic independence because he thought a main reason for blacks' inequality was their lack of civilization. As will be demonstrated later, this view constituted the Washingtonian argument "explaining" black inequality that would later be embraced by the Chicago school of sociology in the 1920s.[39] Washington's leadership was backed by a powerful organization that Du Bois and Monroe Trotter referred to as the "Tuskegee Machine."[40] The "machine" flourished because it was bankrolled by some of America's most powerful and wealthiest whites. Because Washington understood the power of the press, he cultivated newspaper reporters and book editors so that they would use their pages to spread the Tuskegee message far and wide.[41] It was critical, therefore, that Washington maintain top-level experts who specialized in media and publishing. Washington's media reach was so extensive, especially in the black press, that Elliott Rudwick referred to the black press as Tuskegeean-dominated.[42] The Tuskegee Machine also thrived by silencing and co-opting black rivals, planting spies to monitor their affairs, and writing unfavorable articles on them in newspapers and other popular outlets. Most of all, Washington controlled black rivals by controlling the allocation of resources, for he became the gatekeeper determining which Negroes were funded or appointed to important positions.

Washington developed specific strategies for discrediting radical northern black intellectuals who had been highly educated in eastern universities, especially Harvard and other Ivy League institutions. Using newspapers, magazines, books, contacts with influential individuals, and the public sphere, Washington smeared them as unfortunate, misguided, impatient agitators whose heads were filled with abstract, useless book knowledge. An effective Washingtonian tactic was to smear rivals as race hustlers: "Having learned that they are able to make a living out of their troubles, they have grown into the settled habit of advertising their wrongs—partly because they want sympathy and partly because it pays. Some of these people do not want the Negro to lose his grievances, because they do not want to lose their jobs."[43] These northern intellectuals, Washington argued, ignored real solutions while spending their energies fighting windmills. He labeled them as arrogant outsiders who did not understand southern Negroes. Washington possessed little affection for northern cities, viewing them as dens of iniquity that destroyed good earnest country blacks. He preached that blacks should avoid migrating to northern cities and should instead remain in their native southland. For him, the black problem was a southern problem and had to be solved in the South because the future of blacks rested there.

Following the Atlanta speech, Washington became the unquestioned black leader, embraced by white elites and the black masses.[44] Social scientists and white philanthropists gravitated to Washington because his Darwinian stance implied a bright future for white privilege. This admiration of white sociologists, and some blacks as well, was on full display when Booker Washington addressed the Washington Conference of the National Sociological Society in 1903 on the topic "Race Harmony, the City Negro, Rape and Lynchings." When Washington entered the church where the conference was being held, he "was greeted with prolonged clapping of hands." The group chairperson, Kelly Miller, who was chair of Howard University's sociology department, announced, "I noticed that the great Tuskegeeian, Prof. Booker T. Washington, has entered the house, and I move you that unanimous consent be granted him to speak on any subject agreeable to him."[45] The esteemed guest proceeded by espousing his doctrine of racial accommodation and asked that sociologists follow his lead. He reminded them that the majority of Negroes lived in the rural South and that the race problem needed to be solved there even though this meeting focused on city Negroes. He insisted that while agitation and protest had their place, members of this learned society should focus on constructive solutions. He ended by declaring, "We have got to do our duty. In a great many cases you have got to wait patiently for results. If we keep on doing our duty, whether we see immediate results or not, the results will take care of themselves."[46] From the floor, a sociologist wondered whether Washington's method was effective but still concluded, "I believe what you say, that we must construct; we must do, if we can convince the people who are opposed to us that we can do."

Booker T. Washington's leadership had a profound impact on social scientists in the early twentieth century. This was so because his racial doctrines aligned with their scientific racism, which claimed that blacks were at the bottom of the social order because of biological and cultural inferiority. Even though Washington did not earn a college degree and was not a trained social scientist, he was often utilized by white social scientists to legitimate their findings on race. As the historian Francille Wilson points out, "At the meetings of white professional organizations, Booker T. Washington or a close associate might be asked to join a panel when Du Bois or one of his allies was making a presentation. Washington was frequently quoted by northern white academics . . . who felt obliged to deliver a scientific critique of the modernists' environmental thesis."[47] Indeed, while Washington's influence in politics is well known, his impact on social scientific thought is a neglected subject. In this book Washington's impact on sociological scholarship will be closely scrutinized.

Yet Washington's wide-ranging popularity and influence in political and academic circles would not go unchallenged. An intellectually gifted black social scientist and radical activist from the North would challenge the foundations of Washington's leadership and the philosophy on which it was based. I turn to the rise of W. E. B. Du Bois and his pioneering sociology.

CHAPTER 2

Du Bois, Scientific Sociology, and Race

Beginning in childhood, W.E.B. Du Bois imbibed different social and political views than Booker T. Washington. He descended from northern free blacks and became an intellectual who delighted in ideas.[1] As a young man, Du Bois decided to distinguish himself as a man of letters and a master of scholarship.[2] Yet Du Bois's aspirations were not rooted merely in the desire for great personal achievement. He aspired to liberate the oppressed black race by becoming an ambassador in the kingdom of culture, where his scholarship could be used as a weapon for racial liberation. In contrast to Washington, who was trained in industrial education, Du Bois was the quintessential liberal arts devotee who received the best and broadest education possible during the late nineteenth century. Born in 1868 in Great Barrington, Massachusetts, into a relatively poor home headed by his mother, who worked as a domestic, Du Bois earned bachelor's degrees from Fisk and Harvard Universities, studied at the University of Berlin under some of the world's greatest social scientists, and became the first African American to earn a doctorate from Harvard.[3] Du Bois's literary skills surfaced early when at the age of fifteen he became a correspondent for the *New York Globe*, writing columns covering local news of the black community in Great Barrington. Du Bois had high self-esteem, appearing never to doubt his abilities, as evidenced in a notebook entry on his twenty-fifth birthday, where he wondered whether it was the "silent call of the world spirit that makes me feel that I am royal and that beneath my scepter a world of Kings shall bow. . . . I am either a genius or a fool."[4]

15

Du Bois's academic training prepared him to become the founder of scientific sociology in the United States. Only a few isolated classes in sociology were being taught in American universities during Du Bois's attendance at Fisk and Harvard. At Fisk University, in Nashville, Tennessee, where Du Bois was an undergraduate from 1885 until 1888, he experienced southern Jim Crow racism firsthand. These racial experiences, sharply different from his experiences in the genteel racial climate of Great Barrington, where the black community was small and whites were relatively liberal, deepened Du Bois's identity as a black person and caused him to realize that his membership in the Negro race locked him outside white privilege. At Fisk, Du Bois discovered the existence of talented black people who aspired to be free of racism and accomplish lofty goals. He was also introduced to the poor, uneducated, black masses who toiled in circumstances not unlike those of slavery just three decades earlier. These revelations led Du Bois to cast his lot with the oppressed black race and embrace their strivings.

While attending Fisk, Du Bois immersed himself in a liberal arts curriculum, which also included classes on Germany, where he studied that country's history and language. As William Strickland has demonstrated, Du Bois became attracted to German politics and its political leaders, including the German chancellor, Otto Von Bismarck.[5] Because Du Bois was enamored with Bismarck's achievement of uniting a fractured Germany into a great empire, his Fisk commencement speech addressed the political significance of the German chancellor. Following graduation from Fisk, Du Bois attended Harvard as an undergraduate from 1888 to 1890 and completed his graduate work in history in 1895, becoming the first African American to earn a PhD at Harvard. While at Harvard, Du Bois studied with William James, the great scholar of religion and pragmatism. He also studied with the philosopher George Santayana, who introduced him to the German philosophical tradition, and with the Harvard historian Albert Bushnell Hart, who schooled him in the historical approach to scholarship.

At Fisk and Harvard, Du Bois studied philosophy, history, literature, and other liberal arts subjects, although he was most interested in social phenomena that would become the subject matter of the new discipline of sociology. During the late nineteenth century, it was customary for elite scholars interested in social science to study in Europe, especially under the great masters in German universities. Du Bois was acutely aware that given his aspiration to liberate African Americans through scholarship, and the view by whites that Negro scholars were incapable of attaining the highest levels of intellectual achievement, his scientific reputation would be enhanced if he studied social science in Germany at one of its great universities. Thus Du Bois, after seeking a scholarship to study abroad, finally received funds from the Slater Foundation that enabled him to study in Germany. As a result, he participated in the transatlantic exchange of ideas by studying political science at the University of Berlin in 1892–94 under Adolph Wagner and Gustav von Schmoller while being exposed to other leading German scholars including Heinrich von Treitschke, Wilhelm Dilthey, Rudolf von Gneist, and Max Weber. His enrollment there in political science initiated a journey that transformed his worldview and shaped what would be his approach to sociology.

The cruelty of American racism during the last decade of the nineteenth century made it nearly impossible for blacks in the United States to formulate self-evaluations independent of white stereotypes and thus to experience themselves as full human beings. In Du Bois's view, blacks at the dawn of the twentieth century grappled with the question "Am I an American, or a Negro?" This question became especially salient for Du Bois when he first entered Germany and was shocked to discover that in that country he was treated as a social equal of whites.[6] Here Du Bois gained the distance necessary to interrogate America from a new perspective. He explained, "In Germany in 1892, I found myself on the outside of the American world, looking in. With me were white folk—students, acquaintances, teachers—who viewed the scene with me. They did not always pause to regard me as a curiosity, or something sub-human; I was just a man of the somewhat privileged student rank, with whom they were glad to meet and talk over the world; particularly, the part of the world whence I came."[7] Further, his "unhampered social intermingling with Europeans of education and manners" enabled him to undergo a personal transformation and become a world citizen: "I emerged from the extremes of my racial provincialism. I became more human; learned the place in life of 'Wine, Women, and Song'; I ceased to hate or suspect people simply because they belonged to one race or color." In this liberating social climate, he recalled, "I builded great castles in Spain and lived therein. I dreamed and loved and wandered and sang."[8]

Du Bois's experiences of personal liberation in Germany and in Berlin in particular might seem surprising given just four decades later that country constructed concentration camps and launched its Holocaust against Jews to ensure Aryan white supremacy. But, in fact, Germany was far more liberal in its racial views at the turn of the twentieth century than it would be four decades later. Du Bois's experiences in

Germany as a student appear to have been typical for African Americans who visited that country during this time. In 1903, a decade after Du Bois left Germany, his sociological protégée Richard R. Wright Jr. underwent a similar transformation there. As Wright recalled, "Study in Germany was epoch-making in my life. I associated with students, men and women, who knew little or nothing about race prejudice; who, while curious about my color, never looked down upon it."[9] Wright made it clear that his novel racial experiences were not superficial: "I forgot American prejudice, for even the Americans in Germany treated me as a human being. I made it a point not to look up Americans and not to speak English. The barbers argued for an opportunity to cut my hair and shave me, without charge. Germans invited me to sit in train compartments with them, join them in all sorts of celebrations, etc. I was even asked to join the White-Black Club, whose purpose was to encourage intermarriage between Germans and Africans."[10]

Germany during the period when Du Bois and Wright were students was a far more liberal country racially and politically than early twentieth-century America. During the 1890s and early 1900s, Germany tolerated multiple political parties, and their members were able to express and enjoy their liberal freedoms. Such freedoms did not exclude doctrines of anti-Semitism in the academy, where it was espoused by some professors such as Heinrich von Treitschke. But at this time Germany boasted a relatively tolerant social environment and had not yet become rigid in its racial distinctions. This climate enabled Du Bois and Wright to become liberated and transformed psychologically into full human beings.

Another factor spurred Du Bois's and Wright's liberation in Germany: the harshness of American racism. During this period, the installation of the Jim Crow order proceeded swiftly and the number of lynchings of blacks escalated. By the second decade of the twentieth century, the American eugenics movement was consolidating strength as it developed the organizational and ideological infrastructure for its mission. The movement drew its inspiration from the English scientist Francis Galton, who in 1901 proclaimed he had developed the science of eugenics, which could identify the fittest human beings. In his view and that of his followers, a superior race of human beings could be produced through proper breeding and sterilization. Upper-class Western whites were "discovered" to be the superior stock of humans who deserved to be propagated through breeding across generations. They met the rigorous standards espoused by social Darwinists, whereas the

Negroes of the world automatically did not, given their innate biological and cultural inferiority.

The doctrines of eugenics fit well with the emerging Jim Crow system of racism and with the need to replace slavery with a docile black labor force exploitable by capital and an insecure white working class. Many powerful whites, including American social scientists, some of whom were distinguished founders of sociology, were attracted to eugenicist doctrines and hastened to organize an American eugenics movement. The first American sociological journal, the *American Journal of Sociology*, founded by the Chicago sociologist Albion Small, exposed sociologists to Galton's eugenics. The journal's lead 1904 article was by Galton: entitled "Eugenics: Its Definition, Scope, and Aims," it enumerated the principles of his new science.[11] Galton declared that eugenics "must be introduced into the national conscience, like a new religion. It has, indeed, strong claims to become an orthodox religious tenet of the future, for Eugenics co-operates with the workings of nature by securing that humanity shall be represented by the fittest races."[12] In the first highly visible textbook of American sociology, *Introduction to the Science of Sociology*, published in 1921, Robert E. Park and Ernest Burgess reprinted Galton's article, exposing it to a wide range of social scientists and generations of sociologists.[13] Eugenics clearly got an appreciative audience in the American academy and in sociology in the early decades of the twentieth century.

By the time German political elites began building up the ideological foundations for what would become the Nazi Holocaust, American white racism and the eugenics movement served as models for that country's system of white supremacy. To a significant degree, Hitler's racial science was imported from the United States, and the American eugenics movement identified with and supported the development of German Nazism.[14] Small wonder that Du Bois experienced racial liberation in Berlin while there as a student: at that time, racism was far more characteristic of the United States than of Germany, and the trip to Germany allowed Du Bois to escape it.

THE GERMAN HISTORICAL SCHOOL OF ECONOMICS

A crucial intellectual influence that prepared Du Bois to pioneer American scientific sociology was the German historical school of economics (GHSE) and its second generation of social scientists led by Gustav von Schmoller. This socialist-leaning wing of the School of Economics at the

University of Berlin rejected classical economics, arguing that it was the purveyor of abstract concepts such as the "free market" that did not exist in the empirical world. Schmoller, who became Du Bois's primary German mentor, and the other members of his group rejected grand theories and deductive reasoning. These scholars were quintessentially sociological, for they argued that social reality was a product of culture, customs, historical processes, institutions, and human agency. Axel Schafer captured the approach of the school: "They taught their American students to think of the economic organization of society as the reflection of specific ethical and customary views of a culture, not as the result of universal economic laws. They exhorted their students to study and understand economic life in the context of social customs, values, and institutions. They urged them to look at culture, rather than nature; at the environment, not genetics; at historical differences, not universal laws; and at ethical change, not moral absolutes."[15] In contrast to building abstract theoretical systems based on deductive reasoning, GHSE scholars advocated conducting careful empirical research focused on clearly defined questions. They insisted on a paradigm shift in which social science research would abandon the deductive approach and replace it with inductive reasoning. Sociological generalizations were to be based on empirical findings rather than on a priori systems of invented "natural" laws. The GHSE argued that these empirically based, objective generalizations constituted the scientific principles capable of guiding enlightened social reform.

During the closing decades of the nineteenth century, the GHSE conducted empirical research using qualitative and quantitative methods, including interviews, ethnographic research, and statistical analysis. This multimethods approach contrasted sharply with American social science research at the time, which relied almost exclusively on qualitative methods. As Camic and Xie have demonstrated, "In the late nineteenth century, American academic scholarship in the nascent social sciences still consisted mainly of historical and comparative methods pursued by going to the library or the study or the archives."[16] Moreover, in America during this period, quantitative analyses had not penetrated the natural or social sciences. A statistical approach to the sciences first developed in the mid-nineteenth century in Europe, where its pioneers argued that statistical and mathematical approaches constituted the cornerstone of the scientific enterprise. American pioneers of the statistical approach received their quantitative training in Europe before transplanting those methods to American science.[17] By the turn of twentieth century, America had only a handful of scholars trained in statistics who could conduct quantitative research and train students in those methods.

When Du Bois entered the University of Berlin's school of economics in 1892, he became one of the rare American social scientists being trained in statistics and quantitative analysis. By the time Du Bois arrived there, the multimethods approach of the GHSE already included and indeed required statistical training for students. Its proponents were publishing series of studies utilizing statistical analyses, such as articles from the acclaimed pioneer of American statistical analysis in the social sciences Richmond Mayo-Smith, who had been trained in statistics at Heidelberg and the University of Berlin.[18] While in Germany, Du Bois participated in seminars on statistics and performed statistical analysis. Regarding his 1893 doctoral dissertation, "Agriculture in the Southern United States," supervised by Schmoller, Du Bois wrote, "It is a statistical inquiry into the relative economic advantage of the large and small farm."[19]

Du Bois's training at the University of Berlin prepared him to lead the way in introducing quantitative methods into American social science and particularly sociology through both his research and the training of his students. Yet Charles Camic and Yu Xie, in their account of the original small group of social scientists who pioneered American statistical analyses, describe only the role of Mayo-Smith, Franklin Giddings, James Cattell, Franz Boas, and Henry Moore and ignore that of Du Bois.[20] Mayo-Smith and Giddings are given the credit for introducing statistics into the new discipline of sociology during a time when Du Bois was using statistics in his studies and in the classroom.[21]

Du Bois appropriated the emphasis of Schmoller and his school on careful studies that would rely on the collection of data through a variety of empirical methods to develop general principles that could serve as a basis for scientific reform.[22] Schmoller and his colleagues debated policy implications of their scientific work and developed policy recommendations for political leaders on pressing social problems. This policy dimension of the GHSE did not escape Du Bois's attention, for he already believed that scientific knowledge would help liberate oppressed blacks in America.

Undoubtedly Du Bois, who became a member of the GHSE's Verein für Sozialpolitik (Social Policy Association) where intellectual and policy issues were debated, was aware of dissensions and rivalries among senior professors in the GHSE over theoretical and methodological issues. But he seems to have avoided these contentious debates while embracing the school's core scientific principles, perhaps partly because he knew he had a relatively short time to study at the university and partly because he was concerned with what were for him more pressing intellectual and political issues: the establishment in America of a truly scientific social science that could constitute the intellectual foundation on which to liberate his race. As he shuttled between Wagner's and Schmoller's seminars and conducted research, he presented work at the meetings of the Verein that focused on the race problem in America. As he related, during this period "Above all I began to understand the real meaning of scientific research and the dim outline of methods of employing its technique and its results in the new social sciences for the settlement of the Negro problems in America."[23] In Berlin he concentrated on becoming a first-rate social scientist. As Frances Broderick wrote, "W. E. B. Du Bois went to Europe in 1892 an historian; he returned two years later a sociologist."[24]

THE MEANING OF RACE

Upon returning to "'nigger'-hating America," Du Bois embraced his life's work: the production of careful sociological studies of African Americans steeped in empirical data that could be used to discredit the dominant sociological and popular doctrine that blacks were forever stuck at the bottom of human civilizations because nature made them inferior.[25] The production of such knowledge, he reasoned, would lead to the general enlightenment that would end the oppression of his race. As he recalled, "I was going to study the facts, any and all facts, concerning the American Negro and his plight, and by measurement and comparison and research, work up to any valid generalization which I could."[26]

The scientific meaning of race was the issue that immediately drew Du Bois's attention. In the late nineteenth and early twentieth centuries, sociology was under the sway of grand theories developed by Comte, Spencer, Sumner, and Chicago school sociologists. Social Darwinism, embraced by the white founders of American sociology, claimed that society could be explained by natural laws.[27] Social Darwinists extended evolutionary theory to stress natural selection, survival of the fittest, and differentiation as the basic processes determining human behavior.[28] Grand theories, including social Darwinism, posited that a holistic "society" existed as an independent reality and embraced a deductive analytic strategy to "explain" its nature and functioning. Such theorizing based its proofs, not on empirical research, but on speculation and intuition.

Du Bois's sociology of race was deeply rooted in his conceptions of the theoretical and methodological nature of the new discipline of sociology. At the turn of the twentieth century, American social science was in its infancy, attempting to chart out its most basic theoretical and methodological orientations. The various national associations of the American social sciences were not organized until around the turn of the twentieth century, with the American Sociological Society being organized in 1905. Leading American and European natural and social scientists were interested in future directions of science and the relationship between the natural and the social sciences. Many of them desired to be involved on the ground floor where these weighty issues were being contested so they could put their individual stamp on the forms that the sciences might take. A large gathering of scholars assembled at the International Congress of Arts and Science, Universal Exposition, held in St. Louis in 1904. They hailed from around the world and constituted the leading experts in every branch of science. Among the German sociologists attending were Werner Sombart, Edgar Jaffe, Ferdinand Tönnies, and Max Weber. For Weber, this was an important event because it was his first public appearance since his recuperation from a six-year debilitating bout with mental illness. University of Chicago sociologists—W. I. Thomas, Charles Henderson, and Charles Vincent— were well represented at the congress. Albion Small, chairman and founder of Chicago's sociology department, served as a vice president of the congress and functioned as a major organizer of its social sciences division. The first American sociologist to hold a named chair, Franklin Giddings, was an important conference participant representing Columbia University. Regarding the caliber of participants and the expectations for their contributions, a congress organizer declared that the addresses would be "prepared by the highest living authorities in each and every branch."[29]

Du Bois was not invited to or consulted for the congress to chart new directions for the sciences. A former German colleague of Max Weber who had moved to Harvard, Professor Hugo Munsterberg, a guiding light of the congress, explained that it had the "definite task of bringing out the unity of knowledge with a view of correlating the scattered theoretical and practical scientific work of our day."[30] Few scholars were more prepared to contribute to these discussions than Du Bois. Indeed, Du Bois had been taught by many of the best American and

European scholars playing leading roles in the congress. At the time of the conference, he had published major scientific studies that had received critical praise both nationally and abroad. At age thirty-six, he had published far more works than most of the white scholars given prominent platforms at the congress. While there is evidence that Du Bois attended the congress, he did not make public presentations.[31]

Although Du Bois was not invited to participate in the St. Louis conference, he had important reasons to attend. His agenda included meeting over breakfast with the German sociologist Max Weber. Additionally, Du Bois was curious about how the discipline of sociology would be defined. The conference occurred when American social sciences and sociology were just emerging in the United States. Their future and stature were not at all clear, nor had their relationships with the natural sciences been determined. Sociology's future and scientific status were even less clear, and for Du Bois the conference reflected this uncertainty: "The Congress of Arts and Sciences at St. Louis last summer served to emphasize painfully the present plight of Sociology; for the devotee of the cult made the strange discovery that the further following of his bent threatened violent personal dismemberment. His objects of interest were distributed quite impartially under some six of the seven grand divisions of Science: economics, here; ethnology, there; a thing called 'Sociology' hidden under Mental Science, and the things really sociological ranged in a rag-bag and labeled 'Social Regulation.' And so on."[32] The mission of the conference was to address the status of the social sciences and its subfields so their futures could be charted.

Du Bois noted how the leading sociologists at the conference sought to address the troublesome theoretical and methodological challenges faced by the new discipline. From his critique of these efforts a year later, it is clear that he attended many of the conference's panels and forums to determine if his colleagues presented solutions to overcome the impasses confronting sociology. The conference provided Du Bois with evidence that sociological conferees were not even close to solving these issues but actually headed in the wrong direction. He utilized what he learned at the conference to fuel his own unique sociological approach and to provide trenchant critiques of the sociological status quo.

As this book will demonstrate, Du Bois's exclusion from the congress by his white contemporaries was not an isolated event but rather an instance of a pattern that persisted for over a century. The uninvited, marginalized Du Bois had definite views about the topics debated at the congress that he set down in an essay entitled "Sociology Hesitant," but it was not published during his lifetime. In this document, written around 1905, Du Bois chronicled his disagreements with the scholars at the congress. He presented theoretical and methodological solutions that he argued sociology would need to adopt if it was to bear analytical and programmatic fruit.[33]

At the congress, the system-building theories of Auguste Comte and Herbert Spencer loomed large in discussions regarding the future of sociology. Du Bois began his critique by arguing that Comte and Spencer's grand theories erred by positing an abstract "society" as a mystical whole that was the object to be studied rather than the concrete deeds and actions of men.[34] Du Bois described the quest for such grand systems as metaphysical wanderings and concluded that "Spencer and his imitators have done good, inspiring, but limited work."[35] But those limits, in his view, were fatal "because their data were imperfect—woefully imperfect: depending on hearsay, rumor and tradition, vague speculations, traveller's tales, legends and imperfect documents, the memory of memories and historic error."[36] Reflecting on the debates at the conference, Du Bois claimed that such sociological reasoning was flawed by an unscientific methodology that generated unsound data. He argued that for the new science of sociology to be scientific it had to be based on empirical data rather than armchair theorizing and what he called "car window sociology," quick and superficial generalizations about complex social phenomena like the impressions one might gather by glancing at scenes through the window of a fast-moving automobile. These approaches, argued Du Bois, only led to sterile concepts such as "'Consciousness of Kind,' 'Imitation,' the 'Social Imperative,' and the like."[37]

The concepts that Du Bois lists here represented the efforts of the first American sociologists to produce the one sociological principle driving all social interactions and social structures. The magical principle, reasoned each of these founders, was driven by natural laws operating in the same manner as those uncovered by natural scientists. Relying on armchair conjectures and inspiration, scholars competed furiously with each other regarding whose conceptual creation would be considered the supreme sociological key to understanding a universal social reality. Thus Franklin H. Giddings introduced the concept of "consciousness of kind" as "a state of consciousness in which any being . . . recognizes another conscious being as of like kind with itself"; on this basis, human beings established their own distinct social groupings in which they led their collective lives.[38] The French sociologist Gabriel Tarde and his American followers advanced the principle of "imitation" as the fundamental sociological mechanism driving humankind.[39] University of Pennsylvania sociology professor Samuel McCune Lindsay entered the fray with his concept of the "social imperative," defined as "the modifying influence which makes the individual act differently in the presence of his fellow man from the way in which he would act under the same circumstances if he were alone."[40] For Lindsay, the social imperative trumped all other units of sociological investigation, including the family, social man, or the social type. Albion Small argued for his principle of "interest" that drove social reality.[41] For Du Bois, these first principles were wrong-headed; they mistook abstractions for reality. Sociology was the science of human action, not an enterprise seeking to explain abstractions that begot more abstractions in a futile effort to discover universal laws.

By rejecting Spencerian organicism, Du Bois also made clear his rejection of social Darwinism: "The elaborate attempt to compare the social and animal organism failed," he wrote, "because analogy implies knowledge but does not supply it—[it] suggests but does not furnish lines of investigation."[42] Du Bois believed the main reason sociologists became trapped in the search for natural laws was their inferiority complex regarding natural scientists. He depicted sociologists as dumbfounded when confronted with questions such as "Is this science? Where are your natural laws? What sort of a science is a science without laws?"[43] Indeed, these were the kinds of questions that had been raised at the St. Louis Congress in 1904.

The search for comprehensive incontrovertible laws was inconsistent with Du Bois's conception of sociology. He argued that sociology should be developed as the science of human action, which would seek to understand both patterned behavior that unfolded in lawlike fashion and unpredicted lines of human action driven by chance. Chance factors were also crucial because human agency helped shape the outcomes of human behavior: "For a thousand and a thousand years, and today as strongly as, and even more strongly than, ever, men, after experiencing the facts of life, have almost universally assumed that in among physical forces stalk self-directing Wills, which modify, restrain, and re-direct the ordinary laws of nature. The assumption is tremendous in its import. It means that, from the point of view of Science, this is a world of Chance as well as Law."[44] Du Bois argued that sociology's task was to study and measure the interactions between social patterns that consistently structure human action and chance, or, in contemporary language, between structure and agency.[45] He believed that both dimensions of human behavior could be studied scientifically by sociology.

Throughout his career, Du Bois sought a dynamic sociology because in his view a static, mechanistic sociology based on universal laws of human behavior failed to capture social reality.[46] Du Bois's conception that sociological theory should account for the role of human agency in social events made it possible for him to undertake a "public sociology" approach that informed his academic sociology as well as his extensive career of social change activism.

Du Bois, therefore, broke from the dominant theoretical stance by arguing that there were no universal laws mechanistically governing human behaviors. His focus on the powerful role of human agency in human affairs was innovative when sociology was developing in America at the turn of the twentieth century. In this period, sociologists struggled to get a foothold inside academia and be recognized as legitimate in the same manner as natural scientists. To receive such recognition, sociologists felt compelled to demonstrate that human behavior was propelled by natural laws as sure as those governing ants or plants. Thus, one year following the congress, a group of pioneering sociologists founded the American Sociological Society to advance the professional interests of the new discipline. Its first president, Lester Ward, considered by some as the father of American sociology, gave the society's inaugural address. Ward claimed that sociology had proven that human behavior, like the inorganic behavior studied by the natural sciences, was guided by natural laws. He urged sociologists who aspired to professional status to be unintimidated by arguments that sociology was not a real science:

> The place of sociology among the sciences has been definitely fixed. It stands at the summit of the scale of great sciences arranged in the ascending order of specialty and complexity according to the law of evolutionary progress. It rests directly upon psychology, in which it has its roots, although it presents a great number of striking parallels with biology, chemistry, physics, and even astronomy, showing that there are universal laws operating in every domain of nature. The motor principle of sociology is psychic, and the study of this principle has shown that social phenomena are produced by the action of true natural forces, which, when abstraction is made of all perturbing elements, are found to be as regular and reliable as are the forces of gravitation, chemical affinity, or organic growth.[47]

Ward recognized that human behavior was both dynamic and static and that sociologists needed to study both dimensions. For him, the static aspect encompassed the study of social order while the dynamic dimension required study of the domain of social transformation, where processes of change modified social structures and human institutions. Nevertheless, Ward's conception of social dynamics differed from Du Bois's view of human chance. For Ward, both aspects were governed by natural laws because social statics and social dynamics had been discovered and formulated and their workings described by sociologists. Yet Ward was uncomfortable with the energy that social dynamics unleashed: "The social energy is so powerful as to exceed its proper bounds and threaten the overthrow of the social order, and would do so but for some effective curb to its action. The motion power of society has to be guided into channels through which it can flow in harmony with the safety of society. The guidance has been furnished by the higher mind or intellect of man."[48] For Ward, it was crucial that sociology discover the laws of socially transformative forces so those forces could be mastered and directed by responsible agents of the social order.

Scholars of the origins of American sociology agree that the white founders sought to uncover universal laws because they were upwardly mobile middle-class individuals who hungered for the legitimacy and recognition enjoyed by "hard" scientists in the business of formulating natural laws at work in the universe. Thus Anthony Oberschall concludes that the early founders were insecure and excessively self-conscious about their lack of professional legitimacy.[49] Breslau similarly asserts that "the social sciences faced special problems of legitimation, and their very presence in the new universities was by no means certain. They therefore imitated the established natural sciences in order to appear 'scientific.'"[50] They dreamed up natural laws of human behavior as part of a quest for cultural authority that would confer on them the status of "real" scientists.

Du Bois did not share the professional insecurities of the white founders. In 1900, while addressing graduates at Atlanta University regarding the need for sociological researchers, Du Bois revealed his conception of the new science:

> The study of society as it is carried on today is a slow and difficult task. No sociologist claims to present in his science any such finished system of laws and measurement as chemistry or astronomy—it is rather a great field of study where careful observers are daily counting, measuring and searching— gathering the data which another age will systematize and interpret. . . . It [sociology] has discovered no great or startling laws of human action and may never do so—but it has collected a mass of material of supreme interest and value, and of such a nature that no modern thinker who is interested in the condition and destiny of beings can afford to ignore its methods and results.[51]

As early as 1897, Du Bois offered a similar description of sociology's task, cautioning that it was not scientific in the same way as the work of the natural sciences: "But if you mean by sociology a vast and fruitful field of inquiry into the mysterious phenomena of human action, which has yielded evidence of the working of scientific laws to some extent, and promises much more for the future—if such a work deserves, as many think, the name of science, then Sociology is one of the greatest of sciences."[52] Du Bois had no need to posture as a "real scientist" building a system of natural laws to legitimate sociology. He was satisfied with the more modest ambition of elucidating human action in ways that took into account both its patterned, lawlike character and its unpredictable rhythms produced by human agency.

Du Bois rejected the idea that such socially transformative forces operated according to natural laws and could be rationally controlled in advance. This did not mean, however, that understanding human agency was beyond the reach of sociology. Rather, human agency had to be studied as a creative force capable of generating new directions and possibilities. Thus Du Bois insisted that the domain of the sociologist included the study of both patterned social structures and the unpredictable creative role of human agency. Moreover, he insisted that the sociologist, to arrive at sociological generalizations, had to study the deeds and interactions of real human beings rather than metaphysical constructions. Being true to his German historicist roots, Du Bois discarded the straitjacket of grand theories, including social Darwinism, and replaced them with an inductive method seeking sociological knowledge based on clearly defined empirical research. Clearly, Du Bois's conception of sociology at the dawn of the twentieth century prefigured the midcentury call by Robert Merton to construct sociological theories in the middle range rather than to pursue abstract grand theories.[53]

DU BOIS AND RACE

Du Bois formulated a social constructionist view of race. However, not all Du Boisian scholars interpret Du Bois as a social constructionist, especially in terms of race. I argue that Du Bois's sociology of race was rooted in the fundamental postulate that the people who in his political and historical moment were defined as "Negroes" were not inherently inferior to any other so-called race on earth, including "white Americans," as they were being called in the United States. Nevertheless, this argument is at variance with a prominent literature developed by social scientists and philosophers arguing the opposite. This alternative view claims that a biological conception lies at the heart of Du Bois's race analyses and that, contrary to his numerous claims otherwise, he believed what his white contemporaries contended, that blacks were racially inferior. This view has been given classic expression by the philosophers Anthony Appiah and Gooding-Williams and the political scientist Adolph Reed Jr. and the sociologist Jerry Watts.[54] Accompanying these claims is the argument that Du Bois was an elitist who had contempt for the black masses and viewed them as inferior to culturally refined individuals like himself. These scholars purport to prove these claims by using texts from Du Bois's own pen.

I take issue with these scholars and will demonstrate that their claims cannot be sustained. They privilege a selective assortment of isolated phrases and concepts extracted from Du Bois's writings and present them as pillars of Du Bois's thought. My differences with these scholars are based on an analysis of Du Bois's entire corpus of sociological work and particularly his work on the sociology of race, where his unique approach radically differentiates him from his social science contemporaries.

From certain characterizations of the black masses espoused by Du Bois it might appear that Appiah, Gooding-Williams, Reed, and Watts have grounds for arguing that Du Bois considered blacks to be an inferior race. In early writings Du Bois at times referred to blacks as "backward," of "low social grade," "undeveloped people," "ignorant," in a state of "race-childhood," "primitive folk," and in need of "guidance" from culturally superior groups, including selective whites. These characterizations, according to the critics, show that Du Bois, though usually considered to be a champion of black liberation, actually loathed the black masses and agreed with his white scholarly forebears and contemporaries that blacks were an inferior race. Because such serious charges deserve intense scrutiny, I turn to an investigation of their merits, but not before some caveats concerning language usage and politics. At the close of this discussion I explicate how Du Bois's choices of words and descriptions have had negative unintended consequences.

When analyzing terminology used by Du Bois over a century ago, some contemporary scholars have tended to unwittingly blame Du Bois for not using social constructionist language that had not been invented. It was possible for Du Bois and other scholars in the early twentieth century to use a vocabulary not meant to convey essentialism, even though today no constructivist would use it. Hence there is a need for caution against a contemporary reading of what Du Bois *should have been writing about* in those times, given the current vocabularies available to scholars writing today.[55] Such caution, however, does not erase the need to examine whether Du Bois's scholarship was driven by race essentialism or by an innovative sociological approach.

Du Bois is often thought to have been elitist because of his strategy to achieve black liberation. Du Bois argued that an educated elite—a "talented tenth"—was the group capable of leading black people to overthrow racism. He wrote, "The Negro race, like all races, is going to be saved by its exceptional men. The problem of education, then, among Negroes must first of all deal with the Talented Tenth; it is the problem of developing the Best of this race that they may guide the Mass away from the contamination and death of the Worst."[56] For Du Bois, slavery had produced illiteracy and ignorance among the black masses, so that they lacked the intellectual and material resources necessary for liberation. Therefore, those blacks who acquired advanced and broad educations were to be the leaders of the masses. As we will see, these alleged deficits were not thought to inhere within black people in particular. Rather, they were products of social development and existed in all racial groups at a similar level of social development. However important these issues of language and politics were, it was Du Bois's sociological analysis that made clear he did not view the black masses as inherently a racially inferior group.

In an article entitled "The Uncompleted Argument: Du Bois and the Illusion of Race," Appiah contends that Du Bois did not formulate a social constructionist analysis of race.[57] According to Appiah's reasoning, Du Bois clung to a biological definition of race even as he superficially substituted a socio-historical approach. According to Appiah, "We need to make clear that what Du Bois attempts, despite his own claims to the contrary, is not the transcendence of the nineteenth century scientific conception of race—he relies on it."[58] Appiah seeks to establish this claim by dissecting Du Bois's famous 1897 definition of race as a "vast family of human beings, generally of common blood and language, always of common history, traditions and impulses, who are both voluntarily and involuntarily striving together for the accomplishment of certain more or less vividly conceived ideals of life."[59] Appiah's main argument is that if Du Bois really believed that race was socially constructed by factors such as common history, language, customs and traditions, long collective memories, and common experiences of oppression and discrimination, then he would not need to invoke biological notions of "common blood" at all.

Consequently, Appiah claims Du Bois held the same biological conception of race as his white intellectual forbearers and contemporaries. Appiah accuses Du Bois of a sleight-of-hand intellectual maneuver when he repeatedly appears to privilege sociological explanations of race: these "only lead us back into the now familiar move of substituting a sociohistorical conception of race for the biological one; but that is simply to bury the biological conception below the surface, not to transcend it."[60]

Yet the causal language in Du Bois's analysis of race overwhelmingly privileges sociological explanations:

> What is the real distinction between these nations [races]? Is it the physical differences of blood, color and cranial measurements? Certainly we must all acknowledge that physical differences play a great part, and that, with wide exceptions and qualifications, these eight great races of to-day follow the cleavage of physical race distinctions. . . . But while race differences have followed mainly physical race lines, yet no mere physical distinctions would really define or explain the deeper differences—the cohesiveness and continuity of these groups. The deeper differences are spiritual, psychical, differences—undoubtedly based on the physical, but infinitely transcending them. The forces that bind [races] together . . . are, then, first, . . . race identity and common blood; secondly, and more important, a common history, common laws and religion, similar habits of thought and a conscious striving together for certain ideals of life. The whole process which has brought about these race differentiations has been a growth, and the great characteristic of this growth has been the differentiation of spiritual and mental differences between great races of mankind and the integration of physical differences.[61]

In this passage, Du Bois seeks to define and account for the constitutive qualities of race—those that explain how races cohere and maintain that group feature through time. These constitutive qualities, for Du Bois, are the "deeper differences" driving race phenomena, and sociological factors—a common history, common laws and religion, similar habits of thought, and a conscious striving together for certain ideals of life—are more important in determining race because in a causal sense they "infinitely transcend" biological factors. As we proceed, I produce additional evidence that Du Bois formulated a view of race consistent with a social constructionist view. Suffice it to say here that nowhere in Du Bois's race analysis are biological factors elevated in causal significance over sociological ones. Appiah is right that by introducing talk of "blood" into the definition of race, Du Bois creates a tension between the biological and the sociological. Yet that tension never rises to a level where biology trumps sociological explanations of racial categories and racial outcomes. If biological causation were paramount for Du Bois, we would find elaborate analyses of the role that "blood" played in determining racial outcomes; we would find formulations purporting to explain how preceding genealogical trees crucially determined subsequent racial outcomes in succeeding generations. Since we find, instead, that Du Bois produced an elaborate sociological analysis explaining racial dynamics, we can conclude that Appiah's charge is unfounded.

In an essay on Du Bois's concept of "double consciousness," Reed suggests that Du Bois did not formulate this concept from thin air.[62] It was common, he argues, for leading scholars and activists, black and white, male and female, around the turn of the twentieth century to describe their inner lives in terms of dual selves coexisting in tension. Those dual selves were seen as rooted in dichotomies of femininity versus masculinity and lower races versus superior races. It was common, Reed points out, for women, men, whites, and blacks to assign superior reasoning and cultural abilities to men and to whites. Reed claims that Du Bois absorbed these ideas current in dominant intellectual discourse and thus fell in line with those who assigned racial superiority to whites.[63] Drawing on scattered passages from Du Bois's writings that refer to blacks disparagingly, Reed concludes that Du Bois, just like other leading scholars of the period such as sociologists W.I Thomas, Edward Ross, and Robert Park, "defined blacks as comparatively primitive and undeveloped as a race," considered their state to be a "race-childhood," and saw them as "emotional" and in need of white tutelage.[64]

Reed claims that Du Bois's views on race—evidenced, for him as for Appiah, by the language of black inferiority that Du Bois sometimes employed to describe the black masses—flowed directly from an acceptance of the Lamarckian theory of the inheritance of acquired characteristics. In the late eighteenth century the biologist Jean-Baptiste Lamarck had developed his own theory of evolution, arguing that in order to adjust to changing environmental conditions organisms changed their habitual patterns of using their powers, and that such changed patterns could be passed on to their offspring in the form of developed or discarded characteristics. Over long periods such organismic changes could become enduring qualities of a population. Although Lamarckianism was to some extent supplanted by Darwin's theory of natural selection and Mendel's discovery of genes as mechanisms of inheritance, the period between Darwin's death in the 1880s and the discoveries in genetics of the 1920s and 1930s featured numerous challenges to Darwinism and a revival of Lamarckian theory that has been called neo-Lamarckianism.

And as James B. McKee has shown in his definitive history of racial theory at the beginning of the twentieth century, sociological thinking was at this time very much "entangled with Lamarckianism."[65] This was a "soft theory" of evolution because it posited that the mechanisms of inheritance were not strictly genetic; adaptive changes to environmental conditions could eventually lead to alteration of a population's inheritance. The conceptual shift occurred precisely when biological theories of black inferiority were being discredited. Neo-Lamarckian theory is important because it provided social scientists of the early twentieth century with a theoretical foundation to continue claiming that blacks were inferior because their common history had produced a collective, heritable temperament that was marked by inferior racial traits. Neo-Lamarckian theory allowed white sociologists to continue to "play the dozens" with black people, as the Princeton sociologist Howard Taylor has described for more contemporary sociological approaches to inequality: "a game of one-upmanship whose aim is 'to cleverly insult someone by insulting members of one's family, usually by making derisive comments, preferable of a sexual nature, about one's mother.'"[66] The theory merely replaced unalterable biological racial traits with acquired racial traits that had become encoded in biology and would take perhaps centuries of altered environmental conditions to change.

Although Reed states that Du Bois's "basic views on race proceeded explicitly from the convention of neo-Lamarckian social science," he actually does not provide direct evidence for this claim.[67] He presents no proof that Du Bois or his students corresponded with Lamarckian scholars or even cited them. Reed claims, for example, that in a 1904 lecture entitled "Heredity and the Public Schools" Du Bois shows his support for the "soft inheritance" approach of neo-Lamarckians,[68] yet Du Bois in fact makes no statements in the article that would support a biological approach to race. To the contrary, throughout the article Du Bois argues that sociological factors are the basic determinants of racial dynamics. Indeed, he states outright that heredity cannot be invoked to explain differences in educational performance between black and white children. Not only do their differing social circumstances provide sufficient explanation, but no hereditary differences between the races in physical development can be found: "What now are the facts in the case and the fair deductions? First, as to sheer physical heredity, are the black races degenerate or undeveloped specimens of humanity? The answer to this is clear and unequivocal and has never for a moment been disputed by any scientific evidence; the Negro races are from every physical standpoint full and normally developed men; their stature and muscular development, their keenness of sense and their physical measurement show absolutely no variation from the European type sufficient to base any theory of essentially human differences upon."[69]

As with Appiah, if Reed's claims were accurate we would expect Du Bois to produce a body of work demonstrating how the inheritance of acquired characteristics determined racial inequality. Indirectly, Reed acknowledges that no such Du Boisian approach exists when he says that "Du Bois did not attempt to detail the biochemical mechanisms through which alleged racial characteristics were generated and solidified within populations, as Thomas and others did."[70] As I will demonstrate, Du Bois did not produce such formulations because he did not advance any claims that racial hierarchies rested on biological foundations. Du Bois headed in a completely different direction: he formulated a sociology of race showing that racial hierarchies rested on edifices of power, discrimination, and entrenched oppression.

Another philosopher, Robert Gooding-Williams, has analyzed Du Bois's scholarship with a keen eye toward understanding his approach to race. After thorough examination, Gooding-Williams reached some conclusions consistent with Appiah's claims: like Appiah, he draws on Du Bois's writings to argue that Du Bois viewed the black masses as backward people unable to meet the standards of an advanced white civilization. He makes a seemingly convincing case that Du Bois's elitism toward the black masses was extensive and permeated his scholarship.[71] But unlike Appiah he does not think Du Bois viewed the black masses as culturally backward because they were a black race. Rather, for Gooding-Williams Du Bois viewed the racism that blacks encountered as the cause of delayed social development. Du Bois, according to Gooding-Williams, rejected the intellectual heritage of the nineteenth century that viewed race as biologically determined and broke with his contemporaries by conceptualizing races sociologically. "For Du Bois mental and spiritual differences have historical and social causes (law, religion, and so forth) that are not reducible to biological racial differences. In fine, he takes these causes to be causally independent of biological racial facts."[72] The philosopher Lucius Outlaw concurs with Gooding-Williams on this important issue.[73]

Gooding-Williams highlights Du Bois's language regarding the black masses as derogatory but does not place it within the context of the early twentieth century, when a social construction vocabulary did not exist. Even more important, Gooding-Williams, like the other scholars discussed, fails to examine Du Bois's structural analyses of caste and white oppression and how these negatively affected cultural conditions of the black masses. Thus Gooding-Williams asserts that Du Bois expressed arrogance toward the lower classes but fails to engage with Du Bois's structural analyses of the culture of the oppressed, which demonstrate that racial oppression trumped cultural factors as a determinant.

Watts reaches conclusions much like Reed's and Appiah's concerning Du Bois's view of the black masses but on different analytic grounds. According to Watts, Du Bois's "cultural distaste for the black masses is repeatedly displayed in *Souls of Black Folk*,"[74] and he attributes that alleged distaste to deep and pervasive personal insecurities: "One cannot understand the richness of *The Souls of Black Folk* without confronting the anguished, almost racially/culturally obsequious, status-grasping motivations in Du Bois' use of arcane, highbrow Western humanistic language."[75] Moreover, Watts claims that Du Bois's race analyses reflect his search for personal recognition from white oppressors because he longed to be embraced as the exceptional Negro. This account of Du Bois's *Souls of Black Folk* contrasts sharply with the usual view of this work as an eloquent call for recognizing black humanity and the need for black liberation. In rejecting this view of *Souls*, Watts maintains: "The voice that Du Bois appropriated in the hope of generating a serious reading of the text is supposedly used in the service of racial uplift. One could just as easily reverse the reading and argue that the elitist Du Bois was using the plight of the subjugated black neopeasantry as a backdrop to highlight the uniqueness of his own problematic status as a black man-of-culture."[76]

To clinch his argument, Watts selects from Du Bois's works phrases regarding the black masses that are very similar to those selected by Appiah and Reed. He cites this passage: "I should be the last one to deny the patent weaknesses and shortcomings of the Negro people; I should be the last to withhold sympathy from the white South in its efforts to solve its intricate social problems. I freely acknowledge that it is possible, and sometimes best, that a partially undeveloped people should be ruled by the best of their stronger and better neighbors for their own good, until such time as they can start and fight the world's battles alone."[77] However, Watts cites this quote without examining Du Bois's next sentences which rejects white guidance:

> I have already pointed out how sorely in need of such economic and spiritual guidance the emancipated Negro was. . . . But the point I have insisted upon and now emphasize again, is that the best opinion of the South to-day is not the ruling opinion. That to leave the Negro helpless and without a ballot

to-day is to leave him not to the guidance of the best, but rather to the exploitation and debauchment of the worst; that this is no truer of the South than of the North,—of the North than of Europe: in any land, in any country under modern free competition, to lay any class of weak and despised people, be they white, black, or blue, at the political mercy of their stronger, richer, and more resourceful fellows, is a temptation which human nature seldom has withstood and seldom will withstand.[78]

Thus Watts fails to understand a fundamental dimension of Du Bois's analysis of the need for "Negro" guidance. In this passage, Du Bois does not address the essential nature of black people or the alleged intrinsic nature of "races" for any other racial group. Rather, he addresses class dynamics in the context of a capitalist economy—or what he refers to as "modern free competition"—and the role of power and exploitation exercised over lower economic classes. But for Du Bois, there is a special twist regarding poor black workers in the early twentieth century, and that is the condition whereby class exploitation is joined with exploitation based on racial prejudice. In an article dissecting race inequality, Du Bois instructs readers to see more than class exploitation; in addition, he writes, "You must see the color line. It stands at the depot with 'waiting room for white people' and 'waiting room for colored people,' and then the uninitiated might lose sight of it; but it is there, there and curiously wandering, but continuous and never ending."[79] The color line produced diminished wages for black farm laborers; it also controlled the spaces their bodies occupied and the absence of justice they experienced in the courts and the public square. In short, Watts mistakenly sees Du Bois's characterizations of the black masses as expressing pejorative essentialist race qualities. He also mistakes Du Bois's searching sociological analysis as a quest for personal status that Du Bois supposedly was desperately seeking from white oppressors. In so doing, Watts, like Appiah and Reed, ignores Du Bois's sociological analysis of race and labors under a grave misconception regarding Du Bois's assessment of the masses.

Du Bois's sociology of race is the hallmark of his scholarship and radically differentiates his analyses from those of his contemporaries that flourished over the ensuing century. A systematic examination of Du Bois's sociology of race makes clear that he proceeded from a social constructionist framework. Talk of biology and inherited racial traits is absent, and such traits are attributed no causal power. In contrast to Appiah, Reed, and Watts, and to Gooding-Williams to some extent, historical specificity is crucial in Du Bois's accounts of racial dynamics and assessments of the black masses. This is not surprising, given that besides earning a doctorate in history, Du Bois while at Harvard and the University of Berlin was exposed to the role of history in human affairs. He insisted that if analysts were to grapple intelligently with race they were compelled to focus on "the greater problems of human development in society." Moreover, to understand the development of a people, Du Bois argued, "we must seek to know what human advancement historically considered has meant and what it means today, and from such criteria we may judge the condition, development and needs of the group before us."[80] Like his fellow German historical school contemporary Max Weber, Du Bois paid close attention to developmental tendencies regarding race, including how such tendencies were fundamental in the development of African Americans.[81] Thus historical time and social development were key sociological principles driving Du Bois's sociology of race.

Du Bois's scholarship of race early in the twentieth century addressed a historically specific population just decades removed from slavery: "The basic question is, How soon after a social revolution like emancipation ought one reasonably to expect the appearance of habits of thrift and the accumulation of property? Moreover, how far is the accumulating of wealth indicative of general advance in moral habits and sound character, or how far is it independent of them or in spite of them?"[82] In examining recently freed slaves, Du Bois delved into their past conditions of servitude and their postemancipation status to determine whether race or sociological factors accounted for their subordinate position in the social order. He found that the first generation following slavery was actually not free structurally or culturally. Structurally, black people after emancipation were constrained within a system of economic and social domination. Culturally, they were severely crippled by a social heritage inherited from two centuries of slavery.

The economic bondage former slaves encountered was a caste system initially constructed by white slave masters and refashioned by the southern white aristocracy to control the now-emancipated slaves. It was a caste system, according to Du Bois, because American slavery initially operated through a Slave Code that did not tie bondage to skin color. However, once the slave system became regulated by a Black Code, a caste of race replaced the caste of condition.[83] This caste system equating subordination with black skin doomed African Americans to centuries of class and racial oppression. In Du Bois's analysis, this tight linkage between physical traits (the biology of black skin and the bloodlines that created people without black skin who were nevertheless classified as black) and the condition of bondage and inferiority was a political accomplishment created through codes, laws, and economic contracts. This caste system followed the freedmen as they moved from formal slavery to neo-slavery following emancipation: "The most piteous thing amid all the black ruin of war-time, amid the broken fortunes of the masters, the blighted hopes of mothers and maidens, and the fall of an empire,—the most piteous thing amid all this was the black freedman who threw down his hoe because the world called him free. What did such a mockery of freedom mean? Not a cent of money, not an inch of land, not a mouthful of victuals,—not even ownership of the rags on his back."[84] As a result, emancipated slaves became economically dependent on white masters by entering exploitative arrangements of debt peonage and sharecropping that kept them perennially in debt and able to live only a "hand to mouth" existence. Moreover, without the vote, legal protections, and education, the black masses trapped by caste were defenseless neo-slaves within a new system of oppression. Du Bois discovered little substantive difference between formal slavery and the new slavery of emancipation: "And after the first flush of freedom wore off, and his true helplessness dawned on the freedman, he came back and picked up his hoe, and old master still doled out his bacon and meal. The legal form of service was theoretically far different; in practice, taskwork or 'cropping' was substituted for daily toil in gangs; and the slave gradually became a metayer, or tenant on shares, in name, but a laborer with indeterminate wages in fact."[85] Du Bois argued that these social conditions severely hampered blacks by throwing them into competition with white workers who had been taught to despise them. These workers trampled over blacks as they struggled to make ends meet in a fierce capitalist system engaged in an incessant quest for profit. Therefore, for Du Bois, economic exploitation, the lack of political power, and the absence of education determined racial inequality and not inherited race traits or some other essentialist racial characteristics.

Du Bois recognized that systems of domination produce and are sustained by cultures of subordination that drastically curtail challenges from below and derail social development of the oppressed. What Du Bois's critics fail to recognize is that when Du Bois spoke of the development of blacks he was referring to their development not merely as a race but as a social group. Du Bois analyzed black development in a comparative context, comparing it with similar processes that people and nations have undergone globally and historically. He argued that all nations developed through a series of overlapping stages because "in the life of advancing peoples there must go on simultaneously a struggle for existence, accumulation of wealth, education of the young, and a development in culture and the higher things of life."[86] These stages of development applied to all racial groups as they matured culturally and socially through time.

For African Americans, the stages of group development were rudely interrupted by devastating forms of oppression, including the slave trade, over two centuries of slavery, and the radical ruptures caused by the Civil War and emancipation. For Du Bois, these social disruptions were culturally cataclysmic: "A nation that breaks suddenly with its past is almost fatally crippled. No matter how crude or imperfect that past may be, with all its defects, it is the foundation upon which generations to come must build. Beauty and finish and architectural detail are not required of it, but the massive weight of centuries of customs and traditions it must have."[87] In Du Bois's analysis, a negative achievement of American slavery was the upheaval of the social institutions and cultural foundations that existed in the African fatherland. This included the near dissolution of the African family, native languages, and the myriad customs and habits that had previously guided the Africans. Centuries of slavery embedded a culture of broad ignorance and submission into African Americans, making them "ignorant of the world about them, of modern economic organization, of the function of government, of individual worth and possibilities,—of nearly all those things which slavery in self-defence had to keep them from learning."[88] From this perspective, such ignorance stemmed not from an inherited racial temperament but from a system of domination that required ignorance for its survival. Therefore, if the black masses needed "guidance" to overcome their "child-like" stage of social development, their cultural ignorance had been imposed upon them; "Nor does it require any fine-spun theories of racial differences to prove the necessity of such group training after the brains of the race have been knocked out by two hundred and fifty years of assiduous education in submission, carelessness, and stealing."[89]

Du Bois did not deny that African Americans a few decades removed from slavery suffered from cultural ignorance. Yet he was not surprised, given that such ignorance sprang from oppressive social forces aimed at keeping blacks ignorant. Addressing defects in black cultural capital head on, Du Bois related that his studies had led him to examine this condition "in all its degradation and uncleanness," but he also concluded, "I cannot but see a plain case of cause and effect. If you degrade people the result is degradation, and you have no right to be surprised at it."[90] Du Bois was clear that cultural degradation did not arise from biological or culturally transmitted traits. Rather, it sprang from an oppression that kept blacks illiterate and uneducated and from the narrow horizons inherent in the experiences of people too poor to travel in Jim Crow cars and too illiterate to read the books that would enable the imagination to soar. Because of the origins of these cultural deficiencies, Du Bois defiantly declared: "Nor am I called upon to apologize for these people, or to make fun of their dumb misery. For their condition there is an apology due, witness High Heaven; but not from me."[91]

Du Bois's descriptions of the "dumb misery" of the black masses might in retrospect appear judgmental, elitist, and inappropriately derogatory. Yet whenever Du Bois dwells on the ignorance or backwardness or primitiveness or undeveloped nature or "childlike-ness" of blacks, he explains it as a consequence of white oppression. His analysis of the stereotype of blacks as "shiftless" is illuminating:

> To the car-window sociologist, to the man who seeks to understand and know the South by devoting the few leisure hours of a holiday trip to unravelling the snarl of centuries,—to such men very often the whole trouble with the black field-hand may be summed up ... "Shiftless!" They have noted repeatedly scenes like one I saw last summer. We were riding along the highroad to town at the close of a long hot day. A couple of young black fellows passed us in a muleteam, with several bushels of loose corn in the ear. One was driving, listlessly bent forward, his elbows on his knees,—a happy-go-lucky, careless picture of irresponsibility. The other was fast asleep in the bottom of the wagon. As we passed we noticed an ear of corn fall from the wagon. They never saw it. . . . . A rod farther on we noted another ear on the ground; and between that creeping mule and town we counted twenty-six ears of corn. Shiftless? Yes, the personification of shiftlessness. And yet follow those boys: they are not lazy; to-morrow morning they'll be up with the sun; they work hard when they do work, and they work willingly. They have no sordid, selfish, money-getting ways, but rather a fine disdain for mere cash. They'll loaf before your face and work behind your back with good-natured honesty. They'll steal a watermelon, and hand you back your lost purse intact. Their great defect as laborers lies in their lack of incentive beyond the mere pleasure of physical exertion. They are careless because they have not found that it pays to be careful; they are improvident because the improvident ones of their acquaintance get on about as well as the provident. Above all, they cannot see why they should take unusual pains to make the white man's land better, or to fatten his mule, or save his corn.[92]

In one example after another, Du Bois shows how behaviors that would ordinarily be explained by racial stereotypes are actually rational because oppression provides few incentives to act otherwise. To be an efficient slave was to act irrationally because it increased the power of one's oppressor. Du Bois did not sugarcoat the negative effects of white racism on black people, for to do so robbed the devil of his due.

Du Bois's sociological analyses, based on surveys, ethnographic research, massive interviews and participant observation, took him behind cultural stereotypes of the black masses, enabling him to realistically describe the conditions with which they struggled, conditions that were unknown to the public and most social scientists:

> We seldom study the condition of the Negro to-day honestly and carefully. It is so much easier to assume that we know it all. Or perhaps, having already reached conclusions in our own minds, we are loth to have them disturbed by facts. And yet how little we really know of these millions,—of their daily lives and longings, of their homely joys and sorrows, of their real shortcomings and the meaning of their crimes! All this we can only learn by intimate contact with the masses, and not by wholesale arguments covering millions separate in time and space, and differing widely in training and culture.[93]

Du Bois's sociological studies of the masses do not square with the views attributed to him by Appiah, Reed, and Watts. Du Bois's data led him to conclude that the black masses tended to be hardworking and honest but only barely literate and desperately poor. He emphasized their humanity as individuals, stating, "We often forget that each unit in the mass is a throbbing human soul . . . [that] love and hates, . . . laughs and weeps its bitter tears, and looks in vague and awful longing at the grim horizon of its life."[94] In contrast to critics who claimed that he saw the masses as biological and cultural primitives, he described them as a population who, despite stifling oppression, were resolutely advancing in their social evolution: in only one generation since slavery, "the Negro . . . forms the chief laboring force of the most rapidly developing part of the land. He owns twelve million acres of land, two hundred and fifty million dollars worth of farm property, and controls as owner or renter five hundred millions. Nearly three-fifths of the Negroes have learned to read and write. An increasing number have given evidence of ability and thoughtfulness."[95] For Du Bois, the figures indicating black advancement meant that the development was distinct and markedly in the right direction, and that, if blacks were given justice and help, no honest man could doubt the outcome.

A large part of Du Bois's intellectual project involved documenting the great strides made by the black masses in all phases of life just one decade following slavery. Another dimension of that project was to prove the black masses were not culturally inferior but culturally challenged by historical contingencies. Thus Du Bois warned that "to assert dogmatically that the present distribution of culture is a fair index of the distribution of human ability and desert is to make an assertion for which there is not the slightest scientific warrant."[96] Regarding the abilities of the black masses, Du Bois agreed with a recently emancipated young boy, Richard R. Wright Sr., who, when asked in 1868 to provide his assessment of the newly freed slaves, responded: "Tell them we are rising!"

Appiah, Reed, Gooding-Williams, and Watts assume that when Du Bois referred to whites as possessing superior civilizations, he meant that they were racially superior to blacks. They imply that Du Bois engaged in moral judgments suggesting that whites had a "better" or "higher" civilization. Yet this is a misreading of Du Bois's conception of civilization. Degrees of civilization for Du Bois were determined by a population's literacy rate, knowledge of economic activities, social organization, and knowledge acquired beyond local setting. If a population was high on these dimensions, it ranked high in civilizational achievements. Even so, for Du Bois, such "higher" cultures were not automatically "better" or more worthy in a humanistic sense. In fact, "higher" cultures might be morally corrupt and even more barbaric than "lower" cultures.

Thus Du Bois considered white American and European civilizations that colonized and discriminated against people of color to be barbaric and backward. Speaking of caste oppression by whites, Du Bois declared that "this outrageous programme of wholesale human degeneration is not outspoken yet save in the backward civilizations of the southern United States, South Africa and Australia. But its enunciation is listened to with respect and tolerance in England, Germany and the northern states."[97] Pointing to the failures of American white civilization, Du Bois cried out, "Merciful God! in these wild days and in the name of Civilization, Justice, and Motherhood,—what have we not seen, right here in America, of orgy, cruelty, barbarism, and murder done to men and women of Negro descent."[98] Though the white man's civilization "boasted much" of moral superiority and though the modern white man "took himself and his own perfectness with . . . disconcerting seriousness," "We whose shame, humiliation, and deep insult his aggrandizement so often involved were never deceived. We looked at him clearly, with world-old eyes, and saw simply a human thing, weak and pitiable and cruel, even as we are and were."[99]

This examination of Du Bois's sociological approach to race demonstrates that biology played no role in his causal analysis of racial inequality. Instead, what we find is a political sociology stressing power, economic exploitation, and social oppression as producers and sustainers of racial inequality. Moreover, Du Bois's students such as Monroe Work, Richard R. Wright Jr., Edmund Haynes, and Mary White Ovington followed their mentor in rejecting biological factors as determinants of racial inequality. For example, Wright concluded in his social study of the blacks of Xenia, Ohio, that "the future will see the Negroes better their condition as their environment becomes better."[100]

Du Bois's race analysis is dynamic because it stresses how historical specificity and developmental tendencies influence and shape race and class dynamics. It also takes culture into account by emphasizing how social oppression creates cultural deficits among the dominated, thus encouraging cultures of domination to take hold in ways that stunt a group's social development and its capacity to engage in collective action.[101] Although Du Bois's choice of language such as *primitive, childhood,* and *low grade of culture* in his early works has led some scholars to highlight tensions within his sociological approach, their theories are based on a failure to recognize Du Bois's larger sociological framework for understanding culture and on a mistaken apprehension that his language supports biological and cultural determinist arguments regarding race inequality. Even worse, such language has provided grist for the mills of racists intent on using the dean of Negro scholars' words to support their own beliefs. Reed confirms that as early as 1904 Du Bois abandoned language suggesting essentialist interpretations of black oppression.[102] Indeed, Du Bois expressed embarrassment for having used such language as a young scholar.[103] It should be borne in mind, however, that at the turn of the twentieth century constructivist language did not yet exist and social Darwinism permeated intellectual discussions of race inequality. Despite these difficulties, Du Bois developed a potent sociology of race that transcended the biologistic and cultural determinism driving race analyses at the turn of the twentieth century.

Appiah, Reed, and Watts fail to grasp Du Bois's transcendence of determinism because they ignore the body of sociological analysis produced by Du Bois and his students and focus instead on terminology that they believe conveys the essence of Du Bois's analyses. They take this position even in the absence of any declarations by Du Bois that blood and ancestry determined racial inequality.

In actuality, Du Bois's analysis anticipated the contemporary social constructionist view of race. The historian Tom Holt captured this aspect of Du Bois's thinking: "Those who contend, therefore, that DuBois embraced certain elements of the nineteenth-century conceptions of race, even as he struggled to free himself from their biological genesis, are only partially correct. They are wrong in not crediting DuBois with going a much greater distance in refiguring the nineteenth-century 'race idea' that he had inherited. But even more important is our own intellectual loss in not recognizing and building upon DuBois' insights into the relation between 'the race idea' and history."[104] Indeed, as we will come to see, while Chicago school sociologists were still asserting that biological factors played important roles in racial dynamics, Du Bois was insisting, "There are no races, in the sense of great, separate, pure breeds of men, differing in attainment, development, and capacity."[105]

Unlike white sociologists, Du Bois had a vested interest in distancing himself from social Darwinist thought. In his autobiographical *Dusk of Dawn*, Du Bois recalls: "At Harvard, I began to face scientific race dogma: first of all, evolution and the 'Survival of the Fittest.' It was continually stressed in the community and in classes that there was a vast difference in the development of the whites and the 'lower' races; that this could be seen in the physical development of the Negro."[106] Du Bois related the disgust he felt while visiting a museum where he observed "a series of skeletons arranged from a little monkey to a tall well-developed white man, with a Negro barely outranking a chimpanzee."[107] In addition to its fatal analytical flaws, social Darwinist thought was personally reprehensible to Du Bois because it defined black people as inferior. Thus, on scientific and ideological grounds, Du Bois elevated racial analysis to the sociological plane and discarded social Darwinist explanations of race.

THE PHILADELPHIA NEGRO AND "THE NEGROES OF FARMVILLE": PIONEERING TEXTS OF MODERN EMPIRICAL SOCIOLOGY

In 1899, Du Bois published *The Philadelphia Negro*. Now recognized as a classic, it is usually depicted as the first study of an urban black community. But its status as America's first major empirical sociological study has rarely been acknowledged. Du Bois made clear the broad scientific aims of his sociological works:

The American Negro deserves study for the great end of advancing the cause of science in general. No such opportunity to watch and measure the history and development of a great race of men ever presented itself to the scholars of a modern nation. If they miss this opportunity—if they do the work in a slip-shod, unsystematic manner—if they dally with the truth to humor the whims of the day, they do far more than hurt the good name of the American people; they hurt the cause of scientific truth the world over, they voluntarily decrease human knowledge.[108]

Du Bois felt that studies of African Americans should be conducted in the most careful and systematic manner and anchored in observations and comparisons. He always maintained that racial transformation was sorely needed in America and the world. But he insisted that scientific research on race be based solely on scientific criteria, especially in America given the volatility and entrenched biases associated with the race problem.[109] He warned that "students must be careful to insist that science as such . . . has but one aim: the discovery of truth. . . . Any attempt to give it a double aim, to make social reform the immediate instead of the mediate object of a search for truth, will inevitably tend to defeat both objects."[110] However, he was not advocating for an "objective" science where the scholar steers clear of "meddling" in the real world because those concerns taint the authenticity of science. At the top of his scientific agenda was the production of a *critical* social science: "Most unfortunate . . . is the fact that so much of the work done on the Negro question is notoriously uncritical; uncritical from lack of discrimination in the selection and weighing of evidence; uncritical in choosing the proper point of view from which to study these problems, and, finally, uncritical from the distinct bias in the minds of so many writers."[111] Scientists had to seek first the truth utilizing the best available theories and methods. Regarding sociology and social change, Du Bois stated, "The sole aim of any society is to settle its problems in accordance with its highest ideals, and the only rational method of accomplishing this is to study those problems in the light of the best scientific research."[112] Scholars had the responsibility to make scholarship available to scientists across the world so it could be evaluated on purely scientific grounds. But like Marx, Du Bois believed that once the scientific truth was established, the point of knowledge was to transform the world. Efforts seeking racial changes could be effective only if based on scientific findings derived from carefully conducted research.

Du Bois employed demanding scientific standards while researching and composing *The Philadelphia Negro*. In so doing, he broke new sociological ground. The book was a study of the black population in the Seventh Ward of Philadelphia at the close of the nineteenth century. Its first seminal contribution was its empirical methodology. Departing from the armchair conjectures and flashes of intuition customary at the time, it rested on an empirical base: not only extensive interviews with all families in the ward but also surveys, archival data, and ethnographic data from participant observation. Indeed, Du Bois emerged from *The Philadelphia Negro* as the first number-crunching, surveying, interviewing, participant-observing and field-working sociologist in America, a pioneer in the multimethods approach. He cross-checked his quantitative and qualitative data to ensure accuracy by eradicating undetected errors associated with a particular method. Thus he also pioneered the data-gathering technique known as triangulation.[113]

The Philadelphia Negro was steeped in historical and comparative analyses. It was not by happenstance that Du Bois's sociology was deeply rooted in historical analyses; he had been trained as a historian at Harvard and had earned his doctorate in that field. Thus he studied blacks during slavery, charted their migration to Philadelphia, and explored the complex ways through which they constructed an urban community in a large northern city. He explained, "One cannot study the Negro in freedom and come to general conclusions about his destiny without knowing his history in slavery."[114] Comparative analysis was required because during this period social scientists conceptualized blacks as subhuman. To address this fallacy, Du Bois compared the development of Philadelphia blacks with that of the city's European immigrants, showing similarities at comparable stages of development. He pointed out that when social context and developmental conditions were similar black outcomes on major indices were comparable to those of European immigrants.

Du Bois was aware that white sociologists possessed little knowledge of black institutions and cultural processes. They tended to view black communities as distorted and inferior copies of white communities.[115] In *The Philadelphia Negro* Du Bois showed this conception to be sociological nonsense by analyzing the black community's institutions and culture. Sociologists of the period usually ignored class distinctions among blacks, thus treating them as a homogeneous mass. Du Bois analyzed the black class structure and demonstrated how it shaped the community and its stratification dynamics.[116] He developed a novel sociology of work and occupations analysis by exploring stratification and mobility processes within the black community.[117]

Du Bois analyzed the conditions of black women and the unique challenges they faced in the labor market. *The Philadelphia Negro,* therefore, focused attention on gender relations.[118] In this work, Du Bois also developed a sociology of demographics, population, and health to scrutinize death rates and the health status of black Philadelphians.[119] He analyzed "how the African American slums were experiencing population turnover as more affluent African Americans were moving out and being replaced by African Americans migrating from the 'country areas.'"[120] As we will see, this line of inquiry anticipated future ethnic succession models and provided a sustained sociological analysis of the urban community. Du Bois analyzed black crime, revealing that it was largely rooted in social conditions rather than in biological and social degeneracy, as white social scientists usually claimed.[121] In developing a novel sociology of religion, Du Bois analyzed the social organization and cultural processes of the black church and laid bare its role as the community's central institution, affecting all aspects of black life.[122] He subjected other community organizations, including a wide range of voluntary associations, to fine-grained analyses,[123] and he examined leisure by analyzing the recreational activities of black Philadelphians.[124]

The Philadelphia Negro was not exclusively an analysis of the black community. It also focused on racial power relations and demonstrated that oppression and discrimination trapped blacks in a vicious cycle of subordination.[125] The rich data from *The Philadelphia Negro* were the empirical basis for Du Bois's construction of an intricate sociological narrative clearly identifying the racial dynamics that existed at the beginning of the twentieth century and that continue to drive contemporary American race relations. The sociological frames that emerged were largely structural and cultural, pinpointing how white discrimination and prejudice produced a peculiar and powerful social environment that crippled Philadelphia's black community. *The Philadelphia Negro* was characterized by novel inductive theorizing, for it flew in the face of social Darwinist theories that blamed racial inequality on black inferiority.

Yet it would be a mistake to view *The Philadelphia Negro* and Du Bois's scholarship generally as merely black sociology. Du Bois sought to explicate the human condition by interrogating the color line in America and globally. For him, that color line was a social divide structuring social inequality between the haves and have-nots. It was as important for dominant white groups to understand that color line as it was for oppressed people of color across the globe. As Du Bois put it in the "Forethought" to *The Souls of Black Folk*, "Herein lie buried many things which if read with patience may show the strange meaning of being black here at the dawning of the Twentieth Century. This meaning is not without interest to you, Gentle Reader; for the problem of the Twentieth Century is the problem of the color line."[126]

While completing *The Philadelphia Negro*, Du Bois also traveled south and conducted a classic study of Farmville, Virginia's rural black community.[127] The first empirical study of rural sociology in the United States, it examined questions similar to those explored in *The Philadelphia Negro* and employed the methodologies it had pioneered.[128] This strategy enabled Du Bois to compare a rural and an urban community before the turn of the twentieth century. Du Bois believed that to understand American race relations the sociologist had to focus on both North and South and rural and urban communities because together they reflected an unbroken chain of social processes operative in both milieus. This approach was to remain a distinguishing feature of Du Bois's sociology.

The Philadelphia Negro analyzed the city as a setting where spatial arrangements revealed racial dynamics. Through his extensive use of maps, Du Bois captured how spatial configurations of Philadelphia were shaped by racist practices generated by the color line. His geographical analysis documented the high levels of racial segregation in the city and how segregation resulted from decisions made by economic elites to protect white interests. Unlike the urban analysts of the Chicago school three decades later, Du Bois documented racial configurations within city spaces as planned phenomena rather than as outgrowths of natural ecological processes:[129] the locations of neighborhoods and businesses were products of those who possessed money and power. This was true even within the black community because middle- and upper-class blacks separated themselves spatially from the black lower classes to the extent possible given the dictates of Philadelphia's color line. Evaluating Du Bois's analysis of the city, the urban sociologist Mary Pattillo commented that "movement across space was key for DuBois and surely predated the Chicago School spatial concepts of human ecology, invasion and succession, and concentric zones."[130] The Du Boisian scholar Marcus Hunter concurred:

> Long before scholars such as Robert Park (1915), St. Clair Drake and Horace Cayton (1945), William Julius Wilson (1987, 1996), and Douglas Massey and Nancy Denton (1993) (to name a few) imagined ethnic and racial urban

enclaves as comprising entities unto themselves, Du Bois (1899) characterized urban Black enclaves as "a city within a city" (p. 5). Employing and examining this spatial concept, Du Bois's *The Philadelphia Negro* provides an oft-overlooked analytic bridge between the varied directions taken by urban scholars. Emphasizing the persistent impact of race, historically and contemporarily, Du Bois's analysis offers a path to examine the spatial organization of urban America.[131]

Thus in the *Philadelphia Negro* Du Bois pioneered an urban sociology that remains relevant for contemporary urban analysts.

The Philadelphia Negro was an original treatise based on empirical methods and sociological analysis. It contained analysis in what would become major subfields of modern American sociology, including stratification, class, race, gender, work and occupations, crime, demography and population, institutions, religion, and leisure. These multiple areas were analyzed with a novel multimethod triangulated set of data. This was a quintessential pioneering study because, as Mia Bay has argued, "Since white sociology's natural laws and negative assessments of black capacity tended to be based on evolutionary theory rather than any sort of empirical evidence, American social science offered no research models for DuBois as he set up his study of Philadelphia's black population."[132] Thus, by utilizing his analytic training gained from the Schmoller wing of the German historical school, Du Bois engaged in bold intellectual innovations, producing the first classic of American scientific sociology.

Other scholarly influences besides the GHSE were directly relevant to the production of *The Philadelphia Negro*. As he conducted the research, Du Bois was aware that sociology needed new intellectual directions to reach its potential as a new illuminating discipline. *The Philadelphia Negro* represented Du Bois's first sustained effort to produce a sociological study that broke from the tradition of armchair grand theorizing. Yet, as Randall Collins has argued, intellectual work is always influenced by scholarly activities embedded in historic and contemporaneous networks.[133] Despite the intellectual isolation and racism Du Bois encountered throughout his career, he was influenced by scholarly networks, and so was *The Philadelphia Negro*. As we have seen, Du Bois's educational experiences at Fisk, Harvard, and Berlin helped shape his intellectual orientation. Beyond those experiences, particular works, and intellectual networks, influenced *The Philadelphia Negro*.

By the time Du Bois commenced research for *The Philadelphia Negro* in 1896, Charles Booth had published eight of his seventeen volumes of *Life and Labor of the People in London*.[134] These were groundbreaking works conducted by a large research team that examined the poor of East London. They pioneered particular empirical methods, including statistical surveys and interviews that were used to determine the size of the population of poor East Londoners and to explore the social conditions that circumscribed their lives. Moreover, Booth's volumes pioneered the use of color-coded maps to produce powerful visuals of the people and the social conditions they encountered. Therefore, *Life and Labor of the People in London*, first published during the last decade of the nineteenth century, contained extensive quantitative and qualitative data derived from house-to-house interviews and questionnaires.

Booth's empirical research on the poor broke from the armchair speculation typical of the period. Future social science researches, especially of urban communities, were deeply influenced by Booth's pioneering research.[135] Surveys, interviews, and maps became standard features of many future studies. These methods enabled researchers and activist-scholars to depict oppressed populations through trenchant visuals and accuracy not previously achieved.

The American settlement movement, which developed in London before being transplanted to America, made effective use of empirical techniques pioneered by Booth. Hull House, founded in Chicago in 1889, became the model inspiring the spread of settlement houses across America.[136] The settlement movement was usually though not exclusively organized by talented women who had backgrounds in social science, especially in the emerging field of sociology.[137] Jane Addams, the charismatic and brilliant leader of Hull House, modeled her settlement after the famous Toynbee Hall in London. Hull House leaders were well aware of Booth's studies of the urban poor and its use of survey methodology and maps. In 1894, Hull House leaders produced a volume that examined poor immigrant communities in downtrodden neighborhoods just beyond the settlement's doorstep.

In 1895, Jane Addams published *Hull House Maps and Papers* (*HHM&P*), which examined the social conditions of the poor in Chicago's Nineteenth Ward. Sklar asserts that "until the publication of the multi-volume *Pittsburgh Survey* in 1909, *HHM&P* represented the state of the art of social science analysis of working-class urban life in the United States."[138] Like Booth's studies in London, *HHM&P* utilized scientific methods including surveys, questionnaires, and maps to produce data-driven essays that captured social conditions confronting Chicago's poor.[139] Indeed, the book's skillful use of maps was its most distinctive feature, "the American equivalent of Charles Booth's stunning 'Descriptive Map of London Poverty,' published in five parts in 1891."[140] Thus ensuing empirical studies of urban communities could not afford to ignore the pathbreaking contributions made by *HHM&P.*

Another project that produced multivolume examinations of urban communities in the early twentieth century was the GroBstadt-Documente, headquartered in Berlin. This effort, led by Hans Ostwald, led to the publication, between 1904 and 1908, of a series of fifty-one volumes with the aim of capturing everyday life in Berlin and several additional European cities.[141] A collection of forty writers, none of whom were professional social scientists, published books on the people and institutions of modern European cities. These were usually based on ethnographic research and firsthand personal documents, and their analyses tended to focus on classifying "social types" of urban dwellers (such as bohemians or unmarried mothers).[142] Although these volumes produced rich empirical data on modern city life, they had little impact on professional social science in Europe or the United States. However, their choice of an urban focus and their use of personal documents and ethnography would influence the Chicago school.[143] Although publication of these works began five years after *The Philadelphia Negro*, their appearance is another indicator that Du Bois's classic was produced during a period in which scholars and reformers were turning attention to empirically based studies of urban communities.

The studies, which launched a survey movement, made contributions to this emerging tradition. *The Pittsburgh Survey* was the outcome of a large research team of seventy-four individuals who studied the impact of industrialization on communities of steelworkers in Pittsburgh.[144] This work was initiated in 1907 when a large research team entered the field collecting data on the working class and its living conditions by utilizing surveys, interviews, maps, and photographs. In 1914, the results were published in six volumes collectively known as *The Pittsburgh Survey*. This impressive effort was soon adopted in other cities, initiating the survey movement. Like the other efforts, *The Pittsburgh Survey* reflected the interest of social scientists and reformers in establishing a scientific reservoir of data to address the impact of rapid industrialization, labor strife, and explosive racial and ethnic tensions in the early twentieth century. Nevertheless, neither the GroBstadt-Documente nor *The Pittsburgh Survey* influenced Du Bois's *The Philadelphia Negro* because Du Bois's book predated them by five and ten years respectively. By the time these projects published their results, Du Bois had produced numerous studies at Atlanta University.

Du Bois formally acknowledged the influence of Booth's *Life and Labor of the People in London* on *The Philadelphia Negro*, and that influence is unmistakably present in its pages. Du Bois used techniques like Booth's to collect and analyze his data. Further, the use of numerous graphs, tables, maps, and charts pioneered by Booth was replicated in Du Bois's study. Thus Du Bois was one of the first American social scientists to make use of the empirical methods pioneered by Booth.

Du Bois was also directly influenced by Hull House's publications and leaders. These female leaders and Du Bois shared bonds of oppression, one based on race, the other on gender. Both he and the leaders of Hull House were marginalized from mainstream academia and the emerging sociology programs at prestigious institutions including Chicago, Columbia, and Pennsylvania.[145] Du Bois had no choice but to work at financially impoverished black institutions, while women in the settlement movement developed their own female-based institutions known as settlement houses. Yet a certain freedom derived from this marginalization because Du Bois and settlement leaders could avoid the intellectual censorship otherwise imposed by dominant white male leaders.[146] Du Bois had less freedom than the women did because he battled both white racism and efforts of black leaders to silence his challenging voice. Because of oppression and marginalization, Du Bois and settlement leaders like Addams viewed scholarship and social change differently than dominant white male scholars. Whereas white male scholars, given their privileged position and the rewards they inherited from the status quo, were wary of efforts to use science to promote social change and considered such aims as detrimental to objectivity and detachment, Du Bois and settlement leaders, though believing that the purpose of research was to generate scientific knowledge using the best methods and theories available, viewed scholarship as having the additional goal of informing struggles against oppression. Du Bois and settlement leaders frequently shared forums where they debated and discussed both scholarship and social activism.

The *Philadelphia Negro* profited from these associations and intellectual exchanges. Because he was familiar with the works produced by settlement houses, including Hull House's groundbreaking *Maps and Papers*, Du Bois incorporated insights from their findings, especially as these related to gender. *HHM&P* had even more impact on *The Philadelphia Negro* than the Booth studies did. Isabel Eaton, who participated in the research and writing of *HHM&P*, was chosen to write a section of *The Philadelphia Negro* on black domestic service work: an important contribution given that large numbers of black women worked as domestics and experienced the economic and sexual exploitation associated with that occupation.[147] Clearly, Booth's work and *HHM&P* directly contributed to the quality of Du Bois's first social science classic.

Yet it would be misleading to conflate the contributions of *The Philadelphia Negro* with those of other empirical studies produced at the dawn of the twentieth century. Whereas *Life and Labor of the People in London* and *HHM&P* examined specific social problems, *The Philadelphia Negro* was a comprehensive sociologically informed community study.[148] The former two studies, as products of research teams covering disparate issues, lacked a broad conceptual framework and a distinct sociological argument at a time when sociology was seeking to find conceptual focus. In contrast, as anthropologists Faye V. Harrison and Irene Diggs pointed out, "The method and theoretical point of view which Du Bois articulated for this study helped to lay foundations for research that changed the discourse on race and culture in the social sciences in the United States."[149] However, as we will see, that contribution would not prevent *The Philadelphia Negro* from being largely ignored by mainstream white social scientists for decades.

CHAPTER 3

The Du Bois–Atlanta School of Sociology

Du Bois's goal following the publication of *The Philadelphia Negro* was to establish a research program at a university for sociological research on the nation's black population. He was eager to produce a body of scientific knowledge to combat scientific racism. He wished to locate this research center in a leading white university so it could be nurtured by the resources and prestige such an institution could provide. After realizing that white institutions were not interested in research exploring African Americans, Du Bois hoped several would at least collaborate with such an effort housed at a black university. Both dreams vanished because white universities at the turn of the twentieth century did not hire or collaborate with black scholars, even the brilliant Du Bois. White scholars were not interested in the collaborative project Du Bois proposed. A brief history of Du Bois's early experience in academia sheds light on race and social science at the turn of the twentieth century.

During the last decades of the nineteenth century, Du Bois obtained a bachelor's degree from Fisk, one of the leading historically black universities and a bachelor's, a master's, and a doctorate from Harvard; he also undertook advanced graduate work at the University of Berlin, where he was not granted a doctorate solely on the basis of a technicality.[1] His experience helped him understand the great differences between research-rich white universities and cash-strapped black institutions, many of which functioned as glorified high schools. His ambition to be a great man of letters and literature, enabling him to lift an oppressed race, needed the intellectual fuel and financial capital of the great white universities. After earning a doctorate from Harvard and publishing a book based on his prizewinning dissertation, Du Bois faced the bitter truth that racism stood between his ambitions and landing a professorship at a white university. Like other accomplished black scholars of the period, he could hope to gain employment only at a black university.

Du Bois secured his first position in 1894 as professor of classics at Wilberforce University, a small religious black college located near Xenia, Ohio, where he taught Latin, Greek, German, and English. He yearned to teach sociology there but was not permitted to do so because of the conservative nature of the institution and its lack of recognition that sociology was important.[2] Even though sociology was an amorphous ill-defined field without a definite intellectual direction at the time, Du Bois was clear that his lifework and ambition fell within sociology.[3] Even while studying at Harvard, which did not have a sociology department, Du Bois found his way to sociology through history and philosophy.[4] He explained that at Wilberforce, "try as I might, . . . the institution would have no sociology, even though I offered to teach it on my own time."[5] The two years Du Bois spent at Wilberforce were restrictive intellectually, given its narrow curriculum and lack of resources required for the production of impeachable scholarship.

Du Bois next held an untenured position as assistant instructor in sociology beginning in 1896 at the University of Pennsylvania. At the time, the university and the College Settlement of Philadelphia decided that a study of the city's Negro population was needed. Du Bois was identified as the scholar capable of conducting the research and producing a successful study. *The Philadelphia Negro* derived from this arrangement between Du Bois, Penn's sociology department, and the university. Du Bois's position was merely an affiliation enabling him to conduct the study. Du Bois was deeply disappointed that the position was so marginalized it did not enable him to teach at the university. Recalling the experience, he wrote, "It goes without saying that I did no instructing save once to pilot a pack of idiots through the Negro slum."[6] Further, "In this appointment there was one fly which I have never mentioned; it would have been a fine thing if after this difficult, successful piece of work, the University of Pennsylvania had at least offered me a temporary instructorship in the college or in the Wharton School. . . . White classmates of lower academic rank than I, became full professors at Pennsylvania and Chicago."[7]

ESTABLISHING A SCIENTIFIC SCHOOL OF SOCIOLOGY

With *The Philadelphia Negro* completed in 1897, Du Bois headed to another historic black college, Atlanta University, where he was appointed as professor of economics and history. Here he developed a sociology department, taught sociology, and built a research laboratory in sociology. Du Bois remained at Atlanta for thirteen years, making a name in social science, letters, literature, and activism while pioneering the first scientific school of American sociology. The rudimentary elements of a sociology department had been organized at Atlanta by Dean John Hincks, a professor of economics and history. That early effort faltered when Hincks died in 1895. When Du Bois arrived in 1897 as Hincks's replacement, he began developing Atlanta's sociology department and its curriculum and securing its physical plant in Stone Hall.

In Atlanta, one of the era's locales for race riots and lynching, Du Bois embraced his campus, writing of its majestic setting:

> The hundred hills of Atlanta are not all crowned with factories. On one, toward the west, the setting sun throws three buildings in bold relief against the sky. The beauty of the group lies in its simple unity: —a broad lawn of green rising from the red street and mingled roses and peaches; north and south, two plain and stately halls; and in the midst, half hidden in ivy, a larger building, boldly graceful, sparingly decorated, and with one low spire. It is a restful group, —one never looks for more; it is all here, all intelligible. There I live, and there I hear from day to day the low hum of restful life.[8]

In Atlanta University's serene and austere classroom and laboratories, Du Bois explained that he found "nothing new, no time-saving devices, simply old time-glorified methods of delving for Truth, and searching out the hidden beauties of life, and learning the good of living."[9] Yet accompanying the searches for truth and beauty lurked conservative forces intent on defining and restricting the university's liberal arts program. Within a decade, those forces controlled the university's purse strings enough so that Du Bois would abandon pure science to engage in power politics via a protest organization in New York City.

Though stung by the University of Pennsylvania's racism and rejected by all major white universities, Du Bois accepted the professorship at Atlanta University with the intent of pursuing his lifelong goals. The university was a historic black institution located in the heart of black Atlanta. It was a leading, though resource-starved, black university that refused to segregate its faculty and its sprinkling of white students. As a result, Georgia's state legislature punished it by withholding needed funds.

But the university held attractions for Du Bois because its location near the center of one of America's leading black communities and its proximity to a dynamic city provided an ideal setting in which to study the Negro Problem.[10] The city surrounding the university contained all elements of that problem, making it an ideal location to establish a sociological laboratory. Moreover, at the time Hampton, Tuskegee, and Atlanta Universities had already launched annual projects where data were collected on black communities and analyzed during annual conferences.

However, the Atlanta Conferences differed profoundly from those of Tuskegee and Hampton, which focused on industrial education. The mission of the Tuskegee and Hampton conferences reflected Booker T. Washington's goal of perfecting industrial education among the rural southern masses. Their goal was to improve farming techniques and provide industrial education. At these conferences, farmers, domestic workers, blacksmiths, brick masons, weavers, and washerwomen gathered to share practical knowledge attained in industrial work settings. The attendees engaged in building bonds of solidarity necessary for the great work of moving a "crude and primitive" people toward acquiring civilization that white people would respect. The Tuskegee and Hampton conferences embraced the goal of gaining practical knowledge; pure scholarly pursuits were not their forte, and their leaders had no desires to pursue such a mission.

In contrast, the president and board of trustees of Atlanta University decided that its annual conferences would focus on black urban life, given that many of its graduates lived in cities. The goal of the Atlanta Conference was to collect data on urban black life each year and to analyze it at annual meetings to shed light on black city life. At the outset, the Atlanta Conferences were conceived as a scholarly enterprise embedded in a social scientific framework.

The Du Bois–Atlanta school of sociology was guided by a scholarly principle: sociological and economic factors were hypothesized to be the main causes of racial inequality that relegated black people to the bottom of the social order. The school was preoccupied with racial inequality because its social scientists were mostly African Americans who, like all black people, experienced excruciating racial oppression. Beside lynchings and other terrorist violence, prison, and starvation wages, that oppression rested on the widely accepted claim by whites that blacks were genetically and culturally inferior. Thus to build an intellectual school on the scholarly principle that race inequality stemmed from white racism and that black people were equal to whites was a radical undertaking. Even more threatening to white supremacy, the Du Bois–Atlanta school was convinced that the sociological causes of race inequality could be proven through systematic research. The proponents of the school contended that racism was based in white ignorance and that sociological research was the scientific weapon that could dismantle Jim Crow and racial discrimination. As Du Bois saw it, "The world was thinking wrong about race because it did not know. The ultimate evil was stupidity. The cure for it was knowledge based on scientific investigation."[11] The Du Bois–Atlanta school placed all its bets on truths that they believed the new discipline of sociology would uncover.

Black intellectuals and other informed blacks immediately embraced sociology with a zeal absent in the white community.[12] Blacks scanned the academic horizons, incessantly seeking to learn where the new discipline was being taught and how they could journey to the appropriate campuses to learn the theories and methods of sociology. Scholars who hungered for the knowledge that they thought would free black people made enormous sacrifices, traveling long distances to enroll in summer programs where sociology was taught; endured racism at white campuses; spent precious resources to absorb the substance of the new discipline; and separated the sociological knowledge from the racist ideas of white professors struggling to reconcile long-held beliefs with sociology's unsettling intellectual viewpoints.

Therefore, a rare phenomenon occurred at the dawn of the twentieth century: the leaders of an oppressed people one generation removed from slavery embraced an intellectual discipline as a weapon of liberation. They trekked to Chicago, where they were taught W. I. Thomas's principles of social interaction and the importance of how people defined social situations. At Chicago they were also exposed to the sociology of religion rooted in the social gospel taught by professors Albion Small, Charles Henderson, and William Rainey Harper. At the University of Pennsylvania they attended sociological lectures taught by professors Samuel McCune Lindsay and Carl Kelsey. At Yale they heard lectures by William Graham Sumner on the rightness and truth of folkways and mores. At Columbia they heard the sociologist and eugenicist Franklin Giddings attempting to prove that human behavior could be explained by the principle of "consciousness of kind." Once they finished various forms of sociological training at white universities, they rushed home and developed sociology courses within the curriculum of segregated black schools so that the masses could be exposed to this secular religion and its promise for social transformation.

Yet while these black sociology students attended white universities, they were most riveted by Du Bois, who declared he was "bone of the bone and flesh of the flesh of them that live within the Veil."[13] As they mastered the graduate requirements of the white pioneers of American sociology, they followed the rising sociological star of Du Bois, whom their parents and the larger black community hailed as the great scholar to be emulated. After all, he had done it correctly by earning a degree from Fisk and was the first black to earn a doctorate from Harvard and study in Germany under great social scientists. But more than his degrees, it was Du Bois's scholarship that set fire to the sociological imagination of the young black students. *The Philadelphia Negro* rapidly became a scholarly masterpiece that young scholars admired and set out to emulate. The same held true for the stream of early studies including "The Negroes of Farmville" and *The Black North*. Du Bois rapidly became a scholarly icon for blacks as he published one work after another as a young professor at Atlanta University. The 1903 *Souls of Black Folk* in particular conferred a lofty status on Du Bois. One reader, an educated black minister named Francis Grimke, was moved to write Du Bois, "More than ever do I feel that God has raised you up at this juncture in our history, as a race, to speak to the intelligence of the country on our behalf."[14] Similarly, a talented black student at Cornell, Jessie Fauset, wrote Du Bois that she was glad he had published *Souls* because "We have needed someone to voice the intricacies of the blind maze of thought and action along which the modern educated colored man or woman struggles."[15] Du Bois's innovative methodology and his sociological arguments concerning racial inequality seized the interests of other black sociologists and social scientists. Young scholars began publishing their own studies using Du Bois's work as the model. While they trained at the fabled Ivy League universities in the North, they were drawn by the magnetic force of the Atlanta University program. It was there that Du Bois was developing the scientific school of sociology in which some of these young scholars would participate.

Du Bois was not the first to advocate the necessity of collecting and marshaling empirical data to disprove claims of inferiority promoted by white social scientists. Pioneering black intellectuals had believed that empirical data could sustain a counterargument that sociological and economic factors, not defective genes or culture, were determinants of race inequality. Indeed, Du Bois's first mentor, Alexander Crummell, encouraged him to think along sociological lines as he explored race.[16] Richard Wright Sr., who in the late 1890s served as president of Savannah State College and who was an alumnus and member of Atlanta University's board of trustees, had developed an incisive sociological argument concerning the inequalities blacks faced. Wright was the central figure who had originally conceived of a social scientific laboratory with the mission of explaining black inequality in American cities.[17] With this sociological insight as his guiding principle, Wright began the Atlanta Conferences in 1896 and established the first team of researchers who collected data, culminating in the first two monographs that came out of the conferences.[18] Therefore, it was Wright who crafted the original scientific mission of the Du Bois–Atlanta school as well as an embryonic organizational framework from which to launch it. Wright was instrumental in hiring Du Bois at Atlanta University to establish sociology and expand the scientific study of race.[19] Thus, while sociology was developing in white America, a sociological orientation among some black intellectuals that aligned with the new discipline was already present. Although Du Bois provided the intellectual energy leading to the "takeoff" phase of this scientific project, his initiative fit into a framework that had already developed.

From the outset, the Du Bois–Atlanta school promoted the use of multiple research methods, including fieldwork where researchers entered communities and systematically collected data that served as the foundation on which sociological generalizations were to be formulated. Du Bois pioneered this method in *The Philadelphia Negro*, "The Negroes of Farmville," and numerous studies during his tenure at Atlanta. He developed an explicit research strategy to guide his school very similar to the approach adopted two decades later by the Chicago school, which has received credit for being the original model. In 1897 Du Bois presented a two-pronged research plan to the Federal Bureau of Labor Statistics. In a letter to Carroll Wright, who headed the Bureau, Du Bois stated, "I have been for the last month giving considerable thought as to method of studying certain aspects of the industrial development of the Negro."[20] His "Plan A" called for a series of small preliminary studies of "the economic situation of a typical town containing from 1,000–5,000 Negro inhabitants." Following a research phase designed to ascertain accurate information on a limited scope of issues including occupations, wages, home ownership, hours of labor, economic history, cost of living, organizations, and crops, these community studies were to be published. Plan B envisioned a larger project modeled after *The Philadelphia Negro* but based on the research methods used in the smaller studies. This research plan, partially funded by the government, guided the sociological studies produced over a decade by the Atlanta Sociological Laboratory.

The investigative tools of the Du Bois–Atlanta school encompassed surveys, interviews, participant observation, organizational documents, and census data. These were the empirical techniques that the first generation of black students undergoing graduate training in white universities wanted to master. Through such means, they believed, crucial data for overthrowing racial ignorance and stereotypes would be gathered. Thus Monroe Work, while earning a master's degree in sociology at Chicago under W.I. Thomas and Albion Small, eagerly kept an eye on the groundbreaking research projects headed by Du Bois at Atlanta. As he would later recall, during this period, "I dedicated my life to the gathering of information, the compiling of exact knowledge concerning the Negro."[21] The author of a study of early black sociology notes that "while still a student at the University of Chicago, Monroe Work started collecting all the empirical data he could find on black life, systematically storing it away in envelopes and notebooks; this data gathering would eventually become a central part of a career as the first comprehensive bibliographer of black American culture."[22] His Chicago classmate R.R. Wright Jr., who would earn a doctorate at the University of Pennsylvania, shared Work's desire to conduct empirical studies in the black community.

AN ERASED GENERATION OF BLACK SOCIOLOGISTS AND A SETTLEMENT SCHOLAR

Several scholars who apprenticed with Du Bois constituted the first generation of black sociologists. Work, Wright, and Haynes in Du Bois's Atlanta school made notable intellectual contributions to the field, yet this "hidden generation" of sociologists has been erased from the sociological record. Typical histories of black sociology, after covering Du Bois, move rapidly to the 1920s and 1930s, when the famous trinity of Charles S. Johnson, E. Franklin Frazier, and Oliver Cox were educated at white universities under the guidance of white mentors. Because each of these sociologists was advised by Robert Park at Chicago, he generally receives credit for having produced the first generation of black sociologists.[23] But, as we have seen, to proceed as if the first generation of black sociologists emerged from Chicago in the 1920s and 1930s requires skipping over an entire generation of black sociologists mentored and trained by W.E.B. Du Bois. The historical obscurity of Work,

Wright, and Haynes is striking, given their early contribution and outstanding intellectual achievements. Brief profiles of these pioneers reveal the irony of their historical obscurity.

Monroe Work, the son of slaves, earned an AB degree from the University of Chicago in 1902 and was the first black sociologist to earn a master's degree in sociology from the same institution in 1903. Work was also the first black sociologist to publish in the *American Journal of Sociology*, with his article on black crime in Chicago appearing there in 1900.[24] A superb mathematician, Work became an empirical social scientist publishing scores of quantitative and qualitative articles in some of the leading social science and history journals, including *Social Forces, Annals of the Academy of Political and Social Sciences*, and *Journal of Negro History*. Work was a "data hound" who insisted that you cannot argue with the facts. In 1903 he became a professor at Savannah State, a college founded and headed by Richard R. Wright Sr., father of his classmate Richard R. Wright Jr.

Work became an important member of Du Bois's research team, conducting studies on race and crime, the black church and politics. He presented scholarly papers at the Atlanta annual conferences, and his work was published by the Atlanta Studies series. He was a committed scholar who conducted fieldwork for the Du Bois–Atlanta school, supplying it with primary data on which to base its analyses. Referring to a 1906 study in which he participated for $2.50 per day, Work informed Du Bois: "I am sorry I could not remain longer. The work was very interesting and we have got some of the most valuable material that has been collected in a study of this sort. If there is any further assistance I can render you in this study I shall be pleased to do so. I will help to work out any phase you wish."[25] Work was also an early political ally of Du Bois, agreeing with him that Booker T. Washington's industrial strategy was not sufficiently broad to liberate the race. He accepted Du Bois's invitation to become a founding member of the Niagara movement, organized in 1905.

Work relocated in 1908 to Tuskegee Institute, Booker T. Washington's famous school advocating industrial education, where he founded the Department of Records and Research.[26] Over his long career at Tuskegee, Work became famous as the chronicler of blacks throughout the diaspora. For a quarter of a century, Work founded and edited the *Negro Year Book*, the "Bible" for accurate, empirical, data on black people. Given his many sociological accomplishments, he deserves recognition as a pioneering sociologist of the twentieth century.

Richard R. Wright Jr. was a second-generation family member of the Du Bois–Atlanta school, given that his father—a former slave and an alumnus and trustee member of Atlanta University—was a founding member of the original Atlanta Studies and the original Atlanta Conferences. The senior Wright, it is to be recalled, played an important role in recruiting Du Bois to Atlanta University in 1897. The elder Wright admired Du Bois and was impressed with his credentials as the first African American to earn a doctorate from Harvard and study abroad in Germany. The senior Wright was an accomplished intellectual and educator with long-term service as an administrator and a college president. He informed his son that Du Bois was a great intellectual he should emulate. The son grew up reading Du Bois's scholarship and wanted to become a scholar and study in Germany like his hero. After completing undergraduate studies at his father's university, Wright enrolled at the University of Chicago in the School of Divinity, where he was introduced to the tenets of the social gospel and studied sociology. He pursued the ministry as well as utilizing it as a platform to attack racism. The junior Wright earned his bachelor of divinity degree in 1901 and an MA in 1904 from the University of Chicago. He sailed to Germany in 1903, where he studied religion at the Universities of Berlin and Leipzig. Like Du Bois a decade earlier, he experienced freedom from America's racism in Germany as liberating and as enabling him to become a citizen of the world.

In 1905 Wright entered the University of Pennsylvania, where he pursued a doctorate in sociology and conducted an empirical study on blacks as Du Bois had done earlier. Because of the immense sociological knowledge he had gained at Chicago and working on research projects with Du Bois, Wright was far more expert on race and the "Negro Problem" than his University of Pennsylvania adviser, Professor Carl Kelsey, who taught on the American Negro. Wright recalled his experience in Kelsey's class: "The discussion became so embarrassing that we agreed that he would outline his day's lecture to me before holding his class. Thus, he could eliminate what he called the 'emotional areas' and what I called the 'areas of ignorance and prejudice'—that was our secret agreement which I contended was not one hundred percent professional but at least it helped us 'get along with the class.'"[27] Wright became the first African American to earn a doctorate in sociology at the University of Pennsylvania in 1911.

Following graduate studies, Wright continued to produce scholarly studies in a variety of venues, including *Annals of the Academy of Polit-*

ical and Social Sciences, Southern Workmen, and *Bulletin of the U.S. Department of Labor,* as well as religious journals and proceedings. Wright also became a major administrator, serving as president of Wilberforce College, the first institution where Du Bois held a professorship. In 1938, Wright was elected bishop of the A.M.E. Church, one of the most powerful positions in the black religious community. In these roles, Wright intensified his activism against racism by applying lessons learned from the social gospel and from sociological knowledge he gained over decades. He was close with sociologists and activists in the women's settlement movement. Like them, Wright utilized both academic sociology and social work, viewing them as complementary pursuits.[28] Wright spread the message of the Du Bois–Atlanta school of sociology far beyond academe in his efforts to change America.

George Edmund Haynes was an early member of the Du Bois–Atlanta school of sociology and a member of the first generation of black sociologists. Haynes attended Fisk, which was Du Bois's alma mater, earning a bachelor's degree in 1903. While at Fisk, Haynes developed a relationship with Du Bois described by the historian Francille Wilson: "George Edmund Haynes was an early admirer and lifelong correspondent of W.E.B. Du Bois. . . . Du Bois took a personal and active interest in Haynes's educational and career choices, serving first as Haynes's mentor and informal advisor and later becoming a colleague and friend in much the same fashion as he had done for R.R. Wright Jr. and Monroe Work."[29]

Like Wright and Work, Haynes initially desired to enter the ministry to utilize the pulpit as an avenue to advocate racial change. Following consultation with Du Bois, however, Haynes changed career plans and pursued a career as a social scientist. He earned a master's degree in sociology from Yale in 1904 after studying with William Graham Sumner. He acquired additional sociological knowledge at the University of Chicago before heading to Columbia University to earn the terminal degree. In 1911, Haynes earned a doctorate in economics and sociology, making him the first African American to earn a doctorate from that institution. His doctoral dissertation, which he published the following year, firmly established his reputation as an expert on black migration and northern blacks in the tradition of Du Bois. Expertly trained in quantitative methods, Haynes produced important scientific articles and books on black migration and conducted numerous surveys shedding light on black migrants' economic opportunities. Not content to merely study the difficult transition of southern migrants to city life, Haynes became deeply involved in social work to address their hardships. In 1911, he co-founded the National Urban League, whose mission was to assist migrants in their adjustment to urban life in large cities.

In 1913, Haynes began a four-year stint as head of Fisk University's social science department. His mission, as described by Francille Wilson, was to "offer sociology and black history to all undergraduates and to select the best students for advanced study in sociology and social work." In Haynes's view, "Black leaders also needed to be acquainted with both the methodology of the social sciences and the principles of social work."[30] Haynes embraced the Du Bois–Atlanta school's view that sociology was to be utilized as a liberating force. His work at Fisk sought to disseminate the techniques and substance of the new field of sociology. As Earl Wright has demonstrated, Haynes's work in the training of black students in sociology in the early twentieth century was pioneering because at the time most universities, including prestigious white institutions such as Harvard and Berkeley, had not yet developed departments of sociology.[31]

It was not long before the federal government recruited Haynes because of his expert social science knowledge. In 1918, Haynes became special assistant to the secretary of labor, making him the first African American to hold a subcabinet post in the federal government. In this capacity, Haynes produced numerous studies addressing the economic plight of black people. During his decades as a government official, Haynes remained an active social scientist and eventually accepted a professorship in sociology at the City College of New York for nine years beginning in 1950.

The first "erased generation" of black sociologists produced scholarship germane to the Du Bois–Atlanta school that provided sociological analyses of blacks in both the North and the South. Schools of thought cannot develop if necessary resources are unavailable. The publication of groundbreaking research advancing new theoretical frameworks and methodologies is the driving force opening up possibilities for new schools of thought to develop. Rival interpretations of phenomena differing foundationally from existing paradigms are the hallmark of new intellectual schools.[32] New methodologies can spur the development of schools because they enable scholars to generate empirical findings that challenge dominant paradigms. Du Bois's scientific school of sociology incorporated both novel theory and distinct methods. The school's conception that blacks were not an inferior race and that racial categories were socially constructed challenged the scientific racism of the era. The school's multimethod approach generated quantitative and qualitative data to assess its theoretical positions. This approach contrasted sharply with those used at other universities, where it was common to privilege only one methodological technique. The insistence on scientific rigor and exact measurement of social phenomena also set Du Bois's school apart from other sociological enterprises that did not explicitly confront methodological issues. Du Bois and his colleagues were convinced that careful, systematic research would disprove the ideology of African American inferiority and would undermine the system of racial oppression predicated on it.

Du Bois laid the intellectual foundations of his school by publishing pathbreaking studies incorporating novel theoretical frameworks and a multimethod approach and spanning both rural and urban sociology. With regard to rural sociology, this chapter focuses on "The Negroes of Farmville, Virginia: A Social Study" (hereafter "Farmville") and the model it provided for generating similar studies. With regard to urban sociology, it focuses on *The Philadelphia Negro* and the series of studies Du Bois published examining the black North in 1901. These early works led to the development of America's first scientific school of sociology.

"Farmville" was published in 1898, a year before *The Philadelphia Negro*. It examined the social organization of a small rural community in Virginia, including its class structure and its layers of community institutions, and probed the culture and subjective worlds of the black population, concluding that the people possessed hope and optimism for the future. Du Bois's pioneering multimethod approach was evident in the study: "Du Bois lived with the Farmville Negroes, joined their social life, visited their homes, and asked each family and individual 21 questions concerning birth, sex, and age of each family member, occupation, wages, employment, landownership, and church attendance."[33] To make sure the study contained detailed, systematic, information, Du Bois "collected data on many other subjects such as wages, family income and budgets, value of black property, secret and beneficial societies, slums, gambling, liquor, local prostitution, and group, social, and religious life."[34] The study demonstrated that in rural black America, despite the presence of a vibrant community, the color line was sharply drawn, relegating blacks to the bottom of the social order.

"Farmville" provided an exemplary model for future research: as Jonathan Grossman noted, "This little research gem served as the model for many later studies."[35] Indeed, "Starting in January 1901, the

Department of Labor published four studies by other investigators modeled on Du Bois' Farmville, Va., report, and a fifth study based on Du Bois' theme of the Atlanta investigation of black self-betterment."[36] Here we witness a school of thought developing because an intellectual leader published original scholarship, blazing a path for other scholars to follow. Using "Farmville" as the model, Du Bois's student Richard R. Wright Jr. conducted a study of a northern black community entitled "The Negroes of Xenia, Ohio: A Social Study"; it examined that community's structural and cultural makeup as did "Farmville" and reached similar conclusions regarding the racial oppression of blacks in Xenia. Grossman declared Wright's investigation to be "an excellent study." Du Bois's "Farmville" also became a model for scholars on the other side of the color line.[37] A substantial number of Du Bois's studies following "Farmville" were published by the Bureau of Statistics of Labor under its director Carroll D. Wright. Being an expert statistician, Wright recognized Du Bois's statistical expertise and made census data with meager funds available to Du Bois to conduct research and publish pioneering studies. Du Bois then opened this channel for research and publication to his students.[38] With "Farmville," Du Bois added a pioneering rural study to his developing school that would be greatly boosted by the publication of The Philadelphia Negro a year later.

The Philadelphia Negro (1899) has been acclaimed as the first scientific study of urban blacks. Yet this attribution is narrow because The Philadelphia Negro, along with Hull House Maps and Papers (1895), was one of the first empirically based scientific studies of American sociology. Though white sociologists largely ignored it, two decades later they celebrated The Polish Peasant in Europe and America (1918–20) as the first great empirical study of American sociology, thus stamping Chicago as the pioneering school in this regard. Lewis Coser, for example, called The Polish Peasant "a monumental achievement, the earliest major landmark of American sociological research."[39] In doing so he epitomized the practice among white scholars of obscuring Du Bois's prominent role in the birth of American sociology.

The Philadelphia Negro examined the transition of poor blacks into Philadelphia as they migrated from the rural South. As The Polish Peasant would do two decades later, it investigated the institutional and cultural processes that made their transition possible. The Philadelphia Negro also examined the white racism and discrimination faced by Philadelphia blacks, obstacles that differed drastically from those faced by European immigrants. Du Bois demonstrated that the urban spaces of

Philadelphia were habitats created not by natural forces but by racial conflict and vested interests.[40] He analyzed the larger environment in which the political and economic struggles were waged and the internal structures and culture of the black community. However, it is less well known that Du Bois followed up *The Philadelphia Negro* with a series of three studies of northern black communities published in the *New York Times* in November and December 1901. These studies, analyzing black communities in New York, Boston, and Philadelphia, underscored the importance of northern race dynamics and emphasized that a substantial proportion of the black population lived in cities. Many white sociologists focused on southern blacks because they embraced Washington's claim that blacks were a southern rural people and that their future would be determined in the South, yet southern blacks were even then migrating to large northern cities, and soon they would be doing so in unprecedented numbers.[41] Du Bois's northern studies identified the need for research on urban black communities if race was to be fully understood. By studying New York and Boston, Du Bois found that the conditions uncovered by *The Philadelphia Negro* were widespread throughout American cities. While there were differences, the three black communities were strikingly similar. Black immigrants established a semblance of community autonomy because they "built negro churches, organized negro societies, settled in negro neighborhoods, and hired out to work in gangs."[42] Yet in all three communities, systematic discrimination meant "that the northern negro receives less wages for his work and pays more rent for worse houses than white workmen, and that it is not altogether a matter of fitness that confines his work chiefly to common labor and menial service."[43] Du Bois focused on the "policy of refusing negroes remunerative work" because it was the major cause of poverty, crime, idleness, lack of education, and weak families. These *New York Times* articles broadcast findings first discovered in *The Philadelphia Negro* to a larger audience of scholars and the general public.

The scholarly influence of *The Philadelphia Negro* and the *Times* articles on young black social scientists and on white women in the settlement movement was immediate. In 1911 Wright completed his dissertation, "The Negro in Pennsylvania: A Study of in Economic History," at the University of Pennsylvania and published it as a book under the same name in 1912. Following Du Bois, Wright provided painstaking statistical and qualitative data for his analysis of black Pennsylvanians. The data revealed there was no "Negro Problem":

"The 'Negro Problem'—that condition which is peculiar to Negroes, and common to them—is rather found in the attitudes of the white race toward the Negro; an attitude of a majority which seeks to shut out a minority from the enjoyment of the whole social and economic life."[44]

Wright's account of how he came to undertake his study shows that one woman in the Chicago settlement movement, the white female sociologist Frances Kellor, was familiar with *The Philadelphia Negro* and held it in high esteem: "One day a former University of Chicago schoolmate of mine, Miss Frances Keller [*sic*], told me that the University of Pennsylvania was looking for a colored man to take a fellowship in sociology and to do research in Negro-American conditions in Pennsylvania, following the work so well done by Dr. W.E.B. DuBois on 'The Philadelphia Negro.' She advised me to apply."[45] Wright took Kellor's advice because he had previously worked on numerous research projects headed by Du Bois and he admired his scholarship.

George Edmund Haynes, another intellectual protégé of Du Bois who knew him and was familiar with his scholarship, produced his dissertation in sociology and economics, "The Negro at Work in New York City," at Columbia University in 1911 and published it as a book in 1912. Haynes relates that his study on black New Yorkers was influenced by Du Bois and Wright: "Conditions among Negroes in Philadelphia have been adequately studied in the work of Dr. W.E.B. DuBois and Dr. R.R. Wright, Jr. It is to be hoped that some time soon the need of similar inquiries in other cities—East, West, North and South—may be realized and that provision may be made in this way for the guidance of the growing impulses of those who wish to better conditions in urban centers."[46] Haynes's study was based on data collected using multiple methods: the analysis of census reports, including unpublished schedules for 2,500 families of the New York State Census of 1905; block-to-block canvassing; and compilation of records of business enterprises that were obtained by personal interviews.[47] For Haynes, it was essential for the study to be based on "painstaking investigation." As Du Bois had argued in the *Times* articles, Haynes asserted that "Negroes will continue to migrate to the urban centers and . . . they will come to the cities in comparatively large numbers to stay." According to Haynes, black New Yorkers early in the twentieth century were disproportionately poor and disadvantaged because of "greater handicaps due to [their] previous condition of servitude" and "the prejudiced opposition of the white world that surrounds [them]."[48] Haynes's economic sociology emphasizing work and poverty contributed to the body of early research produced by the Du Bois–Atlanta school.

Monroe Work was a Du Bois protégé influenced by his mentors' early publications. Work's biographer reports that he "became involved in the Atlanta Studies while still a student in Chicago."[49] Work became a central member of Du Bois's school in its early days, working closely with Du Bois and other colleagues to produce numerous studies on northern and southern black communities modeled after Du Bois's pioneering scholarship. In his studies of Negro crime in northern and southern cities, Work demonstrated that crime rates were determined not by racial traits but by social conditions.[50] Work also conducted studies on the black church in northern and southern communities, demonstrating what Du Bois had long argued, that churches were the central institution in the national black community.[51] Like Du Bois, Work argued in "The Importance of Sociology for the Negro" that "sociological research could provide a great service to blacks through the compilation of factual data, since no group had suffered more from a lack of knowledge concerning themselves."[52] Work embodied the intellectual and political values of the Du Bois–Atlanta school because he dedicated his life "to the gathering of information, the compiling of exact knowledge concerning the Negro."

This first generation of black graduates from white sociology departments looked toward Atlanta, where Du Bois was engaged in pioneering empirical research not being conducted elsewhere, and valued Du Bois's approach over that of white sociologists. Du Bois incorporated them into his research projects. Two decades before E. Franklin Frazier, Charles Johnson, and Oliver Cox emerged on the sociological stage, this first generation conducted field research for Du Bois, wrote research reports, read papers at annual conferences, and engaged in scholarly debates. They energized Du Bois's school of scientific sociology and provided it with scholarly expertise. They were joined at Atlanta by two tiers of volunteer researchers: college-trained undergraduates who had received their bachelor's from historically black colleges and Du Bois's undergraduate and graduate students at Atlanta.

Du Bois took a deep interest in those students, and it was not unusual for him to know them personally, either through their parents or through associations he had established with them while they were attending segregated undergraduate institutions. Du Bois often became their mentor, providing advice on career choices, research projects, and funding sources and shepherding their work to publication.[53] These students idealized Du Bois as a role model and studied his work thoroughly, internalizing its methodology and theoretical orientations. They also embraced Du Bois's activism and the ways he utilized his scholarship to inform social change work. As a result, some of these students became major scholars, while others became educational leaders and some even college presidents.

Currently there exists no sustained analysis of how such important and pioneering figures could be erased from the collective memory of sociology for a century. Yet this erasure speaks volumes about the power of racism in American science. Clearly Du Bois's pivotal scholarship was not the only casualty of racism because his entire school of scholars and researchers suffered similar fates. Their marginalization from mainstream social science was so complete that their contributions have gone unrecognized. However, Du Bois's mentoring of this generation, which enabled them to flower intellectually, is an enduring legacy of his school. Even more significant, this hidden generation, who were partially trained by first-generation white sociologists including Small and Thomas at Chicago, Sumner at Yale, Giddings at Columbia, and Kelsey at Pennsylvania, accessed Du Bois and his ideas and then advanced his arguments even as they were pursuing their studies at Chicago and other elite white universities. This trend would continue two decades later when the second generation of black sociologists was trained at Chicago by Robert Park.

Du Bois did not restrict his mentoring to black scholars trained in his school. Numerous white scholars and leaders contributed to the Atlanta school by writing reports, reading scholarly papers, and attending its annual conferences. Mary White Ovington, a white intellectual and activist, was influenced by Du Bois's writings, including *The Philadelphia Negro,* the *New York Times* articles, and the Atlanta Studies. In 1911, Ovington published a study entitled *Half a Man: The Status of the Negro in New York.* Ovington concentrated on economic status of black New Yorkers, carefully examining their employment opportunities and working conditions. She found racial discrimination to be a serious problem throughout New York and especially in the labor market. More than other researchers, Ovington devoted detailed attention to conditions of black women in New York, including a chapter titled "The Colored Woman as Bread Winner" where she contrasted their economic and labor market experiences with those of white women. Black women were largely restricted to domestic work and other menial tasks. In a moving passage, Ovington described the condition of black women:

If the Negro civilization of New York is to be lifted to a higher level, the white race must consistently play a finer and more generous part toward the colored woman. There are many inherent difficulties against which she must contend. Slavery deprived her of family life, set her to daily toil in the field, or appropriated her mother's instincts for the white child. She has today the difficult task of maintaining the integrity and purity of the home. Many times she has succeeded, often she has failed, some-times she has not even tried. A vicious environment has strengthened her passions and degraded her from earliest girlhood. Beyond any people in the city she needs all the encouragement that philanthropy, that human courtesy and respect, that the fellowship of the workers can give,—she needs her full status as a woman.[54]

Although containing gender stereotypes, this assessment captures the unique oppression black women faced in large northern cities in the early twentieth century. Because Ovington was a member of the settlement movement, like Jane Addams, Isabel Eaton, Florence Kellor, and numerous others who studied and sought solutions to gender inequality, she was sensitized to gender discrimination.[55] Ovington's study tended to be descriptive given its reliance on secondary data, but it was nonetheless a major contribution to the understanding of a northern black community during the first decade of the twentieth century. The study was an important addition to the Du Bois–Atlanta's school offerings in urban and economic sociology.

Ovington revealed how her book was influenced by black social scientists associated with the Atlanta school and by Du Bois himself. As the junior Wright recalled, "Miss Ovington, a young woman, studying race relations came to my mission and went away to write *Half a Man* which she says was inspired by our conversation, and to devote a full life of over 40 years in trying to get the black man considered as a whole man."[56] In her book Ovington praised Wright's "careful study" on the conditions of northern blacks and described him as having the "right to speak with authority."[57] She also commended Haynes for "an intensive study, shortly to be published, on the wage-earners and business enterprises among Negroes in New York."[58] Du Bois's own decisive role in the production of Ovington's book is revealed in a letter Ovington wrote to Du Bois stating, "I want very much to talk with you. You see, you have talked to me through your writings for many years and have lately made me want to work as I never wanted to work before, but I need now to ask directly for advice."[59] Later she informed Du Bois, "I have received the Atlanta publications, Nos. 1, 2, 5, 7 & 8." She also told him that she had read his *Times* articles and other writings on blacks in the North.

Du Bois was generous with his time mentoring scholars associated with his school. In her autobiography, Ovington recounts that in 1904 Du Bois invited her to attend the Atlanta Conference. Excitedly, she accepted: "I would be entertained at the university. Would I Come? Of course I Would!"[60] While at the conference, Ovington "could always turn to the Du Bois apartment. There, if the Doctor and Mrs. Du Bois were away, I would browse in their excellent library."[61] Thus Du Bois mentored across the color line, enabling scholars like Ovington to contribute numerous publications in the tradition of the Atlanta school. This early work culminated in Ovington's becoming a co-founder of the National Association for the Advancement of Colored People (NAACP), where she worked for decades with Du Bois to dismantle racism. Clearly, Du Bois was not an isolated thinker but a productive intellectual embedded in scholarly networks. In the early days of sociology when sociologists were seeking intellectual direction to explain just what a sociologist was, Du Bois was developing the scientific methods and the connections that would enable him to build America's first school of scientific sociology.

In a national study of sociology courses and departments at the turn of the nineteenth century, Frank Tolman documented Du Bois's extensive research activities. He reported that "graduate study of the social problems in the South by the most approved scientific methods is carried on by the Atlanta Conference, composed of graduates of Atlanta, Fisk, and other institutions. The aim is to make Atlanta University the center of an intelligent and thoroughgoing study of the negro problems. Five reports of the conference have been published, and a sixth in preparation."[62] Tolman stated that Chicago had developed the most advanced and differentiated graduate program. Early in the twentieth century, sociology graduate students at Chicago were dependent on local charities to provide them with methodological training and opportunities to conduct research. For black students at white universities, Du Bois and his sociological laboratory at Atlanta provided opportunities to become proficient in scientific methodologies and "hands-on" research. The Du Bois–Atlanta school attracted these students interested in a sociology they believed capable of lifting a race out of oppression.

The annual research projects and the Atlanta Conferences presented the ideal frameworks for Du Bois to build a research center. Both had been launched two years before Du Bois's arrival; thus Du Bois had some latitude to reshape them. Although the Atlanta Studies series and its conferences had been organized by R. R. Wright Sr., they were headed by George Bradford, a white Atlanta University trustee and Boston businessman. Because Bradford had no academic training and little discretionary time, the future and scope of the studies and the annual conferences were limited. After just two years of operation, the two enterprises were in jeopardy. Du Bois, immediately upon arrival, took control. As he later explained, "This program at Atlanta, I sought to swing as on a pivot to one of scientific investigation into social conditions primarily for scientific ends."[63] Du Bois did so by developing what he called the "Laboratory in Sociology at Atlanta University," with the mission to conduct annual studies addressing a specific research topic each year.[64] The vision was for these studies to be generated continuously for one hundred years, with each being repeated every decade to capture longitudinal changes. The intellectual strategy was that pioneered in *The Philadelphia Negro* where data were collected by multiple methods, including surveys, interviews, participant observation, and ethnographic materials. This approach enabled the researcher to triangulate data to ferret out errors. The inductive method was utilized to guide data analysis and the construction of sociological generalizations. Wright considered Du Bois's approach to the studies to be consistent with his original vision.

For thirteen consecutive years, Du Bois and his research teams conducted annual studies exploring particular issues affecting African Americans, discussed them at the annual conference with scholars and local and national leaders, and revised them for publication. The research teams consisted of Du Bois's Atlanta-trained graduate and undergraduate students, alumni of select black colleges, community leaders, and trained social scientists. In the early days of the new discipline, Du Bois also exposed black women to sociological research as he instructed them at the university and assigned research responsibilities to them in the field.[65] Because of Du Bois's groundbreaking work with the Laboratory and his scholarly charisma, a wide range of black scholars sought out research roles in his Atlanta projects.

For more than a decade, the Laboratory produced a significant body of sociological scholarship on African Americans. While Atlanta served as the principal site for study, research extended far beyond it. Thus, in one study on crime, Du Bois found that "in 10 Georgia counties crime was increasing, while in 56 counties crime was decreasing."[66] In another study examining black self-help, Du Bois chose "nine southern cities of varying size and . . . selected in them such organizations of Negroes as were engaged in benevolent and reformatory work."[67] This scholarship provided primary data and formulated new interpretations of black America regarding social organization, class, religion, crime, health, occupations, education, demography and population, leisure, migration, family, urbanization, and culture.

In these early years of American sociology, no comparable research programs existed that produced empirical research on African Americans. For example, the University of Chicago's sociology department, founded in 1892, did not produce a dissertation on blacks until 1919, and very few followed that one.[68] In contrast, as early as 1898, students at Atlanta University enrolled in sociology and related classes to master the new methods and theories of sociology as they prepared to become researchers. These efforts bore fruit: for over a decade, field researchers from the Laboratory in Sociology at Atlanta entered research sites in numerous communities and collected data that served as the foundation of published scholarship.

The Negro Artisan, published in 1902, provides an example of the extensive research activities conducted at Atlanta University in the early twentieth century. The future for African Americans appeared bleak at this time because Jim Crow was taking root throughout the South and lynching was on the rise. Black voters in the South had been disenfranchised. Most blacks had become victims of sharecropping arrangements where they barely eked out a living. The black leader Booker T. Washington insisted that manual labor and the appeasement of whites were the only routes to liberation. White social scientists comforted white elites by producing "scientific" studies predicting black extinction because moral, mental, and physical degeneracy was reaching irreversible proportions. Du Bois, however, surveyed the racial horizon and concluded that the claims of the prophets of black doom were greatly exaggerated. As he wrote in *The Negro Artisan*'s introduction, "The twelfth census has, let us hope, set at rest silly predictions of the dying out of the Negro in any reasonably near future. The nine million Negroes here in the land, increasing steadily at the rate of over a 150,000 a year, are destined to be part and parcel of the Nation for many a day if not forever."[69] As a sociologist, he believed that a careful scientific study of Negro artisans would reveal concrete reasons for optimism about the race. But Du Bois made clear that "a careful study of the conditions and needs of the Negro population—a study conducted with scientific calm and accuracy, and removed so far as possible from prejudice or partisan bias," was to be the guiding force of the study rather than unfounded optimism or fear.[70] In discussing the black population, he wrote, "We must no longer guess at their condition, we must know it."[71]

The research for *The Negro Artisan* was thorough. Professional sociologists, college graduates who were trained researchers, and students from black colleges conducted nine extensive surveys of the artisans themselves, their children, their employers, and labor union leaders. Thirty-five field researchers, known as correspondents, collected data in thirty-two states and in Canada and the Caribbean. The surveys as well as interviews and participant observation provided the basis for extensive reports. The data were classified by region, gender, and educational levels so that subgroups could be analyzed. Organizational and institutional histories were collected so artisans could be analyzed within a historical context that compared their conditions in slavery to their conditions in freedom. Census data and government reports made possible the use of charts and graphs to map the distribution and status of these skilled workers.

Du Bois reasoned that the future of black artisans could not be accurately projected without information from black children regarding their occupational aspirations. Because he understood that the socialization of children significantly influenced their career choices, he had six hundred students in the public schools of Atlanta, Georgia, write answers to the following questions:[72]

1. What kinds of work do you do at home?
   Do you sew? Do you sweep?
   Do you cook? Do you tend chickens?
   Do you wash? Do you work in the garden?
   Do you iron? Do you keep flowers?
2. Have you got a hammer and saw at home?
   Do you use them?
   Have you any other tools at home?
3. Do you ever make little ornaments to hang on the walls, or to put anywhere in the house?
4. What do you like to do best?
5. What are you going to do when you grow up?
6. How old are you?
7. What is your name?
8. Where do you live?

Speaking of the children's participation, Francille Wilson wrote that the study contained "what is apparently the first published research on black children, offering an all too brief portrait of turn-of-the-century working-class home life and occupational aspirations."[73]

The data allowed Du Bois and his collaborators to reach important conclusions regarding black artisans. First, they were not becoming extinct: their numbers were increasing in certain regions, while declining in others. Second, industrial schools were important to the training of artisans but were often too costly and ineffective. Liberal arts education was crucial because artisans needed to understand the world as well as build things upon it. This was not a finding that gave comfort to Booker T. Washington's hopes of expanding his leadership by building more schools concerned exclusively with industrial education. Finally, Du Bois found that white racism, especially within labor unions, was a major barrier limiting the choices and careers of black skilled workers.

Beyond its practical and political significance, *The Negro Artisan* was a groundbreaking sociological work because it produced empirical data and arguments that contradicted popular claims of the day. It was a study that enabled voices of ordinary people to be heard through their extensive quotes embedded in the monograph. Above all, it revealed that it was possible for a team of researchers—all black—to take to the field, collect data systematically, and produce a masterful sociological work. The first generation of black sociologists took notice and made themselves available to the young scholar at Atlanta so they too could become highly skilled sociologists. As Wilson argued, "The most lasting impact of *The Negro Artisan* . . . was its influence on other black scholars."[74] It joined *The Philadelphia Negro,* "Farmville," and *The Souls of Black Folk* as pioneering classics that helped launched Du Bois's Atlanta school. Thus, each year during the first decade of the twentieth century, studies from the Atlanta Sociological Laboratory rolled off the presses at Atlanta University as Du Bois shuttled between communities, lecturing on the social change implications of his scientific studies.[75]

THE ATLANTA CONFERENCES

In the spring of each year, scholars and leaders from across the nation converged at Atlanta University to participate in a conference where they would debate the intellectual and practical implications of that year's research findings. They also formulated resolutions that advocated social change.

Rather than being tangential to the scholarly activities of the research laboratory, the annual Atlanta Conferences operated in tandem with them as a scholarly enterprise. As conference convener and corresponding secretary, Du Bois organized the conferences, paying attention to minute details. For example, in February 1910 Du Bois was concerned with the quality of the visuals at the upcoming May conference. Before overhead projectors and PowerPoint technologies existed, Du Bois dispatched Atlanta University's president a letter listing items he required, including a "reflectograph to throw charts on a screen during the conference instead of hanging them around the Walls."[76] Like Small at Chicago, Du Bois was an institution builder who created favorable conditions at his school that enhanced the work of colleagues and students. Once details were settled, major scholars and leaders gathered to engage in serious, stimulating debates over issues of science, race, and inequality.

Annual conference participants included leading black scholars such as Monroe Work, Eugene Harris, Savannah State College president R. R. Wright Sr., Howard University sociologist and dean Kelly Miller, and John Hope, the future president of Morehouse and Atlanta University. Black and white leaders including Booker T. Washington, Georgia governor Allen D. Candler, and Charles William Eliot, the twenty-first president of Harvard University, attended the conference. Leading scholars and activists of the settlement movement also attended, including Sophonisba P. Breckinridge; the movement's influential leader and founder Jane Addams; Florence Kelley, a superb empirical sociologist and the guiding scholar of *Hull House Maps and Papers*; and Mary White Ovington, who several years later would issue a call culminating in the formation of the NAACP. Mary Church Terrell, NAACP founder and leader of the National Association of Colored Women's Club, participated in the conferences. Leading white scholars from prestigious universities and important institutions participated. An examination of the participation of Walter Willcox, Frank Sanborn, Franz Boas, and Jane Addams provides a sense of the important role that the conferences played in the Du Bois–Atlanta school of sociology.

WALTER WILLCOX, FRANK SANBORN, FRANZ BOAS, AND JANE ADDAMS IN ATLANTA

Walter Willcox's attendance at the conference in 1905 is especially notable because it underscores how important these early conferences were and the influence Du Bois exercised through these scholarly meetings held at the dawn of the twentieth century. Willcox served as an influential professor of economics for four decades at Cornell University, begin ning in 1891. He was a leading academic economist and president of the American Economic Association, which served as the professional home for early sociologists before the American Sociological Society was organized in 1905. Willcox was a central figure in the American Statistical Association, serving as its president in 1911, and was a pioneering American demographer, serving as a statistician for the Census Bureau for over three decades beginning in 1899. In this capacity, he presided over numerous studies of the American Negro.[77] Although positioning himself as a liberal, Willcox was an active member of the American eugenics movement and was actually a racist who predicted that because blacks were inferior Darwinian law would inevitably lead to their extinction.[78] Nevertheless, Du Bois did not exclude scholars from the conferences because their views differed from his own. The annual conferences considered a variety of viewpoints on the topics they researched, and although Willcox held racist views, he was considered to have a valuable viewpoint, especially given his stature as a leading economist and official at the Census Bureau. Du Bois invited Willcox to attend the 1905 conference, but Willcox hesitated until receiving instruction from Cornell's president: "I have just had a conference with President Schurman regarding your invitation to attend the Conference at Atlanta, May 30th. He was away from Ithaca until two days ago. He strongly advised me to accept the invitation and that solves the only question remaining in my mind. You may therefore count upon my presence unless something entirely unforeseen arises to prevent it."[79] Although Du Bois's scholarship emanating from Atlanta University could be ignored by the mainstream, his scholarly status, recognized by presidents of elite universities, could not.

Another highly influential scholar, Frank Sanborn, who differed from Willcox politically, was attracted to the Atlanta Conferences. Sanborn was a social scientist and founder of the American Social Science Association (ASSA) in 1865. This organization was an incubator of modern American social sciences, including sociology. Sanborn was also member of a small group that helped finance John Brown's October 16–18, 1859, raid on Harper's Ferry. When he agreed to participate in the Atlanta Conference in 1904, Atlanta's president took notice, writing to Du Bois, "I think we are very fortunate in getting Mr. Frank B. Sanborn to speak at the Conference and also to give the Commencement address. His connection with humanitarian and charitable work for so many years, including prison reform, especially fit him for the former, while his association with the old line of abolitionists and all the Concord philosophers will make him an interesting personality to present on our Commencement platform."[80] The Atlanta Conferences enriched academic life at Atlanta University given that influential and famous scholars often addressed the commencements held at the time of the conferences.

A closer examination of Sanborn's participation at the conference as reported in the ASSA's journal is illuminating. Sanborn's social science approach, like Du Bois's, insisted on the collection of facts and the importance of their use in social reform.[81] At the Ninth Atlanta Conference in 1904, Sanborn, in his capacity as secretary of the ASSA, presented a rich and expertly argued paper titled "Negro Crime." Sanborn reported the conferees' reaction to his paper: "Joining in the discussion, Mr. Sanborn said that he had taken part in a most interesting and instructive Conference at the Atlanta University May 21, 1904, in which the questions concerning negro crime were treated by negroes themselves (ministers, school-teachers, and others) with a directness and practical good sense not always seen by him in meetings of the Prison Association since 1870, when it was organized by members of the Social Science Association."[82] Sanborn identified as the editor of the Atlanta Studies "W.E.B. Du Bois, a colored native of Massachusetts, who was educated at Harvard and in Germany." Speaking of the pioneering study on black crime that was to result, Sanborn concluded, "Some extracts from this work will have a bearing on one marked aspect [black crime] of the race question much debated of late."

The intellectual engagement at the 1906 conference between Du Bois and Franz Boas, the Columbia University anthropologist considered to have engineered a paradigmatic shift regarding race in the social sciences, reveals the impact of the scintillating exchanges on conference participants. While attending that conference, on the theme "Health and Physique of the Negro American," Boas delivered a stunning commencement address to the Atlanta University graduates challenging them to reject claims of black inferiority. Boas stated that ancient Africans had shown inventive genius in constructing stupendous kingdoms featuring technological breakthroughs that lifted human civilizations to new heights. He beckoned the graduates to follow in the footsteps of their African ancestors and achieve greatness because history had proven they were not inferior to the white man. This was, indeed, an unorthodox race message boldly espoused in Jim Crow Atlanta. Du Bois recalled the impact it had on him:

> I remember my own rather sudden awakening from the paralysis of this judgment taught me in high school and in two of the world's great universities. Franz Boas came to Atlanta University where I was teaching history in 1906 and said to a graduating class: You need not be ashamed of your African past; and then he recounted the history of the black kingdoms south of the Sahara for a thousand years. I was too astonished to speak. All of this I had never heard and I came then and afterwards to realize how the silence and neglect of science can let truth utterly disappear or even be unconsciously distorted.[83]

It was rare, indeed, for Professor Du Bois to be too astonished to speak.

The relationship that flowered between Du Bois and Boas at the 1906 conference documents the scientific and political value of these pioneering gatherings. Prior to 1906, Du Bois and Boas's first contact occurred when they exchanged letters regarding Du Bois's invitation for Boas to speak at the conference. Boas accepted the invitation because he believed "the Atlanta Conference was an opportunity to present really new evidence and new points of view on the Black problem."[84] Although the two men were aware of each other's work, the Atlanta Conferences enabled them to initiate a unique personal and professional relationship that lasted over three decades.[85] That relationship was made easier because both scholars had experienced discrimination and had chosen to become public intellectuals addressing social inequality. At the conference, Boas and Du Bois discussed the causes of race inequality and what could be done to eradicate it.

A decade older than Du Bois, Boas had been born into an upper-middle-class Jewish family in 1858. Because he was a Jew, Boas experienced anti-Semitic discrimination in both Germany and the United States.[86] Like Du Bois, Boas had attended German universities where he was taught by philosophers and historians who themselves had been influenced by scholars who took history seriously, including Goethe, Hegel, Marx, Nietzsche, and Kant. Like Du Bois, Boas was influenced by his professors to think inductively and to develop a deep historical and sociological imagination.[87] Boas also shared with Du Bois a set of deeply held democratic values that led him to plead the cause of the oppressed. Like Du Bois, Boas became a public intellectual utilizing social science to initiate social transformations. Boas's stature as a highly influential anthropologist, and as a white man, was important to Du Bois's mission to use social science scholarship effectively to liberate his race and to keep Booker T. Washington in check. In return, Du Bois's prominence as a scholar and a black leader provided Boas with a platform to showcase his pioneering scholarship on race and culture. That platform offered Boas additional leverage to assist in the great struggle to bring racial justice to a society catastrophically flawed by racism.

The intellectual similarities in Du Bois's and Boas' scholarship on science and race made for a near-perfect scholarly marriage. Boas rejected the social Darwinist thesis that all races traveled through identical stages on their journey from savagery to high civilization. He was vociferous in his postulate that races were not groups whose biological heritage placed them at different levels on an evolutionary hierarchy.[88] To the contrary, race outcomes for Boas were determined by historical and sociological circumstances. Thus all racial groups were products of their culture and social surroundings. As a result, there existed no superior and inferior races but only groups with different cultures. Culture in this sense was not an ultimate, highly developed state that human groups reached if properly endowed. Each race, argued Boas, possessed an independent culture, so there were as many cultures as there were distinct groups. Therefore, the existence of universal criteria by which cultures could be judged was a logical and sociological impossibility.[89]

An affinity between Du Bois and Boas was their rejection of doctrines declaring black Americans inferior. Boas was clear that white racism, rather than flawed genetics or black cultural practices, was the cause of racial inequality. He argued, "When, finally, we consider the inferior position held by the Negro race of the United States, . . . we must not forget that the old race-feeling of the inferiority of the colored is as potent as ever and is a formidable obstacle to its advance and progress. . . . It is hardly possible to say what would become of the Negro if he were able to live with the whites on absolutely equal terms."[90] Boas advanced this radical position during the height of black oppression and scientific racism. It was a time when social scientists weighed the size of black skulls, brain cavities, and facial configurations, always concluding that the measurements proved black inferiority. While white scholars and statisticians predicted that black genetic inferiority would destroy the black race, white mobs lynched blacks and led riots destroying their property and their hopes.[91] Boas's approach to racial inequality, formulated as early as the mid-1880s and espoused by a white scholar of European origins, challenged white social scientists and the virulent racism that was so widespread in America.[92]

Boas's challenge rested on science rather than conjecture and armchair theorizing. As Du Bois did for sociology, Boas insisted on a scientific anthropology based on careful measurement and rigorously executed inductive studies. Boas and Du Bois challenged social Darwinists to prove racial inferiority scientifically. They both took scientific rivals to task by exposing their pseudoscience, fuzzy and inaccurate measurements, and biased, abstract formulations. Both scholars used the most rigorous scientific techniques of their day, thus injecting science into sociology and anthropology. For example, Boas demonstrated that brain sizes and the qualities of the cephalic cavities between racial groups overlapped so extensively they could not account for racial outcomes because internal variation within races outweighed differences between them.

Du Bois recognized in Boas a kindred spirit and a social scientist who espoused ideas similar to his own. Thus Du Bois summoned Boas to the Atlanta Conference in 1906 because through him he could further transmit and advance his scientific agenda promoting racial change and bolster his case against Booker T. Washington. Indeed, Washington's accommodationist message supported social Darwinism rather than the claims of social equality espoused by Du Bois and Boas. Furthermore, Du Bois, always the scholar, was anxious to be exposed to innovative scholarship, and Boas had produced work that broke with the scientific racism of the day. Du Bois knew a "good" white man when he saw one precisely because they were so rare. Boas, while serving as a museum curator, had vigorously attacked the racist classifications of human groups displayed in exhibits that Du Bois also despised. And because, as the old postbellum saying goes, "The white man's ice is always colder," Boas's scientific findings would gain more credence among more people than those of Du Bois.

Yet racism in America and abroad limited the similarities between the pioneering sociologist and the anthropologist. Boas did experience anti-Semitism that made it difficult for him to obtain a suitable professorship in Germany, and although he journeyed to America seeking a position in the merit-based country that preached equal opportunity, discrimination against Jews followed him to the United States. William Rainey Harper, president of the University of Chicago, denied Boas a professorship. It was difficult for Boas to attain work at other universities as well. All the same, the anti-Semitism that Boas encountered paled in comparison to the racism Du Bois encountered. Boas's white skin provided him with racial privileges unavailable to Du Bois. Boas secured a professorship at Clark in 1889, where he remained until 1892. He then accepted an academic position that Du Bois could only dream of: he was hired at Columbia as a lecturer in 1896 and became professor of anthropology in 1899, remaining there until his death in 1942. At

Columbia, Boas was thrust into a position of power where he utilized considerable intellectual resources and trained gifted graduate students. These students, who included Margaret Mead, Melville Herskovits, Alfred Kroeber, Ruth Benedict, Zora Neale Hurston, Otto Klineberg, and Ashley Montagu, became renowned scholars in their own right and produced influential scholarship, demonstrating the merits of Boas's scientific approach. At Atlanta University, in contrast, Du Bois barely had resources to train undergraduates and a few master's students. While these students were indispensable to the mission of the Du Bois–Atlanta school, they were greatly outnumbered by the privileged young white students attracted to Boas and nourished by one of the world's greatest research universities.

Boas also differed from Du Bois in aspects of his thinking on race. As a creature of those racist cultures in which he was socialized, Boas could not free himself completely from racism in his thinking. In that sense, he was imprisoned by his own cultures. Charles Brigg has argued that "if culture produces incarceration, anthropologists are uniquely qualified to bust people of out jail."[93] But when it came to race, Boas could not break cleanly from the biases inherent in social science. Thus in 1909 Boas argued, "I do not believe that the Negro is, in his physical and mental make-up, the same as the European. The anatomical differences are so great that corresponding mental differences are plausible. There may exist differences in character and in the direction of specific aptitudes."[94] Throughout his career, Boas argued that slight physical differences between blacks and whites played a small, but important, role in preventing them from accomplishing at the level of the most gifted white people.[95] Thus, argued Boas, blacks, because of slightly smaller head sizes than whites on average, could not produce men of high genius at the same rate as whites.

When Boas addressed the Atlanta Conference before hundreds of inquisitive blacks the evening before his Atlanta University commencement address, he argued against black inferiority but also trotted out his theory about races' skull size and men of genius.[96] Du Bois and other highly accomplished African Americans at the conference were not enamored with this Boasian line of thought.[97] When Boas concluded, they sat tightly on their hands rather than applaud the professor who was becoming famous for espousing theories of racial equality.

During the commencement address the following day, Boas made amends. After writing his mother and wife anxiety-filled letters and fretting throughout the day about his pending remarks, Boas revised his address so as to hit the right tone.[98] On that occasion, he did not disappoint. While describing superior ancient African kingdoms, Boas remarked, "It seems not unlikely that the people that made the marvelous discovery of reducing iron ores by smelting were the African Negroes. Neither ancient Europe, nor ancient western Asia, nor ancient China knew the iron, and everything points to its introduction from Africa."[99] Given such declarations, the black audience broke into ringing, prolonged, applause as Boas returned to his seat, pleased that he had gotten a good reception and had broadened the horizons of thousands of students, their professors, and guests. Indeed, it was this riveting message of black greatness that rendered Du Bois momentarily speechless. The 1906 Atlanta Conference was indeed a success; it cemented a scholarly and personal bond between Du Bois and Boas that lasted for three decades, enabling them to be comrades in their battles against racism, cultural parochialism, and undemocratic values.

Stimulating exchanges and the building of important scholarly relationships were routine occurrences at the Atlanta Conferences. Thus, two years following Boas's presentations, Jane Addams, the Hull House leader, sociologist, and author, traveled to Atlanta for the Thirteenth Annual Conference. Addams expressed "a certain diffidence" in speaking on the conference topic of "The Negro Family" and stated that "with such a careful sociologist as Dr. Du Bois at the head of your department, I am quite sure you would be quick to detect my ignorance if I tried to say very much about a subject which has been handled so well."[100] She focused primarily on describing difficulties of adjustment to US city life in the immigrant families among whom she worked and pointed out that the destruction of African family traditions through slavery held at least the advantage of freeing black people from the more backward influences of such traditions. Though she did not directly express her solidarity with black people, she acknowledged as "heart-breaking" black people's difficulties in obtaining "equal opportunity and a square deal."[101] The Atlanta Conference marked the beginning of a long personal and professional relationship between Addams and Du Bois in which they joined hands to fight for racial and class transformation.[102]

When the American Sociological Society was organized in 1905, the Atlanta Conferences had already conducted national scholarly meetings for nearly a decade, attracting major scholars to present research and debate major issues of the day. Thus Du Bois's school was embedded in the early social science movement that laid the foundations of modern American sociology.

An additional attraction of the conferences for leading scholars-activists such as Boas and Addams was their political edge. Indeed, Du Bois had taken more than his intellectual direction from the German historical school of economics. The German school's research and political wing, the Verein für Sozialpolitik, formulated resolutions designed to influence policies of the state. This is why Schmoller and his associates came to be known as socialists of the chair. In this environment, Du Bois learned not only how a research organization was run but also how to use scientific findings in efforts to guide social change.

The Du Bois–Atlanta school's annual conference formulated resolutions each year to address racial oppression. A glimpse inside the Eleventh Conference, with the theme of "Health and Physique of the Negro American," reveals how the political and the scientific meshed. This conference hosted Boas, the leading expert on racial measurements. Such measurements had been presented as foundational evidence by social scientists to prove black inferiority. To be sure, the matter of racial inferiority was both scientifically and politically charged. The conference selected Boas, R. R. Wright Jr., and Du Bois to formulate the resolutions. After poring over extensive data and scholarly papers, the Resolution Committee concluded: "The Conference does not find any adequate scientific warrant for the assumption that the Negro race is inferior to other races in physical build or vitality. The present differences in mortality seem to be sufficiently explained by conditions of life; and physical measurements prove the Negro a normal human being capable of average human accomplishments."[103]

Conference resolutions were politically charged because they were elaborated in an environment where Jim Crow oppression was being consolidated. Scientific racism, espoused by scholars of the day, provided political actors the ideology to justify the oppressive regime. Indeed, the consensus regarding the claims of black inferiority was shared across American social science. At the University of Chicago the ideology masquerading as "science" was embraced by W. I. Thomas, Charles Henderson, George Herbert Mead, and John Dewey and was promulgated at Columbia by Giddings and his student Howard Odum.[104] It is instructive to keep in mind that the consensus regarding black inferiority cut across all academic disciplines during the first half of the twentieth century. Mark Aldrich has described it:

> A turn-of-the century biologist or anthropologist might subscribe to any of a wide variety of views on Negro-white racial differences. Blacks might be termed the result of arrested development and hence permanently inferior.

Or they might be described as imperfect Caucasians who would someday evolve through a genetic, cultural, or neo-Lamarckian process into a higher type. Climate and Negroes' African background might be stressed as determining factors in their behavior, or the selective properties of two hundred years of slavery could be noted. These and many other areas of contention existed within an almost unchallenged larger scientific consensus: important racial differences did exist, and the darker races were inferior.[105]

After summarizing the political intensification of racism during this period, Aldrich concludes, "The academic disciplines were, of course, by no means exempt from these currents; the period also witnessed the high tide of scientific racism in biology, anthropology, sociology and economics." Aldrich identifies economics as a major bastion of scientific racism: "Along with other scientists and social scientists, economists helped provide the intellectual rationale for the increasingly open and popular oppression of black Americans."[106]

In the year before the conference, Du Bois had openly challenged the scientific racism inherent in the extinction hypothesis, widely held by Walter Willcox's influential school of economics, in a paper entitled "The Future of the Negro in America" and had sent a copy of the paper to Willcox. Willcox, in reply, accused Du Bois of bias and painted himself as the objective scientist who remained agnostic on the causes of racial inequality. Du Bois responded:

> The fundamental difficulty in your position is that you are trying to show an evaluation of the Negro problem—only from inside your office. It can never be done. You have simply no adequate conception of the Negro problem in the south and of Negro character and capacity. When you have sat as I have ten years in intimate soul contact with all kinds and conditions of black men you will be less agnostic. I have my prejudices but they are backed by knowledge if not supported. . . . If you must [go] on writing about and promising judgment on this problem why not study it? Not from a car-window and assembled dispatches as in your pamphlet on crime but get down here and really study it at first hand.[107]

As Darity points out, "There were *no* intellectual defenders of 'the Negro' among the economists. . . . Only W.E.B. DuBois contested the Willcox School's hegemony on matters of race in America."[108] Du Bois did not merely call for scientific sociology; he advocated for scientific social science. As this exchange shows, Du Bois's school of sociology operated on the belief that a scientific approach, as advocated at Atlanta University, would produce objective research findings that would blow up the premises of scientific racism and lead to the political overthrow of racial oppression. If the evidence got a hearing, its truth would ultimately prevail.

After issuing resolutions challenging scientific racism, the proceedings closed by stating the scholarly aims of the conferences: "The Conference above all reiterates its well known attitude toward this and all other social problems: the way to make conditions better is to study the conditions. And we urge the systematic study of the Negro Problem and ask all aid and sympathy for the work of this Conference in such study."[109] Thus, in step with the German historical school, Du Bois embraced ideas driving the new scientific approach to the social sciences; he also embraced a similar organizational and political template to guide social change efforts based on scientific sociology. These sustained scholarly activities signaled the presence of a groundbreaking sociology absent elsewhere in America. The Laboratory in Sociology at Atlanta University and its annual conferences were landmarks in the history of scientific sociology in America.

THE SOULS OF BLACK FOLK

The Atlanta Studies and the Atlanta Conferences created the foundation on which rose a unique, empirically based American sociology of race. Early in Du Bois's tenure at Atlanta University, he pioneered a new genre of sociology when, in 1903, he published *The Souls of Black Folk*. *Souls* was a stunning work that conveyed sociology through a poetic literary style combined with the cold, dry analysis of scientific sociology. Long before Coser and others formally introduced the idea of sociology through literature and elaborated its use as a teaching tool, Du Bois directly engaged in producing sociology through a literary format.[110] Generally, this approach involves selecting great pieces of literature rich in sociological significance and arranging them in a logical sequence with appropriate introductions and commentaries that make them attractive to readers. The intent is to convey weighty sociological ideas in a fashion far more attractive than dispassionate arguments and dense statistical tables.

In *Souls* Du Bois merged social scientific skills with considerable literary talents to produce a broadly appealing hybrid work linking the humanities and social sciences. This style enabled him to convey complex concepts such as "double consciousness" in a form culminating in classical statements long admired by succeeding generations of readers. Thus, exploring how the black experience created a social psychological duality at the core of African Americans' subjective experiences, Du Bois wrote:

> The Negro is a sort of seventh son, born with a veil, and gifted with second-sight in this American world,—a world which yields him no true self-consciousness, but only lets him see himself through the revelation of the other world. It is a peculiar sensation, this double-consciousness, this sense of always looking at one's self through the eyes of others, of measuring one's soul by the tape of a world that looks on in amused contempt and pity. One ever feels his two-ness,—an American, a Negro; two souls, two thoughts, two unreconciled strivings; two warring ideals in one dark body, whose dogged strength alone keeps it from being torn asunder. . . . The history of the American Negro is the history of this strife,—this longing to attain self-conscious manhood, to merge his double self into a better and truer self.[111]

This idea of oppression creating a double consciousness has become widely used in the social sciences and humanities. In *Souls* Du Bois employed a literary style to convey intricate sociological analyses of music, rural sociology, leadership, education, and the centrality of human agency as expressed through African Americans. *Souls* soon became a classic deeply influencing understandings of race and inequality in African American studies, the social sciences, and humanities. It, too, was a pioneering contribution made by Du Bois's Atlanta school of sociology.

DU BOIS THE PROFESSOR

Teaching sociology at Atlanta University was another pioneering contribution Du Bois rendered at the turn of the twentieth century. He was among the first professors to teach sociology to black students in the United States at the secondary, undergraduate, and graduate levels.[112] As a professor at Atlanta University, Du Bois exhibited qualities of aloofness, arrogance, and bluntness. His manner of dress alone set him apart as he strode across the campus wearing a dapper suit, a top hat, and gloves, sporting a manicured Vandyke moustache and goatee, and twirling a cane. Regarding his bluntness, a future Morehouse president, Benjamin Mays, recalled, "When people would walk up to him and ask him if he remembered them. Du Bois' tart reply was usually, 'why should I?'"[113] By Mays's account, Du Bois "didn't bite his tongue. . . . He was tactless . . . blunt. . . . He didn't dress it up. . . . He called a spade a spade . . . He didn't make it sound good enough to be palatable, . . . He was not the back slapping kind. . . . He was in a way a lone wolf . . . a scholar type. Even though he championed the cause of the man farthest down, he was not a good mixer with the man farthest down."[114]

Yet as a professor, Du Bois displayed multiple dimensions of his personality. In intimate settings, decked in his smoking jacket, he interacted warmly with his graduate students. One student remembered that he was a "charming host . . . thoughtful and entertaining. He told anecdotes and showed that he did understand his students. . . . He seemed very relaxed in his apartment, very witty and permissive." A graduate student related that when students were in intimate settings with Du Bois "the atmosphere was different from the classroom. . . . We were special and he let us know it."[115] There is one aspect of Du Bois's teaching on which students, professors, and administrators agreed: it was demanding, and scholarly expectations were high. One student described Du Bois as an excellent teacher "because he had a skill of trying to make you think . . . and he pulled on your intellectual powers with broad reading and open discussion. There was a lot of give and take in the classroom. The classes were usually small and met in his office. He stimulated your thinking."[116] Du Bois gave himself high marks as a teacher: "I was, for instance, a good teacher. I stimulated inquiry and accuracy. I met every question honestly and never dodged an earnest doubt. I read my examination papers carefully and marked them with sedulous care."[117]

Du Bois's meticulousness as a teacher is apparent in the charts and graphs that he prepared with his students. For example, as part of his gold medal–winning exhibit for the 1900 Paris Exposition, Du Bois and his students produced detailed hand-drawn artistically colored graph and charts (see figures 1–3) that depicted the journey of black Georgians from slavery to freedom.[118]

Atlanta University president Horace Bumstead explained the reasons why Du Bois's work "became a memorable part of the Institution": "One was the inauguration, for the first time in any American college, of a thoroughly scientific study of the conditions of Negro life, covering all of its most important phases, and resulting in a score of annual *Atlanta University Publications,* conceded to be the highest authority, both in this country and in Europe. . . . Even more important than this, was the stimulating personal influence of Doctor Du Bois upon our students. He had acquired his own education where the highest standards prevailed, and he would tolerate no lower ones in his own classrooms."[119]

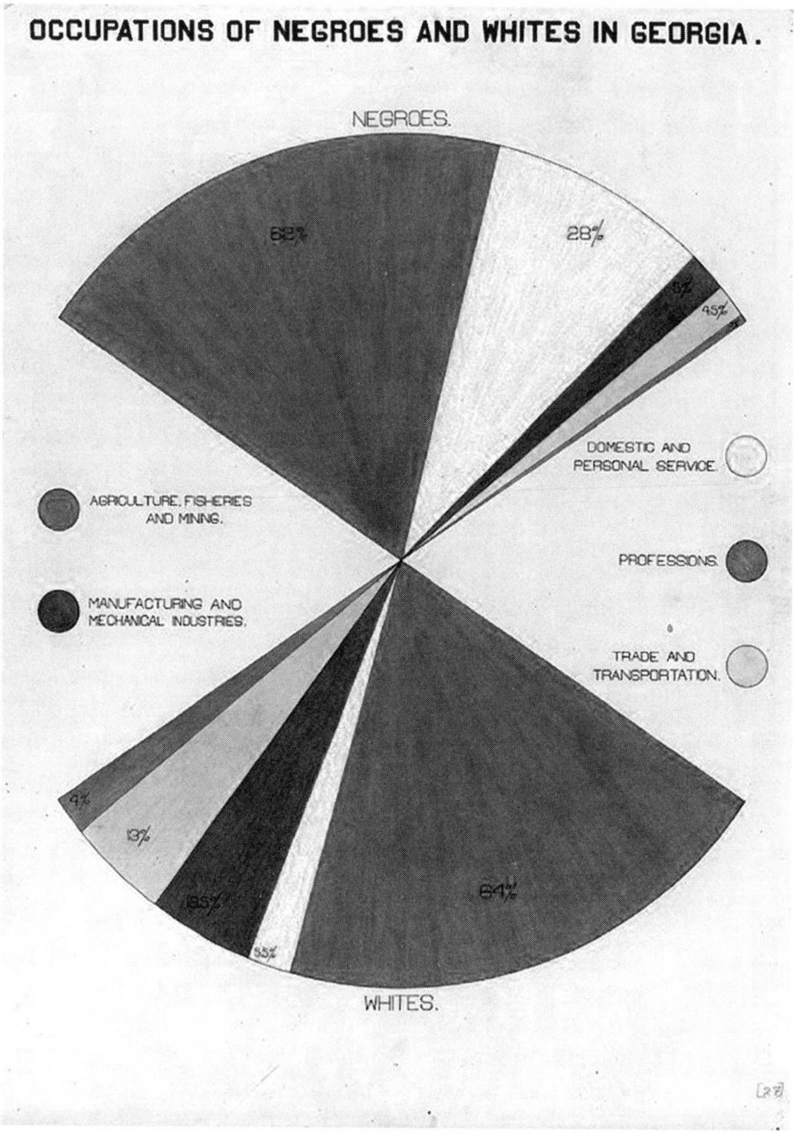

FIGURE 1. A hand-drawn chart by Professor Du Bois and his Atlanta University students comparing occupations held by blacks and whites in Georgia. It was part of the exhibit Du Bois presented at the 1900 Paris Exposition that won a gold medal.

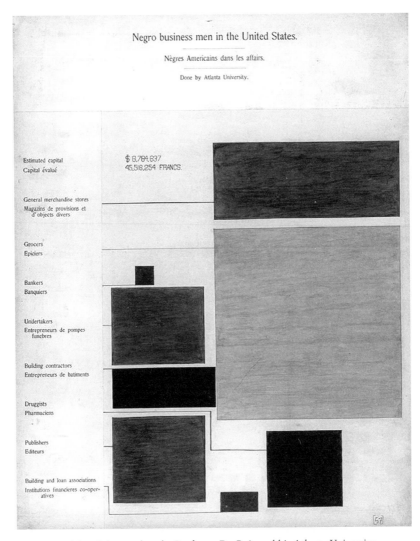

FIGURE 2. A hand-drawn chart by Professor Du Bois and his Atlanta University students depicting the distribution of black businessmen across occupations in Georgia. It was part of the exhibit Du Bois presented at the 1900 Paris Exposition.

Du Bois's teaching and scholarship were mutually reinforcing and inextricably linked activities. In the classroom, Du Bois encouraged students to think critically and sociologically. Significant numbers of them became field researchers who collected data for the Atlanta University Publications monographs. Both scholarship and teaching were hallmarks of America's first scientific school of sociology.

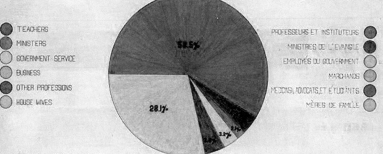

FIGURE 3. Hand-drawn statistical charts by Professor Du Bois and his Atlanta University students illustrating the conditions of the descendants of former African slaves residing in the United States. It was part of the exhibit Du Bois presented at the 1900 Paris Exposition.

THE DU BOIS–ATLANTA SCHOOL: A LANDMARK IN AMERICAN SOCIAL SCIENCE

At the end of the first decade of the twentieth century, Du Bois's scientific school encountered serious roadblocks. Yet it would be a mistake to overlook or underestimate the school's achievements. Perhaps detractors can, at times, best judge one's contributions. Thus the notable white journalist Ray Stannard Baker, in an article condemning Du Bois's radical leadership, nevertheless conceded that Du Bois "is today one of the able sociologists in this country. His economic studies of the Negro made for the United States Government and for the Atlanta University Conference (which he organized) are works of sound scholarship and furnish the student with the best single source of accurate information regarding the Negro at present obtainable in the country. And no book gives a deeper insight into the inner life of the Negro, his struggles and his aspirations than 'The Souls of Black Folk.'"[120] Similarly, in 1901 Booker T. Washington praised *The Philadelphia Negro* and other studies produced by Du Bois at Atlanta University. He assessed these works as valuable and quoted from them liberally.[121] Speaking at the fifth Atlanta Conference, Washington declared: "For several years I have watched with keen interest and appreciation the work of these annual conferences, and the whole country should be grateful to this institution for the painstaking and systematic manner with which it has developed from year to year a series of facts which are proving most vital and helpful to the interests of our nation. The work that Dr. DuBois is doing will stand for years as a monument to his ability, wisdom and faithfulness."[122]

Thus both friends and foes recognized Du Bois's scholarly brilliance and original contributions. Yet given severe funding problems and time constraints, the Atlanta Studies were uneven in quality and at times suffered from undertheorizing.[123] To be sure, they could have been strengthened through the use of more sophisticated methodologies. But even here it is important to bear in mind that Du Bois was a pioneering methodologist without models to follow. He was aware of methodological limitations of his work and pledged to improve them as more experience was obtained. In this vein, Francille Wilson wrote, "One reason that *The Negro Artisan* was a better study than previous Atlanta University monographs was that it fit more neatly into and synthesized the best practices from Du Bois's other research on labor and economic conditions."[124] Du Bois's awareness of the pioneering role of *The Philadelphia Negro* and the Atlanta Studies was evident in his statement that "the significance of these studies lay not so much in what they were actually able to accomplish, as in the fact that at the time of their publication Atlanta University was the only institution in the world carrying on a systematic study of the Negro and his development, and putting the result in a form available for the scholars of the world."[125]

To grasp the full significance of Du Bois's school of sociology, one must recognize that sociology was not usually a part of the curriculum in southern universities until the 1920s. Edwin Alderman, an expert on higher education who served as president of three southern universities, including the University of North Carolina, complained in 1901 about the lack of any "training in the higher universities in the South of the cultured youth in scientific study of social phenomena. Our students have been in the habit of approaching these studies empirically and emotionally. They must learn to approach the study of social questions scientifically and methodically. They must become conscious of society as an organism just learning to know itself. There are no departments of sociology in Southern colleges. This fact is both startling and hurtful."[126] Addressing the lack of knowledge of sociology among southern students, Alderman concluded, "They do not bring to the consideration of such questions the trained habit of mind, the trained orderliness of thought, that is needed for their mastery."[127] (He was considering only white youth here because Negroes, in his view, needed only to follow the practical educational model developed by Booker T. Washington.) According to Alderman, "There is needed a new social spirit, a new type of man, with a new equipment of power to inform and influence and guide this spirit. . . . This real sort of scholar is needed to aid in the transformation of unthinking, careless, white men, without tastes or wants or desires, into men with ideals." But as Clarence Bacote points out in his history of Atlanta University, the scholar that Alderman sought already existed. "In 1901 . . . Dr. Edwin A. Alderman stated with regret that there was not a single southern college that had a scientific course in sociology. This was not true, unless President Alderman had reference to white institutions only, for the Department of Sociology at Atlanta University under the direction of Dr. Du Bois had been engaged in systematic study of social phenomena since 1898."[128] Indeed, "On his arrival Du Bois entered upon his duties with much zeal and determination, and in a short time succeeded in fulfilling the assignment expected of him; he organized a strong Department of Sociology and brought efficiency to the work of the conferences and of the accompanying publications."[129]

It is ironic that a small black university, without adequate funds and considered inferior by whites, introduced scientific sociology to the South under the leadership of a new type of sociological scholar. An additional irony is that given Jim Crow, Du Bois awakened the sociological imagination in black students whom he was training to become members of the "talented tenth" so they would be equipped to free the black masses from their oppression. Meanwhile, the elite southern white youth that Alderman cherished would wait two decades before their introduction to the sociological perspective at southern white universities.[130] The situation was not much different in the North. Only a few sociology departments—Chicago, Kansas, and Columbia—existed outside the South that were founded roughly at the same time as the department at Atlanta University. And these departments in the North at the turn of the twentieth century tended not to be empirically based. Martin Bulmer, the historian of social science and the Chicago school, reveals this when he concludes that *The Philadelphia Negro* "was unique in its intensity of study, and there was nothing comparable being produced at the time from Columbia under Giddings or Chicago under Small."[131]

Du Bois's visibility in the larger society made it impossible for white sociologists to entirely escape his influence. As David Levering Lewis wrote of Du Bois during the first decade of the twentieth century, "With two large, critically acclaimed monographs published by age thirty-one, a major essay in Weber's arbitral *Archiv* at thirty-seven, his scholarship discussed in large-circulation newspapers and middlebrow periodicals, and his Stone Hall office becoming a stopping-off point for the famous, the influential, and the merely curious on southern learning safaris, Du Bois's professional achievements placed him in the vanguard of social-science scholarship in America."[132] Thus when Du Bois's name was mooted for inclusion in a social club of white liberals whose members were concerned with the race question, Giddings, the first American sociologist to hold a named chair in sociology in 1911, wrote President Ware of Atlanta University that "it is desirable to know with great positiveness the candidate's reputation as a man of integrity and honorable character." Because Giddings believed the inclusion of Du Bois would have considerable weight, he insisted, "We need to know [w]hether, in your judgment, the cause of the negro would be prejudiced by the election of Dr. DuBois to such a club?"[133] But liberal white clubs aside, the white founders of American sociology ignored the work of their black colleague in the South as he pioneered scientific sociology. At the dawn of the twentieth century, the power of American racism was greater than scientific merit in determining which scholars would be recognized as sociological pioneers and which would be denied. Although the studies produced by the Du Bois–Atlanta school were visible in select venues in America and abroad, they failed to attract the attention of white sociologists because they originated from black scholars situated in a segregated small southern black school. Even more devastating, the Du Bois–Atlanta school was forced to operate on a shoestring budget that required him to literally beg for funding.

Here Booker T. Washington enters the picture because he profoundly affected the trajectory of the Laboratory in Sociology at Atlanta University. For Washington, Du Bois and Atlanta University represented precisely the type of liberal arts education that was irrelevant for solving the race problem. By the time Du Bois established his school, Washington had become the gatekeeper determining which institutions and which scholars received funds. Without his nod, new funds headed in opposite directions and old ones dried up. On one occasion Du Bois sought funds from a well-positioned philanthropist to initiate a journal. Du Bois recalled: "Mr. Schiff wrote back courteously, saying: 'Your plans to establish a high-class journal to circulate among the intelligent Negroes is in itself interesting, and on its face has my sympathy. But before I can decide whether I can become of advantage in carrying your plans into effect, I would wish to advise with men whose opinion in such a matter I consider of much value.'"[134] According to Du Bois, "Nothing ever came of this, because, as I might have known, most of Mr. Schiff's friends were strong and sincere advocates of Tuskegee."[135]

Studies produced by Du Bois were not projects that Washington urged philanthropists to support, especially during the early years of the twentieth century when Du Bois became increasingly critical of Washington, thereby initiating the epic Washington–Du Bois controversy. As this ideological struggle exploded, Du Bois found that securing adequate funding for his Atlanta school became impossible. Meager funding always affected the quality and scope of Du Bois's studies, but by 1905 it threatened the very existence of the school itself and even Atlanta University. In an open letter to Atlanta University's president published in a leading black newspaper in 1903, Washington warned: "If Atlanta University intends to stand for Dr. Du Bois' outgivings, if it means to seek to destroy Tuskegee Institute, so that its own work can have success, it is engaged in poor business to start with; . . . Tuskegee will go on. It will succeed . . . not withstanding the petty annoyances of

Du Bois and his ilk. . . . Let [the president of Atlanta University] prove himself by curbing the outgivings and ill-advised criticism of the learned Doctor who is now in his employ."[136]

Du Bois kept his studies going for another decade, but they were restricted by serious financial difficulties. Beyond a doubt, Washington made his mark on the development of American sociology by smothering its first scientific school. But despite it all, the Du Bois–Atlanta school, led by a pioneering black sociologist and his researchers, made its own, more positive mark on the discipline, even though its influence was forced to travel subterranean routes before bursting into mainstream recognition a century later.

CHAPTER 4

The Conservative Alliance of Washington and Park

In 1905 Robert Ezra Park accepted a job with Booker T. Washington at the Tuskegee Institute as director of public relations and as his ghost-writer. Park's association with Washington significantly shaped the trajectory of modern American sociology. The position at Tuskegee was extremely important because it enabled Park to crucially affect perceptions of Washington's leadership and to undermine his rivals. The ideal hire needed to be a fluid and prolific writer well versed in media. Because of these exacting criteria, Washington first offered the post to W. E. B. Du Bois, who rejected it despite tremendous pressure from Washington and his allies to accept. Du Bois refused because his self-confidence and important scholarly achievements led him to believe that he was destined to be a historic actor as scholar and black liberator. His accomplishments at the time included three influential books, numerous published studies, leadership of the Laboratory in Sociology at Atlanta University, and national visibility as a popular lecturer. Du Bois decided that remaining free of Washington would advance his career far more than serving as Washington's ghostwriter. Du Bois also feared that a Tuskegee position would compromise his political independence because he was rapidly becoming the most important critic of Washington's politics of accommodation.

At the time Park was offered the position at Tuskegee his self-confidence had seriously eroded. Despite being four years older than Du Bois, he had few professional accomplishments. Park recalled that "as his earlier ambitions faded . . . he felt the 'shades of prison walls descend' and faced the melancholy truth of maturity, that he would never 'disturb the course of history.'" As Park recalled: "I had come to the conclusion that I couldn't do anything first rate on my own account. I decided the best thing to do was to attach myself to someone who was doing something first rate. Washington was not a brilliant man or an intellectual, but he seemed to me to be doing something real. So I went."[1]

In the fall of 1905, Park reported to Tuskegee for duty. This was a propitious opportunity because Washington was at the zenith of his power, clearly recognized as the leader of American blacks at home and respected abroad. His advice to US presidents, governors, congressmen, and captains of industry determined which blacks received treasured appointments and philanthropic funds. Park was well suited for the position because his previous work as a newspaper reporter for over a decade covering numerous cities had given him valuable media contacts and expertise in navigating the press. Park was also a scholar who, like Du Bois, had been taught at Harvard by some of the same people and had studied under famous social scientists in Germany. Although Park's educational career will be discussed later, it is important to mention at this juncture that Park received his master's degree from Harvard in philosophy in 1889 and a PhD in the same field from the University of Heidelberg in 1904.

Park also accepted Washington's offer because it would enable him to closely observe Negroes and southern race relations. As St. Clair Drake put it, Park would "receive a profound post-doctoral education" at Tuskegee."[2] Indeed, Winifred Raushenbush, Park's biographer, has noted that "it was Washington who suggested to Park the proper focus of his studies should be 'the Negro and the South.'"[3] Park later recounted that "until I met Booker Washington, except for what I had learned from books, I knew nothing either about Negroes or about the South. But what one can learn about Negroes and the South from books, as I was soon to discover, is not enough. Under these circumstances my journey to Tuskegee assumed—particularly as I travel very leisurely, reading all the local newspapers and talking with everyone I meet— something of the character of a voyage of exploration and discovery."[4] For seven consecutive years, Tuskegee provided the social laboratory for Park to familiarize himself with race and for Washington to serve as his mentor. The Tuskegee experience proved critical in the development of Park's sociological imagination and his subsequent understandings of race.

At Tuskegee, Park enjoyed access to southern black communities unavailable to other white scholars. Reflecting on the experience, Park wrote, "At Tuskegee I was, it seemed, at the very center of the Negro world. I had the access to most everything that was likely to throw light on the processes that were slowly but inevitably changing Negro life and the South."[5] While under Washington's tutelage, Park was welcomed in black homes, churches, rallies, conferences, and leadership circles. Black people welcomed him because he was a representative of Tuskegee and a friend of their greatest leader. Because of Park's affiliations with Washington, certain blacks shared their innermost worlds with this northern white man. After seven years at Tuskegee, Park was surely one of the white sociologists who was most knowledgeable about black people and race relations. This wide and deep knowledge served Park well as he matured as a scholar and came to be recognized as the premier sociologists of race in America.

As Park conducted "fieldwork" in the South, he absorbed Washington's views concerning African Americans and race relations. Those views profoundly shaped Park's intellectual understandings of race. The first principle he adopted from Washington was that blacks were a primitive people lacking the advanced civilization possessed by American whites. In a letter to Washington, Park confided: "The Negro has risen in the scale of civilization to the point where he kept slaves. So far as I know the Negro is the only savage people who has done so. A system of government based on slavery is essentially higher than one based on the mere tribal or family relation. The Southerner will appreciate that."[6] In a 1913 letter to Washington, Park expressed the same judgment: "No one can know much about the Negro race ... until he has become acquainted with the masses of the Negro people as they are in the black belt counties of the south. They are a strong, vigorous, kindly and industrious people; simple minded, wholesome and good as God made them. They are very different from the people of the cities."[7] According to this view, blacks, given their alleged primitiveness, had to work their way up from the bottom to prove themselves worthy to whites and to earn their respect and fair treatment.

Washington viewed blacks as a quintessentially rural, southern people. He considered northern cities to be dangerous for blacks because of their widespread temptations to wickedness and their lack of opportunities as compared to agricultural and manual jobs available in the rural South. In Washington's eyes, the race problem was a southern problem whose solution could be found only in the South. In 1903 he told the

Washington Conference of the National Sociological Society, "I hope you will always bear in mind that the great body of our people live in the South. There are eight million and more of us down there. And the problem is there. If you can help us to bear our conditions, I hope you will keep in close touch and sympathy with those who are striving for better conditions right there in the South."[8] In a letter to Washington Park expressed his agreement: "Fortunately the great majority of the race still live in the country and if they can be educated there, where they can grow up slowly and naturally, and be kept out of the cities where they will be forced along at a pace that will make them superficial and trifling, the race problem will eventually solve itself. In my opinion the hope of the race is these people in the country districts."[9] This restricted geographical perspective profoundly shaped Park's sociology of race.

Washington maintained that the black community constituted a nation within a nation. Park's embrace of this conceptualization eventually led him to argue that black culture was the basis for development of a nationalistic racial consciousness that would pursue blacks' group interest politically.[10] Even Park's academic approach to teaching and supervising research at Chicago was heavily influenced by Washington's teaching methods and philosophy employed at Tuskegee to teach black students.[11] Tuskegee emphasized concrete "hands-on techniques" and real-life experiences.[12] Park appropriated this approach and encouraged his students to go out in the real world and conduct empirical research.

Most importantly, the development of Park's famous race relations cycle grew from his studies and observations while at Tuskegee. Washington emphasized that social changes in race relations occurred only gradually, usually over centuries, and that outside agitators, political activists, reformers, do-gooders, and intellectuals could not hasten them by interfering. It was from Washington, wrote Park, "that I first gained some adequate notion of how deep-rooted in human history and human nature social institutions were, and how difficult, if not impossible it was, to make fundamental changes in them by mere legislation or by legal artifice of any sort. It was the first time I realized that social problems, in so far as they are not problems of administration or of policy, are problems of fundamental human nature and culture."[13] Park drew from Washington's approach the insight that "behind and beneath the superficial pattern and external aspect of Southern life was the working of a great historical process, a process which was slowly but inexorably changing traditional units in this, as in every other part of the U.S., including the traditional relations between the races."[14]

Thus Park's influential theory of race relations cycles was very much shaped by Booker T. Washington. Scholars of intellectual thought, race relations, and the Chicago school have overlooked Washington's crucial intellectual influence on Park.[15] But this oversight is certainly not Park's fault, for he reiterated Washington's influence repeatedly in his writings and exchanges with colleagues. On one occasion he declared, "I have studied, first and last, under some very eminent teachers. . . . However, after reviewing my experiences in more universities than I care to mention, I came to the conclusion that I learned most about methods of teaching and most about life while I was studying at Tuskegee under the general supervision of Booker Washington."[16] Park concluded in his "Autobiographical Note" shortly before his death that "I think I probably learned more about human nature and society, in the South under Booker Washington, than I had learned elsewhere in all my previous studies."[17] Drawing on his Tuskegee experience, Park insisted, "Sociology must be empirical and experimental. It must, to use Booker Washington's expression, 'learn by doing'; it must explore, invent, discover, and try things out."[18] Park, therefore, made clear that Washington had the greatest influence on his thinking and pedagogy, outranking the influence of teachers at Michigan, Harvard, and even Germany.

TWO INVISIBLE SHIPS PASSING IN BROAD DAYLIGHT

A curious, seemingly inexplicable thing happened in the early days of American sociology. The arguably two greatest scholars of race during the twentieth century—Du Bois and Park—passed each other like invisible ships in broad daylight, seemingly unaware of each other. But can this really be true? This puzzle can be solved by examining the triangular relationship of Washington, Du Bois, and Park.

During the first decade of the twentieth century, an epic ideological struggle erupted between Washington and Du Bois. Du Bois began it in his 1903 classic *The Souls of Black Folk*, where he criticized Washington's industrial program as narrow and questioned whether it was the best, or only, solution to the race problem.[19] Insisting that blacks needed both industrial and higher education to advance, Du Bois rejected Washington's acquiescence to racial segregation and demanded the franchise for blacks, arguing that without full social equality they would remain oppressed. At the height of the controversy in 1905, Du Bois and a cadre of highly educated and radical-leaning blacks from across the nation organized the militant Niagara movement, which demanded full rights for African Americans. Washington considered the new movement to be a direct attack on his leadership. It was.

When Park arrived at Tuskegee in the autumn of 1905, he stepped directly into the line of fire. One of Washington's major battle strategies was to attack opponents in the press, and "Park's primary function was always to maintain the flow of articles, books, and press releases."[20] As a former newspaper reporter, Park hit the ground running in Tuskegee: "Exploiting more directly his old newspaper contacts, [he] worked at the classic public relations job, planting stories and references favorable to Tuskegee in the daily press. Park followed up formal news items with editorials discussing the valuable work done at Tuskegee, writing them himself or supplying information for them, as the editors chose."[21] Thus it was Park's occupational duty to be a political ally of Washington during the Du Bois–Washington controversy. This was not difficult for him because his views on race aligned with those of Washington. Park adopted Washington's view that the northern radical intellectuals were outside meddlers who did not understand the South or the common man.[22] Park's writings reveal that he and Washington viewed Du Bois, and his ilk, as arrogant snobs who promoted their unwise abstract notions as the solution to the race problem. For them, the real leader of the black masses—Washington—already had devised wise solutions to the race problem.

Washington's stance, and Park's support of it, are evident in a letter Washington wrote to his personal secretary, Emmett Scott, in 1908 about an article by a leading white journalist, Ray Standard Baker, that was about to be published in the *American Magazine*. Baker praised Washington as the leader of the black masses north and south and accused Du Bois and his northern intellectual allies of being snobbish mulattoes who could not relate to the masses. Washington told Scott, "Mr. Baker was kind enough to let me see the proof of the article which he has written concerning Du Bois and myself. I have read it very carefully. It is a fine article, clear and clean-cut, and I am satisfied with his treatment of the subject. He certainly has a way of getting at the truth. When Du Bois, Trotter and his crowd read what Baker has written I think they will squirm. I wish you would let Dr. Park read this."[23]

Park's response to a horrendous race riot in Atlanta in 1906 further reveals how Park aided Washington in smearing Du Bois. That riot involved thousands of whites killing and injuring large numbers of black people. It was devastating to Du Bois, who received word of it in Lowndes County, Alabama, while supervising fieldwork and collecting data for a large study of African Americans in that area.[24]

The riot became the pretext for Park to launch a smear campaign against Du Bois. As Park's biographer Raushenbush recounts: "Park stated in one of his diaries that Du Bois, then a professor of sociology at Atlanta, hid in a country farmhouse during the riot, whereas Washington went to the scene immediately to see what he could do to calm things down. Park commented: 'Washington was a man of courage; he was no white man's nigger.'"[25] Du Bois's account, however, flatly contradicts Parks: "In 1906 I rushed back from Alabama to Atlanta where my wife and six-year-old child were living. A mob had raged for days killing Negroes. I bought a Winchester double-barreled shotgun and two dozen rounds of shells filled with buckshot. If a white mob had stepped on the campus where I lived I would without hesitation have sprayed their guts over the grass."[26] The depths of this sentiment are even more revealing because philosophically Du Bois abhorred violence.[27]

The evidence confirms that Park's account was not accurate. David Levering Lewis, after meticulously reviewing the archival evidence, concluded that Du Bois, rather than hiding out till calm was restored, had "rushed to the city by train to sit on the steps of South Hall [at Atlanta University] to protect Nina and Yolanda [his wife and daughter] with a shotgun." Further, Washington, rather than hurrying from New York to help his people, had "stayed put for several more days, issuing deeply pained, even-handed condemnations of black racists and white rioters."[28] Park's biographer also confirms that Park had it wrong. Though he says, "Washington showed extraordinary courage going to Atlanta during the riot," he admits that "what Park says about Du Bois is not wholly accurate."[29]

Five years following the riot, Washington continued to utilize Park's claims about Du Bois's cowardice to discredit him. In a letter to Timothy Fortune, a close Washington adviser and editor of the *New York Age,* Washington approved Fortune's handling of the smear, stating, "Du Bois did run away from Atlanta. All the time that the riot was going on, Du Bois was hiding at the Calhoun School in Alabama—a school which I was responsible for establishing some fifteen years ago. He remained there until the riot was over and then came out and wrote a piece of poetry bearing upon those who were killed in the riot."[30] Approving of these and other accusations that Fortune made against Du Bois, Washington wrote, "I am glad that you went for Du Bois in the way that you did." Fortune responded to Washington, "I have put Dr. Du Bois in a ragged hole in this town" and added, "But I felt that it was necessary to discredit Du Bois in the matters I have before taking up the other and more vital matters." Fortune assured Washington that Du Bois would have troubles "when we get done with [him]."[31]

Washington and Park kept close watch on Du Bois not only for political but also for scientific reasons. Du Bois was one of those rare persons in history whose leadership was based on scholarship rather than guns and charisma. Washington understood that Du Bois could use his scholarship to discredit Washingtonian ideas such as the principle that industrial education was the most effective strategy to achieve black liberation. White scholars usually endorsed Washington's leadership because it was congruent with their beliefs in black inferiority and their scholarship that claimed to prove it. Although Washington had earned no advanced degree, white scholars often invited him and his designees to participate on scholarly panels, especially when Du Bois was a participant.[32] It was commonplace for white scholars to accept Washington's "scientific views" over those of Du Bois. For example, in a joint report commissioned by the American Economic Association, Du Bois and the Cornell economist Walter Willcox disagreed over the wealth blacks had amassed. On the basis of his scholarly research, Du Bois refused to accept Willcox's data, arguing that they were inaccurate. Willcox responded by writing Washington to obtain confirmation that Washington agreed with his estimates. Washington replied that Willcox's numbers were closer to reality than were Du Bois's.[33] Willcox, delighting in Washington's support, responded, "Thank you for your letter of November 9th about the amount of property accumulated by negroes. . . . At present I am not disposed to agree with Professor Du Bois that they are too small."[34] Willcox then submitted the report, which, though supported by the powerful black leader, was disputed by the leading scholar of black Americans.

Thus Park, the scholar who preached objectivity and calm scholarly detachment a few years later at the University of Chicago, thoroughly embraced a political ideology while working with Washington. It was an ideology designed to neutralize Du Bois while elevating a conservative alternative. Ideologically, Park identified with his fellow journalist Ray Stannard Baker, who considered Washington a "leader of men . . . organizing the practical activities of the race" and Du Bois as "the lonely critic . . . holding up distant ideals" such as equality.[35] Park came to thoroughly identify with Washington's views and adopted them as his own. The two were close personally because of the enormous time they shared while traveling nationally and internationally and working in close quarters at Tuskegee. Indeed, on one occasion they shared a bed in Europe because two rooms were not available at the hotel.[36]

Park stood in opposition to a wide range of black intellectuals and radicals who criticized Washington because he viewed Washington's stance on race as wiser sociologically and pragmatically. He agreed with Washington that blacks were best suited for industrial education, and he believed that Du Bois and black radical intellectuals had it wrong when they thought the historical process could be hurried by agitation and protest. For Park, it was Washington who correctly understood the historical process by which primitive blacks could be eased into civilized society and who realized that a solution to the "Negro Problem" consequently required patience rather than intervention by misguided radicals.

Because Park's job as ghostwriter required anonymity, direct evidence of the newspaper stories Park planted attacking Du Bois with the intent of making him irrelevant and invisible often failed to appear on the historical record. But one can be sure they were numerous, and his negative views about Du Bois were apparent in books he ghostwrote for Washington. The historian Fred Matthews notes that "as press agent and principal 'ghost,' Park could not help but take an active part in the struggle between Washington and his 'radical' civil libertarian opponents, led by W. E. B. DuBois and William Monroe Trotter" and adds that "there is no evidence that Park found this role unpleasant, since his experience at Tuskegee had reinforced his distaste for moral reformers who relied on the word, on political agitation, rather than the 'evolutionary' solution of concrete improvements in Negro education and community life."[37]

Park had a vested interest in rendering Du Bois irrelevant and invisible as a political actor and as an influential scholar. His adoption of Washington's views on race occurred both politically and intellectually: he fused these dimensions of Washington's thought so that it constituted, for him, a single storehouse of sociological and political wisdom. And in each realm it is clear that, as Matthews points out, "Park's view of race relations always followed the Washington doctrine closely."[38] Mary Jo Deegan, a rare scholar of the Chicago school who understands this aspect of Park's work, explains: "Park's loyalty to Booker T. Washington profoundly shaped the political agenda of the race relations analyses, and Park's animosity toward the great sociologist W. E. B. Du Bois limited the application of the latter's more egalitarian and militant ideas within the discipline especially in the core ethnographies."[39] Upon his arrival at Chicago's sociology department, Park transplanted Washington's doctrine into the Chicago school of sociology and continued to marginalize Du Bois's pioneering sociology.

PARK AND THE CHICAGO SCHOOL

Park's Tuskegee experience and the knowledge of the Negro he acquired while working with Washington were important factors in his appointment at the University of Chicago and subsequent legacy as the leader of the Chicago school. In April of 1912, Park organized an International Conference on the Negro for Washington at Tuskegee under the theme of "Education for the Primitive Man." It explored how education could help advance primitive black races the world over.[40] Black and white leaders throughout the African diaspora attended the conference. Such wide participation was guaranteed given the connection between the Jim Crow order and European colonialism. Uppermost on the minds of whites was the need to determine if Washington's approach was applicable to both forms of white domination. W.I. Thomas, responding to an invitation from Washington that Park conceived and dispatched, attended the conference. Thomas spoke on the genesis of cultural traits of backward races, while Park delivered the keynote on the education that primitive man needed if he was to advance.[41] Immediately the two scholars recognized their like-mindedness and agreed they could enjoy being colleagues in Chicago's sociology department. Thomas broached the idea to his colleague and department chairman, Albion Small, who arranged for Park's employment.

Thomas initiated efforts to recruit Park. In terms of academic training, Park possessed appropriate credentials to join Chicago's faculty. He had received a bachelor's from the University of Michigan in 1887 after studying under John Dewey. For the next decade, Park had served as a newspaper reporter working in large cities, including Detroit, Denver, New York, Chicago, and Minneapolis. After his journalism career, Park pursued graduate study, earning a master's degree in philosophy in 1899 at Harvard, where he studied under William James, George Santayana, and Josiah Royce, the same professors who had taught Du Bois. Like Du Bois, Park traveled to Germany to study under the pioneers establishing the new social sciences. In the spring of 1900, Park took courses with the great sociologist Georg Simmel in Berlin, where he developed a sociological perspective focusing on structural forms of social interaction that would inform his academic work throughout his career. Park then moved to Strassburg, where he studied with the famous social psychologist Wilhelm Windelband, who supervised his dissertation, "The Crowd and the Public." Park followed Windelband to Heidelberg University in 1902 and earned his doctorate there in 1904.

Upon returning to the United States, Park taught as an assistant in Harvard's department of philosophy from 1903 to 1904 before accepting his position under Booker T. Washington at Tuskegee.

Despite his impressive education, Park at age forty-nine had no major sole-authored publications and possessed few of the scholarly achievements meriting an academic professorship at Chicago. In contrast, by age forty-five Du Bois was world famous, having published *The Philadelphia Negro, The Souls of Black Folk*, over a dozen pioneering sociological studies at Atlanta University, and major articles in numerous journals and magazines. Yet Park's lack of academic achievements did not deter Thomas, who immediately turned to the department chair, Albion Small, urging him to recruit Park. Small consulted with William Rainey Harper, a friend, colleague, and president of the university, exploring ways to bring Park to Chicago. In 1914, Park accepted a lectureship and commenced teaching a course entitled "The Negro in America" at Chicago. Park was promoted to full professor in 1923 and remained at Chicago until his retirement over two decades later.

When he moved from Tuskegee to Chicago in 1914, Park entered a new world as far as academia was concerned. Although Tuskegee was lauded as a great institution because it was the citadel of black accommodation, it was a small black institute bereft of the prestige and resources attached to Chicago and Ivy League institutions such as Harvard. Park was aware of how he was disadvantaged by the lack of prestige associated with his affiliation with an "inferior" black school. When denied a research opportunity from the Stokes Foundation while at Tuskegee, Park wrote Washington: "I was impressed . . . with the fact that the reason I did not get the job or was not going to get the job, was because I did not seem to represent science. Perhaps also, there was a distrust of the ability of anyone connected with a negro school to do scientific work. This suggests the advisability of my making some connection with Chicago University. Mr Thomas has proposed it. Then, when I wanted to do sociological work from Tuskegee, I would have a title and the backing of the University."[42]

Washington understood that Park could enhance his leadership with a connection to the University of Chicago. As he wrote to his personal secretary Emmett Scott, "We can get a strong and striking news item for the colored papers out of the fact that Dr Park is being employed as an associate professor at the University of Chicago. . . . Our friends will soon see the significance of our having a man who thinks as we do in such an important position as a professor at the University of Chicago.

Dr. Thomas tells me Dr. Park is making a great hit with his work. Of course the letter ought to be dated from Chicago."[43]

Most small black colleges fared even worse than Tuskegee, especially if they veered from the industrial approach promoted by Washington. This certainly was the case for Du Bois as he labored at Atlanta University begging for nickels and dimes to support his ambitious research agenda. At Atlanta, Du Bois was trapped in poverty and a degraded status while Park became a professor at Chicago, a bastion of white privilege and academic prestige.

Indeed, the University of Chicago had been prestigious from its very beginning in 1892, thanks to the riches of John D. Rockefeller and the creative intellectual vision of William Rainey Harper, its young president. By the time Park arrived, the sociology department was well established, housing a core group of influential professors, most of whom, like Du Bois and Park, had been educated in elite universities and had studied under the great German masters of social science. Moreover, a creative and gifted set of interdisciplinary faculty, including George Herbert Mead and John Dewey in the social sciences and humanities, were nestled in a shared milieu at Chicago, fully engaged with the sociology faculty.[44] They were surrounded by talented graduate students seeking to be trained in sociology so they could make their intellectual mark by carrying forth Chicago's brand of sociology. Finally, the city of Chicago was a key resource because, like Atlanta for Du Bois, it provided Chicago sociologists with a social laboratory to study numerous facets of human behavior.

Because Harper had access to considerable resources, he invited the chair of sociology, Albion Small, to found a sociology journal. Thus the *American Journal of Sociology* came into being, serving as a key instrument through which a national sociological community would be organized and Chicago sociology made dominant.[45] In addition, the University of Chicago Press provided a publishing outlet for Chicago faculty and heavily subsidized the journal.[46] Research funds were bountiful at Chicago, supported by enterprises such as the Rockefeller Spelman Foundation, the Social Science Research Association, and other local and national philanthropic organizations.[47] Chicago professors were highly paid, receiving salaries far above those of their counterparts at other universities. Department heads such as Small were hired in the early 1890s with a salary of $7,000, nearly six times the $1,200 received by Du Bois for heading a sociology department and a research center for twelve years beginning in 1898.[48] Chicago faculty enjoyed light teaching loads so they could conduct research, publish, and train graduate students. Research funds were abundant at Chicago. In 1908 Professor W.I. Thomas received the enormous amount of $40,000 for an undeveloped research project on immigrants to which he was not fully committed.[49] In contrast, at Atlanta Du Bois worried about how to fund his ambitious research program on $5,000 a year, which included his annual salary.[50] At Chicago, Park inherited resourceful networks, apprentices, and funds that enabled him to thrive while building an empirically based sociology program. Two decades earlier, Du Bois complained about the unavailability of resources to fund his school in Atlanta and the lack of professional recognition for its achievements: "So far as the American world of science and letters was concerned, we never 'belonged'; we remained unrecognized in learned societies and academic groups. We rated merely as Negroes studying Negroes, and after all, what had Negroes to do with America or science?"[51] Throughout the twentieth century, white scholars at elite universities enjoyed privileges that contrasted sharply with the meager resources and low status experienced by black scholars working in segregated black schools.

THEORETICAL FOUNDATIONS OF THE CHICAGO SCHOOL

The Chicago school was guided by two major theoretical principles formulated mainly by Park. The first was that sociology was an objective science whose mission was to formulate natural laws determining human behavior. The second was a unique social Darwinism that combined evolutionary principles with social interaction analyses. Chicago sociologists clearly set forth the first principle, that sociology was a science not differing from the natural sciences, but not the second, their approach mixing evolution and social interaction analyses, even though it was central to their analytical formulations. Before I go on to critique Chicago sociology, a caveat is in order. I agree with Deegan that a "great man" theory does not capture the intellectual foundation and achievements of the Chicago school.[52] Many of those contributions were made by other Chicago sociologists, including Small, Burgess, and Thomas, and by interdisciplinary scholars such as Mead and Dewey. Yet I privilege Park because he is widely recognized as the Chicago school's leading theoretician and because he most clearly embodied and transmitted the essence of the collective enterprise to students and succeeding generations of sociologists.

Before Park's arrival, prominent Chicago sociologists reached the conclusion that grand theories and the search for a master explanatory principle based on intuition and speculation had failed to advance sociology as a science. As Small summed up the situation in 1916, during the final decade of the nineteenth century and the first decade of the twentieth some American sociologists had come to realize the futility of grand sociological theories and the lack of an empirical agenda: "It seems to me," he wrote, "that our situation was weak at the time in our unpreparedness to strike out in search of social causes, and our virtual standing still in our tracks peering about for the *social cause*."[53] Small approvingly quoted a critic who in 1902 had asserted, "Sociology must define itself either as a body of doctrine, as a point of view, or as a method of research. It has tried to develop itself as a body of doctrine, and it has failed in the attempt. . . . It has yet made no serious attempt to develop itself as a method of research, and must develop itself on these lines, and show its fruitfulness before it can demand consideration at the bar of science. This critic advised sociologists to "develop sociology as a method of research as rapidly as possible."[54] Small agreed, calling for the building of an objective science because sociologists "have been seduced into moralizing when our job demanded analyzing. . . . But sermonizing does not make astronomy, nor botany, nor child psychology, nor sociology; no more does it furnish a worthy program for the pursuit of either science."[55] Yet all the calls for an objective science rooted in empirical research ignored the fact that Du Bois had already initiated such a program beginning with *The Philadelphia Negro* in 1899 and had already published a body of empirical studies during the first decade of the twentieth century.

Park easily fit into the Chicago orientation. In 1921 he and Burgess defined sociology as "a natural and relatively abstract science that "seeks to arrive at natural laws and generalizations in regard to human nature and society, irrespective of time and of place."[56] Furthermore, they wrote, "Sociology . . . seeks to explain, on the basis of a study of other instances, the nature of the process involved. . . . By nature we mean just that aspect and character of things in regard to which it is possible to make general statements and formulate laws."[57] Thus sociology was to apply the same logic to the study of human beings as scientists did to the study of natural phenomena. Further, the view of sociology as an "abstract" science meant that its approach was to be deductive. However, Park and Burgess did not explicitly acknowledge this; they left the impression that sociology proceeded inductively because of Chicago's emphasis on empirical research.

But because the Chicago approach also emphasized natural laws of human behavior, and because natural laws transcended time and place, historical and comparative contingencies had to be minimized. As Lee Braude has described this deductive approach to theory building: "The observer brings categories of analysis and interpretation to his data that do not necessarily derive from other bodies of data or from any data, but from the logical manipulation of variables which may bear no relation at all to the empirical world. So, too, the interactionist approach espoused by Park and Burgess is an interpretation of data which may equally obscure phenomena under investigation or eliminate relevant sociological concerns from investigation."[58]

A central component of the Chicago approach was the call for "objectivity." Sociologists were to avoid corrupting their scholarship with social work or religious proselytizing. They were not to become "do-gooders" crusading to make the world better. While training his students, Park "told them flatly that the world was full of crusaders. Their role instead was to be that of the calm, detached scientist who investigates race relations with the same objectivity and detachment with which the zoologist dissects the potato bug."[59] Park's ridiculing of reform-oriented sociologists, coupled with his insistence that sociology was an objective natural science aimed at discovering "universal social natural laws," encouraged the undertheorizing of human agency characteristic of the Chicago school.

The concept of social interaction was central to Park's sociology. While studying social science in Germany during the closing decade of the nineteenth century, Park was influenced in his sociological approach primarily by Georg Simmel. Simmel stressed identifying social forms and their sociological properties. These forms encompassed a variety of social processes that incubated and crystallized through social interaction. Drawing on Simmel, Park argued that society itself emerged from social interactions through which individuals were engaged in a process of ceaseless reciprocal influencing. Symbolic communication was the medium through which social interactions flowed, enabling people to engage in a perpetual dance of mutual influence. And as Simmel wrote, "If, therefore, there is to be a science, the object of which is to be 'society' and nothing else, it can investigate only these reciprocal influences, these kind and forms of socializations."[60] The goal of the Parkian approach was thus to identify social forms and unravel their mysteries by analyzing the social interactions that created them.

Park, and the Chicago school, imbibed a heavy dose of social Darwinism. Although the Chicago school is celebrated for breaking from the past by emphasizing a distinct sociological orientation and stressing social processes and empirical research, the centrality of evolutionary social Darwinism to Park's approach meant that the Chicago school developed as a hybrid enterprise that embraced irreconcilable contradictions. The wonder of it all is that Park seemed not to discern them.

Social Darwinist sociologists argued that a hierarchy of races existed with superior races at the top, less superior ones in an intermediate position, and inferior ones locked at the bottom. In this scheme, races differed in terms of both mental and physical characteristics. Higher races inherited both superior genes and a socially transmitted superior culture. European superior races, unlike primitive peoples, had civilizations because their cultures had been "generalized, rationalized, and made generally intelligible."[61] For social Darwinists, it was not possible to alter the racial hierarchy because it had been formed by unchanging natural laws under which a powerful natural selection process ensured the survival of the fittest.[62]

Park followed the lead of the social Darwinists by uncritically accepting their racial hierarchy paradigm. For him, white Western Europeans, including American whites, were the superior races because they had developed sophisticated civilizations. European peasants, including those who migrated to America, occupied an intermediate position because their previous exposure to European culture served as the foundation on which they could successfully assimilate into the superior white culture through additional exposure and education.[63] Africa, by contrast, was populated by savages. Therefore, Africans and their descendants were different biologically and culturally from Europeans, with unique racial temperaments and low levels of culture. Blacks occupied the bottom rung of the racial hierarchy because of crippling physical qualities and a lack of civilization. Park was clear about where he personally fit into this racial hierarchy, for he referred to the white race as "our" superior civilization.[64] Indeed, even as Park endorsed manual labor for blacks and simple folktales for their children, he exposed his own children to Plato, Shakespeare, and Homer as well as opera and classical music.[65] In Park's eyes, what was cultural nourishment for white children was a waste of time for black children toiling on southern plantations.[66]

Park smuggled this conception of an evolutionary racial hierarchy into the core analytic structure of his famous race relations cycle. He followed Simmel in theorizing that basic social processes inhered in particular social forms. These forms—competition, conflict, accommodation and assimilation—were foundational in Park's analysis. They determined outcomes of race and ethnic relations in the modern world and would do so for humankind in the future. Viewing the social world from the standpoint of those atop white empires, Park was emphatic about how these forces operated through the race relations cycles with mathematical certainty and universality for all times and places: "This principle may be very simply stated: Every stronger ethnic or social group strives to subjugate and make serviceable to its purpose every weaker element which exists or may come within the field of its existence. This thesis of the relation of heterogeneous ethnic and social elements to each other, with all the consequences proceeding from it, contains within it the key to the solution of the entire riddle of the natural process of human history."[67] These evolutionary assumptions fueled Park's race relations cycle. The sociologist Everett Hughes has correctly argued that even though Simmel and Park's dissertation adviser Windelband had influenced his thinking, Park "also worked a new concept of evolution into it—evolution as itself a product of interaction. This idea is the leading one of the new school of evolutionary biologists."[68]

Park elaborated the four social processes in detail. The first in the cycle, competition, "is the elementary, universal and fundamental form. . . . Competition is *interaction without social contact*" and is "the process through which the distributive and ecological organization of society is created. Competition determines the distribution of population territorially and vocationally."[69] Human competition mimics the plant world, where the struggle for existence unfolds with the participants completely unaware of each other. When participants become aware of each other, the second process, conflict, begins. As a form of interaction, it "is a contest in which contact is an indispensable condition. . . . Conflict is always conscious, indeed, it evokes the deepest emotions and strongest passions and enlists the greatest concentration of attention and of effort."[70] Unlike competition, which is continuous and impersonal, conflict is intermittent and personal and constitutes a political struggle between rivals. Since conflict is disruptive, it tends to move toward resolution by accommodation, "the process by which the individuals and groups make the necessary internal adjustments to social situations which have been created by competition and conflict. When changes thus effected are decisive and are accepted, conflict subsides and the tensions it created are resolved in the process of accommodations into profound modifications of the competing units, i.e., individuals and groups."[71] Accommodation is solidified when subordinate groups accept and internalize their lowly position within a system of unequal social arrangements. Finally, assimilation "is a process of interpenetration and fusion in which persons and groups acquire the memories, sentiments, and attitudes of other persons or groups, and, by sharing their experiences and history, are incorporated with them in a common cultural life."[72] Assimilation occurs gradually and is based on the most intimate associations, which serve as the foundation on which the content of the personalities of previously unassimilated persons undergoes profound transformations, making them one with the host culture.

According to Park, "The race relations cycle which takes the form, to state it abstractly, of contacts, competition, accommodation and eventual assimilation, is apparently progressive and irreversible." Human agency may affect the cycle "but cannot change its direction; cannot at any rate reverse it."[73] Thus Park asserts that this cycle is a predestined process of evolution through which racial groups must travel as they march to their ultimate destiny of becoming assimilated.

But what are races and ethnic groups? Park does not offer clear distinctions between racial and ethnic groups, often using both concepts interchangeably. Yet his concept of race is dominant in his theorizing. It is surprising, given Park's preoccupation with racial dynamics, that he fails to grapple explicitly with what races actually are. Nevertheless, his writings on race show that he saw races as embodying distinct characteristics, including racial temperaments, prejudice and antipathies, dispositions, and instincts. His distinctions between primitive and civilized races are also paramount in his race analyses.

For Park, racial temperaments are key determinants differentiating racial groups. Contrary to scholars who argue that biology is almost absent from Park's analysis of race, his concept of "racial temperaments" reveals that he conceptualized races mainly in biological terms. Defining racial temperament, Park states, "This temperament, as I conceive it, consists in a few elementary but distinctive characteristics, determined by physical organization and transmitted biologically."[74] Thus his conception of race is consistent with the social Darwinist thesis that basic racial characteristics are biologically inherited. Indeed, in 1919 Park stated, "The question remains still to what extent so-called racial characteristics are actually racial, i.e., biological, and to what extent they are the effect of environmental conditions," and answered that question emphatically: "Fundamental temperamental qualities, which are the basis of interest and attention, act as selective agencies and as such determine what elements in the cultural environment each race will select; in what region it will seek and find its vocation in the larger social organization."[75] Moreover, racial temperament determines in the long run a racial group's culture, in the case of the individual his vocation; it also determines what a racial group, "to state it pedagogically, . . . will learn."[76] Innate racial temperament determines a race's aptitude, taste, and talents.[77] These are powerful wide-ranging biological claims. If racial temperament determines one's culture, job, talents, taste, overall interests, and what one can learn, then what on earth is left? In essence, Park argues that an evolutionary natural selection mechanism drives racial differences: racial temperaments function as biological switches that channel the abilities and cultural propensities of races. Park grants that it is through society that races inherit a social heritage, yet a member of a particular race necessarily "transmits by interbreeding a biological inheritance."[78]

Park's evolutionary biological determinism is conveyed through his emphasis on racial predispositions and instincts. He argues that racial inheritances cause races to smell different and that this is sociologically significant because the distinctive odor of a race "becomes, in certain cases, the sensuous basis for racial antipathies."[79] Racial instincts loom large in Park's definitions of racial prejudice and antipathies because "race prejudice may be regarded as a spontaneous, more or less instinctive, defense-reaction, the practical effect of which is to restrict free competition between the races."[80] Thus biological instincts rather than racial discrimination and domination are primary in determining racial inequality. Behind racial antipathies "are deep-seated, vital, and instinctive impulses."[81] In discussing mulattos and other "mixed-bloods," Park argued that they were superior to full blacks because their social location allowed them to associate closely with the superior white race. Additionally, their biological inheritance contributed to their superior intellect and achievements.[82]

As the next chapter shows, Park's preconceptions concerning race and his failure to carry out the empirical research that he advocated led him to numerous erroneous conclusions about black people in America. Du Bois, in his own work, would challenge both these conclusions and their premises.

CHAPTER 5

The Sociology of Black America

Park versus Du Bois

Robert Park's sociology portrayed African Americans as an inferior race. Indeed, the image of blacks emerging from Park's sociology is one of a population handicapped by a double heritage of biological and cultural inferiority. Moreover, even after considering the cultural formulations of the anthropologist Franz Boas, who argued that racial outcomes were determined by historical and social factors, Park conceded only that "so far as this is true we are perhaps warranted in regarding them [black racial characteristics] as modifications of transmitted tradition due to innate traits of the people who have produced them."[1] For Park, "The difference between one culture and another is not very great as long as both are European,"[2] but the difference between blacks and whites, especially white Anglo Saxons, was profound: indeed, he claimed that it was "difficult to conceive two races farther removed from each other in temperament and tradition than the Anglo-Saxon and the Negro."[3]

Park used various descriptors of the black population and people of color, including *primitives, folk people, aliens,* and *savages.*[4] All these labels referred to a people who, when contrasted to civilized Europeans, lacked civilization. Primitive people were incapable of using abstract ideas and rational principles and were driven by undisciplined and uncontrolled wild passions, appetites, and instincts.[5] They survived as creatures of nature responding to immediate stimuli emanating from intense personal and emotional bonds. Their innate racial temperament made them unable to direct attention to intellectual matters like science and technological techniques because "selective attention and the disposition to act consistently—and eventually according to some formal rule or code—seem to be the fundamental traits that distinguish human beings from the lower animals, and, perhaps, primitive from civilized man."[6]

Park also contrasted primitive peoples, with their simple, concrete conceptions, to what he considered to be the ultimate urban group, the Jews: "The intellectual characteristics of the Jew and his generally recognized interest in abstract and radical ideas are unquestionably connected with the fact that the Jews are, before all else, a city folk."[7] Jews were fortunate because "civilization . . . is a product of the city. . . . In the modern world of city-dwellers the rural community is a place to be born but is not a place to live."[8]

Yet cities could not confer their benefits on all racial groups: as centers of advanced civilization, they required special types of civilized persons to inhabit them. White immigrants could adapt to city life, but blacks could not because their biologically inherited temperaments prevented them from developing the self-control needed both to participate in the civilizational wonders that great cities offered and to repress their wild urges, passions, and instincts that the temptations of the city would unleash. For Park, as for Washington, blacks who migrated to cities, rather than acquiring civilization, could only succumb to the vice, disease, crime, and other evils rampant in city life. Blacks should be staying in the southern rural settings that were appropriate for them because it was questionable whether they were even capable of being civilized. It is ironic that Park was writing at a time when blacks were seeking personal, economic, and political freedom from southern Jim Crow by migrating to northern cities. While Du Bois was analyzing the sociological conditions of urban and rural blacks, Park fixed his sociological gaze on the rural South, where he believed blacks existed in an intellectual twilight, and claimed, like Washington, that African Americans' best prospect was to stick to manual labor.

Park argued that blacks differed from immigrants not only because they were more primitive but because they lacked a cultural homeland and thus could not bring an ancestral culture to America. Ancestral traditions, which Park viewed as "a treasure to be preserved" and "an organism to be renewed and perpetuated," were crucial for immigrants because they served as transitional bridges between the old ways of life and those of the host society.[9] But in Park's view, slavery had stripped blacks of every vestige of African culture: "My own impression is that the amount of African tradition which the Negro brought to the United States was very small. In fact there is every reason to believe, it seems to me, that the Negro, when he landed in the United States, left behind him almost everything but the dark complexion and his tropical temperament."[10] Park explored black religion to "prove" that African cultural traditions did not survive the treacherous Middle Passage and American slavery.

In contrast, Du Bois's numerous studies of blacks convinced him that African cultural traditions were not only present but influential in the African American family, church, and music during and after emancipation. Du Bois argued that these traditions strengthened blacks to cope with the vicissitudes of slavery and Jim Crow. Regarding the family, the anthropologist Niara Sudarkasa points out that Du Bois "was the first scholar to stress the need to study the black family in America against the background of its African past."[11] Du Bois's own introduction to his painstaking studies of the black family explains: "In each case an attempt has been made to connect present conditions with the African past. This is not because Negro-Americans are Africans, or can trace an unbroken social history from Africa, but because there is a distinct nexus between Africa and America which, though broken and perverted, is nevertheless not to be neglected by the careful student."[12]

Following an exhaustive historical and empirical analysis of the black church, Du Bois concluded:

> At first sight it would seem that slavery completely destroyed every vestige of spontaneous social movement among the Negroes; . . . indeed, it is usually assumed by historians and sociologists that every vestige of internal development disappeared, leaving the slaves no means of expression for their common life, thought, and striving. This is not strictly true; . . . gradually, after two centuries, the Church became Christian, with a simple Calvinistic creed, but with many of the old customs still clinging to the services. It is this historic fact that the Negro Church of to-day bases itself upon the sole surviving social institution of the African fatherland, that accounts for its extraordinary growth and vitality.[13]

Similarly, Du Bois wrote of black spirituals, which he called "Sorrow Songs," that "the music of Negro religion still remains the most original and beautiful expression of human life and longing yet born on American soil. Sprung from the African forests, where its counterpart can still be heard, it was adapted, changed, and intensified by the tragic soul-life of the slave, until, under the stress of law and whip, it became the one true expression of a people's sorrow, despair, and hope."[14]

In an 1918 essay on the conflict and fusion of cultures, Park addresses, from an opposing perspective, the same topics of black music and the black church that Du Bois addressed, but he avoids directly engaging with Du Bois's arguments and cites him only once. According to Park's thesis, "The fact that the Negro brought with him from Africa so little tradition which he was able to transmit and perpetuate on American soil makes that race unique among all peoples of our cosmopolitan population."[15] No other groups, he argued, "have been so utterly cut off and estranged from their ancestral homeland, traditions and people." In contrast to Du Bois, for example, Park claimed that "the plantation Negro's religion was a faithful copy of the white man's" and that even though the Sea Island Negroes, "who speak a distinct dialect and retain certain customs which are supposed to be of African origin, practice a religion that has undoubtedly the characteristics of primitive ritual, . . . this does not mean that it is African in origin. It seems to me more likely that it is to be interpreted as a very simple and natural expression of group emotion, which is just beginning to crystalize and assume formal character."[16] Park was convinced that black American religion sprang from an innate racial temperament that blacks inherited biologically; it was not a socially transmitted cultural tradition.

In this view, blacks merely imitated white religion and adapted it for their purposes. Park ignored Du Bois's research ferreting out the connections between black religion and liberation struggles led by religious revolutionaries including Nat Turner and Denmark Vesey;[17] instead he declared, "The restlessness which this situation [the restrictiveness of slavery] provoked found expression, not in in insurrection and rebellion—although, of course, there were Negro insurrections—but in his religion and in his dreams of another and freer world. I assume, therefore, that the reason the Negro so readily and eagerly took over from the white man his heaven and apocalyptic visions was because these materials met the demands of his peculiar racial temperament and furnished relief to the emotional strains that were provoked in him by the conditions of slavery."[18]

Park's view of black religion as an otherworldly oriented apolitical force that served as an emotional release for otherwise dangerous tensions would be embraced by succeeding generations of white sociologists. It would prove to be erroneous, however, for it took root precisely when the structural and cultural forces in the black community that would drive the civil rights movement were gathering strength. What was thought to be an "apolitical" church would turn out to play a central role in generating a movement that transformed America.[19]

Park addresses Du Bois's treatment of black spirituals only indirectly. For instance, whereas Du Bois explored how spirituals were laced with protest themes expressing black aspirations on earth, Park describes them as significant primarily for their "ecstatic visions of the next world." Whereas Du Bois depicted spirituals as creative masterpieces, Park repeatedly describes them as primitive and naive compared to European folk songs. And whereas Du Bois called spirituals "Sorrow Songs," Park states, "It is true that the slave songs express longing, that they refer to hard trials and great tribulations, but the dominant mood is one of Jubilation. 'Going to sing, going to shout. Going to play all over God's Heaven.'"[20] Park adds that these songs "tend to justify the general impression that the Negro is temperamentally sunny, cheerful, optimistic." He concludes, "It is interesting to note in this connection that nowhere in these songs do we discover the slightest references to Africa."[21]

But Park's argument is based on assertions and the testimony of questionable informants. His "evidence" comes from the report of an English visitor; a book by a white Army colonel, Thomas W. Higginson, who headed a black regiment; a book written by a music critic, Henry E. Krehbiel, who was educated by his father; and a book entitled *Social and Mental Traits of the Negro*, by the white sociologist Howard Odum, who shared Park's view that blacks were inferior.[22] Park does not reference Du Bois's study *The Negro Church*.[23] Du Bois's *Souls of Black Folk*, which contains a chapter on black spirituals and religion, is mentioned briefly but not addressed systematically.[24] Indeed, writing well over a decade after Du Bois's groundbreaking works addressing the black church, religion, and survivals of African culture, Park makes clear whom he considers to be the authority on black spirituals: "The first and most interesting account we have of these Negro spirituals is that of Col. Thomas Wentworth Higginson in his *Army Life in a Black Regiment*. He collected them from the lips of his own black soldiers as they sung them at the campfire at night. He was almost the first to recognize that these rude plantation hymns represented a real literature, the only real literature the American Negro has produced, until very recent times."[25] So much for Park's scientific sociology! Subsequent social scientific works have confirmed Du Bois's findings: African cultural traditions survived the Middle Passage and slave experience and continued as enduring features of black American religion.[26]

Park's claim that American blacks lacked a cultural homeland was significant because it portrayed blacks as empty cultural vessels whose salvation depended on their assimilating the superior culture of whites. Given the claims of black inferiority in Park's framework, blacks had no choice but to copy white culture, but surely this would entail a mighty struggle given the sophisticated skills an inferior race would need to acquire in order to appropriate a superior white culture. At best, blacks could become only inferior cultural copies of their superiors. This line of argument reveals that for Park biology trumped sociology as an explanation for racial outcomes. Slavery had stripped blacks of their African culture but left in place their biologically derived African racial temperaments that negatively influenced their social development.

According to Park, racial temperament was responsible for blacks' intellectual inferiority, lack of ambition for social change, and lack of entrepreneurial spirit. It caused blacks to embrace "an interest and attachment to external, physical things rather than to subjective states and objects of introspection; in a disposition for expression rather than enterprise and action."[27] Expanding on this, Park asserted elsewhere in the same essay that "everywhere and always it [black race] has been interested rather in expression than in action; interested in life itself rather than in its reconstruction or reformation. The Negro is, by natural disposition, neither an intellectual nor an idealist, like the Jew; nor a brooding introspective, like the East African; nor a pioneer and frontiersman, like the Anglo-Saxon. He is primarily an artist, loving life for its own sake. His *métier* is expression rather than action. He is, so to speak, the lady among the races."[28] Although Park did not address gender inequality directly, this passage suggests he thought women, like blacks, were handicapped by distinct temperaments.

According to Park, blacks, unless deracinated in northern cities, were willing prisoners of white domination: he wrote in the *Introduction to the Science of Sociology* that "the [black] masses . . . accept the superiority of the white race as a race . . . as a mere matter of course" and that both the Negro and the "average southern white man" recognize the white race's superiority without giving it a moment's thought because "the status of superior and inferior is simply an inherited part of [their] instinctive mental equipment."[29] In a 1926 book review Park makes clear his belief in the biological basis of white superiority when he states that "the reason why the symptoms of racial decay are not more pronounced is probably that European civilization is still living on its biological capital, on the qualities bred into the Nordic stock by the severest natural selection."[30] A critic of some aspects of eugenics, Park nevertheless claims that "the eugenist program, as it is ordinarily propounded, is in the interest of civilization."[31]

It is sobering to ponder Park's negative judgments about blacks given his close associations with black leaders and the masses and his declaration that the experiences made possible by Booker T. Washington allowed him "to get acquainted with the actual and intimate life of the Negro in the South. . . . I became, for all intents and purposes a Negro myself."[32] It is equally sobering that by implication Park held similarly negative views about women, given that he was married to a woman who was an intellectual, sociologist, and renowned activist.[33] There can be little doubt that social Darwinism, racism, and white male privilege had seeped deeply into Park's "calm," "detached," and "objective" sociology.

Park's heavy reliance on a biologically based social Darwinist theory fused with a social interactionist perspective shaped the logic of his race relations cycle. Like Weber's conception of the historic march of bureaucratization and Marx's formulation of a worldwide class struggle, the race relations cycle as envisioned by Park was an inevitable epic phenomenon ushering in modern civilization across the globe. Park's sociology was driven by major developments including European colonization of Africa and Asia, the incorporation of millions of European immigrants into American society, and the ever explosive homegrown American race problem. For Park, European colonialism was causing the overthrow of governments, high levels of brutality, and simmering conflicts across continents; European immigration to America was stirring class and ethnic conflicts; and America's race problem was leading to lynchings, race riots, and ceaseless tensions between blacks and whites. Park's race relation cycle represented an intellectual effort to formulate a conceptual framework that would explain these tumultuous developments and their consequences in the modern world.

Park conceptualized the race relations cycle as the conveyor belt of civilization.[34] Like the classical European sociologists, he accepted the distinction between Gemeinschaft, a parochial, relatively homogeneous community characterized by personal ties among members who shared a sense of moral responsibility to the group, and Gesellschaft, a heterogeneous civil society, like that of the great American and European cities, characterized by formal, impersonal roles and an emphasis on individual self-interest.[35] For Park, the overwhelming majority of backward groups were societies of color strewn across Asia and Africa. They were augmented by European peasants who shared in the civilization of

Europeans generally but had not completely transitioned from Gemeinschaft to Gesellschaft and thus were not completely integrated into its modern civilization, where rationalization, modern industry, written language, and scientific technique were dominant. According to Park, his race relations cycle captured the stages through which advanced European civilization would spread across the world.

Violence, forceful overthrow of governments and tribal councils, disruption of local economies, intense human exploitation, streams of migrations, and implementation of slavery, caste, and colonialism were for Park the conduits through which Europeans nations brought civilization to backward populations of the world. Thus global political and social upheavals constituted a civilizing process despite their devastating short-run effects on backward peoples. Such catastrophes were the collateral damage backward peoples had to endure in order to obtain the white man's superior civilization. As Park put it, "Civilization is built up by the absorption of foreign ethnic groups, by undermining them, and by secularizing their cult and sacred order."[36] This civilizing impulse was the motivation for colonizing Africa and Asia and for instituting and perpetuating American slavery.

In this view, Africans' capture by European slave traders, their experience of the brutal Middle Passage, and the ensuing 250 years of American slavery were all part of the civilizing school through which African savages had to pass in order to join the modern world. As pointed out earlier, Booker T. Washington himself held this view, seeing slavery as the experience that had enabled black people to advance by bringing them into proximity with the most advanced civilization on earth. As a Washington protégé, Park absorbed this view and incorporated it into his race cycle theory.

Park theorized that slavery had provided blacks with the exposure and experiences they required to take the initial steps toward civilization. Though he conceded that conflict occurred during the implementation of colonialism and slavery, he viewed such conflict as inevitable and creative. Ultimately, however, Park considered slavery and the establishment of a racial caste system as formations representing the accommodation stage in the race relations cycle. Accommodation, it should be recalled, occurred when individuals and groups made the necessary internal adjustments to social situations created by competition and conflict. For Park it was the third stage in a progressive cycle occurring just before the most advanced stage, assimilation. According to Park, during the slavery era no race problem existed in the United States because slavery, despite its gross inequalities and brutalities, enabled slaves and their masters to make internal adjustments that generated peaceful relations.[37]

For Park, accommodation occurred during slavery when slave masters and slaves developed intimate, warm, personal associations, characterized by kind and sympathetic personal relationships. Such cozy relations required slaves to accept their wretched conditions and to fully accept the superiority of their white masters. Here Park followed the lead of his old mentor. Washington extolled the so-called intimate relationships between masters and slaves and highlighted slaves' loyalty to their masters. He maintained that slaves proved their loyalty by raising their young and being gentle caretakers of their old.[38] Again, Park followed in Washington's footsteps, arguing, "The sentiment of the Negro slave was, in a certain sense, not merely loyalty to his master, but to the white race."[39] Furthermore, the slaves' inherited racial temperaments caused them to form "allegiances to the state, of which they were only indirectly members, or at least to their masters' families, with whom they felt themselves in most things one in sentiment and interests."[40] Such internal adjustments, according to Park, softened the racial conflicts that arose from slavery and resolved the tensions that slavery created.

Park has often been viewed as an innovative sociological scholar whose analysis broke from outdated presociological thought. This is not at all the case, however, for his views on slavery, which merely repeat the proslavery arguments of the period's mainstream, racially biased social science scholarship. The obvious parallel is with the work of Park's contemporary Ulrich Bonnel Phillips, the most prominent historian of slavery. For Phillips, slaves were inferior, docile creatures who were loyal to their masters.[41] In a 1944 review of Phillips's work, Richard Hofstadter wrote: "Phillips chose to portray the Negro slave as a singularly contented and docile 'serio-comic' creature. His casual treatment of the slave's resistance to slavery and in particular of slave revolts was accordingly inadequate, and highly misleading, not merely as to the character of the slave but also upon critical aspects of race relations."[42] Phillips described those "race relations" of slavery as consisting of educative arrangements enabling the barbaric slave to ease into the superior white civilization. For Phillips, slavery was a period of tranquil accommodations that should not have been rudely shattered by the Civil War. Thus Park's and Phillips's views of slavery meshed seamlessly. With regard to slavery it was Du Bois, as we will see, who was the innovative scholar given that his analysis of the regime revealed its brutal nature and the fierce resistance of slaves to this most undemocratic form of white supremacy.

Park claimed that slavery became a period where two highly unequal parties fused their interests, sentiments, and personalities so that the subordinate one became fully assimilated to the dominant.[43] Yet in his view this most advanced stage in his progressive cycle was followed by one of the most retrograde regimes known to humankind, Reconstruction. Park never explained how the cycle could go backwards at this juncture. But following Washington's lead, he argued that the upheavals of the Civil War and then Reconstruction caused the race problem to return by destroying intimate, peaceful relations between master and slave and dismantling the racial assimilation that blacks had achieved.[44]

While at Tuskegee, Park became familiar with Washington's dictum that blacks constituted a "nation within a nation." Park appropriated this idea and applied it to the post-Reconstruction black community and other minority communities, arguing that when they were isolated from the dominant group they developed nationalistic ideologies. Such communities might organize internally and engage in conflict to realize their interests. This became true for the black community especially during the Harlem Renaissance period in the North. Yet Park never fully developed an analysis of urban blacks because he accepted Washington's view that blacks were primarily a southern people.

Summing up, Park's sociology of race portrayed blacks as inferior culturally and biologically. They were prisoners of the workings of a predetermined race relations cycle that changed gradually and was not amenable to human intervention. Moreover, blacks lacked agency to overthrow oppression because they had no cultural past and were burdened by a fixed biological temperament that rendered them loyal to their oppressors. Following Washington, Park viewed militant black leaders and intellectuals, such as Du Bois, as misdirected agitators meddling with social processes that had evolved according to their own internal logic. Under Washington's tutelage, Park came to believe that change occurred slowly because such processes were deeply rooted in social structures and human culture.[45] Indeed, Park's idea of a race relations cycle germinated while he studied the Negro's relationship with white folk at Tuskegee under Washington's direction. Having initially developed the core ideas of the race relation cycle at Tuskegee, Park applied this sociological schema to world history: "I became convinced, finally, that I was observing the historical process by which civilization, not merely here but elsewhere, has evolved, drawing into the circle of its influence an ever widening circle of races and people."[46]

THE DU BOISIAN SCHOOL MEETS
THE CHICAGO SCHOOL

Du Bois's sociology of race was developed two decades before that of Park and the Chicago school. Although Du Bois produced pioneering work on sociology and race, Park and Chicago school sociologists ignored it, so that their conceptualizations remained largely unaffected by Du Bois's contrasting approach. As will be shown below, in some cases Du Bois's ideas did influence those of Park, but he rarely acknowledged this publicly. If Park had engaged Du Bois's work, he would have discovered stark differences between how the two men defined sociology and race and outlined a sociology of black Americans. A brief examination reveals the irreconcilable differences between Park's and Du Bois's approaches.

As we have seen, Du Bois conceived sociology as an inductive science that could derive valid generalizations only from careful and accurate empirical studies. For Du Bois, it was unproductive for sociologists to develop formal laws of human behavior and assert their universality irrespective of time and place. Du Bois argued that generalizations had to emerge from empirical research anchored in data rather than from preconceived formal laws. He warned that it was naive for the social sciences to use natural sciences as their model given fundamental differences between human behavior and natural phenomena. As discussed earlier, Du Bois also rejected a sociology that did not incorporate human agency at the core of its conceptualizations because he saw human behavior as characterized by an element of chance.[47] Human action's influence on social structures made it impossible for universal laws to be applicable outside history and social context. A valid sociology, argued Du Bois, required the study and measurement of patterned behavior and an examination of how human agency affected those patterns.

Du Bois, in contrast to Park, broke from social Darwinism, especially claims that biology and cosmically driven forms of interaction determined race dynamics and racially based social conditions. Unlike Park, Du Bois did not offer biological conceptualizations such as racial temperaments to explain race differences. Like Boas, he rejected claims of biological and cultural inferiority as explanations of race and gender inequalities, arguing that any such inferiorities derived from exploitation, domination, and human agency exercised by both oppressors and the oppressed. While Park clung to the heritage of nineteenth-century thinkers who stressed natural racial hierarchies and biological determinism, Du Bois foreshadowed the current social constructionist approach, which emphasizes race as a social construct and highlights the role of power in establishing and maintaining racial inequalities.

Du Bois parted ways with Park regarding American slavery. He did not believe that slavery completely stripped blacks of an African cultural heritage. As we have seen, he argued that while slavery partially crippled blacks culturally, African culture nevertheless expressed itself in black music, literature, family, and in a dominant institution of religion.[48] Given such cultural survivals, the black American personality was no tabula rasa onto which blacks copied the culture of the white man. Du Bois argued that blacks had developed unique souls enabling them to produce original gifts that enhanced the kingdom of culture worldwide. Blacks, in Du Bois's view, were able to fashion a world of their own making precisely because they constructed it upon cultural traditions socially inherited from Africa.

Du Bois's analysis of American slavery differed radically from Park's and Washington's view that slavery was the bringer of civilization to black people and that slaves generally had warm, intimate associations with their masters. Du Bois pointed out that in some instances house servants and members of the master class did develop sympathetic relationships. However, those relationships involved only a minority of slaves and by no means characterized the slave system. Du Bois viewed slavery as a cruel institution of domination and exploitation and provided evidence that blacks resisted it and exercised decisive agency to participate in its overthrow. Rather than a civilizing process, slavery, for Du Bois, was "a nasty business that engaged directly in the barter of human flesh" given that it was the "deliberate commercial breeding and sale of humans for profit."[49] Instead of intimate warm relations, slavery perpetuated conditions that were "in a very real sense the ultimate degradation of man."[50] Du Bois stated his views of slavery emphatically in his response to the charge that blacks' political record during Reconstruction showed they never should have received the vote allowed to them by the Fifteenth Amendment: "It was not the Emancipation Proclamation but the Fifteenth Amendment that made slavery impossible in the United States and those that object to the Fifteenth Amendment have simply this question to answer: Which was best, slavery or ignorant Negro voters? The answer is clear as day: Negro voters never did anything as bad as slavery. If they were guilty of all the crimes charged to them by the wildest enemies, even then what they did was less dangerous, less evil and less cruel than the system of slavery whose death knell they struck."[51]

In Du Bois's view slaves were not loyal to their master "naturally" or voluntarily. Slave owners wielded enormous power and so thoroughly and brutally enforced slavery that slave communities often functioned as armed camps. Du Bois's scholarship regarding slave revolts, slaves' important roles as abolitionists and revolutionaries, the Underground Railroad, and fiercely fought battles by black soldiers in the Civil War was too extensive for him to accept the apologetic renderings of slavery presented by Washington and Park. It was no surprise to Du Bois that slaves streamed into the Union Army in great numbers to overthrow their masters.[52]

Du Bois also pointed out that slavery made possible the oppression of the entire working class by dividing white and black laborers along racial lines.[53] Racial prejudice, unlike the social psychological defense mechanism Park believed it to be, was in Du Bois's view a powerful weapon used by the dominant group to achieve and maintain power. Du Bois's approach to slavery and race generally is best seen as a political sociology stressing power, violence, exploitation, ideological dominance, and class relations.

Du Bois did not share Washington and Park's negative view of Reconstruction as a period that reintroduced the race problem and destroyed relations of racial assimilation that had formed during slavery. For Du Bois, slavery marked the beginning of the race problem that had endured and was continuing as the central issue throughout the world during the twentieth century. Reconstruction was a progressive period where experiments in democracy and racial equality were undertaken.[54] It was an era that sparked high levels of creative agency and black leadership. For these reasons, Du Bois argued, northern and southern whites consolidated power and crushed the brief regime of Reconstruction.

Du Bois, unlike Washington and Park, did not view blacks as primarily a southern rural people. His *Philadelphia Negro* analyzing an urban northern community was paralleled and followed by numerous studies of rural blacks in the South, but whereas Washington and Park viewed southern and northern blacks as distinct groups embedded in different social relations, Du Bois argued that the same fundamental social realities confronted both groups.[55] His fieldwork enabled him to present more complex portraits of African Americans on plantations than Park, who emphasized their biologically driven sunny dispositions and their loyalties to white oppressors. Du Bois found African Americans trapped in slavelike conditions of inescapable debt and harsh treatment: "They are not happy, these black men whom we meet in this region. There is little of the joyous abandon and playfulness which we are wont to associate with the plantation Negro. At best, the natural good-nature is edged with complaint or has changed into sullenness and gloom."[56] In Du Bois's research he encountered angry black men such as the one who declared, "Let a white man touch me, and he dies; I don't boast this,—I don't say it around loud, or before the children,—but I mean it. I've seen them whip my father and my old mother in them cotton-rows till the blood ran."[57] Thus widespread prejudice and rampant discrimination circumscribed blacks' life chances and influenced their culture and social organization in both North and South, both on farms and in cities. What differed regionally were only the mechanisms through which injustice and discrimination were imposed upon the darker race. For Du Bois, the race problem was global and in the American context required a nationwide solution.[58]

Du Bois's approach also contrasted with the logic of Park's race relations cycle. According to Park's theory of that cycle, racial groups worldwide would eventually assimilate into the culture of white Europeans. Du Bois rejected this ideal of the fusion of all races in a gigantic cultural melting pot.[59] Rather, he posited that different cultures were relatively autonomous and had their own contributions to make to human civilization. Here he agreed with Boas, who early in the twentieth century had argued that "we should learn to look on foreign races with greater sympathy and with a conviction that, as all races have contributed in the past to cultural progress in one way or another, so they will be capable of advancing the interests of mankind if we are only willing to give them a fair opportunity."[60] Du Bois's argument of cultural autonomy made him a pioneer of what Manning Marable characterizes as cultural pluralism.[61] While Park, seeing the world through the eyes of white rulers, advocated the triumph of a single superior white European culture, Du Bois envisioned a future for humankind that would interweave numerous cultures in a tapestry of diversity.

Finally, Park's sociology usually lacked scientific precision and objectivity because it was seldom based on empirical data. Du Bois had warned sociologists twenty years earlier of the pitfalls and biases lurking in studies of race in the United States, speaking specifically of the fatal dangers inherent in a sociology depending on "hearsay, rumor and tradition, vague speculations, traveller's tales, legends and imperfect documents, the memory of memories and historic error."[62] For Du Bois, such approaches, based on speculations rather than "hands-on" research in the field, represented what he called "car-window" sociology.[63] These warnings were especially applicable to ideas Park appropriated from an enormously powerful black conservative leader who had vested interests to protect.

Yet despite the warnings Park fell into the analytical and methodological traps identified by Du Bois. Though he had loudly demanded that sociologists engage in detached scientific scholarship based on empirical research, Park succumbed to the habits of grand theorists, often relying on intuition, impressions, opinions, and travelers' tales told by individuals with ideological axes to grind and power to protect. Park's race relation cycle was based on deductive theorizing, not supported by empirically based research. When making grandiose claims about black people, Park often conceded that these were his impressions, opinions, and beliefs, and he often based them on accounts from others who were not trained scholars. In so doing, given his towering influence on generations of scholars, Park miserably failed Du Bois's standards that race scholarship should be based on systematic data, careful measurement, and unbiased analysis. Du Bois had stated that social scientists who did otherwise "do far more than hurt the good name of the American people; they hurt the cause of scientific truth the world over, they voluntarily decrease human knowledge."[64] Although Du Bois was committed to scientific sociology, he advocated that knowledge be utilized to engender social change. Because he was convinced that social scientific knowledge could inform social change, he rejected the so-called objective sociology of Park and his scorn for activist scholars as useless do-gooders.

DU BOIS: THE PREEMINENT PUBLIC SOCIOLOGIST

Even before the turn of the twentieth century, Du Bois had become a public intellectual who developed sociology relevant to social change and utilized it in his efforts to emancipate the oppressed.[65] In so doing, Du Bois broke radically from those social scientists who promoted their investigations as pure objective scholarship. This was true for the Chicago school, whose scholars followed Park's advice that "their role . . . was to be that of the calm, detached scientist who investigates race relations with the same objectivity and detachment with which the zoologist dissects the potato bug."[66] Du Bois inhabited a different world from white social scientists; he was often the victim of racism, and he abhorred the pain it inflicted on him personally and on his race. Speaking of a horrific lynching, after which he saw the victim's knuckles on display in the window of a local grocer, Du Bois wrote: "One could not be a calm, cool, and detached scientist while Negroes were lynched, murdered and starved."[67] This standpoint led Du Bois to pioneer public sociology, becoming the discipline's first preeminent public scholar long before such a role was lucrative and celebrated.

In the twenty-first century, several sociologists have argued that sociological knowledge should be brought outside academic confines and injected into the public arena. They claim that academic sociology is too insular, and they believe that professional sociology's task of developing core principles, bodies of knowledge, methodologies, and empirical findings should be paired with the task of expressing to the world those important things sociology has to say that could help humanity face its problems and move toward solutions.[68] They argue that sociology should engage publics beyond the academy in dialogue about matters of political and moral concern and should create publics and forge identities for movements of social change.

Unbeknownst to many of these public sociology advocates, they are attempting to reclaim a heritage pioneered by Du Bois a century ago. Du Bois developed his sociology to serve as a weapon of liberation to change white minds, awaken blacks to the power of education, and reshape how blacks saw themselves. As early as 1895 after returning from Germany, Du Bois revealed his intent to advocate for change: "I returned ready and eager to begin a life-work, leading to the emancipation of the American Negro. History and the other social sciences were to be my weapons, to be sharpened and applied by research and writing."[69]

As a public sociologist, Du Bois organized and founded historic publics and social movements including the National Negro Academy, the Niagara movement, the NAACP, and four Pan-African Congresses held in Europe and America during the 1920s. A century before the political philosopher Charles Mills concluded in *The Racial Contract* that racism was a global system of white supremacy that oppressed people of color around the world, Du Bois reached the same conclusion. From this international perspective, he founded and led organizations to fight against racism globally.[70] These organized publics and social movements initiated major efforts to overthrow racism nationally and internationally and were driven by sociological scholarship. Writing in the

"Manifesto of the Second Pan-African Congress" presented to people of color from many parts of the world in London in 1921, Du Bois utilized findings from his scientific studies to assert: "The absolute equality of races, —physical, political and social—is the founding stone of world peace and human advancement. No one denies great differences of gift, capacity and attainment among individuals of all races, but the voice of science, religion and practical politics is one in denying the God-appointed existence of superior races, or of races naturally and inevitably and eternally inferior."[71] In a similar vein, Du Bois used an intersectional analysis in the *Crisis* to address the disenfranchisement of women: "The statement that woman is weaker than man is sheer rot: It is the same sort of thing that we hear about 'darker races' and 'lower classes.' Difference, either physical or spiritual, does not argue weakness or inferiority."[72] Separating himself from white sociologists who claimed that sociology should be scientifically pure and conducted by calm, detached scholars, Du Bois rejected a science that was a slave of racial and capitalist oppression and imperialism.[73] He disseminated this knowledge through the innumerable lectures he presented and the thousands of articles he published in newspapers and periodicals. A central conduit for his public sociology was magazines: he was one of the first to convey sociology through literature and journalism.

Du Bois, a founder of the NAACP, became the director of its department of research and publicity in 1910. In this capacity, he founded the *Crisis* magazine and edited it for a quarter century. The *Crisis* became Du Bois's major vehicle for merging sociological scholarship and activism. Through this magazine he used his scholarship, as well as that of others, to educate the world about the devastating effects of racism and inequality. Many contemporary scholars claimed that by educating the public in the *Crisis* Du Bois was no longer acting as a scholar but had turned propagandist. Yet Du Bois and other scholars reviewed major scholarship in the magazine and offered searing critiques especially regarding works advocating the black inferiority thesis. In the *Crisis*, Du Bois highlighted cutting-edge social scientific ideas, explaining their contributions and limitations. He also expounded on his theories of race, class, and gender inequality for a popular audience. In the *Crisis* were explanations of how ruling classes eroded the power of labor by dividing black and white workers, making possible the exploitation of both groups. Du Bois explained how women's disenfranchisement was a tool for promoting racism, sexist, and capitalist domination. He pointed to the role ignorance played in oppressing people and sought to develop the knowledge people needed for their liberation. He sought to disentangle social factors that produced wars from those that promoted peace. He analyzed protests nationally and internationally, always interested in the lessons of social change that they provided.

The analyses disseminated through the *Crisis* were intended to spur social action and social movements that could build a more just and equal world. The magazine counseled the oppressed to engage in unceasing protest and agitation. It published literature and scholarship aimed at building and promoting race, feminist, and class consciousness. Its pages were opened to scholars and writers—E. Franklin Frazier, Franz Boas, Jane Addams, Zora Neale Hurston, Alain Locke, Langston Hughes, Claude McKay, and many others—whose ideas promoted progressive thinking. Many of the writers who birthed the Harlem Renaissance, such as Jesse Fauset, who became full-time literary editor for the *Crisis,* were first published by Du Bois in the *Crisis.* The *Crisis* not only openly supported activists and movements for change but repeatedly called for action to attack inequality.

Du Bois's public sociology refused to condescend to the public. Yet he made sure his ideas were presented clearly and provocatively so that they could reach large audiences. He employed different genres to appeal to readers, including poems, novels, interviews, plays, and literary works. As a result, the *Crisis* became an instant success and by the 1920s had thousands of subscribers, many of whom were African Americans. One subscriber stated, "I know in my family the *Crisis* was the magazine to read and take leadership from." Another confided, "I don't know where the Bible was in the house but I knew where the *Crisis* was."[74] Never before, or since, has there been such an effective organ that disseminated a sociological perspective to millions.

Du Bois's achievements in organizing publics and social movements have been influential in American and world politics. His pioneering public sociology demonstrated that the discipline could combine science and activism to engender change. In so doing, Du Bois enhanced sociological scholarship, demonstrating that sociology was capable of diffusing its important messages to the world outside academia.

PARK'S AND CHICAGO'S MARGINALIZATION OF DU BOIS

A cardinal sin of science is for scholars to ignore scholarship bearing directly on their scholarship. Park and the Chicago school committed this sin by marginalizing Du Bois's work. Park is widely considered the father of American race studies, especially in sociology. There are obvious reasons why this view is feasible, given that he was probably the first scholar to teach a course devoted exclusively to the Negro at a white university.[75] Unlike other white sociologists of the period, Park was the only scholar to closely observe blacks and race relations directly and in depth during his tenure at Tuskegee. His close association with Booker T. Washington enabled him to speak authoritatively on race and African Americans. Park also appeared to be the unquestioned pioneer of race studies because of his access to graduate students, colleagues, financial resources, and a social science infrastructure through which he projected his sociology broadly. Thanks to his Tuskegee experience and newspaper background, Park effectively disseminated his sociological perspective because at Tuskegee he had learned the value of being a member of an organization through which ideas could be projected far and wide.

Park's reign as king of race studies was made possible by both American racism and his own agenda. The effective pursuit of that agenda enabled Park and the Chicago school to render Du Bois's scholarship invisible. An analysis of Park's success in marginalizing Du Bois's sociological scholarship sheds light on a nation rocked by tumultuous racial conflicts. I begin with two questions: First, to what extent did Park ignore Du Bois's scholarship? Second, why did Max Weber, a continent away, embrace Du Bois's scholarship while Park ignored it? The first question is taken up in this chapter; the second will be addressed in the chapter that follows.

Park was familiar with Du Bois's scholarship and was aware of Du Bois's status as a major black leader. He knew that Du Bois had emerged as the principal rival of his mentor, Booker T. Washington. It was Park's job to keep close watch over the ideas espoused by Du Bois and his radical colleagues and to communicate them to Washington.[76] Washington was familiar with Du Bois's scholarship and interacted with him at conferences and intimate settings. At the beginning of the Washington–Du Bois controversy in 1903, Du Bois published his *Souls of Black Folk* (hereafter referred to as *Souls*). It was widely read and reviewed and became an instant classic that has been continuously in print since its publication. This work was of particular interest to Washington and Park because it contained Du Bois's first public attack on Washington's leadership. When Park arrived at Tuskegee in 1905, the rivalry between the two leaders was at fever pitch and the attention garnered by *Souls* was immense. Park must have read *Souls* because he cited it several times and used it as a text in the first class he taught on race at the University of Chicago. Likewise, Park was familiar with Du Bois's *Philadelphia Negro* because he cites it in the bibliography of the 1921 *Introduction to the Science of Sociology* (hereafter referred to as *Introduction*), which he edited with Ernest Burgess. In *Introduction*, Park shows familiarity with Du Bois's annual Atlanta Studies, citing the 1908 *Negro American Family* from that series. Also in the bibliography of *Introduction* Park cites *Darkwater*, a volume Du Bois published in 1920. Park's first sociological article, "Negro Home Life and Standards of Living," was published only eighty-six pages apart from an article by Du Bois, "The Negro in Literature and Art," in the same issue of *Annals of the American Academy of Political and Social Science*.[77] It is unlikely that Park was unaware of Du Bois's article in the very same journal as his own. Thus the historical record is clear: Park was familiar with Du Bois's scholarship.

Park and Burgess's text is the appropriate starting point from which to explore the extent to which Park ignored Du Bois's prolific scholarship.[78] *Introduction* introduced sociology to a national academic audience. Coser concluded that it was the most important textbook-reader in the early history of sociology.[79] Likewise, Faris wrote that "the direction and content of American sociology after 1921 was mainly set by the Park and Burgess text."[80] Deegan concurred, writing that the volume was dubbed the 'Green Bible' for its near-sacred status. . . . It guided all Chicago ethnographies, and most sociologists, between 1921 and 1941."[81] The "Green Bible" set forth Park and Burgess's thesis that sociology was an abstract science.

Introduction was conceived as a monumental work that would span the major topics of sociology and include the major contributors to sociology worldwide. As Raushenbush details, "The *Introduction* is a 1,000-page book organized around fourteen sociological themes illustrated by the 196 readings. The index lists over 1,700 writers. Biologists, philosophers, and men of letters, as well as sociologists, are quoted. There are extracts from diaries and private journals. Of the ten writers most frequently cited one is German, Simmel; two are English, Darwin and Spencer; three French, Durkheim, Tarde, Le Bon; and four American, William Graham Sumner, Charles Cooley, Park himself, and William I. Thomas."[82] Other major contributors included W. I. Thomas and the founder of eugenics, Francis Galton. Thus the "Green Bible" contained a dazzling array of thinkers and writers cutting across cultures and through the ages. The authors chosen constituted a "who's who" list that clearly preferred to err on the side of inclusion.

Yet Du Bois, who by 1921 was world famous, having published several classic books and numerous important articles in visible outlets, did not make the cut for inclusion in the "Green Bible." There were no selections chosen from his prolific writings, which included dozens explicitly sociological in content and logic. Park and Burgess did not quote him. His name in the index appeared four times only because of references to his writings in bibliographies following chapters. And even in the index the eugenicist Galton had more entries (five). Thus the "Green Bible" provides yet another instance of how Du Bois, like an Old Testament prophet crying out in the wilderness, and expressing views of critical importance to his society, was nevertheless marginalized and largely unheard.

The silence regarding Du Bois's work is evident throughout Park's writings and those of the Chicago School generally. In Park's collected papers on race and culture, spanning four hundred pages and consisting of twenty-nine papers written over a span of more than thirty years, Du Bois is listed in the index six times. Two mentions refer perfunctorily to Du Bois as a leader and editor; another refers to a text that criticized Du Bois for not understanding the superficiality of Negro slave songs; and two others refer to a text that cites a couple of Du Bois's formulations favorably.[83] The final entry refers to a footnote where Du Bois is accused of failing to acknowledge the preeminent role of more intelligent "mixed bloods" in black leadership, which Du Bois conceptualized as the "talented tenth." In this comprehensive volume, Park spends less than two paragraphs on Du Bois's work, and those paragraphs are superficial. Therefore, Park's collected papers on race provide additional proof that Park never engaged Du Bois substantively throughout his scholarly career.

The same record of silent treatment holds true for other sociologists of the Chicago school. Andrew Abbott concludes that during the early years of sociology as a discipline, Small controlled the *American Journal of Sociology* and usually published only articles written by a few close associates.[84] That this founding sociological journal did not review *The Philadelphia Negro* reveals Du Bois was not one of the associates. In its May 1898 issue, the journal published a small excerpt of Du Bois's article "The Study of the Negro Problems," which had been published in the *Annals of the American Academy of Political and Social Science*.[85] But "During the sixteen years Du Bois was associated with the Atlanta publications, only two were reviewed by . . . the *American Journal of Sociology*."[86] *Souls* did garner a short review in which the author reported that "Professor DuBois approaches the many-sided negro question with the confidence and conviction of a master, and with the grace and beauty of a poet."[87] But following this praise came the claim that the real strength of *Souls* resided in its "unbiased consideration of the negro's emotional nature" because "there can be no doubt of the preponderance of misdirected emotionalism is evidenced in the rapidity with which the negro swings from love to hate, from laughter to tears."[88] There is no mention of Du Bois's prophetic prediction that "the problem of the Twentieth Century is the problem of the color-line," which has endured over a century as the most profound insight of *Souls*. Nor did the University of Chicago Press play any significant role in publishing Du Bois's work.[89]

Yet another revealing indicator that the Chicago school turned a blind eye to Du Bois's pioneering scientific sociology is Small's failure to mention Du Bois's work in his 143-page article in the *American Journal of Sociology* examining fifty years of American sociology from 1865 to 1915.[90] It was during the latter years of that period that Du Bois established his Atlanta school and published groundbreaking sociological works. Yet Small laments the lack of empirical work produced by sociologists during the period in which Du Bois published numerous empirical studies. Small complains about the endless meetings where early sociologists tried to transcend grand theorizing and engage in empirical work. Yet he does not mention that Du Bois, during this period, was producing such work while other sociologists were at a loss about which road to travel. Evidently, for Small, Du Bois never entered the domain of sociology during its first fifty years.

Du Bois's *Philadelphia Negro* and Thomas and Znaniecki's *Polish Peasant* address similar sociological issues concerning how populations from rural agricultural backgrounds adjust to city life. Yet Thomas and Znaniecki do not engage or cite *The Philadelphia Negro* in their book, even though it preceded their monumental study by two decades. This omission in *The Polish Peasant* is striking because W. I. Thomas was thoroughly familiar with *The Philadelphia Negro* by 1912, before Park and Burgess joined Chicago's sociology department. In a progressive article published in the *American Journal of Sociology* in 1912, Thomas argued that blacks and women were held back by an oppressive environment rather than biological factors.[91] To make his case on the racial front, Thomas used long quotes from *The Philadelphia Negro* to drive home his argument.[92] Toward the end of his article, Thomas included *The Philadelphia Negro* as one of the important books on the Negro in America.[93] Yet in the 1920 publication of *The Polish Peasant*, Du Bois's groundbreaking study on the urbanization of a rural peasantry received no mention. Ironically, Thomas and Znaniecki concluded their study by issuing a call that in effect erased *The Philadelphia Negro* as a forerunner to *The Polish Peasant*:

> But it is evident that this monograph must be followed by many others if we want our acquaintance with social reality to be complete. Other Slavic groups, particularly the Russians; the French and the Germans, as representing different types of more efficient societies; the Americans, as the most conspicuous experiment in individualism; the Jews, as representing particular social adaptations under peculiar social pressures; the Oriental, with his widely divergent attitudes and values; the Negro, with his lower cultural level and unique social position—these and other social groups should be included in a series of monographs, which in its totality will give for the first time a wide and secure basis for any sociological generalizations whatever.[94]

Given the entire record, this conclusion is inescapable: Park and the Chicago school locked Du Bois out of the intellectual fraternity of sociology by systematically ignoring his scholarship. This exclusion relegated Du Bois to the institutional margins of American sociology because it was accompanied by his exclusion from scholarly networks that functioned as pathways to journal editorships, memberships in learned societies, and presidency of learned societies, including the American Sociological Society. Because of his skin color and his challenges to Park's racist propositions, Du Bois was denied meaningful participation in mainstream American sociology.[95]

Although the erasure of Du Bois from mainstream sociology began in the late nineteenth century, it continued throughout the twentieth. This is clear from an examination of volumes on the origins of American sociology. Prominent among these "origin narratives" are Luther Bernard and Jessie Bernard's *Origins of American Sociology*, Howard W. Odum's *American Sociology*, John Madge's *Origins of Scientific Sociology*, Herman Schwendinger and Julia R. Schwendinger's *Sociologists of the Chair*, and Stephen Turner and Jonathan Turner's *Impossible Science*.[96] These volumes explore the intellectual and institutional origins of American sociology, paying attention to the economic and political context from which sociology emerged. They examine how sociology shifted from grand theorizing to the use of empirical inductive approaches. The controversies surrounding the use of statistical and quantitative methodologies are probed. The major sociological players, who are argued to have founded the new discipline, are placed on stage, with the authors making cases for why their favorite sociologist was a major founder. Though these accounts differ in their emphases, they are strikingly similar with regard to their treatment of Du Bois's pioneering contributions: they either ignore Du Bois as a founder of American scientific sociology or severely diminish his role in the discipline.

In Bernard and Bernard's 860 pages explicating the origins of sociology, and in the Turner and Turner study, Du Bois is not mentioned. In Madge's six hundred pages, Du Bois is mentioned only once, where the author notes that Gunnar Myrdal consulted with Du Bois. Odum and Schwendinger and Schwendinger at least devote some discussion to Du Bois's role in the early years of American sociology.

Odum studied black folk music and Negroes in Philadelphia following Du Bois's pioneering work in these areas, interacted with Du Bois on several occasions, and exchanged letters with him regarding shared intellectual interests. He identifies Du Bois's pioneering role in American empirical sociology, pointing out that, "as originator and editor of the pioneering *Atlanta Sociological Studies* from 1897 to 1910, he was among the earliest to apply sociology to empirical inquiries, producing more than a dozen studies."[97] Odum also recognizes Du Bois's pioneering institutional role: "Keeping in mind that Du Bois began his Atlanta Studies in the 1890's, just about the same time that sociology departments were being developed at Columbia University, the University of Chicago, and other pioneering institutions, the succession of his followers constitutes an important segment of American sociology."[98]

Yet Odum minimizes his praise of Du Bois as founder of American scientific sociology by arguing that Du Bois "contributed powerfully to what we have characterized elsewhere in the book as 'practical sociology' and sociological writings."[99] For Odum, "practical sociology" is a popular sociology that supplies useful materials for scientific sociologists but "do[es] not conform to the more accurate definition of sociology as the scientific study of human society by sociologists."[100] Yet Odum relates an occasion in 1940 when Du Bois conducted a conference addressing social research with "real" scientific sociologists, "collaborators from the Universities of Chicago, North Carolina, Iowa State University, Fisk University, and many others. . . . He appeared more keenly aware of his problems and methods than did his distinguished visitors."[101] Odum, reflecting the ambivalence of white scholars regarding superior black sociological talent, cannot bring himself to acknowledge the founding role Du Bois had played in developing American scientific sociology.

Schwendinger and Schwendinger devote several pages to Du Bois's pioneering role in sociology, especially as a black sociologist.[102] They relate that after Du Bois was appointed at Atlanta University to study black Americans, he "plunged into the work with great energy, and in a short time Atlanta University became the most important center for scholarly research on the black American."[103] Schwendinger and Schwendinger, by using Du Bois's own words, make clear that he was the lone scholar in America producing high-level sociological scholarship on African Americans. The remaining coverage details how powerful white American capitalists, along with the conservative black leader Booker T. Washington, derailed Du Bois's center of research because it ran afoul of their vested interests. The authors correctly conclude that "it is of no mean significance that some of the finest scholarly works on Black Americans were written by Du Bois during the years *following* his employment at Atlanta, while he was engaged in political life *outside* the business-dominated institutions of higher learning."[104] Yet even though Schwendinger and Schwendinger's treatment of Du Bois's pioneering role in sociology is the most positive among the origin narratives, like those it fails to critically examine Du Bois's pioneering scholarship and methodological contributions.

In 1972, the sociologist Anthony Oberschall published an article on the institutionalization of American sociology that comes closest to documenting Du Bois's pioneering role as founder of empirical sociology. Oberschall explains that "the early academic sociologist were textbook writers, not researchers or writers of scholarly publications."[105] Du Bois obviously departed from this genre: "The most professionally executed of the early city investigations was W. E. B. DuBois' *The Philadelphia Negro* (1899). . . . His results were summarized and analyzed in clear tables, charts, and graphs throughout, and backed up with systematic white-black comparisons."[106] Oberschall described the voluminous and meticulously collected data that Du Bois presented in his pioneering urban study. Yet *The Philadelphia Negro* is not just "the most professionally executed of the early city investigations" but the most scientifically based study of the period. Oberschall does recognize that it was racism that denied Du Bois his place as a founder of scientific sociology: "Kept from a well-deserved appointment at the University of Pennsylvania because of his race, he later organized a sociology department and 'sociological laboratory' at Atlanta University. With this base of operation, he and his students conducted a whole series of empirical studies into the condition of different black social strata in the United States at the turn of the century, which represents a lasting contribution to American social history."[107]

Unlike Oberschall's account, the origin narratives cast white sociologists as the pioneers of American sociology. In them, the first-generation founders usually include William G. Sumner, Lester Ward, Franklin Giddings, Albion Small and W. I. Thomas. The second generation consists of Park and Burgess of the Chicago school, who are usually presented as the dominant founders of American scientific, empirical sociology. They are credited with shifting the field from armchair theorizing to empirically based modern science. This claim has prevailed despite the fact that Du Bois landed there first, publishing groundbreaking empirical research two decades earlier. Du Bois's contributions have been cast aside because they originated on the black side of the sociological map and from the pen of a black scholar and his students. This is a story of how scholars embedded in marginalized black educational institutions on the periphery made scholarly history that went beyond that produced at rich white, elite, universities at the core of scholarly prestige in America.

The intellectual networks and ideas of the Du Bois–Atlanta school can be conceptualized as insurgent because they developed outside mainstream sociological networks and provided counteranalyses to those of the mainstream. They were not embraced by mainstream networks, nor did they receive nurturing and resources from those networks. Randall Collins, who has formulated an elaborate network analysis of intellectual schools, argues that scholarly ideas will play no major role in the development and institutionalization of scientific schools if they fall outside elite mainstream networks.[108] For ideas to receive scholarly attention and come to matter, they must be embedded in mainstream intellectual networks. It is those networks that disseminate ideas across generations of scholars. Yet an examination of Du Bois's networks and his Atlanta school makes clear that insurgent forces can have real impact on intellectual thought, including that produced by the mainstream. I will return to this issue in concluding chapters.

DU BOIS'S SUBTERRANEAN INFLUENCE

One more issue must be considered in a comparison of Du Bois's sociology with that of the Chicago school and other white sociologists: To what degree did Du Bois's ideas affect mainstream sociology in the twentieth century but go unrecognized because white sociologists neglected to credit them as Du Bois's ideas? There is little doubt that this practice occurred. However, its frequency and usage are difficult to assess because the subterranean quality of the phenomenon obscures transparency. The scholarly career of Park's concept of the "marginal man" sheds light on the phenomenon.

In 1928, Park published an article in the *American Journal of Sociology* where he introduced the concept of the "marginal man" and developed it theoretically, arguing that it referred to a distinctive personality type that arose in the context of human migration and the development of modern cities.[109] Park defines the marginal man as a cultural hybrid: "a man living and sharing intimately in the cultural life and traditions of two distinct peoples; never quite willing to break, even if he were permitted to do so, with his past and his traditions, and not quite accepted, because of racial prejudice, in the new society in which he now sought to find a place. He was a man on the margin of two cultures and two societies, which never completely interpenetrated and fused."[110] Park credited Simmel for inspiring him, during his study with Simmel in Berlin at the turn of the twentieth century, with his concept of the stranger: "The stranger stays, but he is not settled. He is a potential wanderer. That means that he is not bound as others are by the local properties and conventions. 'He is the freer man, practically and theoretically. He views his relation to others with less prejudice; he submits them to more general, more objective standards, and he is not confined in his action by custom, piety or precedents.'"[111] Simmel's "stranger" shares some characteristics with Park's "marginal man." They both live on the margins, not loyal to or settled within one culture. The two personality types are lodged in a creative structural position that imparts to them unique standpoints from which to assess social relations more objectively than others. Nevertheless, the two concepts differ in emphasis. The "marginal man" is not accepted because of racial prejudice and because he shares the cultures of two distinct peoples, making assimilation nearly impossible. But Du Bois's concept of double consciousness reflects these aspects of the "marginal man" more sharply than the concept of the "stranger" does. Du Bois's concept was explicitly formulated to capture a situation created by racial prejudice that led to the oppression of black Americans. At the turn of the twentieth century, blacks and whites were thought to be distinct races that, like the marginal man, could not be fused into an assimilated amalgamation.

In 1897, in the *Atlantic Monthly,* and again in the 1903 *Souls of Black Folk,* Du Bois introduced and theorized the concept of "double consciousness":[112]

It is a peculiar sensation, this double-consciousness, this sense of always looking at one's self through the eyes of others, of measuring one's soul by the tape of a world that looks on in amused contempt and pity. One ever feels his two-ness,—an American, a Negro; two souls, two thoughts, two unreconciled strivings; two warring ideals in one dark body, whose dogged strength alone keeps it from being torn asunder. . . . The history of the American Negro is the history of this strife—this longing to attain self-conscious manhood, to merge his double self into a better and truer self.[113]

Du Bois claimed that the structural position of those experiencing double consciousness enabled them to attain unique viewpoints because "the Negro is sort of a seventh son, born with a veil, and gifted with second-sight in this American world."[114] The similarities between Du Bois's and Park's conceptions of "double consciousness" and "marginal man" are obvious and significant. Given these conceptual similarities, which scholar influenced the other? The answer is obvious: Du Bois influenced Park. Park was familiar with Du Bois's concept long before he developed his own. In 1923 he indicated that the idea of double consciousness "found a classic expression in Du Bois' *Souls of Black Folk.*"[115] The sociologist Chad Goldberg concludes, "Notwithstanding Park's close ties to Du Bois's rival, the African-American educator Booker T. Washington . . . , Park . . . invoked Du Bois and his notion of double-consciousness a full five years before introducing his own concept of the marginal man."[116] Park's concept of the marginal man gained wide currency in sociology and the social sciences because his students further elaborated and expanded its theoretical and practical significance. Goldberg wrote that "Park's students were also familiar with the notion of double-consciousness" and added that "it was likely under Du Bois's influence that Park and his students identified the mixed-race individual as a marginal man—not by virtue of heredity, they insisted, but because of the social situation in which he typically found himself."[117]

The evidence supports Goldberg's attribution of credit. Louis Worth, an important student of Park, was influenced by Du Bois's formulation of double consciousness. Elizabeth Marvick relates that "at this time also Park's connection with Booker T. Washington helped to form another identification of Wirth—with the American Negro. Wirth himself remembered that, when he was a student, reading W. E. B. Du Bois' *The Souls of Black Folk* had been an important and moving experience for him."[118] Park's student Everett Stonequist was the main scholar to elaborate Park's concept of the marginal man and disseminate it to large scholarly audiences. Referring to the dilemma faced by the marginal man, Stonequist wrote, "Perhaps no one has voiced this inner conflict with more dramatic self-analysis than W. E. B. Du Bois, in *The Souls of*

Black Folk."[119] In the abstract of his 1935 *American Journal of Sociology* article on the importance of Park's formulation of the marginal man, Stonequist wrote, "The marginal individual experiences what Du Bois has analyzed as 'double consciousness.'"[120] Stonequist also concluded that "since these two standpoints are in conflict . . . the individual experiences this conflict. He has something of a dual personality, a 'double consciousness' to use the words of Du Bois."[121]

Because Park was familiar with Du Bois's idea of "double consciousness" and undoubtedly aware of its impact on his own concept of the "marginal man," why have intellectual histories failed to explicate Du Bois's influence on this important sociological concept? The blame rests with Park. In his classic *American Journal of Sociology* article, Park credits Simmel's concept of the stranger for influencing the development of his own concept of the marginal man. Why, then, did Park fail to mention how Du Bois's concept of double consciousness had influenced his own marginal man formulation? Fortunately, several of Park's students did not follow in the master's footsteps; they did not erase Du Bois's concept from the collective memory of the discipline.

As pointed out earlier, there is another intriguing case of erasure. The historical record is clear that W. I. Thomas was familiar with Du Bois's *The Philadelphia Negro* before he and Znaniecki published *The Polish Peasant.* That monumental work examined issues pertaining to the transition of peasants into modern urban life very similar to those analyzed in Du Bois's book. Yet *The Polish Peasant* does not mention Du Bois's pioneering text. The larger question, of course, is, How prevalent was this practice of incorporating Du Bois's ideas into mainstream sociology without acknowledging their source? What we do know is informative: while white sociologists suppressed the credit owed to Du Bois, they could not suppress his ideas—at least some of them.

Another curious omission from Parks and Burgess's *Introduction* was Max Weber's work. By the time *Introduction* was published, Weber was a well-known social scientist in Germany. Park had studied in Germany between 1899 and 1903, and when he arrived there Weber had been appointed to professorships at Freiberg University and Heidelberg from which Park took his doctorate. It would have been impossible for Park to have been unaware of Weber's important work, given the latter's close personal and professional relationships with Simmel, whose formulations drove the theoretical orientation of Park and Burgess's "Green Bible." Indeed, Simmel was a frequent participant in the "Weber Circle" that met in Weber's home to discuss intellectual and political issues of the day. Yet the *Introduction* does not mention Weber's substantive and methodological writings.[122]

By ignoring Du Bois and Weber, Park and Burgess missed an opportunity to incorporate those two scholars' emphases on power, class, and domination. Neither Du Bois nor Weber believed social structures were eternally fixed and irreversible, as Park and Burgess asserted in the *Introduction*. Although Weber described bureaucratic rationality as nearly inescapable, he left the door ajar for potentially transformative human intervention by charismatic leaders or elites atop organizations where decision making was not fully bureaucratized. In short, the Chicago school would have been far more likely to develop a political sociology if they had incorporated Du Bois and Weber's sociology into their thinking at the time when the young discipline was struggling to find its intellectual bearings.

CHAPTER 6

Max Weber Meets Du Bois

A prominent sociological scholar a continent away embraced Du Bois's scholarship and declared him to be one of the greatest sociologists in America. Not only did the famous German sociologist Max Weber, who became world renowned several decades later, include Du Bois in the sociology fraternity; he absorbed Du Bois's sociological insights, using them to significantly enrich his own sociological imagination. Weber's and Du Bois's intellectual paths crossed on several occasions. The first occurred when Du Bois studied in Germany from 1892 to 1894 and attended lectures delivered by Weber. It is true that Weber and Du Bois shared an intellectual environment in Germany and were influenced by many of the same scholarly currents present in this social scientific setting. Nevertheless, the view expressed by Mary Jo Deegan that Weber mentored Du Bois while he was a student in Germany is untrue.[1]

There is no evidence that Du Bois and Weber had either a personal or an intellectual relationship in Germany. The claim that Max Weber served as a major mentor to Du Bois during his student days at the University of Berlin from 1892 to 1894 is not supported by evidence. It implies that Weber was already the great internationally known sociologist canonized as the third of a trinity with Marx and Durkheim, who famously founded sociology. This myth conjures up notions that it was a great privilege for Du Bois to sit at the fount of knowledge embodied in the person of Max Weber. Yet myths often dissipate when confronted with stubborn facts. Weber and Du Bois were contemporaries, with Weber being only four years older than Du Bois. In fact, they were both essentially graduate students during the time they both attended the university. On one occasion, Weber served as a lecturer in a class in which Du Bois was enrolled, but that was because Weber's mentor fell ill and chose Weber as a temporary replacement. This arrangement has contributed to the assumption that Weber was Du Bois's professor and mentor. Yet this conclusion is erroneous, as evidenced by a letter Du Bois wrote to an inquirer seeking to discover whether the two scholars had a relationship while Du Bois was in Germany: "I remember the article [that Du Bois published] in the *Archiv* [Weber's journal] and I am sure it was written at the personal solicitation of Max Weber. I think he visited me in Atlanta. In Berlin, while I was in class I did not have, as I remember, any personal contact."[2]

Du Bois and Weber did share overlapping intellectual interests and graduate school experiences that provided them with multiple opportunities to influence each other. While in graduate school, both were serious scholars of economic and social relations in agrarian societies and how these changed with the rise of modern capitalism. Both scholars studied these dynamics as members of the Verein für Sozialpolitik under the guidance of the same professors of the German historical school of economics. Prior to these studies, Weber had developed scholarly expertise in agricultural relations from his studies of the social conditions affecting Roman farmers. While Weber was a student member of the Verein in the 1890s, this organization of scholars conducted an extensive empirical study of agrarian relations east of the Elbe in Germany, where labor problems were generating intense conflicts between Polish and German agricultural workers. German elites worried that these problems could prevent Germany from fulfilling the international ambitions that they held for it. To understand the underlying issues, the Verein conducted massive surveys of relevant actors to determine which policies should be implemented to address their concerns. The data were then analyzed, interpreted, discussed in seminar formats, and written up in comprehensive reports.

The twenty-nine-year-old Weber was chosen to perform many of these scholarly duties. As Keith Tribe recounts, "Weber was given the tasks of covering the material on the rural labour problem East of the Elbe, recognized as the most important section of the survey."[3] Weber was selected because of his recently published *Habilitationsschrift* on Roman agrarian history, and because he was recommended by August

Meitzen, a prominent scholar on agrarian dynamics and a former teacher of Weber. Tribe describes Weber's scholarship on the Polish labor problem in East Germany as a "substantial bod[y] of work comprising . . . a Verein report of over 800 pages and more than 100,000 words of newspaper articles, conference proceedings, and journal contributions."[4] Thus by the early 1890s Weber was a recognized expert on agrarian societies entrusted by his senior colleagues to execute the most demanding and sensitive scholarship on a rural labor issue that threatened the well-being of Germany's imperial state. He had become an accomplished rural sociologist, though he identified himself as an economist and scholar of political economy.

When the twenty-four-year-old Du Bois arrived at the University of Berlin in 1892, he had developed a deep interest in understanding the interactions of agrarian relations with modern capitalism. These issues were germane to Du Bois because he had decided that his life's mission was to help liberate African Americans from racial oppression. Following his undergraduate studies at Fisk in Nashville, Du Bois, noting that racial oppression was severest in the southern United States, where the overwhelming majority of blacks lived and worked, set out to understand the racial caste system that had emerged in the rural South in the midst of new capitalist markets that had emerged following the Civil War. While studying in Germany in 1892–93, he worked on a thesis entitled "The Large and Small-Scale System of Agriculture in the Southern United States," and in 1893 he read portions of it to the seminar sponsored by the Verein.

Du Bois's major professors, Schmoller and Wagner, were so impressed with Du Bois's thesis that they allowed him to submit it as an early fulfillment for a German doctorate because he had depleted his funds and would have to leave the university before completing residency requirements. Wagner wrote a recommendation urging that the thesis be accepted as meeting the qualification for the doctorate:

> Mr. W. E. B. Du Bois has laid before me his work upon "The Large and Small System of Farming in the [Southern] United States of America"; this careful as well as comprehensive work, resting on a basis of wide study, has impressed me very favorably. The author has succeeded in bringing much material together to prove that American experience offers no ground for the assumption that Agriculture tends to develop toward the large-farming system, as the most advantageous. . . . The work proves that the author possesses talent and diligence, and that he has made good use of the time spent in Germany. . . . The before-mentioned thesis would, without doubt, be received as a Doctor's thesis.[5]

Schmoller concurred:

Mr. William Edward Burghardt Du Bois, who has studied now three semesters at the University of Berlin, wished in course of the Winter semester, '93–94, to pass the doctor's examination; for this purpose he prepared a scientific thesis on the large and small systems of farming in the southern parts of the United States. This work would have been sufficient. . . . The philosophical faculty might, indeed, on the recommendation of Professor A. Wagner and myself, have possibly dispensed with 2 semesters, because we were able to express so favorable an opinion in regard to Mr. Du Bois.[6]

Thus Du Bois, like Max Weber, had achieved distinction in agrarian analyses and was praised for this work by two of the most esteemed scholars in the world. The two scholars' shared interest in rural sociology constituted the foundation for future exchanges between them.

In Germany, Du Bois and Weber were taught by many of the same professors, were mentored by the same scholars of the German historical school of economics, and were involved in many of the same intellectual activities in the context of the Verein. As the Weberian scholar Lawrence Scaff comments regarding Du Bois, "It is noteworthy that his university program of studies closely paralleled Weber's: Du Bois studied primarily with the political economists Schmoller and Adolph Wagner while attending lectures by the two historians Heinrich von Treitschke and Max Lenz. His instructor in statistics was August Meitzen, the man under whom Weber had written his habilitation on Roman agrarian and legal history, *Die römische Agrargeschichte*."[7] Weber and Du Bois both absorbed these scholars' social scientific approaches stressing empirical research and avoiding the futility of searching for "natural laws" and unproven grand theories. They urged their students to carefully investigate the role that history and culture played in social life, including economic activities. To advance this agenda effectively, students were taught to acquire a command of survey methods, statistical generalizations, and skillful interpretation of social structures.[8] It is likely that Weber reinforced these lessons for Du Bois through the class he taught where Du Bois was a student with less experience in the approaches championed by the German historical school. Beyond formal instruction, Weber and Du Bois interacted in intimate settings where ideas were exchanged. They were participants in Schmoller's political economy seminar, and both presented their work in the context of the Verein. Scaff states that in 1893, when Weber presented a report to Verein scholars on the East Elbian labor question, it is quite possible that Du Bois was in the audience.[9]

Weber's and Du Bois's next encounter was in 1904 in St. Louis at the Congress of Arts and Sciences, where Weber presented a paper. That meeting was followed by scholarly dialogues initiated by Weber that were expressed through letters between Du Bois in Atlanta, Georgia, and Weber in Heidelberg, Germany.[10]

Both Du Bois and Weber admired and supported the settlement house movement. They mentored women leaders of this movement and promoted their careers by providing them with publishing opportunities.[11] In this respect they contrast sharply with Park and the second generation of Chicago sociologists, who distanced themselves from "do-gooders" such as Jane Addams and her German counterpart, Alice Salomon, for fear that their objective science would be contaminated by activism designed to change the real world.[12]

When Weber visited America in the fall of 1904, he was at work drawing analytic distinctions between overlapping dimensions of stratification pertaining to class, status, and political power.[13] He was also exploring race and ethnicity and their roles in developing capitalist societies. Weber was keenly interested in the economic and social roles played by agrarian populations in industrializing capitalist economies. At the time Polish agricultural workers were immigrating to East Germany and establishing competitive niches with German workers. This state of affairs created ethnic and economic challenges that came to be known as the "Polish Problem." It was a "minority problem" that foregrounded concerns about ethnic and cultural superiority and ethnic-based hierarchies in German society.

The "Polish Problem" deeply troubled German's intellectuals and its elites, including Weber. While working as a scholar under the auspices of the Verein, Weber had spent considerable time conducting research and publishing studies on the Polish issue.[14] For Weber, who at the time was a staunch nationalist, the "Polish Problem" demanded a solution because it could affect the future of his fatherland. He was concerned that Germans' contact with inferior Poles could cause Germany to undergo a process of "Polonization" that would cause the decline of its superior culture and render Germany a second-rate European power.

Du Bois's own main interest in studying agrarian populations in developing capitalist societies focused on the southern United States. From the outset, Du Bois was preoccupied with the "Negro Problem" that lay at the heart of America's race dilemma. In contrast to Weber, who inherited class and national privileges, Du Bois inherited the pain and shared fate of a racially oppressed minority. Beginning early in his career, Du Bois examined race and grappled with what it meant socio-logically. In a 1897 essay published in the *Occasional Papers of the American Negro Academy,* Du Bois developed the idea that race was largely a social construct that groups developed on the basis of a shared history, culture, language, customs, and religion. Having settled on this sociological approach to race, Du Bois dissected the mechanisms through which racial inequality was produced and sustained. His mission entailed understanding the sociological and political foundations enabling the oppressed to dismantle racial inequality.

In contrast, Weber, as a privileged European nationalist, was anxious that Germany not lose ground to other European nations that were expanding their empires by colonizing Africa, Asia, and South America. As a product of his times, he initially embraced ideologies of white rac-ism and European ethnic superiority. This stance was typical of Euro-pean social scientists of the period. Schmoller, for example, a mentor of Weber and Du Bois, viewed the Negro of Africa and America as consti-tuting the lowest race.[15] Much like Park, the young Weber asserted that biology was a determinant of race inferiority. In this manner, Weber had a foot in the social Darwinist camp that stressed the evolutionary nature of racial hierarchies.

Regarding Weber's social Darwinist thinking early in his career, Wolfgang Mommsen has noted that "Weber did not hesitate to employ the Darwinist terminology of the 'struggle for existence' and the 'sur-vival' of the fittest, in order to describe the inexorable character of this 'struggle of man with man' for elbow room."[16] Weber offered crude characterizations of races he considered inferior, and the Polish immi-grant population often served as his target. He argued, for example, against the importation of Russian-Polish immigrant laborers because one cannot "allow two nations with different bodily constitutions—differently constructed stomachs . . .—to compete freely as workers in the same area. German workers would have to descend a cultural step. . . . There was once great opposition to an importation of Chinese Coolies to the East, but the importation of Poles is a far greater danger to culture, for our German workers would not have assimilated with the Coolies."[17] At times Weber demeaned Poles by invoking animalistic images.[18] He also claimed that Poles were inferior to Germans both physically and mentally.[19]

Weber associated white blood with racial superiority. After exposure to a variety of African Americans during his 1904 visit to America, Weber described encountering "half-Negroes, quarter-Negroes, and one-hundredth part Negroes whom no non-American can distinguish from whites" and stated that he admired Negroes like Washington and Du Bois because of their mixed blood.[20] In a letter to his mother, Weber expressed some of the worst social Darwinist racism when he described the black masses as the "semi-apes one encounters on the plantations and in the Negro huts of the 'Cotton Belt.'"[21] Thus early in his career Weber embraced the notion that biology was an important determinant of racial differences. Yet Weber's racial views underwent change in the second decade of the twentieth century. Du Bois influenced Weber's transformation through the works of Du Bois that Weber read.

By the time Weber visited America, Du Bois had published numerous studies on race and its role in modern society. While Marx had argued that the basic dynamic of modern society was the class struggle, Weber insisted it was the process of bureaucratic rationalization that was sweeping the world in tandem with modern capitalism. As Du Bois surveyed the globe, he focused on a specific phenomenon that enabled European societies to build capitalist empires: the colonization, exploitation, and domination of peoples of color. For this reason he famously stated in 1903, in *The Souls of Black Folk*, that "the problem of the Twentieth Century is the problem of the color-line—the relation of the darker to the lighter races of men in Asia and Africa, in America and the islands of the sea."[22] His sociology, therefore, revolved around explicating the relations between the darker and lighter races and how the structural formation that he conceptualized as the color line was maintained.

The darker races that Europeans colonized usually consisted of agrarian populations exploited within industrializing societies. The key sociological questions sparked by these unequal arrangements concerned the interactions among race, ethnicity, and capitalist market principles based on free labor as embodied in the modern proletariat. These issues concerned Weber as he explored the "Polish Problem," and they concerned Du Bois as he probed the "Negro Problem" in the southern United States. The crux of the issue concerned how race and ethnicity were to be understood sociologically and how these factors affected capitalist markets and the social relations they generated. When Weber visited America, he was interested in how these dynamics unfolded in the United States, especially in the South.[23] He believed that understanding the complex relations between race, ethnicity, and capitalism in the South could shed light on Germany's "minority problem" and suggest the contours of a general theory of how agrarian and capitalist dynamics operated in modern societies. Because Du Bois was the American sociologist making analytic progress on these issues, Weber turned to him for guidance.

On November 8, 1904, after the St. Louis conference and before leaving the United States, Weber reached out to Du Bois asking that he write an article on caste relations for Weber's journal *Archiv für Sozialwissenschaft und Sozialpolitik*. "Until now," he wrote, "I failed in finding in the American (and of course any other) litterature [*sic*] an investigation about the relations between the (so called) 'race-problem' and the (so called) 'class-problem' in your country. . . . We have to meet to-day in Germany not only the dilettantic litterature . . . but a 'scientific' race-theory, built up on purely anthropological fundaments, too,—and so we have to accentuate especially those connections and the influence of social-economic conditions upon the relations of races to each other. I saw that you spoke some weeks ago about this very question and I should be very glad if you would find yourself in a position to give us, for our periodical, an essay about that object. So, I bid you to write me, whether you should be willing to do so, and at what time?"[24]

Weber expressed three ideas in this letter. First, he informed Du Bois that the extant literature on the relationship between race and class in the United States and Germany was largely useless. Second, he saw that literature as useless because its nonsociological approach emphasized biology as a crucial determinant of racial dynamics. Third, Weber sought to establish a scholarly exchange with Du Bois because he was aware that Du Bois and his school had been conducting sociological analyses of race and class for over a half-dozen years. Weber's remarks about the superficiality of American and German literatures on race and class implicitly convey his respect for Du Bois's own expertise on these topics.

Unlike Park and the Chicago school, Weber was inviting Du Bois to publish in the journal that was the leading venue of social science in his country.[25] Weber was interested in Du Bois's lectures because they addressed the relations between an agrarian population located in the American South and situated in an emerging capitalist system rooted in a plantation economy. These were intellectual issues both scholars had addressed during their study at the Verein.

Du Bois's lecture on relations between race and class that Weber refers to in his November 8 letter was one in a series arguing that a racial caste system was being reestablished in the South following Reconstruction.[26] This caste system, according to Du Bois in a later essay on the same subject, was a historical development because it first emerged in Europe and was transplanted in America during slavery: "That problem of the past, so far as the black American was concerned, began with caste—a definite place preordained in custom, law and religion where all men of black blood must be thrust. To be sure, this caste idea as applied to blacks was no sudden, full grown conception, for the enslavement of the workers was an idea which America inherited from Europe and was not synonymous for many years with the enslavement of the blacks."[27] Du Bois argued that as caste developed during slavery dominant whites gradually began "conceiving certain sorts of work and certain colors of men as necessarily connected."[28] Thus this racially based caste system became a coherent set of economic and social relations whereby human beings were divided into classifications of "good and bad, superior and inferior, slave and free."[29] Du Bois concluded that American caste was a political accomplishment rather than an inherent racial phenomenon: "Here then is the new slavery of black men in America—a new attempt to make degradation of social condition correspond with certain physical characteristics."[30]

If Weber had had the opportunity to compare Du Bois's and Park's analyses of America's racial caste, he would undoubtedly have noticed their radically different arguments. For Park, "The caste system, in so far as it has served anywhere to organize race relations, has been a solution of the race problem. It was when, after the abolition of slavery, the caste system broke that the disorders and racial animosities that we ordinarily identify with the race problem began."[31] Where Du Bois saw caste as a system of black oppression, Park saw that same formation as the source of black liberation.

The racial caste system, according to Du Bois, did not evolve inevitably from class dynamics and market forces, even though it became a dimension of stratification that diminished life chances for African Americans while enhancing life chances for white workers and elites. Du Bois stressed that these social relations grew directly from political decisions: the caste idea was "being insidiously but consciously and persistently pressed upon the nation."[32] For Du Bois, certain political moves had to be made—political disenfranchisement, implementation of a narrow vocational education, and the denial of black civil rights—before caste could be imposed upon blacks.

The caste system was supported by an array of justifications and pseudoscientific explanations that obscured the use of brute force. This movement, wrote Du Bois, "has a whole vocabulary of its own: the strong races, superior peoples, race preservation, the struggle for survival and a peculiar use of the word 'white.' And by this it means the right of white men of any kind to club blacks into submission, to make them surrender their wealth and the use of their women, and to submit to the dictation of white men without murmur, for the sake of being swept off the fairest portions of the earth or held there in perpetual serfdom or guardianship."[33] Du Bois analyzed the social Darwinist ideological justification for the caste system, the claim that "civilization is a struggle for existence whereby the weaker nations and individuals will gradually succumb and the strong will inherit the earth. With this interpretation has gone the silent assumption that the white European stock represents the strong surviving peoples and that the swarthy, yellow and black peoples are the ones rightly doomed to eventual extinction."[34] Du Bois described the caste system as including a "systematic effort to instill contempt and kill self-respect" within the darker races and declared, "There are even those who deny its existence as a definite consciously conceived plan of action. But, certain it is."[35]

Du Bois's empirical and theoretical account of the caste system did not apply only to the American South. Regarding Weber, Mommsen declared, "Whatever the particular topic, Weber always undertook a grand sweep through the ages and geographical regions looking for the dispositions or patterns of conduct of a wide range of different civilizations (and cultures) vis-à-vis the economic sphere of life and their developmental potentials, with the additional notice of finding out about the specific features of modernity."[36] Du Bois had a similar scholarly practice. In his analysis of caste, he sought to develop an intellectual framework that captured the central dynamic driving the problem of the twentieth century—the color line—not only in the United States but worldwide. "To be sure," he wrote, "this outrageous programme of wholesale human degeneration is not outspoken yet save in the backward civilizations of the southern United States, South Africa and Australia. But its enunciation is listened to with respect and tolerance in England, Germany and the northern states and nowhere with more equanimity than right here in New York by those very persons who accuse philanthropy with seeking to degenerate white blood by an infiltration of colored strains."[37] Examining the history of caste and its potential, Du Bois concluded: "This movement gathered force and strength during the latter half of the nineteenth century and reached its culmination when France, Germany and England and Russia began the partition of China and the East. With the sudden self-assertion of Japan its wildest dreams collapsed, but it is still to-day a living, virile, potent force and motive, and the most subtle and dangerous enemy of world peace and the dream of human brotherhood."[38]

It was Du Bois, therefore, who had begun exploring relations between what Weber called the "(so called) 'race-problem' and the (so called) 'class-problem'" in the United States—and the world. Du Bois's work interested Weber because it emphasized "the impact of social-economic conditions upon the relations of races to each other." This was the scholarly contribution that Weber and his colleagues sought from Du Bois for the *Archiv für Sozialwissenschaft und Sozialpolitik.*

Du Bois's influence on Weber extended far beyond the article "Die Negerfrage in den Vereinigten Staaten," which graced the 1906 volume of Weber's journal where it was situated between articles by Simmel and Robert Michels.[39] Before departing New York in 1904, Weber sent Du Bois another letter, in which he wrote, "I will with pleasure read the studies about the race problem you kindly promised to send me, and hope to be allowed to ask you also for a report and schedule of the lectures of the Atlanta University, showing if possible the text books now in the social-science-lectures, if I could get them."[40] Weber, an exacting scholar not given to undisciplined rhetorical flourishes, made clear in the same letter that he had read *The Souls of Black Folk* and agreed with Du Bois's stunning prediction regarding the global color line: "I am quite sure to come back to your country as soon as possible and especially to the South, because I am absolutely convinced that the "color-line" problem will be the paramount problem of the time to come, here and everywhere in the world."[41] Upon his return to Heidelberg, Weber expressed his appreciation of the scholarly profundity of *Souls*, stating: "Your splendid work: 'The Souls of Black Folk' ought to be translated in German. I do not know whether anybody has already undertaken to make a translation. If not I am authorized to beg you for your authorization to Mrs. Elizabeth Jaffé-von Richthofen here, a scholar and friend of mine."[42] Du Bois agreed that a German translation of *Souls* was an excellent idea, prompting Weber to respond, "My Dear Colleague! I thank you very much for your kind letter. *We have engaged* a publisher—. . . I beg you to inform your publishers and hope there will be no difficulties."[43] Unfortunately, difficulties did ensue that caused *Souls* not to be translated into German.[44]

In letters Weber requested that Du Bois send additional work and biographical information as well. To accompany the translation of *Souls*, Weber explained to Du Bois, "I should like to write a short introduction about [the] Negro question and literature and should be much obliged to you for some information about your life, viz: age, birthplace, descent, positions held by you—of course only *if you give* your authorization." He continued, "I should like to give in one of the numbers of the 'Archiv' a short review of the recent publications about the race problem in America. Beside your own work and the 'Character-building' of Mr. Booker Washington, I got only the book of Mr. Page ('The Negro, the Southern Problem'—very superficial me thinks) (and) the *Occasional Papers* of your academy."[45] The importance of Weber's mention of receiving publications of the Occasional Papers series published by the American Negro Academy will be discussed shortly.

In a 1905 letter to Du Bois, Weber repeated his desire to obtain more of Du Bois's scholarship. Weber informed his Atlanta colleague that "the library of our University will certainly be very glad to have your University publications. I thank you very much for your useful informations."[46] Weber also sought out further opportunities to meet with Du Bois in person: "Will you not have your 'Sabbath-year' one of the next years? I hope you will come to Germany then, . . . and visit us. And so then, I shall come to the United States, I think, 1907 or 8."[47] Unfortunately the visits never materialized, but Weber's eagerness for more scholarly and personal contact presents a striking contrast to the indifference of Park and the Chicago school, who faced no obstacles of distance: whereas Heidelberg was 4,622 miles from Atlanta, Chicago was only 717 miles.

WEBER, RACE, AND A EUGENICIST

The continuing salience of Du Bois's ideas for Weber six years after the US visit is evident from Weber's scholarly confrontation of a racist eugenicist in Germany. This occurred on October 21, 1910, during the afternoon of the inaugural meeting of the German Sociological Society in Frankfurt, which Max Weber had been a guiding force in organizing. Doctor Alfred Ploetz, who was the founder of the Society for Racial Hygiene in Germany and would become a Nazis ideologue, was the invited speaker. He was a zealous eugenicist and advocate of white supremacy who believed that biology was the principal determinant of race differences and that African Americans were inferior. Like Weber, he had visited America. Ploetz's delivery of his paper, "The Concepts of Race and Society," was to be followed by a response from a panel that included Max Weber, Werner Sombart, and Ferdinand Tönnies, all of whom stood ready to present a sociological analysis of racial outcomes

Plate 1. *Top:* W. E. B. Du Bois (far right) in the group of six speakers at his Harvard graduation, 1890.

Plate 2. *Bottom:* Du Bois as a graduate student (third from the left in the second-to-back row) at the University of Berlin, 1894.

Plate 3. *Top left:* Adolph Wagner, Du Bois's professor at the University of Berlin.

Plate 4. *Top right:* Gustav von Schmoller, professor and mentor of Du Bois, University of Berlin.

Plate 5. *Bottom left:* Booker T. Washington, principal of Tuskegee Institute and black leader.

Plate 6. *Bottom right:* Robert E. Park, Booker T. Washington's press agent and sociology professor at the University of Chicago.

Plate 7. Du Bois at Atlanta University, 1909.

Plate 8. *Top:* Richard R. Wright Sr. and his son, Richard R. Wright Jr., participants in Du Bois's Atlanta school, September 3, 1941.

Plate 9. *Bottom:* Monroe Work, who would become a pioneering scholar of Du Bois's Atlanta school, as a student at the University of Chicago.

Plates 10–14. *Top left:* Richard R. Wright Jr., circa 1930, sociologist, bishop in the A.M.E. Church, and participant in Du Bois's Atlanta school. *Top right:* George Edmund Haynes, a pioneering scholar in Du Bois's Atlanta School. *Middle left:* Lucy Craft Laney, educator and volunteer researcher in Du Bois's Atlanta School. *Middle right:* John Hope, circa 1930, president of Atlanta University and Morehouse College and participant in Du Bois's Atlanta school. *Bottom:* Mary White Ovington, circa 1930, a founder of the National Association for the Advancement of Colored People (NAACP) and participant in Du Bois's Atlanta school.

Plate 15. *Top left:* Jane Addams, Hull House director and participant in Du Bois's Atlanta school.

Plate 16. *Top right:* Florence Kelley, scholar at Hull House and participant in Du Bois's Atlanta school.

Plate 17. *Bottom left:* Franz Boas, anthropologist and participant in Du Bois's Atlanta school.

Plate 18. *Bottom right:* Franklin Benjamin Sanborn, secretary of the American Social Science Association and participant in Du Bois's Atlanta school.

Plate 19. *Top left:* Max Weber, a German social scientist and a founder of sociology.

Plate 20. *Top right:* Alfred Ploetz, eugenicist in Berlin.

Plate 21. *Bottom left:* Kelly Miller, Howard University sociologist and participant in Du Bois's Atlanta school.

Plate 22. *Bottom right:* Gunnar Myrdal, author of *An American Dilemma*.

Plate 23. Board of directors of the *Encyclopedia of the Negro*, 1936.

and to argue stringently against biological theories of race. Of the three, Weber was the most prepared to counter Ploetz's arguments because of his deep absorption of Du Bois's scholarship, from *The Philadelphia Negro* to the Atlanta Studies publications, the Occasional Papers of the Negro Academy, *The Souls of Black Folk*, and Du Bois's essay "The Negro Question." Weber had also gained concrete knowledge of American racism from his visit to the United States.

Ploetz began his talk with what was for him a basic premise: that "the blooming of the race is a necessary foundation for the formation of the society." He added, "Quite naturally I am not referring to an anthropological variation but to biological constancy. And with respect to this one cannot dispute it."[48] Yet Weber did dispute it, shooting back, "We know nothing provable about this."[49] Ploetz, seemingly shocked, tried to explain: "And further . . . the flourishing of society should not be disassociated from the flourishing of the race. This matter can be cleared up by indicating the misunderstanding involved. Professor Weber means the anthropological variation and I am referring to the greater concept of the enduring persistency of life's unity."[50] Weber countered that social institutions and social relationships were absolutely crucial to racial outcomes because "the peculiarities of social institutions are to a certain extent the rules of the game which have factual validity for the chances of survival of definite human hereditary characteristics; for their chances to 'win,' ascend, or (what is not identical, but proceeds by entirely different laws) to propagate."[51] Unfazed, Ploetz insisted that racial outcomes flowed according to the way nature planned them.

But Weber went on to question the value of Ploetz's racial categories by pointing to the messiness of race as a concept in real life:

> Gentlemen, if the concept "race" were to be understood here in the sense in which laymen usually think of it—as the propagation of communities of hereditary types through breeding, then I would be quite personally embarrassed. I feel myself to be a cross section of several races or ethnic nationalities, and I believe there are very many in this group who would be in a similar position. I am partly French, partly German and as French surely somehow Celtically infected. Which of these races then (for the Celts have been characterized as a "race") flowers in me? Which race must flower in me if social circumstances in Germany are to flower?[52]

Weber's revelation of his mixed ancestral background challenged all the attendees and panelists who put stock in notions of racial purity by raising the embarrassing possibility that they, too, were the products of various racial mixtures.

At one point Weber addressed the view, common among those who believed racial antipathies to be biologically based, that whites instinctively disliked the odor of black people:

> Gentlemen, it has for example been asserted (and even asserted in Dr. Ploetz's journal by distinguished gentlemen) that the contrast between white and Negro in North America rests upon "race instincts." I ask for a demonstration of these instincts and their contents. It should disclose, among other things, that the whites "cannot bear to smell" Negroes. I can call upon my own nose as witness; I have with the closest contact, not perceived anything of the sort. . . . The Negro odor is, as far as I can see, an invention of the Northern States in order to explain their turning away from the Negro recently.[53]

When Ploetz asked Weber why the majority of white Americans segregated Negroes in most aspects of social life and stated that if "even the scholars have shut them out from the universities there must be a reason for this," Weber argued that universities' exclusion of blacks was political because it was in "deference to the protest of their white students—quite obviously."[54] As for American racial segregation in general, it was rooted in antiblack prejudices among the masses of white people. And when Ploetz flatly announced, "It is because of [blacks'] intellectual and moral inferiority,"[55] Weber responded: "Nothing of the kind is proven. I wish to state that the most important sociological scholar anywhere in the Southern states in America, with whom no white scholar can compare, is a Negro—Burckhardt Du Bois. At the congress of scholars in St. Louis we were permitted to have breakfast with him. If a gentleman from the Southern States had been there it would have been a scandal. The southerner would naturally have found him to be intellectually and morally inferior. We found that the southerner like other gentlemen would have deceived himself."[56] Ploetz could only reply, "It is no use individualizing in reference to this great question. . . . Just for once look at it as a natural result, as a natural phenomenon."[57]

At the first meeting of the Society, Weber had a larger aim than defeating one highly regarded eugenicist in a debate: he wanted to totally discredit the role of hereditary determinism in the social sciences and in a sociological understanding of race: "Does there exist even today a single fact that would be relevant for sociology—a single concrete fact which in a truly illuminating, valid, exact and incontestable way traces a definite type of sociological circumstance back to inborn and hereditary qualities which are possessed by one race or another? The answer is definitely—note well—no! I would dispute this with all certainty, and I would dispute it until such a fact were described precisely to me." Weber ended the debate by emphasizing the need for clear thinking, insisting that biologically determined race inequality "is a totally unproven assertion no matter which concept of 'society' and 'race' is utilized."[58]

Although Weber occasionally slipped into racialized thinking throughout his career, the sociological view of race that he espoused in Frankfurt endured as a permanent aspect of his thought. Two years later, at the second meeting of the German Sociological Association, Weber argued that "with race theories you can prove and disprove anything you want" and called it "a scientific crime" to attempt to circumvent the hard work of sociological research by "the uncritical use of completely unclarified racial hypotheses."[59] Here, as earlier, his affinity with Du Bois, springing from an influence that had begun a decade earlier, is apparent.

The article that Du Bois wrote for Weber's journal, which synthesized Du Bois's published ideas on race and class, provided Weber privileged access to Du Bois's analysis of race and its interactions with class, economy, political power, and social honor. There is evidence that Weber read numerous other publications by Du Bois that discussed these issues in detail.[60] One set of these, as noted earlier, was Du Bois's "eleven Occasional Papers published to date by the American Negro Academy."[61] These included Du Bois's 1897 pivotal article entitled "The Conservation of Races," which emphasized that social factors—common history, language, traditions and pursuit of collective goals—trumped biology as determinants of racial outcomes.[62]

As we have seen, Weber during his early career opposed Polish migration to Germany and claimed that races and ethnic groups possessed different biological essences that affected their capacities to contribute to society. But a shift occurred in Weber's thinking on race and ethnicity, as is evident in his 1910 and 1912 contributions to the German Sociological Society. That shift was also reflected in his later writings such as *Economy and Society*, where he defined ethnic groups as "those human groups that entertain a subjective belief in their common descent because of similarities of physical type or of custom or both, or because of the memories of colonization and migration; this belief must be important for the propagation of group formation; conversely, it does not matter whether or not an objective blood relationship exists."[63] Here Weber, like Du Bois, presented race and ethnicity as phenomena belonging to the cultural sphere rather than the biological. For both men, race became a socially constructed category affecting behavior and group formation. Du Bois and Weber stressed the importance of the subjective nature of race engendered by shared religion, language, tradition, and feelings of belonging. These factors were crucial in the production of goal-oriented action undertaken by races. Weber included the importance of memories of colonization and migration, while Du Bois emphasized long collective memories. Given these similarities, Weber's access to Du Bois's scholarship on race suggests that his conception of this phenomenon was influenced by the black scholar from America.

There is a striking similarity between Du Bois and Weber's conceptualizations of caste. For Weber caste was an extreme type of status group formation because when it was developed to the fullest it was a closed system whose distinctions were guaranteed not merely by conventions but by laws and rituals.[64] Du Bois expressed a similar idea of caste, in relation to American blacks, as "a definite place preordained in custom, law and religion where all men of black blood must be thrust."[65] The type of inequality produced by caste is nearly identical in both formulations. For Weber, "A 'status' segregation grown into a 'caste' differs in its structure from a mere 'ethnic' segregation: the caste structure transforms the horizontal and unconnected coexistences of ethnically segregated groups into a vertical social system of super- and subordination."[66] But Du Bois had elaborated a similar conclusion earlier: "We are in fact to-day repeating in our intercourse between races all the former evils of class injustice, unequal taxation and rigid caste. Individual nations outgrew these fatal things by breaking down the horizontal barriers between classes. We are bringing them back by seeking to erect vertical barriers between races."[67]

Weber emphasized the distribution of honor within systems of caste. While Du Bois did not use the term *honor*, he did describe how those of high caste were respected in the sense that they had the power to make their views and judgments those accepted by society as a whole. "No sooner does the virus of caste distinction penetrate a nation's vitals," he wrote in a 1904 unpublished essay, "than good and evil in that nation come to be judged from the point of view of the privileged classes alone."[68] For example, he described a growing contempt for education in America, initiated by those in the highest strata, who believed "that good birth ought to bestow certain privileges by a sort of divine right and that the man who wrote the Declaration of independence was a fool."[69] Du Bois's article for Weber's journal similarly described how, with deepening inequality, Americans who once had had some measure of respect for ordinary working people now were "begin[ning] to show not only open contempt for the 'bastard races' but also a growing respect for snobbism and . . . gladly [beginning] to forget the color of their grandfathers' fingernails."[70] That is, they were forgetting that their own forebears might well have been common laborers who were similarly exploited by capitalists. Under the race caste system, working-class whites impose on blacks a brutal oppression similar to the class oppression they themselves had endured.

While Weber rigorously distinguished status from class, he stated that "class distinctions are linked in the most varied ways with status distinctions."[71] In this respect it is likely that he drew on Du Bois, who preceded him in discussing this interactive dynamic in his analysis of caste and class, and power. Du Bois was particularly concerned about the ways that power entrenched itself through mutually reinforcing caste and class distinctions; in his view, caste and class privilege were both growing as increasingly "social and political power [was] concentrated in the hands of the already powerful."[72] He warned that "class hierarchy grows today in America, in the land that was founded as a mighty protest against this folly that rules the world. It grows almost undisturbed, for its victims today are mostly blacks. But the Americans should not for that reason let themselves be lulled into a false security! The Negro question is only one indication of the increasing class and racial privileges and not, as many optimistically believe, its cause."[73]

Weber was interested in how status groups affected market dynamics in capitalist societies because "'status groups' hinder the strict carrying through of the sheer market principle."[74] Du Bois similarly explored how a caste system in the South interfered with the workings of the market, reducing black laborers to "economic serfdom" and deploying them to keep white union laborers submissive. Emphasizing this point years later, Du Bois wrote, "If the laborer was not free, as in the case of the Negro, he had no opportunity, and he inevitably degraded white labor."[75] For Du Bois, the caste system was retrogressive because it prevented people from being judged on merits, restricted mass education and the franchise, and limited the effectiveness of labor unions to protect workers' rights.

Du Bois and Weber's scholarship on race and ethnicity was mutually affected by their intellectual exchanges. But because Du Bois published his ideas on class and caste earlier than Weber, it is likely that the main direction of influence was from Du Bois to Weber. Lawrence Scaff has concluded that American influences, including Du Bois, were critical to

Weber's work: "Reflecting on the major categories of [his] experience [of America, . . . Weber] found ways of abstracting them from the American context and reworking the ideas in parts of his well-known discussions of race, ethnicity, and nationality; class, status and caste; domination and authority and the sociology of religion. The conceptual apparatuses of these discussions, subsequently canonized in American scholarship, certainly owe some of their richness to this formative episode."[76] Thus Weber's works on race, ethnicity, and stratification "certainly owe some of their richness" to Du Bois's work on the topics.

DU BOIS'S INFLUENCE ON WEBER'S POLITICAL VALUES

As early as 1895, Weber emphasized the causal role of culture in racial dynamics but left the door ajar for biological influences on racial outcomes. Indeed, "Weber remained very interested in the possibility of racial explanations of social action to the end of his career."[77] However, as we saw in the German Sociological Society meetings, Weber argued against racial explanations on the grounds that they were unproven and that their explanatory power was weak in comparison to that of sociological factors. By 1917, Weber had begun to express themes consistent with cultural pluralism: "A state [need] not necessarily be a 'nation state' in the sense that it [orients] its interests exclusively in favor of a single dominant nationality. . . . [It can] serve the cultural interests of several nationalities in a way that [is] in full harmony with the interests of the dominant nationality."[78]

It may be true, as Abraham claims, that Weber's reversal was merely tactical. Yet an additional influence was the cultural pluralism Du Bois espoused. A hallmark of Du Bois's scholarship was its repeated finding that no credible scientific evidence proving African American inferiority existed. On this evidentiary bedrock, Du Bois mounted attacks on social Darwinist claims that blacks occupied the lowest rung on an evolutionary scale of the races and that fundamental differences existed between them and the rest of humanity. Du Bois always insisted on the humanity of black people and used his empirical sociology as the scientific platform from which to demand social justice. Du Bois made no exception in his article published by Weber in his "value-free" journal. In it he seized that opportunity to put the political issue of black inequality squarely on the table: "In the struggle for his human rights the American Negro relies above all on the feeling of justice in the civilized world.

We are no barbarians or heathen, we are educable and our education is increasing; our economic abilities have proven themselves. We too want to have our chance in life. Whoever wants to get acquainted with our living conditions, be welcome; we demand nothing other than that one gets acquainted with us honestly and face to face, and does not judge us according to hearsay or according to the verdict of our despisers."[79] Weber, who once exclaimed that superior Germans had "turned the Poles into human beings," was influenced by Du Bois to revise his views on inequality and square them with democratic values.

Thus Weber, a continent away, embraced Du Bois's scholarship and viewed him as an original scholar of the highest order. For Weber, Du Bois had earned his place in the fraternity of esteemed sociologists, where his insights were solely needed. Park and Chicago sociologists, as well as white sociologists generally, in contrast, extended no such recognition to Du Bois. Perhaps this was because they had more to risk than sociologists in Heidelberg, who did not have the same need to block Du Bois's ideas from entering the intellectual marketplace or feel the same pressure to deny a scholar solely on the basis of his black skin.

CHAPTER 7

Intellectual Schools and the Atlanta School

The central thesis of this book is that W. E. B. Du Bois pioneered the first scientific school of American sociology. I have argued that Du Bois's school was suppressed because of the racism of mainstream white sociologists and white supremacy generally. The ideological and material roots of racism were at odds with the message of the Du Bois–Atlanta school, which argued that social conditions, rather than black inferiority, were the causes of racial inequality. That perspective was incompatible with the interests of white sociologists and the white supremacy widespread throughout the larger society. My argument raises a difficult question: Can a school exist if suppressed for a century? As we have seen, most pioneering sociologists, and even contemporary social scientists, possess little knowledge of Du Bois's school. Is it possible for a school to have major intellectual influences despite mainstream invisibility due to the effective marginalization of its intellectual leader and major contributors from the outset? Here an exploration of the factors producing scientific schools and their institutionalization is required. This chapter seeks to illuminate how Du Bois's school matured as an important center of thought despite the absence of conditions conducive to this outcome. Analyses regarding the birth and institutionalization of schools of thought, drawn from the sociology of knowledge developed by Robert Merton, Stephen and Jonathan Cole, Randall Collins, and Pierre Bourdieu, will be applied to advance knowledge regarding Du Bois's school.

In 1957, Robert Merton's presidential address to the American Sociological Association, "Priorities in Scientific Discovery: A Chapter in the Sociology of Science," called for an analysis examining science as a social institution governed by a set of distinct norms and values. Merton argued that the institutional goal of science was to enable its leading scholars to make original contributions to the stock of knowledge. He sought an understanding of the scientific norms that made it possible for the enterprise to reach this goal of producing original and transformative knowledge. Merton argued that throughout history great scientists engaged in bitter protracted struggles contesting who originally made important scientific discoveries. Merton's pivotal contribution was the formulation of a sociological explanation highlighting the institutional motivations generating these contestations rather than the personalities and egos of the scientists.

Merton identified certain institutional norms as motivating top scientists to achieve the important goals of science. The originality of a scientist's contribution was the main quality that generated distinctive intellectual breakthroughs. Merton probed how the institution of science created structured incentives that scientists internalized, incentives that motivated them to produce at the highest levels of originality. As an institution, science accomplished this task by creating prizes and other honors to be awarded to scientists who made important, original contributions. Such rewards provided recognition and esteem for scientists who made contributions of the first rank. These institutional incentives were devices that motivated great scientists to strive for originality because "recognition and fame became . . . symbol and reward for having done one's job well."[1] Thus recognition among one's peers was an institutional norm fundamental to the mission of science. "When the institution of science works efficiently . . . recognition and esteem accrue to those who have best fulfilled their roles, to those who have made genuinely original contributions to the common stock of knowledge."[2] Merton warned, "It is the social institution of science and individual men of science that would suffer from repeated failures to allocate credit justly."[3]

A decade later, Stephen and Jonathan Cole presented evidence that the institutional virtues of American science identified by Merton functioned as they should.[4] In a study of American physicists, they found that the reward system reinforced the best work being done by physicists. Merton identified an elaborate reward system that existed in American science, including honorific awards, memberships in learned societies, positions in prestigious departments, citations, and journal editorships. Because these rewards were issued publicly, they bestowed recognition on particular scientists, given that through symbolic rituals peers witnessed their achievements. Cole and Cole found that the recipients of honorific awards, memberships in honorific societies, and positions in prestigious academic departments were likely to be physicists of the highest quality. They documented a "high correlation between all three kinds of recognition and quality of the work" and noted, "It is the quality of research rather than its sheer amount that is most often recognized through honorific awards."[5] Thus the institution of science was a meritocracy, given that the most deserving scientists received the illustrious awards and prestigious appointments. These rewards underscored the quality of work produced by top scientists, enabling them to continue making transformative contributions to knowledge.

In the Mertonian world, scientists had interests to pursue given their desires to earn awards and prestigious academic appointments coveted by peers. It was the institution of science itself that regulated these rewards and dispensed them fairly, enabling science to prosper. Thus institutional properties of science accounted for scientific breakthroughs and the recognition their originators received. Institutional processes guaranteeing that meritocratic principles would be honored in science were the driving force for scientific excellence and the ability of scientists to attract scarce resources.

In 1962, Thomas Kuhn presented an explosive analysis challenging core Mertonian principles of science. In his *Structure of Scientific Revolutions*, Kuhn likens the processes producing scientific breakthroughs to political revolutions.[6] He rejects claims that science advances cumulatively, promoted by an elaborate reward system that motivates successful scholars to achieve new breakthroughs. Rather, scientists work in distinct communities where they are committed to a paradigm, a theoretical and/or methodological orientation used by scientists to study complex phenomena. Kuhn describes paradigms as "universally recognized scientific achievements that, for a time, provide model problems and solutions for a community of practitioners."[7] Established paradigms attract communities of scholars who conduct scientific investigations within this framework and utilize its theory and methodological approaches. These scientists engage in "normal science" because they do not seek to generate novel theories or methods; their goal is to solve scientific problems fitting within an existing paradigm. Such scientists become conservative researchers providing data and analyses for entrenched paradigms.

A scientific community develops conservative interests in support of the dominant paradigm. These interests include the intellectual properties and elite positions of the original architects of the paradigm and their infrastructure and staff. Existing paradigms open spaces for numerous scientists to build careers by executing the normal science they require. Textbooks, journals, editorships, publishing opportunities, internships, and grants become available to support the dominant paradigm. Thus scientific communities become gatekeepers protecting interests of existing regimes. They work to prevent "outside" publications from exploring problematic gaps between the paradigm's theory and data that point toward the need for regime change. In Kuhn's view, though scientists appear to be disinterested truth seekers, they are political actors with interests to protect and challenges to suppress. Potential scientific revolutions are strongly resisted by established communities of scientists.

Insurgents interested in overthrowing an established paradigm must develop superior ideas that offer better explanations of the phenomena in question. More precisely, to overthrow an existing paradigm, challengers must appear to have theories superior to those of competitors. If the challenging community prevails, it engineers a scientific revolution that overcomes the resistance of the old regime and abruptly ushers in radical scientific change. This revolution is not a linear, cumulative, process regulated by institutional norms dispensing academic prizes. In scientific revolutions, challengers overturn the dominant means of scientific production possessed by the old regime and seize a hegemonic place for themselves, prompting a new round of normal science. For Kuhn, the scientific enterprise is an interest-driven regime like its cousins in the political arena. In this approach, warfare in science is normal given vested interests of scientists. It is expected that scientists will fight to continue enjoying the fruits of their regimes and work to prevent success of scientific insurgents, including suppressing the ideas they champion.

Network analysis has become a leading approach seeking to explain the workings of intellectual schools. Scholars of social networks argue that great thinkers, who make long-standing intellectual contributions, do so through elite social networks shared with other great intellectuals.[8] Through these networks they gather intellectual resources crucial to building careers that affect social thought during their lives and long after their deaths. Therefore, schools of thoughts cannot be understood by examining the genius of intellectuals, because such individuals attain scholarly immortality only if they are strategically embedded within crucial networks. Privileged elite social networks enable intellectuals to stimulate, excite, and influence each other. These networks make it possible for scholars to inherit and shape the intellectual contributions of their forebears and to pass knowledge through the ages. Thus schools of thought originate in social networks that constitute a unique social structure for the production of intellectual achievements.

Randall Collins has formulated a compelling network analysis of intellectual schools in a 2.8-pound book numbering 1,098 pages.[9] His goal is to provide a global and universal theory of intellectual change. Beyond many examples, subplots, and charts mapping intellectual lineages, Collins's thesis can be distilled into a clear theoretical message: intellectual schools throughout human history and across the globe are produced and sustained through elite intellectual networks. Indeed, "The shape of the network, and where individuals happen to be within it, determines what they can do: what they think, and with what creative energy."[10] It is misleading, according to Collins, to focus on individual intellectuals because "we need to see through the personalities, to dissolve them into the networks of processes which have brought them to our attention as historical figures."[11] Intellectual networks have historical continuity stretching across time and space: "The most notable philosophers are not organizational isolates but members of chains of teachers and students who are themselves known philosophers, and/ or of circles of significant contemporary intellectuals. . . . In addition to this vertical organization of social networks across generations, creative intellectuals tend to belong to groups of intellectual peers, both circles of allies and sometimes also of rivals and debaters."[12] Above all, elite intellectual networks are the crucial mechanisms that generate and sustain schools of thought.

In Collins's perspective, networks are main determiners because nestled within them are intellectual resources—cultural capital, texts, vocabularies, styles of argumentation, strategies for addressing rival schools, and intellectual and organizational leaders. Additionally, emotional energy igniting passions and excitement among intellectuals and firing up their creative impulses dwells within intellectual networks. Intellectuals transfer their cultural capital, consisting of educational competences acquired during formal and informal schooling, writing and debating skills, publishing experiences, and personal contacts, into networks. On their own, without the concentrated resources residing in intellectual networks, these scholars are incapable of becoming leading intellectuals. Even when embedded in these crucial networks, intellectuals face stiff competition, causing the majority not to achieve elite network positions. Moreover, opportunities to receive attention within networks are scarce, causing only a few stars to produce numerous, and sustained, publications of the highest rank. As a result, most intellectuals never become leading figures because they cannot match competition from esteemed network leaders. More challenging, networks can shift their intellectual focus, reorganizing it around other eminent intellectuals and causing talented intellectuals to slide into obscurity.

Collins formulates an explanation for why potential intellectual schools fail to develop and become significant actors on the world stage. Such failure occurs because second-rate intellectuals are unable to reach the highest levels of eminence within intellectual networks. These intellectuals are failures because they are followers rather than leaders and are easily left in the cold when the intellectual focus of networks shifts. Access to elite scholarly networks determines winners and losers in intellectual life. Conversely, political power, economic resources, and ideologies are not crucial to success: "Economic and political macrostructures do not explain much about abstract ideas, because such ideas exist only where there is a network of intellectuals focused on their own arguments and accumulating their own conceptual baggage train. It is the inner structure of these intellectual networks which shapes ideas, by their patterns of vertical chains across the generations and their horizontal alliances and oppositions."[13]

Collins argues, "Winning the focus of attention within the contests among philosophers is done with specifically intellectual resources, which are social resources specific to intellectual networks."[14] Political and intellectual struggles are entirely different phenomena. Collins argues that external power struggles and political ideologies have no effect on intellectual schools because when players in the intellectual arena "try to win their way solely with the weapons of external politics, they win the battle at the cost of their intellectual reputations in the long-term historical community."[15] Thus schools of thought rise and fall on the basis of intellectual qualities recognized by network leaders.

While Collins acknowledges that the intellectuals and their schools, existing over thousands of years, that he has studied are almost exclusively male and white, he rejects the view that women and people of color are incapable of thinking at the highest levels: "The issue is not male and female mentalities, which would be a reductionist explanation, but social discrimination on the level of the material base. It is not individuals, whether males or females, let alone of any skin color, that produce ideas, but the flow of networks through individuals."[16]

Collins argues that certain people may be excluded from the pinnacles of intellectual success because of institutional discrimination. Yet discrimination is not his focus because it is of interest only insofar as it determines the absence of certain groups in intellectual networks. Those who fall outside of elite intellectual networks are analytically unimportant because they never had the chance to perform in the arena where profound ideas and schools are generated and transmitted: there exist no forgotten, deserving intellectuals whose "undiscovered" contributions to historical thought have been lost to history. If such intellectuals were never members of important intellectual networks, they could not have produced works of the first rank because it is networks that make it possible for great ideas to be produced and transmitted through time. In this view, "We cannot invoke as a foil a reservoir of 'deserving' but unknown thinkers in the shadows throughout history but as 'creative' as the ones whose names were trumpeted, as if there were some transhistorical realm in which their achievement is measured."[17] For Collins, intellectual masterpieces can be produced only in stellar networks, while pretenders outside those networks never rise to significance.

Collins's narrative concerns the inner workings of elite networks where external political and economic struggles have little import. Because he quarantines intellectual networks outside politics, economic inequalities, and ideological struggles, he presents elite networks as functional equivalents despite national boundaries, historical epochs, ideologies, and social inequalities. Collins's networks have isomorphic qualities because they are bereft of racial, class, and gendered conflicts that affect core network processes, significantly determining intellectual outcomes. Societies have varied in degrees of patriarchy, racism, class inequalities, and homophobia. But for Collins these cultural and structural formations are of little concern because intellectual life and its networks are not closely intertwined with social, political, and economic forces; the two domains rarely touch.

DU BOIS'S SCHOOL AND LESSONS FROM THE SOCIOLOGY OF KNOWLEDGE

In this book, I address the rejection of Du Bois by mainstream academia, especially in his own discipline, and explore why his pioneering school was marginalized. To what extent can the analyses formulated by Merton, Kuhn, and Collins explain Du Bois's intellectual work and his school of scientific sociology? To account for intellectual outcomes, Merton and Collins place major weight on the internal dynamics and organization of intellectual life. For Merton, if intellectuals perform well at the highest levels, the institution of science showers recognition upon them, enabling their rise to the pinnacles of success. It is the achievements by scientists embedded in the institution of science that determine outcomes of intellectual schools. When the institution of science works effectively, those with outstanding performance succeed. When scientific norms are violated by jealous and greedy individuals, scientists are at fault. The institution of science itself generally fares well, ensuring that scientists who make outstanding, original contributions rise to the top of their fields and bask in the glory of their earned reputations.

Collins's approach to intellectual life shares fundamental assumptions with Merton's framework. For Collins, intellectual outcomes are shaped by thinkers and intellectual resources encompassed within networks of intellectuals. It is the responsibility of intellectuals to establish links with unique networks that enhance and transmit their ideas through the ages, ensuring eminence across generations. This analysis denies the importance of intellectual alliances among political and economic elites. Instead, it focuses on intellectuals who occupy elite positions strategically arrayed within intellectual networks. Network connections and their resources enable intellectuals to build enduring schools of thought. Only a few thinkers influence intellectual history because most are not sufficiently talented to perform in the higher echelons of intellectual networks. Collins's theory, like Merton's, is concerned only with processes and resources internal to intellectual communities because those thinkers who are outside elite networks and scientific institutions drop from analysis. Like Merton, Collins decouples intellectual schools from external power struggles and economic resources controlled by societal elites. This logic suggests that Du Bois was not permitted into elite networks because he lacked sufficient intellectual quality or because he was blocked by institutional discrimination. Either way, he lacked entrée into networks capable of catapulting him into long-lasting fame and intellectual influence. Without such network connections, it was impossible for Du Bois to develop an enduring school recognized and honored by scientific peers.

Kuhn's theorizing encompasses some realities Du Bois encountered as an intellectual of the first rank. It examines how paradigmatic revolutions occur and explicitly recognizes the political nature of scientific change, viewing it as not fundamentally different from political revolutions. In this view, scientists are interest-bearing political actors who mobilize resources to realize interests either as incumbents or as insurgents. When change does occur, it is a rupture signaling that an old paradigm has been overthrown. Thus, unlike the analyses of Merton and Collins, Kuhn's analysis highlights the political nature of scientific institutions and emphasizes that revolutionary tendencies inhere in their structures. Moreover, those tendencies may crystallize, exposing irreconcilable intellectual positions that cause established paradigms to be overthrown.

Kuhn's politically based argument brings us closer to dynamics Du Bois encountered as an intellectual actor. However, it falls short because it shares a fundamental assumption with the theories of Merton and Collins: its point of departure is the internal processes and struggles within the intellectual community. The resources and interests at stake lie within the existing scientific community. Kuhn's theory does not connect external power and economic resources with internal dynamics of the scientific community. As a result, scientific revolutions are compared to political revolutions only because they share certain features. Yet as we have seen, Du Bois's story is germane to the racial, political, and economic struggles deeply embedded in twentieth-century America. We need a theoretical approach that accounts for linkages between societal power and intellectual dynamics to understand science in Du Bois's world. Such an approach requires that we focus on the social context in which Du Bois moved and acted and that we grapple with the racial ugliness that confronted Du Bois's scientific endeavors.

Thus a theory making sense of Du Bois's intellectual marginalization needs to address American society and its racial history. To proceed as if Du Bois's intellectual work were not deeply intertwined with America's political, economic, and social history would constitute intellectual dishonesty of epic proportions. From the beginning, America imposed racist oppression on African Americans beginning with two and a half centuries of chattel slavery. When slavery was ended by the Civil War, black people were imprisoned by a Jim Crow regime of economic exploitation, political disenfranchisement, and racial segregation. In addition, the cultural discrimination that Jim Crow imposed on blacks significantly shaped American intellectual life.

America began as a racist society, assigning racial privileges to original white European settlers and eventually ethnic "white" immigrant groups while oppressing people of color, especially Native and African

Americans.[18] To justify brutal oppression, whites formulated a racist ideology based on claims of black inferiority. This racial ideology was meticulously elaborated for African Americans with a "one drop" rule: anyone who had a drop of black blood was black, possessing no rights whites were bound to respect, as specified in the 1857 ruling of the Supreme Court in the Dred Scott case. Blacks came to be despised as a damaged race best kept out of sight except when serving and working for whites. Legally required racial segregation under Jim Crow codified "black invisibility" legally.

As a result, blacks became "invisible" in broad daylight, experiencing the devastating psychological pain of nonpersons. The pain of invisibility became a major theme of black intellectuals. Du Bois formulated the concept of "the Veil" to capture the condition whereby blacks were hidden behind the color line and visible to whites only as a problem:

> Between me and the other world there is ever an unasked question: unasked by some through feelings of delicacy; by others through the difficulty of rightly framing it. All, nevertheless, flutter round it. They approach me in a half-hesitant sort of way, eye me curiously or compassionately, and then, instead of saying directly, How does it feel to be a problem? they say, I know an excellent colored man in my town; or, I fought at Mechanicsville; or, Do not these Southern outrages make your blood boil? At these I smile, or am interested, or reduce the boiling to a simmer, as the occasion may require. To the real question, How does it feel to be a problem? I answer seldom a word.[19]

The writer Ralph Ellison immortalized the condition of black invisibility in his autobiographically inflected novel *Invisible Man*:

> I am an invisible man. No, I am not a spook like those who haunted Edgar Allen Poe; nor am I one of your Hollywood-movie ectoplasms. I am a man of substance, of flesh and bone, fiber and liquids—and I might even be said to possess a mind. I am invisible, understand, simply because people refuse to see me. Like the bodiless heads you see sometimes in circus sideshows, it is as though I have been surrounded by mirrors of hard, distorting glass. When they approach me they see only my surroundings, themselves, or figments of their imagination—indeed, everything and anything except me.[20]

Whether viewed opaquely behind the Veil or unseen because of an impenetrable cloud of social projections, blacks were considered biologically or culturally inferior. White social scientists, including sociologists, shared this view of black inferiority, and the thesis was a prominent feature of their social scientific writings.[21] African Americans' black skin served to alert the world to their alleged inferiority. By definition, blacks were incapable of great intellectual achievements.

Throughout slavery and Jim Crow, the question regarding proper education for blacks persisted. During slavery, education was denied them because it was considered a dangerous tool promoting insurgency. Thus laws were enacted preventing slaves from learning to read and write. Following emancipation, powerful southern whites proclaimed that society should not waste resources exposing ex-slaves to abstract advanced knowledge because it produced uppity niggers seeking social equality. The planter class needed cheap, exploitable, black labor rather than Negroes who challenged the status quo.[22] Outside the South there was more tolerance for black education, but most college and universities educated few blacks, and many did not even admit them. And major universities throughout America did not hire black professors until forced by pressure from the civil rights and Black Power movements.[23] As a result, black scholars had no choice but to build careers in historically black colleges on the periphery of higher education where resources and recognition were scarce.[24]

As shown earlier, Booker T. Washington stepped into the breach to offer an educational solution. He proposed that an industrial education would prepare blacks to one day join whites as members of their advanced civilization. Washington's "solution" garnered immediate white support, but it had devastating consequences for black scholars who wanted to conduct research and publish intellectual work. Industrial education required a different infrastructure than the production of scholarly work. To advance their own scholarship, black professors needed other scholars to debate and conduct collaborative research with. They also needed talented graduate students to mentor and train to produce scholarship. Most of all, given the expenses associated with the production of scholarship, black professors needed funds and facilities to sponsor research projects and pay staff. In short, they required the same resources found at research universities such as Harvard, Pennsylvania, Chicago, and the University of Berlin. Industrial education required only the resources needed to produce blacksmiths, brickmasons, farmers, carpenters, seamstress, and cooks. Washington won the battle, leaving black liberal arts scholars to scrape for resources to produce first-rank intellectual work.

DU BOIS'S ACADEMIC WORLD AND BOURDIEU'S SCIENCE OF SCIENCE

As a Negro at the dawn of twentieth century, Du Bois rode in Jim Crow trains, anguished over black lynching victims, and was exposed to thousands of racial slights and microaggressions as common as sunshine and rain. Like other black scholars, he was restricted to the segregated academic labor market. Relegated to the periphery of American higher education, he was forced to set up shop in an economically poor black university that could not afford to produce sufficient numbers of scholars of the first rank. He labored in an institution with relatively few graduate students and a graduate program not offering the doctorate.

Du Bois faced a unique problem even among black academics. He stood out as the intellectual who challenged Booker T. Washington. Washington determined which blacks received resources from white funders. His power was enormous because he acquired resources to further his own interests, including black industrial education. He did not respond kindly to blacks seeking to usurp his power or promote alternative agendas. In the meantime, Washington's priorities were supported by most white elites because they resonated with white interests. His conservative vision of black education prevailed early in the twentieth century, despite spirited challenges. In short, Washington was a formidable opponent who stood in the schoolhouse door, opposing Du Bois's intellectual agenda.

As discussed, theories of intellectual life stress the need for scientists to possess academic capital to be serious players in the intellectual arena. Yet Du Bois was steeped in intellectual capital earned through schooling and absorbed from his social environment; indeed, his learning often exceeded that of white competitors. He received a first-rate undergraduate liberal arts education from Fisk and Harvard Universities, and at Harvard he was taught by world-class scholars in history, philosophy, and the humanities. The penultimate intellectual capital for a social scientist during this period was that gained from mentoring by world-famous social scientists in Germany. Du Bois was mentored by Germany's most preeminent scholars, who exposed him to the new social sciences and advanced methodologies, including statistics.

It is instructive to contrast Du Bois's intellectual capital with that of a leading white competitor, Franklin Giddings. As the first recipient of an endowed chair in sociology, Giddings taught sociology at Columbia University, where he provided doctoral students training in statistical analysis. For this he is viewed by scholars of science as a major founding father of American sociology, especially with regard to quantitative methods. Giddings descended from a wealthy, well-connected family. During adolescence, he moved with his family to Great Barrington, Massachusetts, the birthplace of Du Bois. The two scholars attended the same high school and absorbed similar New England influences. Yet their paths differed drastically because Du Bois was disadvantaged by the color line, while Giddings profited from it. Racial politics of that time determined what blacks and whites could achieve in intellectual life. Without any advanced degrees, Giddings landed at the top of academia and was given an endowed chair. While serving in this post, he became a charter member of the American Eugenics Society, where he leveraged the position to promote racist views. Du Bois, holder of one of the most prestigious degrees in social science, could secure only an academic appointment at a resource-starved historically black university, where he challenged the scientific racism promoted by Giddings and other white scholars Giddings trained, including Thomas Jesse Jones, about whom we will learn more in the next chapter.

As Merton and Collins emphasized, to become a major player in the intellectual arena a scientist had to be a prolific publisher of influential scholarship. Yet Du Bois was one of the most prolific scholars of the twentieth century, far outproducing most leading white American sociologists of his era. One scholar of Du Bois has estimated that from the time Du Bois reached eighteen years of age until his death seventy-seven years later, he produced a publication on average every twelfth day. Some of these works became classics and are recognized as such a hundred years later. Few white social scientists possessed a résumé matching either the quantity or the quality of Du Bois's scholarship.

Du Bois's publication record contrasts sharply with that of one of his main competitors, Robert E. Park, often considered father of American race studies. As pointed out previously, Park's and Du Bois's educational credentials were similar in that both men attended Harvard and were mentored in Germany by leading social scientists. By the time Park was appointed at Chicago in 1914, Du Bois had published classic works including *The Souls of Black Folk* and *The Philadelphia Negro*. In addition, he had published most of his pioneering annual studies at Atlanta University, as well as numerous other works in scholarly and popular venues. In contrast, when Park arrived at Chicago he was not a widely known intellectual: he had just spent seven years as Booker T. Washington's ghostwriter and had no major sociological publications. Thus Du Bois had more cultural capital and produced more scholarly work than many of the white scholars who are known to intellectual history as the pioneering founders of American sociology. How, therefore, given his prodigious and high-quality scholarship, could his pioneering school be excluded from mainstream sociology and erased from the discipline's memory for nearly a century?

To capture the dynamics preventing Du Bois's scientific school from receiving mainstream recognition and support, we need a theoretical framework centering on power, political ideologies, social hierarchies, material interests, status and identities, and institutional structures and social prestige. The frameworks of Merton, Kuhn, and Collins have been helpful for understanding the internal institutional dynamics of intellectual life, including how those institutions may be transformed by intellectual revolutions. But in Du Bois's story, intellectual networks are only one of the key factors that determined intellectual outcomes. To fully understand why Du Bois's scientific school was marginalized and erased from mainstream sociology, we need a theory of how scientific schools emerge, take root, and become institutionalized that explores the linkages between science and the power structures of the larger society: structures of politics, economics, race, and societal elites. Nothing short of such a focus can account for why Du Bois was denied a broad stage on which to practice his craft in academia.

The French sociologist Pierre Bourdieu provides such a framework in *Science of Science and Reflexivity*.[25] According to Bourdieu, science is situated within a distinct space, the scientific field. In that social space scientists gather, interact, and work producing scientific products. Dynamics present in the scientific field contradicts genteel views of science:

> The idea of the field . . . leads one to call into question the irenic vision of the scientific world, that of a world of generous exchanges in which all scientists collaborate towards the same end. This idealist vision . . . is contradicted by the facts: what one observes are struggles, sometimes ferocious ones, and competitions within structures of domination. The "communitarian" vision fails to grasp the very foundation of the scientific world as a universe of competition for the "monopoly of the legitimate handling" of scientific goods, in other words and more precisely, of the correct method, the correct findings, the correct definitions of the ends, objects and methods of science.[26]

Thus competition and power struggles are germane qualities of the scientific field. But all scientists do not have equal chances of maximizing their interests because inequality is a structural property of the scientific field: "The structure of the distribution of capital determines the structure of the field, in other words the relations of force among the scientific agents: possession of a large quantity (and therefore a large share) of capital gives a power over the field, and therefore over agents (relatively) less endowed with capital (and over the price of entry to the field) and governs the distribution of the chances for profit."[27] In Bourdieu's framework the distribution of resources structures the scientific game.

Capital in this field is both scientific and financial. Scientific capital is symbolic, consisting of rewards assigned through peer review (reputation, prizes, tenure, membership in societies, etc.) rather than markets. Symbolic capital is unique because it is bestowed upon scientists by scientific peers who alone have the training and ability to perceive the originality, rarity, and distinctive value of scientific work. Peer recognition is crucial, for without it a scientist cannot achieve the visibility that attracts fame, resources, and honors: "The notion of *visibility*, used in the American university tradition, accurately evokes the differential value of this capital which, concentrated in a known and recognized name, distinguishes its bearer from the undifferentiated background into which the mass of anonymous researchers merges and blurs."[28] If peers fail to recognize original accomplishments of a scientist, that scholar is disadvantaged because she will not receive adequate resources enabling her to rise in science. Peer recognition translates into assets providing scientists with advantages over competitors: "The structure of the field, defined by the unequal distribution of capital, that is of the specific weapons or assets, bears on all the agents within it, restricting more or less the space of possibles that is open to them, depending on how well placed they are within the field, that is within this distribution."[29] However, recognition by peers and the resources it engenders are not merely the result of a meritocratic game. The flow of recognition and resources is largely channeled toward those holding advantageous position in the scientific field. Some are dominant because of access to superior resources, and others, as challengers, struggle to obtain resources for intellectual work.

For Bourdieu, the structure of the scientific arena ensures that the richer scientists become richer because placement in the scientific hierarchy largely determines who gets rewarded. Those in the most prestigious universities, academic departments, research laboratories, and elite circles are the most cited and receive academic prizes, research grants, and esteem that place them in positions to be successful in future rounds of competition. Famous, well-connected scientists have tremendous advantages over newcomers and those on the scientific periphery. Elite scientists are in positions to build scientific schools and emerge as winners of scientific competition.

Yet scholars are not the only shapers of science, for scholarly decisions are not based solely on scientific grounds. Powerful actors inside and outside the scientific community also exercise influence. Bourdieu, unlike Merton, Kuhn, and Collins, argues that the scientific arena is situated in university hierarchies and power structures in the larger society that are important because of their impact on scientists and their work—"temporal powers over the scientific field such as those of ministers and ministries, deans and vice-chancellors or scientific administrators (these temporal powers tend to be more national, linked to national institutions, particularly those that govern the reproduction of the corps of scientists—such as Academies, committees, research councils, etc. . . .)."[30] Because expensive scientific research requiring expansive infrastructure cannot be funded solely by scientists, they are compelled to seek resources from well-heeled external funders. Given these funding needs, scientists make concessions so that outside elites look favorably upon their requests: "The concessions that scientists have to make, individually or collectively, to activities oriented towards the search for economic resources—grants, contracts, posts, etc.—varies with the dependence of their scientific activity on these resources."[31] This dependence is not great in disciplines like mathematics, but it is considerable in others like sociology.

Additionally, scientists whose work runs counter to dominant ideologies may encounter difficulties in obtaining funding. Ideologically oriented decisions can have strong influences in the social sciences, where scholars investigate social inequality and powerful interests of concern to elites. In twentieth-century America, white elite funders embraced the ideology of scientific racism and sponsored scientists who generated scholarship that supported, or at least did not disturb, their beliefs.[32] As Bourdieu argued, "Judgments of scientific works are contaminated by knowledge of their position of the authors in the social hierarchies."[33] Judgments by elites are also contaminated by the biased knowledge they possess regarding which scholars are worthy because of superior work.

Because scientific activities are inextricably linked to powerful external actors, the scientific field enjoys only relative autonomy. In fact, "Autonomy is not a given, but a historical conquest, endlessly having to be undertaken anew.[34] "The social sciences must endlessly reckon with external forces which hold back their 'take-off.'"[35] To sum up: in Bourdieu's analysis pure science does not exist; some scientists are dominant and others subordinated; intellectual capital and financial interests are paramount; external and internal elites mutually influence each others' actions; hierarchies of domination are prevalent; socially constructed peer recognition abounds; and there are scientific winners and losers. Indeed, "The dominant players are those who manage to impose the definition of science that says that the most accomplished realization of science consists in having, being and doing what they have, are and do."[36]

Bourdieu's insights are relevant for understanding the fortunes of Du Bois's scientific school of sociology. His analysis would suggest that Du Bois's scientific enterprise was doomed from the start because he was an African American when all blacks were considered inferior. As I argued, to be black in the early twentieth century was to belong to a despised group considered so damaged that it required strict quarantine through racial segregation. Here we reach the crux: invisibility and recognition are opposites. Because of the color line, white social scientists did not recognize Du Bois's scientific contributions as original, rare, and distinctive. As a black person, Du Bois was largely invisible, as were his pioneering scientific contributions. Consequently he was not a viable candidate to obtain a stellar scientific reputation, prizes, or appointments in prestigious universities and academic departments. He was not usually chosen for membership in learned societies or given the extended leadership of prestigious sociological laboratories. As Du Bois recalled about himself and his Atlanta colleagues in his autobiography, "So far as the American world of science and letters was concerned, we never 'belonged'; we remained unrecognized in learned societies and academic groups. We rated merely as Negroes studying Negroes, and after all, what had Negroes to do with America or science?"[37] Once Du Bois was pushed out of sight, white scholars did not have to compete with him because in their scientific world he did not rate as a competitor.

Du Bois was disadvantaged because of the positions he held in the scientific field. Atlanta University, a historically black institution, was not included in the set of major universities where Du Bois's white competitors held appointments. Albion Small, W.I. Thomas, and Robert Park stood at the center of academic prestige, given their positions at the University of Chicago. Franklin Giddings, without any advanced degrees, was able to achieve recognition because he held a prestigious chair at Columbia. William Graham Sumner basked in academic prestige because of his professorship at Yale, a leading Ivy League university. These scholars were linked with similar situated scholars at John Hopkins, Pennsylvania, Wisconsin, and other elite universities. At these universities, white scholars benefited by working with resourceful colleagues at their universities and nationally.[38] They derived rewards from mentoring doctoral students, many of whom produced scholarship that reflected favorably on their mentors. In the early years of American sociology, resources required for building illustrious careers and scientific schools were housed in elite white universities.

Du Bois operated on the periphery of American higher education in Atlanta as he battled intellectual obscurity and a dearth of resources. Few elite scientists were aware of his pioneering sociological laboratory or the sociology department he had developed there, even though it was only the third established in the country. Du Bois's pioneering contributions were remarkable despite the chronic funding shortages he confronted while working in the hinterlands of higher education. His difficulties raising research funds arose not only from his marginalized position but from ideological factors: his race perspective differed from that of elite white funders and Booker T. Washington. White funders were comfortable sponsoring the industrial education championed by Washington and utilizing him as the clearinghouse for funding decisions regarding blacks. But Du Bois's bedrock principle that black people were not inferior and should be treated as social equals and that science could be utilized to prove these propositions was not palatable to white funders. The policy implications of this perspective were troubling for leaders of a society committed to white supremacy—so troubling that on one occasion the US Department of Labor not only failed to publish but actually destroyed the manuscript report of a major study that Du Bois had conducted for them, giving as a reason that it "touched on political matters."[39] In contrast, funders were put at ease by scholars of the Chicago school who clung to claims of blacks inferiority and described sociology as an abstract science that required its practitioners to stay detached from social and political issues and to avoid activism.[40] As a result, research funds and eminent scholars flowed into Chicago, enabling them to build what the scholarly world recognizes as the Chicago school. It would take another century for mainstream scholars to realize that despite the odds Du Bois had built a unique and substantively viable scientific school.

As we have seen, Du Bois's scientific school rejected the grand theorizing of nineteenth-century sociology and embraced empirical research utilizing the inductive method. The novel conceptual frame of Du Bois's scientific school maintained that social conditions generated by racial prejudice and discrimination were dominant in determining racial outcomes. This argument directly challenged the dominant paradigm—scientific racism—which maintained that racial inequality resulted from genetics and inherited racial traits. In contrast, at a time when races were considered natural, Du Bois's school viewed them as socially constructed categories and held that they could not be ranked according to "natural" hierarchies. In the contemporary world it is easy to underestimate how accepted claims of race inferiority were in the early twentieth century. Antonio Gramsci examines how cultural hegemony is a powerful force making it possible for dominant groups to rule over the oppressed.[41] The idea of black inferiority that propped up the racial caste system ideologically was not only embraced by whites but internalized by many blacks, leading them to voluntarily take seats in the back of the bus and at the bottom of the job market. The father of black history, Carter G. Woodson, explained how the ideology worked:

> If you can control a man's thinking you do not have to worry about his action. When you determine what a man shall think you do not have to concern yourself about what he will do. If you make a man feel that he is inferior, you do not have to compel him to accept an inferior status, for he will seek it himself. If you make a man think that he is justly an outcast, you do not have to order him to the back door. He will go without being told; and if there is no back door, his very nature will demand one.[42]

Thus Du Bois's scientific school conducted a war with Jim Crow by challenging the ideological grounds on which it stood. However, Du Bois's school sought to wage this ideological struggle at the scientific level by producing findings undermining political domination. After all, it was science that had trumpeted black inferiority, providing scientific legitimacy for those dedicated to black oppression.

On the basis of the analyses of scientific schools already discussed and Bourdieu's analysis in particular, Du Bois should have failed to develop the first scientific school of American sociology. This view is expressed by Martin Bulmer, who argues that Du Bois failed because of racial discrimination that he could not overcome.[43] Bulmer, both a scholar of the Chicago school and knowledgeable about Du Bois's work at Atlanta, published an article entitled "The Chicago School of Sociology: What Made It a 'School'?" He argued that several factors were necessary for a school to develop. First, there had to be a founder and leader with a dominant personality around which the other members clustered. Second, the school had to seek to modernize or renovate the existing discipline. Third, the school had to be based at an important academic site, usually a university located in a great metropolitan area. Fourth, the school needed a publishing outlet such as a journal and access to a publishing press. Fifth, at the heart of a school, a stream of collaborative scholarly activity, often expressed through seminars, needed to occur. Sixth, there had to be an adequate infrastructure to support scholarly endeavors. Finally, to ensure an adequate infrastructure, outside financial support had to be available, because without it no school of empirical research was possible. Bulmer found that all these conditions were present in Chicago's sociology department of the 1920s, making it the first scientific school of American sociology.

Bulmer's analysis implies that all these factors, with the exception of adequate outside financial support, were available at Atlanta University's sociology department headed by Du Bois. Yet according to Bulmer the lack of funding doomed Du Bois's effort to build a school. Bulmer notes that at Chicago outside funds were readily available from the Laura Spelman Rockefeller Memorial and other sources that nurtured the development of the Chicago school. But "lack of support could clearly be a decisive obstacle [to school building], as DuBois's earlier attempts at Atlanta to initiate serious research on black Americans showed."[44] Du Bois seemed to affirm this view when he wrote to an inquirer in 1939 that "I left Atlanta because my work of scientific investigation of the Negro problem did not find sufficient financial support."[45] Yet Du Bois and his colleagues did produce serious research for well over a decade—a period longer than the heyday of the Chicago school. Bulmer's view that Chicago was the first scientific school of American sociology thus seems unjustified. The more challenging issue, however, is to explain how Du Bois and his colleagues were able to build, despite scarce funding, a scientific school at Atlanta that produced pathbreaking scientific scholarship for over a decade. This question is of great importance because inadequate funding is indeed a major obstacle that prevents most such efforts from having a scientific impact.

How, then, did Du Bois overcome this seemingly insurmountable barrier and develop a scientific school? He developed counterhegemonic networks and a counterhegemonic form of capital that have not been identified or analyzed in the literature. Below I turn to an analytic explanation of these strategies.

LIBERATION CAPITAL AND INSURGENT INTELLECTUAL NETWORKS

Bourdieu has shown that scientific and financial capital are crucial to the development of intellectual enterprises. The history of Du Bois's school suggests the existence of yet another form of capital that can be activated to create and sustain intellectual enterprises, one that I will call liberation capital. Liberation capital is a form of capital used by oppressed and resource-starved scholars to initiate and sustain the research program of a nonhegemonic scientific school. It consists of volunteer or nominally paid labors in research and other scholarly activities that are provided by a self-conscious group of professionals and amateur intellectual workers for a subaltern school of thought that seeks to challenge the intellectual foundations of oppression. The providers of liberation capital, most often members of the oppressed group, work together to formulate new research methodologies that facilitate the collection and analysis of critical evidence leading to new theoretical perspectives on the social conditions faced by the oppressed group, as well as programmatic innovations to be used as weapons of liberation. The promise of ultimately reaching the collective goal of group liberation serves as the compensation motivating this cadre of largely unremunerated intellectual workers even when they are faced with professional sanctions for their work. Liberation capital is a necessary condition for a nonhegemonic school to make up the resource deficits caused by refusal of elite funders to support liberation scholarship and the activism in which it is embedded. Through liberation capital, scholars can hold off resource challenges long enough to make it possible for new schools to take root and become influential.

Liberation capital was the basic form of currency that made it possible for the Du Bois–Atlanta school to become a formidable intellectual force. At the turn of the twentieth century, some black leaders and intellectuals were desperately searching for ways to stop and reverse the entrenchment of Jim Crow in the South. Many of them were former slaves or their direct descendants who believed that education was the road to personal freedom and a collective resource to overthrow racism. American sociology, which was developing precisely at this time, promised a scientific understanding of race based on facts and thus appeared to be the intellectual weapon that blacks needed. In its early days, sociology attracted the attention of black community leaders, clergy, and intellectuals because they literally believed that the scientific truth would set them free. Once new research demolished beliefs in black inferiority, the system that disenfranchised black people politically and subordinated them economically would likewise be toppled. Because of this promise, southern black colleges of the early twentieth century incorporated sociology into their curriculum much earlier than white schools did. In a study of the introduction of sociology in southern black colleges, a former president of the American Sociological Society, Luther

Bernard, concluded, "The reason for the Negro interest is, I think, sufficiently evident in the fact that a minority group was trying honestly to understand the social situation in which it found itself."[46] Blacks streamed to sociology because they sought an understanding of racism and how it could be dismantled. Their hopes primed them to contribute liberation capital to build a scientific enterprise combating oppression.

Du Bois mobilized the liberation capital embodied in black leaders, scholars, and students to conduct research for his sociological laboratory. Atlanta had a sizable black middle class of religious and business leaders, community activists, educator, teachers, and college students—a pool of intellectual talent from which he could recruit researchers. Du Bois is often portrayed as an aloof, detached intellectual who developed his ideas and beliefs in isolation. But in fact, Du Bois, over his long career, was embedded in social networks and communities that shaped and influenced him intellectually and politically. We have already examined Du Bois's intellectual and social milieu at the University of Berlin. Cheryl Gilkes and Reiland Rabaka have revealed another important early influence: while Du Bois was a student at Harvard he was connected to networks of black women leaders and their organizations that enhanced his intellectual vision and political savvy to operate in the perilous racial environment of that era.[47] Du Bois made similar kinds of connections when he came to Atlanta in 1896 to teach at Atlanta University and head its sociological laboratory. Upon arrival, he immediately established relationships with black leaders, educators, and students, many of whom would serve as researchers for his scholarly projects. The intellectual labors of these individuals have not been recorded in the historical record, yet as providers of liberation capital they were crucial to the establishment and continuance of Du Bois's school.

In earlier chapters I discussed the role that a variety of scholars and amateurs played in the scholarly activities of the Du Bois–Atlanta school. Here I situate these individuals as providers of liberation by highlighting their contributions to Du Bois's school. The sociologist Earl Wright, in his study "Beyond W.E.B. Du Bois: A Note on Some of the Lesser Known Members of the Atlanta Sociological Laboratory," has provided an account of how these individuals, who included clergy and educational leaders, were recruited as field researchers.[48] Three examples suffice to demonstrate how these recruitments worked. The first is that of Reverend Henry Hugh Proctor. Upon arrival in Atlanta, Du Bois renewed his friendship with this former Fisk classmate, who had become a renowned local pastor and national religious leader. Proctor had earned a BA from Fisk, a bachelor of divinity degree from Yale and a doctor of divinity degree from Clark University. He was a politically active pastor who fought for racial equality alongside Du Bois. Du Bois's research on the black church and its clergy gave him inside knowledge of the powerful roles that black pastors, including highly educated ones like Proctor, played in the community. Proctor understood the value of research and scholarship. As the pastor of a large Atlanta church, he was economically independent and had access to secretaries and administrators and qualified church members to assist in executing research. He also possessed skills of activism and the courage to confront Jim Crow. Proctor became a researcher on Du Bois's team, working in the field, writing scholarly reports, and presenting research papers during the Atlanta Conferences, because like Du Bois he believed that sociological knowledge, combined with political activism, could serve as a weapon against Jim Crow.

Similarly, Du Bois became fast friends with John Hope, another renowned educator and major political activist who participated in pivotal struggles and protest organizations alongside Du Bois. Hope earned his BA degree from Brown University, studied during summers of 1897 and 1898 at the University of Chicago, where he was exposed to Chicago sociologists, and received honorary degrees from Brown University, Bates College, Howard University, Bucknell University, and McMaster University. During his career, Hope served as a professor of classics and as president of Morehouse College and Atlanta University. Like Proctor, Hope became a scholar on Du Bois's team conducting research, writing reports and papers, and participating in annual conferences. Proctor and Hope became providers of liberation capital because they identified with the liberation-oriented scholarship produced by the Atlanta Sociological Laboratory and were aware that those scholarly efforts were being hampered financially by the master gatekeeper Booker T. Washington.

Teachers of elementary and secondary schools were ideal potential providers of liberation capital given their education and involvement in intellectual activities. Lucy Craft Laney, who has been described as "one of the most important African-American female educators in the late-nineteenth-century South," earned her bachelor's from Atlanta University in 1873.[49] She was the recipient of honorary degrees from four universities. Laney established an elementary school in Augusta, Georgia, where she taught generations of students, including scholars who become active in the Atlanta Sociological Laboratory. Like Du Bois, Laney rejected Washington's industrial education approach and advocated for a liberal arts education as a means to achieve liberation. She believed women had an important role to play in the liberation struggle and diffused this doctrine among students and leaders she encountered. Laney became a researcher on Du Bois's team, writing reports and presenting papers at the annual conferences. She embodied liberation capital because she believed that middle-class leaders should solve the race problem and that black sociologists should help direct the struggle. Participating in the Atlanta Conference at its very beginning, even before Du Bois's arrival at Atlanta, she expressed the hope "that the moving spirit of these meetings may be a Moses come to lead [blacks] out of the wilderness" and "that from these meetings may be evolved plans that will bring some relief" to blacks in poverty.[50] Laney joined the ranks of Proctor, Hope, and numerous other community leaders as researchers who helped to firmly establish Du Bois's scientific school of sociology.

As we have seen, Du Bois relied on professionally trained black sociologists to conduct scholarly research and prepare manuscripts for publication. Earlier I examined the role that Professors Monroe Work, Richard R. Wright Jr., and Edmund Haynes played in this capacity. These scholars provided expert statistical and qualitative skills to accompany the theoretical vision of Du Bois's sociological laboratory. Like the community researchers, they conducted research because they embraced the liberation goals of the school, believing sociological knowledge crucial to overthrowing racial oppression. As a result, they joined the Atlanta Sociological Laboratory, making it possible for the school to generate substantial scholarly products at minimal costs.

The Du Bois–Atlanta school relied heavily on research conducted by black college students. At Atlanta University, Du Bois trained undergraduate and graduate students to conduct sociological research, often involving fieldwork in numerous cities. Augustus Dill was one of those students. Dill graduated from Atlanta University with a BA in sociology after being mentored by Du Bois. In 1906, Dill earned a second BA at Harvard in 1908 and a master's degree in sociology in 1909 after returning to Atlanta University. In 1910 Atlanta hired Dill as a professor of sociology, replacing Du Bois, who had resigned to work for the NAACP. Du Bois viewed Dill as one of his best students, and Dill admired his mentor, who "had been [his] inspiration Harvard-ward," for his "intellect, ability and staunch principles [that] had meant much to me."[51] Because Dill had learned his research skills from Du Bois, he became coeditor with Du Bois of four Atlanta studies, *The College-Bred Negro, The Common School and the Negro, The Negro American Artisan,* and *Morals and Manners among Negro Americans.*[52] Recounting these achievements, Dill concluded: "It is our belief that these publications have been of inestimable value to the student of general social conditions as well as to the student particularly interested in the problems pertaining to the black folk of America."[53] In 1913 Dill resigned his position at Atlanta to become Du Bois's office manager at the NAACP and to serve as assistant editor of the *Crisis,* a position he held until 1928. In that year, Dill resigned his position with Du Bois after being arrested for engaging in homosexual activity.[54]

Dill was just one of many students Du Bois taught at Atlanta who became researchers for his school. In Du Bois's classes, they studied the black class structure, myriad social and economic conditions, social statistics, and economics, while learning to interpret census data, construct questionnaires, conduct interviews, and observe the social scene using participant observation and ethnography. Du Bois's researchers also included students at numerous other black colleges. These students became providers of liberation capital because they embraced the responsibility of lifting their less fortunate brothers and sisters out of social degradation and believed that careful study of the conditions blacks faced was a necessary step toward liberation. They continued as researchers long after graduating, thus constituting a cadre of individuals who dispatched data to Atlanta to be analyzed and prepared for publication. Du Bois thanked his student researchers, especially those from Atlanta, Fisk, Howard, Lincoln, Hampton, Tuskegee, Meharry, and other black colleges, writing that their cooperation had "been amply vindicated and rewarded by the collection and publication of much valuable material relating to the health of Negroes, their social conditions, their efforts of reform, their business enterprises, their institutions for higher learning and their common schools."[55]

The students, teachers, community leaders and professional sociologists who worked for the Du Bois–Atlanta school were embedded in an intellectual network through which scholarship was produced. In that sense, Merton and Collins are right to argue that intellectual networks and scientific settings such as universities are crucial to producing excellent science. Yet networks and institutional theory err in the assumption that great science can be produced only in elite institutions and networks. For Collins in particular, intellectuals outside the central elite networks of the scientific establishment cannot produce great works because such productions can occur only through placement in a key network that collectively generates outstanding masterpieces. However, the history of Du Bois's school shows a different outcome. While a network was required to produce original scholarship, it was an insurgent network that certainly was not elite, given that it was centered, not in prestigious and wealthy white universities, but in poor black schools on the periphery of academia. The politics and economics of racism prevented Du Bois and his colleagues from developing their school within elite academia. Thus the standard sociological theories about schools of thought fail to enhance our understanding of why great science can go unrecognized by the mainstream because they neglect the interaction between science and political/economic/racial processes.

The variegated alliances that fueled the endeavors of the Du Bois–Atlanta school are best conceptualized as an insurgent intellectual network (IIN). IINs are constructed by subaltern intellectuals who—because of empire, race, class, and/or gender discrimination—are denied access to elite intellectual networks. The structured interactions, communications, and scholarly products of these networks are excluded from the scholarly discourse promoted by establishment institutions. Because of this exclusion from formally recognized intellectual discourse, IINs draw on liberation capital, using the donated resources and volunteer labor of activists to develop and validate counterhegemonic ideas; provide previously untrained students and others with the scholarly tools; create media designed to make this scholarship visible to both scholars and consumers of these ideas; and seize opportunities to challenge and replace dominant paradigms. It was through IINs that Du Bois mobilized the liberation capital that made it possible for him to build an enduring school of scientific sociology. This was an exercise in the traditional black religious dictum "You must make a way out of no way."

However, it would be inaccurate to minimize the negative effects on scholarly enterprises when research funds are blocked by social discrimination and opposing ideologies. Indeed, on one occasion Du Bois, though praising the efforts of the volunteers, went on to warn that "notwithstanding this success the further prosecution of these important studies is greatly hampered by the lack of funds."[56] The use of liberation capital can be crucial for the production of scholarly work, but it cannot ensure that the best scholarship will always be produced. All the other conditions—a charismatic intellectual leader who serves as a model by producing groundbreaking scholarship, an institutional setting providing an infrastructure to conduct and publish research and the availability of minimal amounts of scholars and students who can be recruited into intellectual activities—must be in place to found an intellectual school, especially one pursuing subaltern goals. Further, liberation capital cannot bridge the funding gap indefinitely. It can, however, supply the additional resources necessary to propel the takeoff phase for the intellectual activities of a school of thought. In the concluding chapter I investigate the legacies of the Du Bois–Atlanta school made possible by the labors discussed in this chapter.

CHAPTER 8

Legacies and Conclusions

As this book demonstrates, Du Bois laid the intellectual foundations of his school of scientific sociology by publishing pathbreaking studies incorporating a novel theoretical frame and using a multimethod approach. We have also seen how Du Bois attracted other scholars to his school, including Monroe Work, Richard R. Wright Jr., Edmund Haynes, and Mary Ovington. Yet these pioneering members of Du Bois's school have been forgotten, erased from the collective memory of sociology and social science. A goal of this work has been to make this distinctive school more widely known and to restore its intellectual contributors to their rightful place as founders of modern scientific sociology. We have explored how Du Bois's enterprise worked so that we might uncover the political, economic, and intellectual factors that shape intellectual schools and determine their ability to have long-term influence. A novel finding is that an intellectual nonhegemonic school can emerge outside conventional routes if certain conditions are established. In so doing, such a school can make important, enduring intellectual and political contributions. This final chapter demonstrates that such enterprises can profoundly affect conventional schools and the larger society. Du Bois's school helped shape sociology, especially the study of race.

BEYOND THE FIRST GENERATION

The Du Bois–Atlanta school profoundly influenced sociology and the social sciences. While at times these influences have been acknowledged,

195

in most instances they have been overlooked. It was relatively easy for mainstream sociologists to ignore Du Bois's contributions because these were effectively marginalized by early generations of white sociologists and by succeeding generations who followed the established pattern. As generations of scholars passed, the school no longer required marginalization because the success of earlier efforts had caused it to drop from sight. Yet its intellectual impact could not be erased completely given the merits of its ideas and given that some scholars, especially blacks, documented the significance of Du Bois's work for the historical record and elaborated its scientific paradigm. In a previous essay I assessed the lasting intellectual influence of Du Bois on generations of black scholars who came to maturity after Du Bois's groundbreaking scholarship and journeyed in his footsteps. They, too, conducted research showing that black people had developed their own communities, race consciousness, institutions, and discontent with racial oppression and that they did not wish to be fully assimilated into white culture.[1]

Black sociologists often appear to have been exclusively the students of white sociologists who served as formal advisers at prestigious white universities. Yet I have shown that the first generation of black sociologists was also mentored by Du Bois and his Atlanta school. It may appear that Du Bois and his school operated as an "invisible college" that quietly produced scholarship along subterranean channels. However, for Work, Wright, Haynes, Ovington, and numerous other members of the school, the scholarly work produced at Atlanta was highly visible and influential. These scholars did not view their work as insignificant labor performed on the academic periphery. Nevertheless, racism obscured the vision of white academics, causing them to overlook original sociological work produced early in the twentieth century.

Robert Park received credit for producing the second generation of black sociologists in part because Du Bois left academia to join the leadership at the NAACP. With his exit, the field appeared wide open for white scholars to train black sociologists exclusively. But Du Bois had blazed a path in the study of race for black social scientists, opening the way for them to flesh out the theoretical and methodological frameworks that he had so carefully developed. The most celebrated of "Chicago's" black sociologists, E. Franklin Frazier, who served as the first African American president of the American Sociological Society in 1948, was deeply influenced by the Du Bois–Atlanta school. This student of Park's expressed his appreciation of Du Bois's influence on what is arguably his most important work, *The Negro Family in the United States*, writing to Du Bois in 1939 just after its publication, "I had the University of Chicago Press send to you a copy of my recent book, the Negro family in the United States. In this book I have noted your pioneer contributions to the study of the Negro family. In fact, my feeling in regard to the work which some of us are doing has been that we are building upon a tradition inaugurated by you in the Atlanta Studies."[2] As Frazier's biographer Anthony Platt notes, "Frazier's acknowledgment of Du Bois' influence was not just a polite gesture. His early work on the family was very much indebted to Du Bois, whose 1908 report was essentially a prospectus for further research and analysis. . . . There is little doubt that Frazier derived his worldview and initial research propositions about the family from Du Bois."[3]

St. Clair Drake and Horace Cayton's *The Black Metropolis* is another sociological masterpiece bearing the influence of the Du Bois–Atlanta school.[4] The book focuses on many topics analyzed in *The Philadelphia Negro* and Du Bois's other sociological works. The authors use the color line as an organizing principle of analysis and acknowledge the importance of Du Bois's conception of it. They also acknowledge their debt to *The Philadelphia Negro*, which they describe as "the first important sociological study of a Negro community in the United States,"[5] for their own nuanced elaboration of the class structure in Chicago's black community, noting that "all serious students of Negro communities since Du Bois have been concerned with the nature of social stratification among Negroes and with the relative importance of the various factors upon which power and prestige within Negroes communities are based."[6] In this classic study, Drake and Cayton, like Du Bois earlier, conceptualized race in the United States as a caste system that structured relations between black people as well as between blacks and whites.

Earlier I detailed Du Bois's pioneering analysis of America's system of racial oppression as a caste system. Lloyd Warner did not take up this idea until over three decades later, yet in social science's collective memory he is unjustifiably credited with having introduced this concept into race literature.[7] It was Du Bois's caste analysis that attracted Max Weber's attention, leading him to request that Du Bois prepare an essay on the topic for publication in his journal in 1906. Additionally, Du Bois's caste formulation assisted Weber in sharpening his analysis of caste stratification. Again, because of race marginalization, the Du Bois–Atlanta school had performed the heavy lifting, only to have the intellectual credit given to white scholars occupying prestigious positions in elite universities.

DU BOIS'S MARGINALIZATION: *AN AMERICAN DILEMMA* AND THE *ENCYCLOPEDIA OF THE NEGRO*

The Du Bois–Atlanta school helped shape the most famous and influential study of race ever produced: Gunnar Myrdal's *An American Dilemma: The Negro Problem and Modern Democracy* (1944).[8] Myrdal's book influenced Supreme Court decisions and shifted racial perspectives of many Americans. It became a classic in social science and remains a landmark study still consulted on matters of race. *Dilemma* was the most comprehensive study of blacks and race produced at the time: it made available reams of data useful for understanding race in mid-twentieth-century America. But its most important achievement was its political message: that white Americans were being hypocritical because they believed in democratic ideals but treated blacks extremely undemocratically. This was unsettling to the book's audience because the messenger was a white European social scientist who boldly exposed the contradiction with evidence not easily disputed. For blacks, the message confirmed what they already knew and suggested that they could do little to change their oppressive conditions. On balance, *Dilemma* was valuable to the nation because it brought new ideas to the table regarding racial discrimination.

Yet the history of the book's making provides an illuminating story of how white scholars and philanthropists denied Du Bois a seat at the high table of scholarship. Indeed, the funding and publication of this heralded study greatly contributed to the marginalization and silencing of Du Bois's scholarship.

Myrdal was well positioned to execute the study, given his sterling academic credentials. He was a distinguished Swedish economist and a broad-minded social scientist with expertise in sociology. He was a successful politician, having served in the Swedish Senate and as a minister of commerce. Yet Myrdal confided he previously had given hardly a thought to America's race problem. Given his lack of familiarity, this white European was not an obvious choice to produce a comprehensive study of such a vexing and complicated issue. Besides, when research was launched for *Dilemma,* distinguished African American scholars could have been chosen, including the great historian Carter G. Woodson and the prominent sociologist E. Franklin Frazier, whose scholarly achievements had won him election as the first black president of the American Sociological Society in 1949. Moreover, there was Du Bois, the most accomplished race scholar in the United States for nearly half a century. These social scientists were committed to understanding race because they believed scientific knowledge could be used to dismantle oppression. For them, "race relations" was not an abstraction but a reality that attacked their personhood and limited their life chances even though they were elite members of their race.

There were also some accomplished white race scholars, including Melville Herskovits, Howard Odum, and Guy Johnson, who could have conducted the study. Although beneficiaries of racial oppression, they had a stake in "race relations" because they were immersed in its turmoil and, as social scientists, were expected to interpret America's race problem. Yet the Carnegie Foundation, in collaboration with other foundations, including the Rockefeller Foundation and the General Education Board (GEB), a conglomerate of several foundations supporting educational initiatives, chose a Swedish economist, Gunnar Myrdal, to conduct the study rather than any American, black or white. Carnegie provided the extensive resources necessary to execute the project: $250,000, an enormous sum for the period.

The Carnegie Foundation had deep interest in funding a comprehensive study on race during the World War II period. The explosiveness of race was exacerbated as the Allied Forces geared up to defeat Hitler's forces, which were tenaciously pursuing white Aryan supremacy. African Americans were restless as they confronted lynching and racial degradation while their men donned the uniform to fight racism in a segregated military. The fear of riots and other racial conflagrations hung heavy in the air. Because these tensions concerned the philanthropic community, it prepared to open its coffers to fund a comprehensive race study.

For decades, Du Bois had pleaded with foundations to fund his own proposed comprehensive race study, an *Encyclopedia of the Negro* that would analyze blacks throughout the world while adhering to the highest scientific standards. In keeping with the overarching conceptual scheme of his school, Du Bois believed that a massive scientific study would prove once and for all that blacks were not inferior and subhuman. While Du Bois proposed to serve as editor-in-chief of the *Encyclopedia*, his board members and contributing scholars would be interracial and recruited from around the world. Du Bois had sought funding for this project for two and half decades, only to be denied by the philanthropic community. In the early 1930s, his hopes for launching his grand idea were rejuvenated, given foundations' new interest in funding such a major study.

The Phelps-Stokes Fund initiated a movement in 1932 to produce an encyclopedia on the Negro. Black scholars familiar with Du Bois's long-standing efforts to initiate the production of just such an encyclopedia were startled to learn that he had not been invited to help lay the conceptual foundations for the project. After they protested, Du Bois was invited to join the group at its second meeting and was elected as chief editor. Du Bois was well positioned to make rapid progress on the encyclopedia because of his preliminary work and his worldwide scholarly contacts. As he recounted: "In 1934 I was chosen to act as editor-in-chief of a new project of the Phelps-Stokes Fund to prepare and publish an *Encyclopedia of the Negro*. I spent nearly ten years of intermittent effort on this project and secured cooperation from many scholars, white and black, in America, Europe and Africa."[9] Shari Cohen described the work Du Bois had accomplished:

> Du Bois planned a four-volume encyclopedia, each volume comprising 500,000 words. Just as he had done in 1909, he secured the cooperation of an impressive array of scholars, including Charles Beard, Franz Boas, John R. Connors, Edith Abbott, Felix Frankfurter, Otto Klineburg, Carl Van Doren, H. L. Mencken, Roscoe Pound, Robert E. Park, Sidney Hook, Harold Laski, Broadus Mitchell, "and scores of others," as Du Bois put it in a letter to the historian Charles Wesley. Du Bois's "Encyclopædia of the Negro" would require a budget of $225,000. It would be written by a staff of between "25 and 100 persons" hired to be "research aides," to be located in editorial offices to be established in New York, Chicago, Atlanta, and New Orleans. They would prepare bibliographies, collect books and manuscripts, and gather and write "special data" and shorter entries. Black and white scholars, primarily located in Europe, America, and Africa, would write longer interpretive entries.[10]

In 1937, Du Bois secured pledges of $125,000 from the Phelps-Stokes Foundation to provide half the funds for the encyclopedia. Du Bois applied to the GEB for the remaining half of the budget. The Rockefeller-controlled GEB rejected Du Bois's proposal. Yet Du Bois was confident the Carnegie Foundation would cover the outstanding funds, and all signals appeared positive for that outcome. As Du Bois sensed his dream of an encyclopedia reconceptualizing the global race problem was close to fulfillment, his spirits soared. But it was not to be.

Rumblings of discontent from influential, well-connected white scholars were being voiced behind Du Bois's back. Questions of his scientific competence were raised. Melville Herskovits's biographer

Jerry Gershenhorn recounts that "almost immediately Du Bois became the center of controversy as the white-controlled philanthropies and several white scholars expressed doubts about his objectivity. In order to offset Du Bois' authority as editor, the board of directors of the project set up an advisory board dominated by whites as a check on the project's, and particularly Du Bois's, perceived propagandistic tendencies."[11] As the opposition intensified, officials at the Carnegie Foundation fretted over Du Bois's alleged lack of objectivity and scholarly detachment. They worried that any American scholar, black or white, would be too emotional to produce a sufficiently scientific and objective study but considered Du Bois in particular, as a defiant political Negro, to be a liability in this regard.[12] Ironically, these accusations were hurled at a reserved scholar who spoke in measured New England tones and who was perceived by students, scholars, and activists alike as aloof. But there was another burning concern: Du Bois's radical activism shook up white scholars and conservative foundation elites, exposing their commitment to the racial status quo.

Surreptitious attacks by Melville Herskovits and Thomas Jesse Jones designed to derail Du Bois's encyclopedia exemplified the racism that mobilized white scholars to delegitimate him. Herskovits was a Jewish anthropologist mentored by Franz Boas at Columbia University. After receiving the doctorate he became an assistant professor at Howard University in 1925. He moved to Northwestern University as an assistant professor of sociology in 1927, achieving full professorship in 1935. In 1938, he helped organize the department of anthropology at Northwestern and began serving as its first chairman. In 1948, Herskovits founded the first program of African studies in the United States at Northwestern and began serving as its first director. In 1954, he was instrumental in establishing the Melville J. Herskovits Library of African Studies, the largest Africana collection in the world. In 1957, Herskovits founded the national African Studies Association and served as its first president. Like the work of his mentor Boas, Herskovits's scholarship sought to prove that blacks were not naturally inferior and that African Americans were beneficiaries of an African cultural heritage that had survived the vicissitudes of slavery and Jim Crow. While Du Bois had pioneered this line of argument, Herskovits has tended to receive the lion's share of credit as its originator. Herskovits's "African survival" argument broke with the views of the Chicago school as expressed by Robert Park and Park's most famous black student, E. Franklin Frazier. In fact, Herskovits became famous when he debated

Frazier, arguing that the latter's claim that African culture was destroyed by slavery was inaccurate and that his research and publications proved Frazier wrong on this critical point. Descendants of Africa, argued Herskovits, were creative and resilient precisely because they retained elements of African culture.

Yet despite his organization building in African studies, and his progressive thesis about blacks, Herskovits believed that black scholars could not be trusted to conduct objective scholarship on blacks and race because they were too emotionally engaged with these topics and because they violated the basic scientific law not to mix activism with scholarship. Herskovits felt that black scholars, given these defects, should not be left alone to develop scholarship in this field; they needed to be supervised and guided by white scholars.[13] Thus he was disturbed by the prospect that Du Bois and his fellow "emotional black scholars" could take charge of an encyclopedia on black people. Because of his views, Herskovits was placed on the white-dominated advisory board of the encyclopedia to keep Du Bois in check. Gershenhorn explains that Herskovits "received an appointment as one of the two representatives . . . on the advisory board. Herskovits, who apparently did not seek the appointment, was brought on board to counter Du Bois and Stokes [president of the Phelps-Stokes Fund], who were perceived as not sufficiently committed to detached scholarship. Waldo Leland of the ACLS [American Council of Learned Societies] questioned the project coordinators' commitment to objectivity and applauded Herskovits's appointment as necessary to enforce a strong commitment to objectivity."[14]

Herskovits wasted little time using his position to "derail efforts by the encyclopedia board to move the project forward."[15] He argued that Du Bois's proposed study was unscientific.[16] Herskovits pretended publicly to support Du Bois and the encyclopedia initiative. Yet "despite his support for black participation and his promise of cooperation to Du Bois, Herskovits moved to undercut him."[17] Herskovits warned the funders that "the encyclopedia would be 'loaded with propaganda, considering . . . the people who are most active in it.'"[18] Gershenhorn concludes, "In making this accusation, Herskovits particularly targeted Du Bois, noting that 'neither Du Bois nor most members of the backing crew are scientists at all, but uplifters.'"[19] Years later, Herskovits admitted he was the 'hatchet man' who had killed the project.[20] However, the "hatchet man" was assisted by others, most notably Thomas Jesse Jones.

Jones was born in Wales in 1873 and moved to Middleport, Ohio, in 1884. He earned an MA and a PhD in sociology at Columbia University in 1899 and 1904 respectively under Franklin H. Giddings, a founder of American sociology who held the discipline's first endowed chair. As mentor, Giddings exercised a decisive influence over Jones intellectually and politically. As pointed out earlier, Giddings was a racist and an influential member and adviser of the American eugenics movement. He believed that Anglo Saxons were a superior race and that the new science of sociology would enable him to discover scientific laws demonstrating the inevitability of naturally derived race hierarchies. Giddings's views contrasted sharply with those of Du Bois's school, which maintained that races and racial hierarchies were socially constructed rather than "natural." Jones was a loyal mentee who internalized his mentor's racial biases, especially claims that people of color were racially inferior.

Jones proved to be one of Giddings's most influential students. In 1902, he moved to Hampton University as associate chaplain and head of the economics and missionary Department. By 1904, he was promoted to head of the department of sociology and history. After leaving Hampton in 1909, Jones worked for the US Census collecting statistics on blacks. By 1913, he moved to the Phelps-Stokes Fund, where he worked for thirty-three years, securing the important educational directorship in 1917 and holding it until 1946. In 1917 Jones published the two-volume influential report *Negro Education: A Study of the Private and Higher Schools for Colored People in the United States*, which greatly determined which policies for black higher education were supported by the philanthropic community.[21] In 1932 he served as a lecturer at South African Universities for the Carnegie Foundation. Through these networks, Jones became influential in the philanthropic community especially in matters pertaining to race in both the United States and sub-Saharan Africa.[22]

At Hampton, Jones promoted industrial education for blacks, as did Hampton's famous alum Booker T. Washington and the school's founder and Washington's mentor, Samuel Armstrong. Jones added a new modification to industrial education by developing a social studies curriculum that was based on the racial doctrines of Giddings.[23] It taught that the new science of sociology revealed races had different dispositions and mental and moral characteristics.[24] Blacks and Indians were disadvantaged by an evolutionary lag and peculiar historical circumstances unrelated to oppression. Jones instructed people of color to accept their subordination as a natural outcome. The newly enlightened pupil, "instead of regarding the difficulties of his race as the oppression of a weaker by the stronger, . . . interprets them as the natural difficulties that almost every race has been compelled to overcome in its upward movement."[25] Jones counseled blacks to avoid politics and activism because they were incapable of altering natural evolutionary processes. In his view, colonialism was advantageous for Asia and Africa because it enabled whites to bring civilization to those backward continents. Thus blacks required industrial education and guidance from whites to successfully adjust to suitable roles assigned by superior whites. In *Negro Education,* Jones advocated for black colleges and universities to abandon liberal arts, considering the impossibility of teaching such subjects to people incapable of abstract thought. Jones's educational ideology was endorsed by southern white elites and supported by philanthropic funds. Indeed, Jones "was regarded with enormous respect by the educational, business and political leaders of the first half of this century. Jones's support among the educational and philanthropic elites is evident from the fact that various foundations paid his salaries for most of his life."[26]

By the time Jones had elaborated his educational policy, Du Bois was a seasoned critic of industrial education as panacea for black subordination, having conducted years of sustained attacks against Washington, who had initiated the strategy as the way for blacks to climb up from slavery. In Du Bois's view, Jones's *Negro Education* report was a dangerous and unfortunate publication.[27] Its advocacy of industrial training as the sole education for black people would forever doom them to be compliant laborers not substantively different than those who had toiled as slaves. Du Bois lashed out at Jones and his policies in editorials and forums, deploring the undemocratic and retrogressive qualities of an industrial education that replaced liberal arts. Du Bois warned that "such a curriculum would 'make Socrates a fool and Jesus Christ a crank' ... and would guarantee that young blacks would 'dream of cornbread and molasses.'"[28] Du Bois critically engaged Jones repeatedly, labeling him an evil genius of the Negro. Indeed, one scholar has described Du Bois's and Jones's lives as constantly criss-crossing and intertwining like a cultural double helix.[29] David Levering Lewis describes Jones as Du Bois's nemesis and claims that the feeling was mutual: as far as Jones was concerned, Du Bois was the definition of radicalism, a brilliant troublemaker bloated with racial pride and devoid of political common sense.[30]

Du Bois, the leading black sociologist, was joined by Carter G. Woodson, the leading black historian, in a sustained battle against Jones's educational recommendations.[31] Woodson, who became known as the "Father of Black History," was born a decade after slavery and earned his bachelor's and master's from the University of Chicago. In 1912, Woodson earned a doctorate from Harvard University, making him the second African American to receive a Harvard PhD following Du Bois. He organized the Association for the Study of Negro Life and History in 1915, founded the *Journal of Negro History* in 1916, established the black-owned Associated Publisher Press in 1921, and created "Negro History Week" in 1926. Woodson was a prolific historian who wrote over a dozen books and numerous articles and other publications.[32] He described initiatives like Jones's as a white-sponsored education designed to miseducate the Negro and instill a sense of inferiority that would make him accept an inferior status and even seek it out: it would be unnecessary to "send him to the back door," since he would "go without being told."[33]

Jones utilized his institutional positions to attack his adversaries, both of whom were committed to producing a black encyclopedia.[34] His first maneuver was to exclude both Du Bois and Woodson from the organizational meeting for the encyclopedia initiated by the Phelps-Stokes Fund. He was aided in this clandestine effort by his protégé Thomas J. Woofter Jr., who had received his doctorate from Giddings in the 1920s. Woofter joined Jones in the foundation world, helping to administer educational grants and promote harmonious unequal relations between southern blacks and whites. Woofter considered himself a leading liberal who promoted black improvement. The views of black scholars contradicted Woofter's self-appraisal, however. W.M. Brewer, editor of the *Journal of Negro History*, made this clear when he reviewed Woofter's book *Southern Race Progress, the Wavering Color Line*. Unfortunately, Brewer noted, Woofter "came under the indoctrination of Thomas Jesse Jones, Director of the Phelps-Stokes Fund and the most evil person that touched Negro life from 1902–1950! The author was Jones's colleague and field investigator of colored education in the south. . . . Woofter, like his mentor and sponsor Jones, also became a white professional leader of colored people. The roles of such leaders were misnomers without any choice of colored people and, therefore, imposed. What is narrated throughout this reporting is crass benevolent paternalism because Jones and Woofter felt no responsibility to the Negroes."[35] E. Franklin Frazier similarly argued that Woofter's book *The Basis of Racial Adjustment* was nothing less than rationalization of the southern white position.[36] And Du Bois's review of Woofter's *Black Yeomanry: Life on St. Helena Island* scathingly characterized it as a "line of so-called sociological research for which there was absolutely no need."[37] Jones's and

Woofter's shared resentments against Du Bois and Woodson united them as a team dedicated to denying funding for the *Encyclopedia*.

The two hatched the plan not to invite Du Bois and Woodson to the first meeting held by the Phelps-Stokes Foundation to explore the encyclopedia project. It was a bold effort because the potential funders were taking up what had originally been Du Bois's idea and because the black scholars who were invited were aware of Du Bois's encyclopedia dream and his previous efforts to realize it. Jones and Woofter took the risk that the snubs would draw resistance because their long-run strategy was to silence Du Bois. As David Levering Lewis notes, "Permanent exclusion of Du Bois from the project was highly untenable, but . . . by not inviting him to the start-up meeting, Jones and Woofter could count on having a far freer hand in concretizing the project's agenda and personnel."[38]

The plan worked because it sowed suspicions in the philanthropic community that Du Bois was a radical race propagandist unable to generate objective scholarship. On the white left wing, Herskovits pushed the same ideas to prevent Du Bois from triumphing. So although Du Bois did participate in the second meeting and was made chief editor of the encyclopedia, by the time he presented his funding proposal to the GEB, the sentiment that he was not scientific was widespread among the foundations, causing them to reject Du Bois's proposal. This outcome meant the project was not likely to survive because the majority of the available funders fell in line with the GEB. Thus Du Bois was denied his scientific dream. The attacks led by sociologists and a sociologically oriented anthropologist demonstrated that white social scientists were not willing to accept him into their fraternity. Du Bois's final hope that officials of the Carnegie Foundation would bail him out was dashed when they too got wind of the allegations targeting Du Bois and rejected the encyclopedia. As Gershenhorn points out, this denial of funding to an eminent black scholar exemplifies a broader agenda of racial politics: "the desire of the white-controlled foundations to circumscribe the permissible bounds of knowledge. According to white arbiters of 'legitimate' scholarship, a Negro encyclopedia would be inflammatory, inferior, inappropriate, incomplete, and insignificant."[39]

Du Bois did make a last-ditch attempt to overcome defeat and accommodate the concerns of the Phelps-Stokes Foundation by agreeing to have a white deputy editor. He first chose Robert E. Park because of his stature in social science. In 1936 Stokes wrote Park that Du Bois strongly favored him for the position and asked whether Park "would be willing to serve as one of the two editors, with Dr. Du Bois as Chairman, in helping to organize the material for the Encyclopedia."[40] His participation would be crucial, Stokes went on, because "a majority of the board has felt from the first, as I think now that all on the Board feel clearly, that it is advisable to have a white scholar of standing and known fairness on Negro problems associated with Dr. Du Bois so as to make people realize that the Encyclopedia will be entirely objective in its treatment of all Negro interracial matters."[41]

Because Park was a famous white scholar, Stokes raised no concerns about his scientific objectivity; it was assumed. However, Stokes did raise the issue of Park's advancing age given that he was seventy-two at the time of the invitation. Park acknowledged that his age was a problem: "I am bound to confess that such scholarship as I may have possessed is fast ebbing. My memory is breaking up like the ice in the river in spring and is rapidly moving out to oblivion." Yet despite senility, Park could not pass over the opportunity to keep Du Bois in check, even if he had to take a position subordinate to Du Bois; he responded to Stokes, "I note what you say as to the advisability of having 'a white scholar of standing and known fairness on Negro problems associated with Dr. Du Bois'"[42] and agreed to serve on Stokes's condition that if age became a problem he would resign. In less than two years, Park resigned from the position, only to be replaced by another white sociologist, Guy Johnson.[43]

Even this accommodation was not enough because white scholars knew Du Bois would control the intellectual substance of the encyclopedia, as he had controlled the content of the Crisis as its editor. As early as 1931, Du Bois had signaled his intentions in a letter to his colleague James Dillard: "As, of course, you realize, I could not for a moment contemplate a Negro encyclopedia dominated and controlled by Thomas Jesse Jones and Mr. Woofter. I do not, of course, want to exclude them or what they represent, but a Negro encyclopedia that was not in the main edited and written by Negroes would be as inconceivable as a Catholic encyclopedia projected by Protestants."[44] Consequently even the appointment of white associates could not mitigate the threat that Du Bois posed, and the project, bereft of white scholars' and philanthropists' support and funding, came to naught.

Myrdal's study supplanted it precisely because the Carnegie Foundation decided to pursue a different direction than Du Bois's proposed Encyclopedia. Nervousness over Du Bois's radicalism and allegations he and his black colleagues lacked scientific objectivity suggested the need for a new study led by a white scientist from outside the United States.

As Shari Cohen concluded, "In opting to look for a foreigner to do the study, Keppel consciously overlooked another project that was being considered for funding at the time—the Encyclopedia of the Negro. . . . It did not however, meet Keppel's criteria of objectivity given DuBois' two decades of civil rights advocacy in the NAACP."[45] According to Lewis, the foundations were looking for an alternative to the *Encyclopedia* that would provide "satisfactory management of the so-called American dilemma by financing and legitimating a new master theorem of race relations that was interpretively progressive but not socially destabilizing."[46] Lewis concluded, "Within a remarkably short time, the study of the Negro . . . found a quite different direction under a Swedish scholar then unknown in the field of race relations, one whose understanding of American race problems was to be distinctly more psychological and less economic than was Du Bois's."[47]

Unlike Du Bois, Myrdal received from Carnegie the financial resources he had requested. Carnegie's president wrote, "It was understood that he should be free to appoint and organize a staff of his own selection in the United States and that he should draw upon the experience of other scholars and experts in less formal fashion."[48] Myrdal acknowledged that "all decisions on practical and financial matters have been taken on the responsibility of the Corporation. The Trustees of the Corporation have been most generous and prompt in appropriating necessary funds for the study."[49] Upon naming Myrdal study director, Keppel rented the forty-sixth floor of the downtown Manhattan Chrysler Building for him so he could set up shop there.[50] Myrdal was given resources to hire as researchers expert black and white social scientists including E. Franklin Frazier, Kenneth Clark, Ralph Bunche, Herskovits, and Woofter. Some of them produced book-length memoranda that served as source materials of data and analysis for *Dilemma*. Apart from Booker Washington, black scholars could not typically obtain this level of funding. Bunche, for example, said of Myrdal's project, "I have had a project on this subject worked out in outline for some years now, but could never get started on it for lack of funds." Although he at first was reluctant to postpone work on his own South African study, the future Nobel Prize winner eventually joined Myrdal's staff and became his director of research and most prolific collaborator.[51]

The racism that prevented funding of black scholars aborted many scholarly ideas during the twentieth century, but it was not a problem the white Swedish economist encountered. In fact, Myrdal believed that Carnegie's selection of himself showed wisdom and openness: "Many will deem it a foolish idea. But more fundamentally it is a new demonstration, in a minor matter, of American moralism, rationalism, and optimism—and a demonstration of America's unfailing conviction of its basic soundness and strength."[52] In addition to supplying Myrdal with ample financial resources, Carnegie's president made clear that Myrdal had full and final say because "the report as finally drawn up and presented to the public should represent and portray his [Myrdal's] own decisions, alike in the selection of data and in the conclusions as to their relative importance."[53]

Ultimately the extensive research of Myrdal and his staff resulted in a groundbreaking work of nearly fifteen hundred pages. Its range and depth were remarkable because Myrdal utilized America's best social scientists to conduct the research and provide analyses of complex race phenomena. Every conceivable aspect of the topic was explored, including economics, politics, religion, ideologies, stratification, education, psychological processes, and sexual behavior. Following in Du Bois's footsteps and those of black scholars influenced by Du Bois, Myrdal studied the black community as a topic in its own right, providing analyses of its institutions, culture, and internal stratification. Because Myrdal had been trained as a member of Stockholm's School of Economics, he stressed theoretical clarity as crucial to understanding massive data collected to unravel human behavior. Although *Dilemma* was steeped in data, its theoretical framework made the book famous and compelling. Readers did not walk away confused over the study's theoretical argument because its provocative thesis was laid out for all to see. The book's introduction presented it in italics: *"The American Negro problem is a problem in the heart of the American. It is there that the interracial tension has its focus. It is there that the decisive struggle goes on. This is the central viewpoint of this treatise. Though our study includes economic, social, and political race relations, at bottom our problem is the moral dilemma of the American—the conflict between his moral valuations on various levels of consciousness and generality."*[54]

For Myrdal, America's race problem did not stem from economic exploitation wielded by the dominant white group to advance their material interests. Nor was the problem an outcome of political inequality, where power rested in the hands of whites while blacks experienced disenfranchisement and were prevented from enjoying privileges and protections provided for members of the polity. Rather, the origin and perpetuation of the race problem for Myrdal was in essence moral. Moral conflict was the issue, not the actual system of oppression. Ideals, rather than material and structural factors, thus played the dominant role in determining the social dynamics of America.[55]

A second crucial component of Myrdal's theory was that it located power and agency only in the oppressor group. Expounding on this position, Myrdal argued:

> It is thus the white majority group that naturally determines the Negro's "place." All our attempts to reach scientific explanations of why the Negroes are what they are and why they live as they do have regularly led to determinants on the white side of the race line. In the practical and political struggles of effecting changes, the views and attitudes of the white Americans are likewise strategic. The Negro's entire life, and, consequently, also his opinions on the Negro problem, are, in the main, to be considered as secondary reactions to more primary pressures from the side of the dominant white majority.[56]

For Myrdal, therefore, the race problem was the white man's burden, and whites' actions alone would decide whether blacks remained subjugated or liberated.

A third and final component of Myrdal's theory was that black people had an inferior, pathological culture: *"In practically all its divergences, American Negro culture is not something independent of general American culture. It is a distorted development, or a pathological condition, of the general American culture."*[57] While Myrdal discerned little value in black culture, he sought to put the matter positively: *"We assume that it is to the advantage of American Negroes as individuals and as a group to become assimilated into American culture, to acquire the traits held in esteem by the dominant white Americans. This will be the value premise here."*[58]

Myrdal was aware of Franz Boas's claim that human cultures could be judged only on their own terms and not in relation to each other, so that one could not be superior to another, but he attempted to dance around this challenge. Boas's cultural relativism, he claimed, was "a wholesome antidote to arrogant and erroneous ideas bound up with white people's false racial beliefs and their justification of caste. But it does not gainsay our assumption that *here, in America*, American culture is 'highest' in the pragmatic sense that adherence to it is practical for any individual or group which is not strong enough to change it."[59]

In hindsight, it is clear that Myrdal erred in crucial respects given future developments and that outcomes in race relations diverged drastically from the predictions and analyses of *Dilemma*. First of all, the system of racial domination had to be forced to change by political and economic action on the part of the oppressed. That change came not from a resolution of moral tensions in the white mind but from the political action initiated by oppressed blacks in the civil rights and Black Power movements. Moreover, those struggles were driven by a creative black culture and its institutions that infused black protest movements. In short, it was the agency of black people that overthrew major dimensions of the Negro problem that occupied Myrdal's attention.

Myrdal's analytic failures can be traced to the intellectual and political biases he brought to his study. In this respect, he and the Carnegie Foundation officials were mistaken that their imported scholar had landed on the forty-sixth floor of the Chrysler Building with a fresh mind ready to perform purely objective social analysis. White European scholars of the twentieth century such as Gunnar Myrdal also harbored emotional commitments and attachments to certain values, even though Keppel could not discern them precisely because he shared them with the outside scholar. I shall dissect Myrdal's biases and suggest that this particular constellation of errors would not have marred Du Bois's *Encyclopedia*.

Myrdal imposed a preconceived theoretical causal model on the "Negro problem" that he sought to explain in *Dilemma*. It claimed that sociological dynamics were generated equally by multiple reciprocal causes: "A deeper reason for the unity of the Negro problem will be apparent when we now try to formulate our hypothesis concerning its dynamic causation. The mechanism that operates here is the 'principle of cumulation,' also commonly called the 'vicious circle.' . . . Throughout this inquiry, we shall assume a general interdependence between all the factors in the Negro problem. White prejudice and discrimination keep the Negro low in standards of living, health, education, manners and morals. This, in its turn, gives support to white prejudice. White prejudice and Negro standards thus mutually 'cause' each other."[60] By this reasoning, black and white actions equally caused the Negro problem, although one group exercised near-complete power over the other. In this view, white economic and political interests did not disproportionately determine the oppression blacks had experienced for centuries. Myrdal absorbed cumulative causation theory while studying in the 1920s for his doctorate at Stockholm University, where he had come under the influence of that school's leading economist, Knut Wicksell, who developed cumulative process analysis.[61] This theory sought to account for how money markets attained equilibrium. Because Myrdal was publishing on cumulative causation theory by 1931, it is clear he was thoroughly familiar and committed to it as a form of analysis long before *Dilemma* was published. Moreover, in pursuing this line of analysis, "Myrdal's approach emphasized the role of values and the importance of noneconomic factors. He saw interdependence between economic and noneconomic factors and criticized the neglect of noneconomic factors by most economists."[62] Thus when Myrdal began researching *Dilemma* he was already inclined theoretically to assign all relevant variables equal weight, viewing them as operating in a vicious circle, rather than to establish causal significance through research and measurement. He was also predisposed to emphasize ideals over material interests.

Myrdal also came to the project with a pro-Western white bias. In particular, he had come to love America as a great society of the West. His admiration had developed while Myrdal and his wife Alva spent time in America as Rockefeller Fellows in 1929–30. As pointed out by Gene Roberts and Hank Klibanoff: "In *Kontakt*, published in 1941, the Myrdals argued that Swedes had much to learn from America about democracy, dialogue, and self-criticism. 'The secret,' they wrote, 'is that America, ahead of every other country in the whole Western world, large or small, has a living system of expressed ideals for human cooperation which is unified, stable and clearly formulated.'"[63]

In the preface to *Dilemma*, Myrdal wrote, "The author . . . loves and admires America next to his own country."[64] Clearly, Myrdal found America's expressed principles—the American creed—endearing and embraced them as ideals worthy to be emulated throughout the West. Consequently he looked to these ideals as the place from which to initiate his theoretical analysis of the Negro problem. If Myrdal had fixed his sights on how white America had engaged in Native American genocide and structured racism to build an economic empire rivaling that of western Europe, it is quite possible that the Swedish economist would have reached different theoretical conclusions as to the engines of American racism. What is clear is that Myrdal's preestablished emotional attachment to the American creed influenced the theoretical vision of *Dilemma*.

Myrdal's Western biases surely influenced his view of African American culture, leading him to view it as distorted and pathological in comparison to white culture. While criticizing Park and other white scholars for their misleading claims of value neutrality, he embraced their arguments that black American culture was an inferior copy of white culture that needed to be jettisoned in favor of that of the superior whites.

Myrdal rejected the analyses of Du Bois and Herskovits that African American culture possessed unique, creative dimensions because it was spiced with cultural ingredients from African ancestral lands and with the endogenous creativity of African Americans. Myrdal chose to side with the soon-to-be discredited arguments espoused by scholars who claimed that blacks were unlike (and inferior to) white ethnic groups because they were culturally adrift with no anchors in prior traditions. Myrdal's argument was consistent with the contention of racist American social scientists that blacks' only hope for a meaningful future was to seek assimilation and lose themselves in a cultural sea of whiteness. Agency was to be found in whiteness.

Myrdal also shared these white social scientists' view that oppression of blacks would lessen over time because of the favorable workings of the minds of white people. For Myrdal, the crux of the Negro problem existed in white people's values and attitudes. Myrdal thus wrote in his study's final chapter, "We started by stating the hypothesis that the Negro problem has its existence in the American's mind. There the decisive struggle goes on. It is there that the changes occur."[65] Prejudiced beliefs were not only irrational but inconsistent with the American creed. Myrdal argued that whites would inevitably act to change their irrational racial beliefs because they wanted to be right and not to feel ashamed of acting incongruently with their most cherished values. Early in his massive tome, Myrdal, convinced of the goodness of white people, gazed at the black future optimistically: "One main conclusion—which should be stressed here since it cannot be reiterated through the whole book—is this: that not since Reconstruction has there been more reason to anticipate fundamental changes in American race relations, changes which will involve a development toward the American ideals."[66] Because black people had experienced centuries of white "goodness," however, they decided that rattlesnakes did not commit suicide.[67] Acting on "rattlesnake logic," black people organized the civil rights movement, whose protests jarringly thrust the nation into closer congruence with the American creed.

Informed speculation suggests how Du Bois's *Encyclopedia* would have compared to *Dilemma*. It would have rejected any theoretical argument claiming that all relevant factors contributed equally to black oppression. Du Bois's own work made clear that white racism based on economic exploitation and political disenfranchisement of blacks produced the color line erected throughout the world by whites to foster white dominance. Du Bois did emphasize the role of values in social life.

But those values consisted of a racial ideology maintaining that white people deserved to rule over blacks because white skin endowed them with certain inalienable rights that had to be respected, whereas black skin endowed blacks with no rights that whites were bound to respect. Thus for Du Bois material and ideal interests were inextricably linked, and both had to be overturned if people of color were to breathe free in America and throughout the diaspora. The *Encyclopedia* would have been a theoretical voyage in political sociology rather than the exercise in white psychology enacted by *Dilemma*.

Myrdal, though he diverged from white American scholars in arguing that social science was not "value free" and should play an interventionist role in addressing the race problem, did agree with Robert Park and the Chicago school on a crucial matter: race was the white man's burden, and blacks, because of racial inferiority, did not possess the agency to address their own oppression. Du Bois, in contrast, would have located robust agency to produce social change within the oppressed black community. He would have considered it pure nonsense for blacks to wait for change that would occur with the resolution of white psychological tensions. Indeed, the defining characteristic of Du Bois's scholarship and activism was his unswerving adherence to the view that the oppressed had agency. For him, African Americans had a duty to press for change through ceaseless protest and agitation. Du Bois's work documented the importance of black participation in the Civil War for the overthrow of slavery and the major contributions that blacks made to the nation during Reconstruction and beyond.[68] Given his awareness of black agency, Du Bois argued that African Americans had made unique gifts to America and the world that no other group was capable of contributing.[69] While *Dilemma* embraced the greatness of white agency, Du Bois urged blacks to revive their historic agency and slay white oppression. David Levering Lewis has captured how the two volumes would have differed on the agency question: "The Myrdalian paradigm held that the American race problem was a problem in the mind of the American white man, his to solve! Can you think of a controlling idea more antithetical to Du Bois?"[70]

Myrdal's dismissal of black agency impoverished his portrayal of a whole people, as the black novelist Ralph Ellison pointed out: "Can a people ... live and develop for over three hundred years simply by *reacting*? Are American Negroes simply the creation of white men, or have they at least helped to create themselves out of what they found around them? Men have made a way of life in caves and upon cliffs;

why cannot Negroes have made a life upon the horns of the white man's dilemma?"[71] And Myrdal's assumptions even led him to misread his own data. Following in Du Bois's footsteps, *Dilemma* analyzed the organizations and institutions of the black community, ranging from black protest organizations to churches and social clubs. Myrdal's rich data from those explorations suggested that the black community did indeed possess agency-laden institutions and cultural capital.[72] Yet Myrdal conceptualized these indigenous forces as conveyors of a pathological and distorted black culture. When he discovered that blacks belonged to more organizations than whites, Myrdal, instead of interpreting this finding as evidence of black organizational capacity, argued that these high rates of organizational participation meant blacks were simply imitating whites by joining organizations. Yet for Myrdal this imitation went overboard, causing blacks to become exaggerated Americans. By denying agency to African Americans, Myrdal claimed that only whites could initiate racial change because blacks were restricted to merely reacting to their racial superiors.

Last, both Du Bois's and Myrdal's volumes would have expressed each author's emotional commitments. The European's emotional commitment to black American equality was front and center in *Dilemma* because it would have enabled the greatest of Western nations to resolve fundamental conflicts with its noble creed. And the emotional commitment of the descendant of Africa to black American equality would have been front and center in the *Encyclopedia* because it would have struck a strategic blow to global racial oppression. The pity of it all was that racism prevented the two volumes from appearing together, revealing the distinct insights of two studies that emerged from different theoretical standpoints and emotional energies.

THE DU BOIS–ATLANTA SCHOOL, *AN AMERICAN DILEMMA*, AND BEYOND

An American Dilemma was deeply influenced by Du Bois's scholarship. Even after being denied his *Encyclopedia,* Du Bois responded favorably to Myrdal's request to review the initial prospectus for *Dilemma.* No stranger to rejection, Du Bois took the high road, telling Myrdal, "It is needless to say that I wish you all success in this enterprise."[73] Du Bois encouraged Myrdal to avoid the typical portrait of blacks as subhuman and to keep in mind that "the Negro is an integral part of American civilization and not simply one of America's problems as something extraneous to the main American scene."[74] In an ironic twist, Du Bois warned Myrdal of the problem of objectivity:

> One of your difficulties in selecting experts is going to be the intense bias of most Americans, black and white, on the Negro problems. Especially when you seek white men trained in scientific lines their science has almost certainly not included any attention to the Negro at all or has been an hasty expansion of certain misconceived ideas. We have suffered from this especially at the hands of statisticians, criminologists and earlier anthropologists. With regards to Negro experts they are naturally limited in number and if the standard is kept tight, as it should be, you have to look long and carefully.[75]

Myrdal considered Du Bois's scholarship to be of foundational importance in the production of his own study. In *Dilemma*, Du Bois is cited eighty-three times but Park only nine. Myrdal made his debt clear: "We cannot close this description of what a study of a Negro community should be without calling attention to the study which best meets our requirements, a study which is now all but forgotten. We refer to W. E. B. DuBois, *The Philadelphia Negro,* published in 1899."[76]

Du Bois could only dream of receiving the enormous funds Carnegie contributed to the production of *An American Dilemma*. Nevertheless, his Atlanta school had an impact on Myrdal's study: through the black social scientists that Myrdal recruited, scientists who had learned their craft by participating in the Du Bois–Atlanta school or by being in critical dialogue with Du Bois's scholarship. By the time Myrdal initiated the study, Du Bois had trained or influenced a number of black experts in black labor studies that Myrdal recruited as researchers and theoretical framers of the study. As Francille Wilson states, "Beginning with Richard R. R. Wright Jr. and Charles Edmund Haynes, Du Bois played a central role in expanding the number of black social scientists by assisting them in finding funds for their doctoral research, getting their articles placed in professional journals and providing introductions to and interventions with their professors and white reformers and philanthropists."[77] Thus the future Nobel Prize winner Ralph Bunche became Myrdal's chief researcher and consultant. Although Bunche did not participate directly in the Du Bois–Atlanta school, he was thoroughly familiar with Du Bois's scholarship on race and fashioned his own as a Marxist alternative to Du Bois's focus on race rather than class.[78]

Du Bois was aware of the important intellectual impact his Atlanta school had on American social science. Writing a review of Frazier's study on the black family in 1940, Du Bois commented:

It is particularly interesting for me to realize how those pioneer attempts to study the American Negro which were begun in Atlanta University in 1896 and carried on for eighteen years were not altogether sterile weeds. Out of these studies have come Carrie Bond Day's *Negro-White Families in the United States* done at Harvard; Charles Johnson's *Negro College Graduate* done at Fisk; Abram Harris' *The Negro as Capitalist*; Horace M. Bond's *Negro Education in Alabama*; and Cayton and Mitchell's *The Black Worker and the New Union*. As a climax to all this comes Mr. Frazier's study of the family.[79]

In short, Du Bois and his largely volunteer labor force often did more through his Atlanta school to produce black scholars who offered an alternative scientific analysis of race than did rich white universities and their famous professors. They constructed a sociology that conceptualized a set of social arrangements where racial equality could dethrone racism and the outmoded view that America's dark citizens were inferior because nature had played a cruel trick upon them.

This book has concentrated on the pioneering role of Du Bois as a sociologist, given that he worked as a sociologist and identified as such. Indeed, he crafted his scholarship in a sociological vein, always advocating the importance of a sociological perspective. However, he was also the quintessential interdisciplinary scholar who utilized history, anthropology, philosophy, economics, psychology, statistics, and the humanities to understand race globally. As Reiland Rabaka has demonstrated, although Du Bois was clearly a sociologist, his scholarship transcended disciplinary boundaries, incorporating insights from a variety of fields to illuminate race and social inequality.[80] As the sociologist Cheryl Gilkes puts it, in the world of scholarship Du Bois played all the positions.[81] While this book focuses on Du Bois the sociologist and explicates the significance of his school in the birth of modern sociology, it could have focused on the extent to which Du Bois affected the study of race across the social sciences and the humanities. In Du Bois's era, social science disciplines were closely intertwined and not clearly differentiated. The disciplines often operated under the same professional organizations while staking out their unique terrain.[82]

This close intellectual and organizational proximity enabled widely educated scholars to influence multiple disciplines. Thus William James, John Dewey, Robert Park, W.I. Thomas, George Herbert Mead, and Franz Boas influenced each other's scholarship. W.E.B. Du Bois excelled in navigating between disciplines, incorporating a variety of disciplinary insights and weaving them into his scholarship. However, such intellectual boundary crossing raises questions about which scholars first advanced pathbreaking ideas that generated paradigmatic shifts. The famous anthropologist Franz Boas is credited for moving the social sciences beyond biological explanations of race to explanations highlighting culture as the determinant of racial outcomes. It is accepted wisdom that Boas's work forever shifted the paradigm in the social sciences regarding determinants of racial inequality. Yet, as I have argued, Du Bois, beginning in the late nineteenth century, advanced and supported with his scholarship the idea that races were socially created categories and that, despite the scientific racism of the day, blacks were not racially inferior. There is thus a legitimate question regarding whether Du Bois should get substantial credit for shifting the racial paradigm. The anthropologist Lee Baker has asserted that Du Bois "anticipated ideas of cultural relativism and the critique of ideas of racial inferiority that emerged from anthropologists at Columbia University during the 1920's."[83] Baker confronts the issue of intellectual attribution head on: "Du Bois's early understanding of the color line was an important precursor for the paradigmatic shift in the social sciences that is rightly credited to Boas. Boas simply had more power than Du Bois in the academy to redirect scientific approaches to race. Boas was white, was viewed as an 'objective' scientist and held sway over scientific societies, editorial boards, and a prestigious department."[84] As Bourdieu argued, scholars' structural position in the scientific field determines which ideas will be recognized and given visibility.

An important legacy of Du Bois's scholarship is the emphasis it placed on racial attitudes and identities. From the outset, Du Bois and his colleagues were interested in the powerful role that beliefs played in determining racial outcomes. They considered it crucial to discredit nonscientific white beliefs in black inferiority. As a result, they produced scholarship uncovering the roots and social consequences of racial attitudes. A leading expert in this field, Lawrence Bobo, who serves as coeditor of the *Du Bois Review* at Harvard, has argued that "Du Bois's sociological analysis of the status of African Americans reflected a foundational concern with prejudice and racial attitudes" and that "it is essential to reconsider and resuscitate this aspect of Du Boisian sociology."[85] Bobo and his colleagues have invigorated this tradition by studying the social psychological foundation of racial prejudice and how prejudice affects labor and housing markets as well as American politics.[86] Bobo embraces Du Bois's influence: "I suggest that the sort of nuanced and organic view of how racial prejudice relates to and influences the structural positioning of African

Americans, as developed by Du Bois in *The Philadelphia Negro*, is sorely needed."[87]

Du Bois's *Black Reconstruction in America* also deeply influenced the field of history. It demonstrated the value of historical analyses utilizing a "bottom-up" approach to reveal how lower and subaltern classes exercise agency and become historical actors.[88] In *Reconstruction* Du Bois demonstrated how black militia played crucial roles in overthrowing slavery by confronting their oppressors on the battlefield. Before Du Bois's groundbreaking book, one scholarly view dominated the interpretation of Negroes during the Reconstruction period. William Archibald Dunning and his influential school of historians argued that Negroes during the Reconstruction wreaked political and moral havoc on American society. It was an argument that justified keeping blacks in check by repressive forces rather than allowing them full participation in government and society, since their exercise of greater powers could only be detrimental to the nation.[89] Du Bois's scholarship documenting black achievements and the pivotal role of black agency during Reconstruction undermined Dunning's influential school and changed scholarly views about blacks during the period.

Du Bois's classic work has influenced the important subfields of whiteness studies and the intersectionality approach. Whiteness studies is based on the premise that racial categories are socially constructed. As this book has demonstrated, Du Bois was the first sociologist to develop the foundation of what has become the social constructionist approach to race. In "The Souls of White Folk" in 1910, Du Bois claimed that "the discovery of a personal whiteness among the world's peoples is a very modern thing,—a nineteenth and twentieth century matter, indeed."[90] He continued that "wave on wave, each with increasing virulence, is dashing this new religion of whiteness on the shores of our time."[91] Du Bois focused on the idea that although whiteness operates as an invisible default racial category, it is, like blackness, an invented category deserving analytic scrutiny. A major emphasis in whiteness studies is that "whiteness" was invented precisely for the purpose of bestowing economic and political privileges on those with white skins. This conceptualization stems from Du Bois's analysis in *Reconstruction*, where he argues that "the white group of laborers, while they received a low wage, were compensated in part by a sort of public and psychological wage. They were given public deference and titles of courtesy because they were white."[92] Formulators of whiteness studies, including David Roediger and Theodore Allen, have acknowledged Du

Bois as their main inspiration and as the intellectual father of whiteness studies.[93] As Decker states, "The rereading of Du Bois's works became the starting point for critical whiteness in the United States in the late 1980s."[94]

Race, class, and gender have become central to a sociological approach seeking to understand social stratification in the contemporary world by explicating the interaction among these systems of oppression and showing how they are mutually reinforcing. This approach to stratification has come to be known as the theory of intersectionality. While it has developed over the last three decades, its intellectual roots are to be found in Du Bois's work nearly a century ago. In 1920 Du Bois wrote, "What is today the message of these black women to America and to the world? The uplift of women is, next to the problem of the color line and the peace movement, our greatest modern cause. When, now, two of these movements—woman and color—combine in one, the combination has deep meaning."[95] Regarding Du Bois's focus on the intersection of oppressions, Angie-Marie Hancock has written that Du Bois "presages intersectionality with a claim that more than one category of difference should be attacked simultaneously, and, more importantly, that the structures of society operate such that these categories mutually reinforce social stratification for its least empowered inhabitants."[96] Cheryl Gilkes has similarly pointed out that "early in the history of sociology, W.E.B. Du Bois emphasized that gender, race, and class intersected in the lives of black women to foster an important critical perspective or standpoint."[97] Although some scholars assert that Du Bois was conflicted over the roles that black women played in society, the consensus remains that he was the first sociologist that engaged in intersectional analysis that continues to be relevant to contemporary intersectionality theory.[98]

Black studies/African American studies is commonly thought to have emerged from the black revolt of the 1960s. It is true that many such programs and departments, especially at elite white universities, resulted from the protests of the civil rights and Black Power movements. Yet the intellectual foundations of the field of African American studies were laid by Du Bois. African American studies by its very nature is interdisciplinary. Du Bois's sociological, historical, and anthropological works established the social science basis for African American studies. Because policing and crime have always been troubling issues faced by an oppressed black community, African American studies has had to confront the issue of black crime. Du Bois pioneered the study of crime and race in America, arguing that high black crime rates resulted from oppressive social conditions rather than racial traits. The criminologist Shaun Gabbidon makes the case that Du Bois's publication of *The Philadelphia Negro* made him not only a founder of "black criminology" but, more generally, "one of the founders of the sociological approach in criminology."[99] Because he was a novelist, journalist, poet, and composer of plays and musical productions, Du Bois also brought a humanist dimension to African American studies. As a discipline, black studies emerged from a people entrapped by oppression and white supremacy. It never had the luxury of engaging in knowledge for knowledge's sake; its mission was also the production of scholarship useful in the black liberation struggle. Du Bois fit the bill for a discipline requiring intellectual power of the highest order coupled with engaged activism for social change. His international perspective led him to found liberation movements nationally and throughout the black diaspora. In scholarship and activism, Du Bois played all the positions.[100]

The Scholar Denied suggests that searching questions need to be raised about contemporary social science, especially race scholarship. As research for this book proceeded, I was surprised by how deeply racism was embedded in American social science during most of the twentieth century. I had expected that social scientists like Franklin Giddings and Edward Ross, both eugenicists and former presidents of the American Sociological Society, would produce racially biased scholarship. However, it was disconcerting to discover that most liberal sociologists and other social scientists of the era also clung to racist views. Indeed, progressive scholars including George Herbert Mead, Melville Herskovits, and even Franz Boas could not completely stay clear of importing the racially biased assumptions of the larger society into their science. An inescapable question emerges: To what extent do progressive white scholars of today unwittingly interject racist biases in their science even while believing they stand above prescientific racial assumptions? The findings here suggest that contemporary white scholars should engage their highest levels of reflexivity to expunge deep-seated racial biases from their work that are embedded in American culture and social institutions. Black scholars as well need to worry about how racist assumptions enter their work because racially biased scholarship that all scholars draw upon has permeated academia historically and has not been eradicated from the modern academy.

Scholars should be aware that racial biases are present in a broad range of scholars using different methodological and theoretical approaches. Thus Giddings, who is considered to be the pioneer of statistical methods in sociology, was deeply racist and used his "scientific statistics" to "prove" black inferiority. By the same token, Robert Park, considered as a major pioneer of qualitative and ethnographic approaches in sociology, clearly imported racist views into his science. White scholars should not assume that being friends or mentors of blacks will keep them from compromising their science with racist assumptions. Indeed, Park had close contact with blacks and was even considered to be a friend of the Negro by blacks and whites. Park said of his period of intense interaction with blacks at Tuskegee that "I became for all intents and purposes, for the time, a Negro, myself."[101] When leaving Tuskegee for the University of Chicago, Park informed Booker T. Washington that "some of the best friends I have in the world are at Tuskegee. I feel and should always feel that I belong, in a sort of way, to the Negro race and shall continue to share, through good and evil, all its joys and sorrows."[102] Yet Park was an American white man who identified with white Western interests. And although he claimed to be an objective social scientist, detached from the politics of the day, he viewed the world through westernized lenses and identified with Western empires. Hence, Park sought to understand the conditions that would enable the white man to rule the world.[103] He argued that African colonization and American slavery were necessary because they provided the apprenticeships through which backward blacks advanced by being exposed to the white man's superior civilization.

Park's stance supports standpoint and black feminist theories that one's social position significantly shapes one's worldview as well as one's science. This is a sobering insight that should be heeded by scholars today. While social scientists strive for objectivity, they should understand that such strivings are tempered by who they are and what their material interests are. As Julian Go demonstrated, American and Western sociology have produced a truncated and biased viewed of the world because they assume that the West has influenced and determined social reality for the rest of the world.[104] What is required now, according to Go, are "new postcolonial accounts of the making and continual remaking of modernity."[105] In the early twentieth century, Du Bois's accounts stood almost alone in analyzing the world from a perspective that did not privilege Western empires as directing the path of modernity. And that is why his scholarship remains relevant for contemporary social science. Perhaps Ralph Waldo Emerson's dictum applies to the contemporary relevance of the Du Bois–Atlanta school of sociology: "If a man can write a better book, or preach a better sermon, or make a better mouse trap than his neighbor, even if he builds his house in the woods the world will make a beaten path to his door."[106] The history of Du Bois's school exemplifies that creativity and original scholarship may take root outside elite universities and associated networks. A major intellectual school like the Du Bois–Atlanta school can be silenced and erased from the collective memory of social science, but it can also be retrieved and revived.

History teaches that American social science has fallen short of functioning as a democratic institution where intellectual merit would be the criterion required for scholars to enter the gates and enrich the stock of knowledge. The ugly realities of racism, sexism, and class bias have infiltrated American social science and stunted its growth. The field, including its social networks, is crucial to intellectual ferment and the building of theoretical schools. However, its institutional processes lose vitality when discrimination erects barriers preventing the circulation of ideas. Patricia Lengermann has underscored the negative consequences occurring when small insular groups control scholarly discourse.[107] She describes how this happened for decades while a small group of elite white men controlled the *American Journal of Sociology* but how ultimately a rebellion sprang up that overthrew the journal's dominance by giving rise to the *American Sociological Review,* enabling a wider range of ideas to be introduced into the discipline. We also know that sociology, and the social sciences, have suffered intellectually because work by earlier generations of women has been erased from the collective memory of the discipline.[108]

But if an innovative scientific school could take root in the worst of times, amid the terrorism of lynch mobs, attacks from elites within the community it sought to liberate, and discrimination from a racist society that withheld crucial resources, then maybe there is hope for all who work to produce knowledge for the purpose of understanding and transforming humanity.

Notes

Throughout these notes, "DBP" stands for the W.E.B. Du Bois Papers, Department of Special Collections and University Archives, University of Massachusetts Amherst Libraries.

PREFACE

1. Du Bois ([1903b] 2007).
2. Du Bois ([1899b] 1973; [1903b] 2007).
3. Morris (1984).
4. Blackwell and Janowitz (1974).
5. Green and Driver (1978).
6. Du Bois ([1899b] 1973).
7. Marable (1986).
8. Lewis (1993, 2000).
9. Sundquist (1996); Katz and Sugrue (1998); Horne and Young (2001).
10. Zuckerman (2004).
11. Reed (1997); Gooding-Williams (2011).
12. L. Baker (1998).
13. Gabbidon (2007).
14. Wilson (2006).
15. E. Wright (2000, 2002a, 2002b, 2002c, 2006, 2008, 2009, 2010).
16. Rabaka (2010).
17. Scaff (2011).

INTRODUCTION

1. Deegan (2001); Abbott (1999); Fine (1995); Bulmer (1985); Coser (1978); Matthews (1977); Faris (1967); A. Hunter (1980). Even though it is widely

accepted that the University of Chicago's department of sociology was America's first and most influential school of sociology, that claim has been challenged. The department at the University of Kansas claims it was the first to open its doors in 1890 and to offer sociology classes; see Sica (1991) and "About Us" at the website of the University of Kansas at http:// sociology.ku.edu/about-us (accessed October 30, 2014). Yale, on its website at the page "Welcome to the Yale Sociology Department," maintains that "in 1875, Yale professor William Graham Sumner (1840–1910) offered the first American course titled 'Sociology'" (http://sociology.yale.edu, accessed October 30, 2014). Yet despite these claims, Chicago is widely perceived as the first American sociology department, and there is little debate that it was the most influential.

2. E. Wright (2002a, 2002b, 2002c, 2006, 2008); Gabbidon (2007); Zuckerman (2004); Rabaka (2010).

3. Green and Driver (1978); Blackwell and Janowitz (1974); Rudwick (1969); Bracey, Meier, and Rudwick (1971); Broderick (1974).

4. Bell, Grosholz, and Stewart (1996); A. Young et al. (2006); Saint-Arnaud (2009).

5. A legitimate question is why I designate this school as "the Du Bois–Atlanta school of sociology" or as "Du Bois's Atlanta school of sociology." In an e-mail of July 21, 2011, Professor Mary Pattillo writes, "I imagine . . . you'll justify why it should be called the DuBois School and not the Atlanta School, as would be suggested by what we now have is the Chicago School, not the Park School." I include "Du Bois" in the school's name because Du Bois played the primary role in developing and sustaining it. At Chicago a major sociology department existed with professors, graduate students, and a sociology journal when Park arrived. Thus Park entered a well-established sociology department where he carved out a niche as a lecturer. In contrast, though an embryonic organizational shell of a school and some intellectual activities existed when Du Bois arrived at Atlanta, the tasks of organizing a sociology department, training students, fine-tuning a research organization, and guiding publications awaited him. Without a guiding template, Du Bois singlehandedly developed the pioneering scientific intellectual orientation that guided his school.

6. McKee (1993).

7. Du Bois ([ca. 1905] 2000).

8. This book's argument concerns specifically the development of scientific sociology in America beginning in the late nineteenth and early twentieth centuries. In an e-mail of April 7, 2011, Arthur Stinchombe pointed out that a tradition of empirical sociology existed in Europe before Du Bois established his sociology in America. He wrote that "Marx & Engels were good empirical workers on the English industrial revolution, and Marx on the French politics of status groups (e.g. Lumpen Proletariat; petty bourgeoisie), Engels on 'The condition of the English Working Class' . . . though both mostly used archives rather than ethnography. And of course Weber was 'empirical' in the sense of knowing a hell of a lot of facts about social relations at various times in history in many parts of the world. 'Empirical' doesn't mean only going out in the field and interviewing, though it does indeed include that." I agree. My contention is that prior to Du Bois's work in Philadelphia and Atlanta, American sociologists were not employ-

ing empirical methodologies and conducting research on which to develop sociological generalizations. Rather, they relied on armchair theorizing and deductive reasoning to construct various concepts "explaining" social reality. This approach was largely dominant in Europe, though there were notable exceptions, as Stinchcombe argues. In later chapters we will see that American sociologists of the early twentieth century were coming to realize that armchair theorizing was leading to a dead end. Thus there was a need for grounded empirical research if the new discipline was to survive as a legitimate discipline. Du Bois pioneered quantitative and quantitative methods in his sociological scholarship.

    9. Thomas and Thomas (1928, 572).

1. THE RISE OF SCIENTIFIC SOCIOLOGY IN AMERICA

    1. See Du Bois (1901b); Liberson (1980); Massey and Denton (1993).

    2. See Du Bois ([1899b] 1973); Chicago Commission on Race Relations (1922); Frazier (1935); Butler (2007).

    3. For an account of race relations in the North, see Du Bois ([1901a] 1969).

    4. See Du Bois (1935, 700–701).

    5. Hoffman (1896).

    6. See Aldrich (1979); Darity (1994); Muhammad (2010).

    7. Du Bois (1897b); Miller (1897).

    8. See Du Bois (1899a); Baldwin (1984); Roediger (2005); Guglielmo and Salerno (2003); Anderson (1988).

    9. See Franklin (1968); Morris (1984).

    10. See Franklin (1968); Meier and Rudwick (1966).

    11. Liberson (1980); Massey and Denton (1993); Sugrue (2010).

    12. Du Bois ([1903b] 2007).

    13. Du Bois ([1903b] 2007, 2).

    14. A. Hunter (1980, 215–16). Although Hunter addressed sociology and class conflict of the period, he failed to attend to race conflict.

    15. See Park and Miller (1921); Thomas and Znaniecki (1918–20); Sanders (1896, 340); Steven Cohen (1991).

    16. Portes and Rumbaut (1990); Thomas and Znaniecki (1918–20); Park and Miller (1921).

    17. Du Bois ([1903b] 2007).

    18. Du Bois (1896).

    19. Du Bois (1915a).

    20. Anderson (1988); Franklin (1968).

    21. See Sugrue (2010).

    22. Washington (1901b); Harlan (1972).

    23. Anderson (1988).

    24. Washington ([1895] 1974, 583–84).

    25. Washington ([1895] 1974, 584).

    26. Washington ([1895] 1974, 585).

    27. Washington ([1895] 1974, 585).

    28. Washington ([1895] 1974, 584). It is curious, indeed, that Washington urged blacks to engage in manual industrial labor following centuries of slavery

as if they would be embarking on an uncharted venture. Alexander Crummell, an early mentor of Du Bois, expressed the irony: "One would suppose from the universal demand for the mere industrialism for this race of ours, that the Negro had been going daily to dinner parties, eating terrapin and indulging in champagne . . . all these 250 years . . . and then, just now, the American people . . . was calling him, for the first time, to blister his hands with the hoe, and to learn to supply his needs by sweatful toil in the cotton fields" (1898, 13). Eleven decades later, Professor Walter Allen similarly commented to me in an April 8, 2011, e-mail, "This is so ironic, given the long, demonstrated dominance, prominence of blacks in manual labor. African Americans built the country; then to be accused of being lazy!"

29. See Williams (2006, 71).

30. Washington (1907, 74–75).

31. Washington (1901b, 16).

32. Washington (1901b, 17).

33. Washington (1901b, 1907).

34. Washington (1911).

35. See Scott and Stowe (1916).

36. Weber (1958).

37. Max Weber to Booker T. Washington, November 6, 1904, in Scaff (2011, 265).

38. Scaff (2011, 111).

39. See Stanfield (1985); McKee (1993); Steinberg, (2007); Morris (2007).

40. Du Bois ([1903b] 2007); Harlan (1983); Lewis (1993).

41. Washington (1911).

42. Rudwick (1972, 69).

43. Washington (1911, 118). This stance by Washington and his ghostwriter, Robert Park, has a familiar ring in the early twenty-first century, where claims that a postracial America has arrived abound, especially in light of the election of Barack Obama as the nation's first black president. In an e-mail of April 8, 2011, Professor Walter Allen pointed out that the "race hustling" argument by Washington and Park has endured for over a century, given that this tactic is used by conservatives in twenty-first-century America as it was by Washington to neutralize the so-called outdated and self-interested views of the "black civil rights establishment."

44. Du Bois ([1903b] 2007).

45. Washington ([1904] 1977, 342).

46. Washington ([1904] 1977, 342).

47. Wilson (2006, 75).

2. DU BOIS, SCIENTIFIC SOCIOLOGY, AND RACE

1. Unlike Washington, Du Bois did not experience slavery and southern Jim Crow during his youth. These contrasting socialization experiences and racial contacts influenced how Washington and Du Bois related to whites and engaged in struggles for racial equality. But it should be noted that numerous black scholars, including Monroe Work, Carter G. Woodson, Zora Neale Hurston,

Charles Johnson, and John Hope, were born in the South. The same holds true for black leaders, including Frederick Douglass, Mary McCleod Bethune, and Martin Luther King Jr.

2. Du Bois (1968); Lewis (1993, 2000).

3. In the late nineteenth century it was customary for elite social science scholars to attend universities in Germany to study with the world's greatest social scientists who were in the vanguard of the newly emerging social sciences. Du Bois was aware of this custom and decided that he would study at the University of Berlin to obtain the best education possible.

4. Du Bois (1968, 170).

5. Strickland (2011).

6. Du Bois (1968, 160).

7. Du Bois (1968, 157).

8. Du Bois (1968, 160, 183).

9. Wright (1965, 46).

10. Wright (1965, 46–47).

11. Galton (1904).

12. Galton (1904, 5).

13. Park and Burgess (1921, 979–83).

14. See Ordover (2003).

15. Schafer (2000, 41).

16. Camic and Xie (1994, 732).

17. Camic and Xie (1994, 797).

18. Seligman (1924).

19. Du Bois to the Honorable, the Trustees of the John Slater Fund, December 6, 1893, in Du Bois (1973).

20. Camic and Xie (1994).

21. See Camic and Xie (1994); Wallace (1989).

22. Schafer (2001).

23. Du Bois (1968, 160).

24. Broderick (1958, 367).

25. Du Bois ([1920] 2007, 8).

26. Du Bois ([1940a] 2007, 26).

27. See Breslau (2007).

28. See Coser (1978).

29. H. Rogers (1904, 9).

30. H. Rogers (1904, 8).

31. Max Weber confirmed he had had breakfast with Du Bois at the conference ([1910] 1973, 312). Scaff also confirms Du Bois's presence at the conference (Scaff 2011, 75–76).

32. Du Bois (2000, 37).

33. Du Bois (2000, 37–44).

34. Du Bois (2000, 39).

35. Du Bois (2000, 39).

36. Du Bois (2000, 39).

37. Du Bois (2000, 40).

38. Giddings (1896, 17–20).

39. Tarde (1903).

40. Lindsay (1898, 46).

41. Small (1905, 425–42).

42. Du Bois (2000, 40).

43. Du Bois (2000, 43).

44. Du Bois (2000, 41).

45. England and Warner (2013).

46. See Coulborn and Du Bois (1942).

47. Ward (1906).

48. Ward (1906, 8).

49. Oberschall (1972, 189).

50. Breslau (2007, 42).

51. W.E.B. Du Bois, "Post-graduate Work in Sociology at Atlanta University," unpublished manuscript, DBP, 14–15, 16.

52. W.E.B. Du Bois, "A Program for a Sociological Society," unpublished manuscript, DBP, 3–4.

53. Merton ([1948] 1968).

54. Appiah (1985); Gooding-Williams (2011); Reed (1992); Watts (2006).

55. I thank Damon Sajnani for bringing to my attention this issue regarding contemporary vocabulary versus the vocabulary of a century ago.

56. Du Bois (1903c, 33).

57. Appiah (1985).

58. Appiah (1985, 25).

59. Du Bois (1897a).

60. Appiah (1985, 34).

61. Du Bois (1897a, 9).

62. Reed (1992).

63. Reed (1992, 133–34).

64. Reed (1992, 115–37, 135).

65. McKee (1993, 61).

66. Taylor (1973, 433).

67. Reed (1992, 132).

68. Reed (1992, 132).

69. Du Bois ([1904b] 2002, 119).

70. Reed (1992, 134–35).

71. Gooding-Williams (2011).

72. Gooding-Williams (2011, 47).

73. Outlaw (1996).

74. Watts (2006, 116).

75. Watts (2006, 122).

76. Watts (2006, 122).

77. Watts (2006, 123).

78. Du Bois ([1903b] 2007, 84).

79. Du Bois (1904a, 297).

80. Du Bois (1904a, 294–95).

81. Weber (1989).

82. Du Bois (1904a, 294).

83. Du Bois (1898b, 4).
84. Du Bois ([1903b] 2007, 70).
85. Du Bois ([1903b] 2007, 70).
86. Du Bois (1904a, 308).
87. Du Bois (1904a, 307).
88. Du Bois ([1903b] 2007, 69).
89. Du Bois ([1903b] 2007, 80).
90. Du Bois (1904a, 305).
91. Du Bois (1904a, 305).
92. Du Bois ([1903b] 2007, 74).
93. Du Bois ([1903b] 2007, 66).
94. Du Bois ([1903b] 2007, 69).
95. Du Bois (1904a, 308).
96. Du Bois (1909b, 152).
97. Du Bois (1909b, 153).
98. Du Bois ([1920] 2007, 17).
99. Du Bois ([1920] 2007, 18).
100. R. Wright (1903, 1029), quoted in Grossman (1974, 23).
101. See Morris and Braine (2001).
102. Reed (1992, 137).
103. See Lewis (1993, 174); Muhammad (2010, 67).
104. Holt (1998, 68–69).
105. Du Bois ([1920] 2007, 47).
106. Du Bois ([1940a] 2007, 49).
107. Du Bois ([1940a] 2007, 49).
108. Du Bois (1898b, 10–11).
109. Du Bois (1898b).
110. Du Bois (1898b, 16).
111. Du Bois (1898b, 12–13).
112. Du Bois (1898b, 10).
113. See E. Wright (2002b, 30; 2008, 197).
114. Du Bois (1898b, 12).
115. See Myrdal (1944).
116. Du Bois ([1899b] 1973, 168–92 and 309–21).
117. Du Bois ([1899b] 1973, 97–146).
118. Du Bois ([1899b] 1973, 323, 333–36, 427–509.
119. Du Bois ([1899b] 1973, 46–65, 73–82, 147–63).
120. Wortham (2009).
121. Du Bois ([1899b] 1973, 235–68).
122. Du Bois ([1899b] 1973, 197–207).
123. Du Bois ([1899b] 1973, 207–33).
124. Du Bois ([1899b] 1973, 309–21).
125. Du Bois ([1899b] 1973, 368–97).
126. Du Bois ([1903b] 2007, 1).
127. Du Bois, (1898a; [1899b] 1973; [1901a] 1969; [1906c] 2006).
128. Du Bois (1898a).
129. See M. Hunter (2013b).

130. Patillo (2012, 18).

131. M. Hunter (2013b, 8–9).

132. Bay (1998, 45).

133. Collins (1998).

134. Booth (1892–97).

135. See A. Hunter (1980, 218).

136. See Addams (1910); Knight (2005).

137. See Deegan (1990).

138. Sklar (1991, 122).

139. Sklar (1991, 122).

140. Sklar (1991, 122).

141. Jazbinsek, Joerges, and Thies (2001, 3).

142. Jazbinsek, Joerges, and Thies (2001, 11).

143. Jazbinsek, Joerges, and Thies (2001, 6–16).

144. Steven Cohen (1991, 249).

145. See Deegan (1990); Sklar (1991).

146. Deegan (1990). For example, the more activist and progressive members of the Chicago school were censored by administrators to make sure that they did not offend elite funders. The firing of W.I. Thomas in 1918 was a clear example of the exercise of such censorship.

147. Eaton ([1899] 1973.

148. Bulmer (1991, 175).

149. See L. Baker (1998, 114).

3. THE DU BOIS–ATLANTA SCHOOL OF SOCIOLOGY

1. Du Bois was not granted a doctorate at the University of Berlin because he was short of a residency requirement and could not secure the funds to complete the program.

2. Du Bois (1968, 187).

3. During the last two decades of the nineteenth century, sociology was a newly developing discipline, and only in the last decade were the first departments established in America. Scholars of the period who aspired to become sociologists usually were in other fields such as economics and political economy. Even in Europe this was the case: Max Weber, for instance, was a professor of economics rather than a sociologist. Yet following his return from the University of Berlin Du Bois always seemed to be clear that his interests fell squarely within the field of sociology.

4. Du Bois (1968, 133).

5. Du Bois (1968, 188–89).

6. Du Bois (1968, 197).

7. Du Bois (1968, 199).

8. Du Bois (1968, 211).

9. Du Bois (1968, 211).

10. In the history-of-sociology literature it is emphasized that the Chicago school flourished because it was located in a great city that could serve as a social laboratory. At the same time Atlanta served as the sociological laboratory

for many of the pioneering studies produced by the Du Bois–Atlanta school. Du Bois accepted the position at Atlanta, in part, because of its location in a great city that could serve as the site for sociological research.

11. Du Bois (1968, 197).

12. During the first decades of the twentieth century, few professional positions were available to African Americans, especially those that would enable one to promote social change. For African American men, the ministry was the primary position to engage in such endeavors. The first generation of black sociologists, including Monroe Work, Richard R. Wright Jr., and Edmund Haynes, pursued the ministry. When sociology emerged, it seemed to be an ideal profession in which to pursue social change. As a result, Work and Haynes changed careers to become sociologists. Wright also became a sociologist, although he remained a minister, becoming an important bishop in the A.M.E. Church. This pattern of first-generation black sociologists having initially been ministers also holds for many first-generation white sociologists.

13. Du Bois ([1903b] 2007, 1).

14. Francis Grimke to Du Bois, October 16, 1903, quoted in Lewis (1993, 644 n.).

15. Jessie R. Fauset to Du Bois, December 26, 1903, DBP.

16. For a discussion of Alexander Crummell's intellectual influence on Du Bois, see Du Bois ([1903b] 2007, 103–9).

17. See Wilson (2006, 24–26).

18. Wilson (2006, 20–31).

19. Wilson (2006, 27).

20. Du Bois (1968, 202).

21. Wilson (2006, 49).

22. Wilson (2006, 49).

23. See McKee (1993).

24. Work (1900).

25. Monroe N. Work to Du Bois, October 1, 1908, DBP.

26. Monroe Work accepted his first professorship at Savannah State in Georgia in order to be close to Du Bois to facilitate collaboration. After several years there he was recruited by Booker T. Washington for a position at Tuskegee Institute. He moved to Tuskegee because of the superior resources available to conduct his research. As a result he became one of the few individuals to work closely with both Washington and Du Bois. For a biography on Monroe Work, see McMurry (1985).

27. R. Wright (1965, 48–49).

28. See Deegan (1990) for a discussion of the settlement movement and activism in sociology.

29. Wilson (2006, 61).

30. Wilson (2006, 85).

31. E. Wright (2010).

32. See Bulmer (1985, 61–62).

33. Grossman (1974, 20).

34. Grossman (1974, 20).

35. Grossman (1974, 20).

36. Grossman (1974, 21).

37. William Taylor Thom was a white college professor at Hollins Institute who taught history and English and specialized in Shakespeare and Chaucer. Thom authored several studies of small black communities modeled on Du Bois's "Negroes of Farmville"; see Thom (1901a, 1901b, 1902). For a discussion of Du Bois's influence, see Grossman (1974).

38. Wilson (2006).

39. Coser (1971, 511).

40. See M. Hunter (2013a); Patillo (2012).

41. See McKee (1993, 145–80).

42. Du Bois ([1901a] 1969, 41).

43. Du Bois ([1901a] 1969, 43).

44. R. Wright ([1912] 1969, 186–87).

45. R. Wright (1965, 47).

46. Haynes (1912, 8).

47. Haynes (1912, 42).

48. Haynes (1912, 144).

49. McMurry (1985, 28).

50. Du Bois (1904c).

51. Du Bois (1903a).

52. McMurry (1985, 28).

53. Wilson (2006).

54. Ovington (1911, 168–69).

55. See Deegan (1990).

56. R. Wright (1965, 47).

57. Ovington (1911, 100, 104).

58. Ovington (1911, 137).

59. Mary W. Ovington to Du Bois, June 10, 1904, in Du Bois (1973).

60. Ovington (1947, 53).

61. Ovington (1947, 55).

62. Tolman (1902, 114).

63. Du Bois (1968, 214).

64. Du Bois ([1903b] 2007); E. Wright (2006).

65. Wilson (2006, 90–114).

66. Gabbidon (2007, 26).

67. Du Bois (1909a, 5).

68. See Faris (1967, 135–40).

69. Du Bois (1902, 12).

70. Du Bois (1902, 1).

71. Du Bois (1902, 1).

72. Du Bois (1902, 12).

73. Wilson (2006, 32).

74. Wilson (2006, 38).

75. E. Wright (2009).

76. Du Bois to Edward Ware, February 4, 1910, Robert W. Woodruff Library, Atlanta University Center.

77. Aldrich (1979, 2).

78. Aldrich (1979).

79. Walter Willcox to Du Bois, April 19, 1905, DBP.

80. Horace Bumstead to Du Bois, May 14, 1904, Robert W. Woodruff Library, Atlanta University Center.

81. See Bernard and Bernard (1943, 585).

82. Sanborn (1905, 21).

83. Du Bois (1939, vii).

84. Zumwalt and Willis (2008, 47).

85. See L. Baker (1998, 100)

86. See L. Baker (1998, 101–5); Williams (2006, 19). Boas encountered difficulties at Clark because of his intellectual and political opposition to scientific racism and because he was a Jew. He resigned in 1892 because he believed that the university's leadership was attempting to censure his challenging scholarship. Concerning Boas's problems in academia, see L. Baker (1998) and V. Williams (2006).

87. L. Baker (1998, 101–6).

88. Stocking (1966); Williams (2006).

89. Stocking (1966, 871).

90. Boas ([1894] 1974, 226).

91. Darity (1994); Muhammad (2010).

92. See Boas ([1894] 1974).

93. Brigg (2005, 83).

94. Quoted in Williams (2006, 31).

95. Williams (2006, 16–47).

96. Regarding genius, Boas wrote, "We find that 50 per cent of all whites have a capacity of the skull greater than 1550 cc., while 27 per cent of the negroes and 32 per cent of the Melanesians have capacities above this value. We might, therefore, anticipate a lack of men of high genius, but should not anticipate any great lack of faculty among the great mass of negroes living among whites and enjoying the advantages of the leadership of the best men of that race" (Boas [1894] 1974, 233–34).

97. Zumwalt and Willis (2008, 53).

98. Zumwalt and Willis (2008, 55).

99. Boas (1916, 83).

100. Addams (1908, 1).

101. Addams (1908, 1).

102. See Zuckerman (2004); Deegan (1988).

103. Du Bois (1906a, 110).

104. See McKee (1993); Morris (2007).

105. Aldrich (1979, 1).

106. Aldrich (1979, 1).

107. Darity (1994, 55); Walter Willcox to Du Bois, March 13, 1904, and Du Bois to Walter Willcox, March 29, 1904, in Du Bois (1973, 74–75).

108. Darity (1994, 61).

109. Du Bois (1906a, 110).

110. Coser (1972); Sullivan (1982).

111. Du Bois ([1903b] 2007, 3).

112. During this period it was not unusual for black colleges and universities to also teach high school students. At Atlanta University Du Bois taught high schoolers as well as undergraduate and graduate students.

113. Yancy (1978, 62).

114. Yancy (1978, 63).

115. Yancy (1978, 61).

116. Yancy (1978, 61).

117. Du Bois (1968, 283).

118. For a discussion of Du Bois's exhibit in Paris, see Du Bois (1900).

119. Horace Bumstead quoted in Du Bois (1968, 210–11).

120. R. Baker (1908a, 222).

121. Washington (1901a).

122. Washington (1902, 5).

123. Rudwick (1957).

124. Wilson (2006, 32).

125. Du Bois (1968, 219).

126. Alderman (1901, 2411).

127. Alderman (1901, 2412).

128. Bacote (1969, 135).

129. Bacote (1969, 132).

130. The first white department of sociology in the South was founded in 1920 at the University of North Carolina, two decades following the founding of the sociology department at Atlanta University.

131. Bulmer (1991, 181).

132. Lewis (1993, 225).

133. Franklin Giddings to Edward T. Ware, November 2, 1911, Presidential Archives, Robert W. Woodruff Library, Atlanta University Center.

134. Du Bois (1968, 224).

135. Du Bois (1968, 224–25).

136. Quoted in L. Baker (1998, 122).

4. THE CONSERVATIVE ALLIANCE OF WASHINGTON AND PARK

1. Quoted in Matthews (1977, 62).

2. Drake (1983, 90).

3. Raushenbush (1979, 43).

4. Quoted in Raushenbush (1979, 41–42).

5. Park (1941, 41).

6. Robert E. Park to Booker T. Washington, January 28, 1908, in Washington (1980, 449).

7. Robert E. Park to Booker T. Washington, May 29, 1913, in Washington (1982, 190).

8. Washington ([1904] 1977, 341).

9. Robert E. Park to Booker T. Washington, May 29, 1913, in Washington (1982, 190).

10. Park (1950c).

11. Park (1941, 41–46).

12. See Park (1941).

13. Park (1941, 41).

14. Quoted in Matthews (1977, 80).

15. It is ironic that Park concluded, "Washington was not a brilliant man or an intellectual," yet claimed he had learned more from Washington than all his professors. As I have argued, Washington's ideas were important in the development of Park's sociology. One reason Park embraced the black inferiority thesis despite his interactions with black intellectuals and leaders may have been that he thought blacks like Washington and Du Bois were superior to ordinary blacks because of their status as mulattoes. For Park's view on this subject, see his "Mentality of Racial Hybrids" ([1931] 1950), where he argues that mixed-bloods constitute a distinct personality type.

16. Quoted in Raushenbush (1979, 173).

17. Park (1950a, vii).

18. Park (1941, 45).

19. Du Bois ([1903b] 2007, 21–29).

20. Matthews (1977, 64).

21. Matthews (1977, 66).

22. See Washington (1911).

23. Booker T. Washington to Emmett Scott, March 2, 1908, in Washington (1980, 459).

24. Du Bois (1968, 227).

25. Raushenbush (1979, 47).

26. Du Bois (1968, 286).

27. As a general principle, Du Bois believed in peace rather than violence and war. For example, he expressed the view, "I think war is worse than hell, and that it seldom or never forwards the advance of the world." Du Bois ([1940a] 2007, 151).

28. Lewis (1993, 335).

29. Raushenbush (1979, 47).

30. Booker T. Washington to Timothy Thomas Fortune, January 20, 1911, in Washington (1981, 555). Here Washington is referring to the poem "A Litany of Atlanta" that Du Bois composed while taking a train back to Atlanta to protect his family during the Atlanta riot of 1906. Du Bois (1906b).

31. Timothy Thomas Fortune to Booker T. Washington, January 23, 1911, in Washington (1981, 556).

32. Wilson (2006, 79). For example, Wilson points out that "at the meetings of white professional organizations, Booker T. Washington or a close associate might be asked to join a panel when Du Bois or one of his allies was making a presentation. Washington was frequently quoted by northern white academics such as Joseph Tillinghast, who felt obliged to deliver a scientific critique of the modernists' environmental thesis" (75).

33. Booker T. Washington to Walter Willcox, November 9, 1904, in Washington (1979, 125).

34. Walter Willcox to Booker T. Washington, November 14, 1904, in Washington (1979, 131).

35. R. Baker ([1908b] 2007, 73).
36. Raushenbush (1979, 55).
37. Matthews (1977, 77).
38. Matthews (1977, 78).
39. Deegan (2001, 21).
40. Raushenbush (1979, 68).
41. Raushenbush (1979, 68).
42. Robert E. Park to Booker T. Washington, December 3, 1912, in Washington (1982, 82).
43. Booker T. Washington to Emmett Scott, October 23, 1913, in Washington (1982, 320).
44. Deegan (2001).
45. Abbott (1999).
46. Abbott (1999).
47. Bulmer (1984).
48. Oberschall (1972, 194–95); Du Bois (1968, 278).
49. Abbott and Egloff (2008, 221 n.).
50. Du Bois (1968); L. Baker (1998); Lewis (1993).
51. Du Bois (1968, 228).
52. Deegan (2001, 13).
53. Small (1916, 795).
54. Small (1916, 796).
55. Small (1916, 853).
56. Park and Burgess (1921, 11).
57. Park and Burgess (1921, 11).
58. Braude (1970, 4).
59. Burgess (1961, 17).
60. Quoted in Park and Burgess (1921, 349).
61. Park ([1925a] 1950, 29).
62. For classic expression of this view, see Spencer (1851) and Sumner (1906).
63. Park ([1918] 1950, 266).
64. Park ([1918] 1950, 266).
65. Raushenbush (1979, 59).
66. At Tuskegee, Park approved of simple literature and rhetorical tasks for young black students. He wrote of an exercise where students employed in one of the industries of the school had to explain their duties to their fellows: "I was probably the more impressed by this sort of rhetorical exercise because it was so entertaining and instructive as compared with the Friday afternoon rhetoricals with their frigid little essays that I remembered of my own school days" Park (1941, 44). According to Matthews (1977, 68), "The Negro students, Park found, responded best to the great Western myths, based on oral tradition, like the *Iliad, Odyssey,* and tales of King Arthur, which were 'large and simple in outline.'"
67. Park and Burgess (1921, 347–48).
68. Hughes quoted in Raushenbush (1979, 83).
69. Park and Burgess (1921, 506, 508).
70. Park and Burgess (1921, 574).

71. Park and Burgess (1921, 509).
72. Park and Burgess (1921, 735).
73. Park ([1926a] 1950, 150).
74. Park ([1918] 1950, 280).
75. Park ([1918] 1950, 281).
76. Park ([1918] 1950, 282).
77. Park ([1918] 1950, 264).
78. Park ([1918] 1950, 282).
79. Park ([1928] 1950, 239).
80. Park and Burgess (1921, 623).
81. Park and Burgess (1921, 623).
82. Park ([1931] 1950, 389).

5. THE SOCIOLOGY OF BLACK AMERICA

1. Park ([1918] 1950, 265).
2. Park ([1943] 1950, 317).
3. Park ([1913b] 1950, 210).
4. See Park (1937b).
5. Park ([1925b] 1967, 43).
6. Park (1937b, 286–90).
7. Park (1915, 589).
8. Park ([1943] 1950, 326).
9. Park and Miller (1921); Park ([1943] 1950, 319).
10. Park ([1918] 1950, 267).
11. Sudarkasa (2007, 31).
12. Du Bois (1908, 9).
13. Du Bois (1915b, 113–14).
14. Du Bois ([1903b] 2007, 91).
15. Park ([1918] 1950, 269).
16. Park ([1918] 1950, 273).
17. See Du Bois (1907, 1909).
18. Park ([1918] 1950, 279).
19. Morris (1984).
20. Park ([1918] 1950, 278).
21. Park ([1918] 1950, 279).
22. See Odum (1910).
23. Du Bois (1903a).
24. Du Bois ([1903b] 2007).
25. Park ([1918] 1950, 275). For Du Bois's groundbreaking works on the black church, see Du Bois ([1899b] 1973; 1903a; 1908, 9; 1915b).
26. See Woodson (1936); Herskovits (1941); Blassingame (1972).
27. Park ([1918] 1950, 279).
28. Park ([1918] 1950, 280).
29. Park and Burgess (1921, 638–39).
30. Park (1926b, 301).
31. Park (1926b, 301).

32. Quoted in Raushenbush (1979, 49).
33. Deegan (2006).
34. See Steinberg (2010); Lyman (1972); Williams (2006).
35. Connell (1997).
36. Park (1950b, 16).
37. Park ([1937a] 1950, 185–86).
38. Washington ([1895] 1974).
39. Park ([1913b] 1950, 217).
40. Park ([1913b] 1950, 210).
41. See Phillips (1918, 1929).
42. Hofstadter (1944, 122).
43. Park ([1913b] 1950).
44. Park (1950c).
45. Park (1941).
46. Park (1950a, viii).
47. Du Bois (2000).
48. Du Bois ([1899b] 1973; [1903b] 2007; 1903a; 1908, 9; 1915b).
49. Du Bois (1935, 11).
50. Du Bois (1935, 9).
51. Du Bois (1909b, 146–47).
52. See Du Bois (1915b, 1909c, 1935).
53. For Du Bois's analysis of racial divisions negatively affecting working-class solidarity, see Du Bois (1935, 700–701).
54. Du Bois (1910, 1935).
55. Du Bois ([1901a] 1969).
56. Du Bois ([1903b] 2007, 61).
57. Du Bois ([1903b] 2007, 62).
58. See Du Bois ([1899b] 1973, [1901a] 1969).
59. See Morris (2007).
60. Boas (1911, 278).
61. Marable (1986); Du Bois (2000, 39).
62. Du Bois (2000, 39).
63. Du Bois (2000, 39).
64. Du Bois (1898b, 10–11).
65. See Morris and Ghaziani (2005).
66. Coser (1971, 372).
67. Du Bois (1968, 222).
68. See Burawoy (2004); Burawoy et al. (2004).
69. Du Bois (1968, 192).
70. Mills (1997).
71. Du Bois ([1921] 1996, 640).
72. Du Bois (1915c).
73. See Du Bois ([1921] 1996, 642).
74. B. Johnson (2003, 140).
75. Upon his arrival at the sociology department at the University of Chicago, the first course that Park taught was "The Negro in America." For discussion of the class, see Raushenbush (1979, 77).

76. Washington (1911, 122–27).

77. Park (1913a); Du Bois (1913).

78. Park and Burgess (1921).

79. Coser (1971, 371).

80. Faris (1967, 37).

81. Deegan (2001, 19).

82. Raushenbush (1979, 81–82).

83. Park (1950c).

84. Abbott (1999, 88).

85. Du Bois (1898b).

86. Rudwick (1969, 305).

87. Steward (1903, 136).

88. Steward (1903, 136).

89. The University of Chicago Press did not publish any of Du Bois's books. The *American Journal of Sociology*, published by the University of Chicago Press, did include an article by Du Bois (1944) and several minor reviews of Du Bois's work.

90. Small (1916).

91. Thomas (1912)

92. Thomas (1912, 738, 746, 748, 750, 751, and 752).

93. Thomas (1912, 771).

94. Thomas and Znaniecki (1918–20, 77).

95. Du Bois was not completely shut out of learned societies. On December 28, 1900, he was elected member of the American Association for the Advancement of Science. This membership commenced shortly after Du Bois began establishing his scientific school in Atlanta. In 1944 Du Bois was elected member of the National Institute of Arts and Letters. Given the late date of this membership, it was not helpful in developing his school. See American Association for the Advancement of Science membership certificate, December 28, 1900, DBP, and National Institute of Arts and Letters diploma, 1944, DBP.

96. Bernard and Bernard (1943); Odum (1951); Madge (1962); Schwendinger and Schwendinger (1974); Turner and Turner (1990).

97. Odum (1951, 378).

98. Odum (1951, 379).

99. Odum (1951, 378).

100. Odum (1951, 384).

101. Odum (1951, 379).

102. Schwendinger and Schwendinger (1974, 503–8).

103. Schwendinger and Schwendinger (1974, 504).

104. Schwendinger and Schwendinger (1974, 507).

105. Oberschall (1972, 213).

106. Oberschall (1972, 217).

107. Oberschall (1972, 218).

108. Collins (1998).

109. Park (1928b).

110. Park (1928b, 892).

111. Park (1928b, 888). Park's quote here is from Frederick J. Teggart's *Theory of History*.

112. Du Bois, (1897c; [1903b] 2007).

113. Du Bois ([1903b] 2007, 3).

114. Du Bois ([1903b] 2007, 3).

115. Park ([1923] 1950, 291).

116. Goldberg (2012, 202).

117. Goldberg (2012, 202).

118. Marvick (1964, 336).

119. Stonequist (1937, 25).

120. Stonequist (1935, 1).

121. Stonequist (1937, 145).

122. Perhaps if Park and Burgess had paid attention to Weber's political sociology they would have emphasized the role that power and domination played in the oppression of racial groups.

6. MAX WEBER MEETS DU BOIS

1. Deegan (1988, 306).

2. Du Bois to Ernst Moritz Manasse, August 1, 1945, in Du Bois (1997, 45).

3. Tribe (1989, 99).

4. Tribe (1989, 88).

5. Adolph Wagner to D.C. Gilman, March 28, 1894, in Du Bois (1997, 27–28).

6. Gustav von Schmoller to D.C. Gilman, March 5, 1894, in Du Bois (1997, 28).

7. Scaff (2011, 103).

8. Scaff (2011, 103).

9. Scaff (2011, 102).

10. See Max Weber to Du Bois, November 8, 1904, in Scaff (2011, 257); Weber ([1910] 1973, 312); Scaff (2011, 98).

11. See Deegan (1988); Schuler (2004).

12. Deegan (1988).

13. Scaff (2011, 112–16).

14. See Bendix (1962, 13–48); Honigsheim (2000); Munters (1972).

15. Zimmerman (2006, 65).

16. Mommsen (1984, 41).

17. Quoted in Zimmerman (2006, 62).

18. Zimmerman (2006, 61).

19. Zimmerman (2006, 63).

20. Quoted in Zimmerman (2006, 56).

21. Quoted in Zimmerman (2006, 56).

22. Du Bois ([1903b] 2007, 8).

23. Scaff (2011).

24. Max Weber to Du Bois, November 8, 1904, in Scaff (2011, 257).

25. Coser (1971, 239).

26. W.E.B. Du Bois, "Caste in America," February 1904, DBP.

27. Du Bois (1909b, 142).
28. Du Bois (1909b, 142).
29. Du Bois (1909b, 143).
30. Du Bois (1909b, 144).
31. Park ([1937a] 1950, 185).
32. Du Bois (1909b, 144).
33. Du Bois (1909b, 153).
34. Du Bois (1909b, 149–50).
35. Du Bois (1909b, 145).
36. Mommsen (2000, 373).
37. Du Bois (1909b, 153).
38. Du Bois (1909b, 153).
39. Bulmer (1991, 182).
40. Max Weber to Du Bois, November 17, 1904, in Scaff (2011, 258).
41. Max Weber to Du Bois, November 17, 1904, in Scaff (2011, 258).
42. Max Weber to Du Bois, March 3, 1905, in Du Bois (1997, 106).
43. Max Weber to Du Bois, May 1, 1905, in Scaff (2011, 260).
44. It is not exactly clear as to why Weber was unsuccessful in getting Du Bois's *Souls* translated into German. Perhaps the outbreak of the Russian Revolution in 1905 distracted Weber from the task, given his preoccupation with that conflict.
45. Max Weber to Du Bois, March 3, 1905, in Du Bois (1997, 106).
46. Max Weber to Du Bois, March 30, 1905, in Scaff (2011, 259).
47. Max Weber to Du Bois, May 1, 1905, in Scaff (2011, 260).
48. Weber ([1910] 1973, 310)
49. Weber ([1910] 1973, 310).
50. Weber ([1910] 1973, 310).
51. Weber (1971, 36).
52. Weber ([1910] 1973, 311–12).
53. Weber (1971, 37).
54. Weber ([1910] 1973, 312).
55. Weber ([1910] 1973, 312).
56. Weber ([1910] 1973, 312).
57. Weber ([1910] 1973, 312).
58. Weber (1971, 37, 34).
59. Quoted in Roth and Wittich (1978, 398 n.).
60. See Scaff (2011, 1998); Chandler (2007).
61. Scaff (2011, 105).
62. Du Bois (1897a).
63. Weber ([1922] 1978, 1:389).
64. Weber ([1922] 1978, 2:933).
65. Du Bois (1909b, 142).
66. Weber ([1922] 1978, 2:934).
67. Du Bois (1909b, 154).
68. Du Bois, "Caste in America," 3.
69. Du Bois, "Caste in America," 8.
70. Du Bois ([1906c] 2006, 283).

71. Weber ([1922] 1978, 2:932).
72. Du Bois, "Caste in America," 3–4.
73. Du Bois ([1906c] 2006, 284).
74. Weber ([1922] 1978, 2:932).
75. Du Bois, "Caste in America," 7; Du Bois (1935, 25). Throughout his writings, Du Bois maintained that capitalists used racism to divide the working class. For example, see Du Bois (1902, esp. 153–80).
76. Scaff (2011, 112).
77. Abraham (1991, 48–49).
78. Abraham (1991, 64).
79. Du Bois ([1906c] 2006, 286).

7. INTELLECTUAL SCHOOLS AND THE ATLANTA SCHOOL

1. Merton (1957, 640).
2. Merton (1957, 639).
3. Merton (1957, 648).
4. Cole and Cole (1967).
5. Cole and Cole (1967, 384, 385).
6. Kuhn (1962).
7. Kuhn (1962, x).
8. See White (1993); Farrell (2001); Amsterdamska (1985); Collins (1998).
9. Collins (1998). I profited greatly from my discussions with my colleague Charles Camic regarding Randall Collins's formulation of intellectual networks, especially his tendency to treat them as isomorphic.
10. Collins (1998, 39).
11. Collins (1998, 4).
12. Collins (1998, 65).
13. Collins (1998, 2).
14. Collins (1998, 13).
15. Collins (1998, 11).
16. Collins (1998, 77).
17. Collins (1998, 58).
18. See Feagin and Feagin (2007); Omi and Winant (1994); Treitler (2013).
19. Du Bois ([1903b] 2007, 2).
20. Ellison ([1952] 1995, 3).
21. See McKee (1993); Morris (2007).
22. Anderson (1988).
23. I. Rogers (2012); Biondi (2012).
24. Saint-Arnaud (2009).
25. Bourdieu (2004).
26. Bourdieu (2004, 45).
27. Bourdieu (2004, 34).
28. Bourdieu (2004, 55–60).
29. Bourdieu (2004, 34).
30. Bourdieu (2004, 57).
31. Bourdieu (2004, 58).

32. For discussions of the bias of elite funders of research, see Stanfield (1985); Deegan (1990).

33. Bourdieu (2004, 57).

34. Bourdieu (2004, 47).

35. Bourdieu (2004, 47).

36. Bourdieu (2004, 62).

37. Du Bois (1968, 228).

38. For example, the members of the Chicago school were surrounded by accomplished and stimulating colleagues. These extended beyond sociology and included leading scholars in geography, anthropology, and philosophy. They also included talented graduate students whom senior scholars could train and collaborate with. Robert Park and his colleagues were embedded in dense networks of scholars who had access to intellectual and material resources. This situation contrasted sharply with that of professors at historically black colleges and universities, who had few resources, limited access to graduate students, and enormous teaching loads spanning courses from high school through graduate levels. The scholarly environment at black schools was not conducive to high rates of publishing and other scholarly activities. It is amazing that scholars like Du Bois accomplished so much with so little.

39. The study that was destroyed was based on a comprehensive analysis of the black community of Lowndes County in Alabama. According to Du Bois's account, when the study failed to appear after he had submitted it, he contacted the Department of Labor and was told that they were not going to publish it because it "touched on political matters." When he asked for its return, he was told it had been destroyed (Du Bois 1968:227). For a discussion of the controversy involved in the disappearance of Du Bois's study, see Wilson (2006, 80–81).

40. See Deegan (1990).

41. Gramsci (1971).

42. Woodson (1933, xiii).

43. Bulmer (1985). *The Scholar Denied* differs from the typical accounts that bemoan the obstacles resulting from the racism Du Bois encountered. Rather, the focus here is on Du Bois's extraordinary scholarly achievements despite those obstacles.

44. Bulmer (1985, 71).

45. Du Bois to Ben F. Rogers, December 20, 1939, DBP.

46. Bernard (1948, 14).

47. Gilkes (1996); Rabaka (2010).

48. E. Wright (2009).

49. Hine (1993, 1:593).

50. E. Wright (2009, 709).

51. Dill (1914, 93).

52. Du Bois and Dill (1910, 1911, 1912, 1914).

53. Dill (1914, 93).

54. David Levering Lewis has discussed the painful decision Du Bois made in accepting Dill's resignation. He writes, "Du Bois closed with the assurance that the 'little incident' had no bearing at all upon his painful decision. More

than thirty years later, however, the editor made a self-reproachful admission in *The Autobiography,* writing of a 'new and undreamed aspect of sex' bursting upon him, of having 'never understood the tragedy of Oscar Wilde,' and of dismissing a 'co-worker forthwith' and spending 'heavy days regretting my act.'" See Lewis (2000, 205).

55. Du Bois (1902, 1).

56. Du Bois (1902, 2).

8. LEGACIES AND CONCLUSIONS

1. Morris (2007, 530).

2. E. Franklin Frazier to Du Bois, August 2, 1939, DBP.

3. Platt (2001, xiv–xv).

4. Drake and Cayton ([1945] 1993).

5. Drake and Cayton ([1945] 1993, 787–88).

6. Drake and Cayton ([1945] 1993, 788).

7. Warner (1936, 234–37).

8. Myrdal (1944).

9. Du Bois (1968, 302).

10. Shari Cohen (2004, 9).

11. Gershenhorn (2004, 149–50).

12. Lewis (2000, 445–49); Gates (2000, 213); Gershenhorn (2004, 143–62).

13. Gershenhorn (2004, 150).

14. Gershenhorn (2004, 150).

15. Gershenhorn (2004, 155).

16. Gershenhorn (2004, 151, 155).

17. Gershenhorn (2004, 152).

18. Gershenhorn (2004, 150).

19. Gershenhorn (2004, 150–51).

20. Gershenhorn (2004, 156).

21. Jones (1917).

22. Watkins (1996, 239).

23. D. Johnson (2000).

24. D. Johnson (2000, 78).

25. Jones (1906, 5).

26. D. Johnson (2000, 90).

27. Du Bois (1918, 173).

28. D. Johnson (2000, 85).

29. D. Johnson (2000, 78).

30. Lewis (2000, 427).

31. Gershenhorn (2004, 143–49).

32. For a biography of Carter G. Woodson, see Goggin (1993).

33. Woodson (1933, ix).

34. There were tensions in Du Bois's and Woodson's scholarly relations. For example, Woodson refused to be on Du Bois's editorial board for the *Encyclopedia of the Negro,* claiming that it had been his idea to produce such a work. He wrote Du Bois, "I should add that the Associated Publishers, drawing upon

data collected for this purpose since 1922 by the Association for the Study of Negro Life and History would bring out its *Encyclopedia Africana* by the end of 1933. We welcome competition, because it is the spice of life." Carter G. Woodson to Du Bois, February 11, 1932, in Du Bois (1973, 449).

35. Brewer (1958, 161).

36. Lewis (2000, 206).

37. Quoted in Lewis (2000, 27).

38. Lewis (2000, 427–28).

39. Gershenhorn (2004, 153).

40. Anson Phelps Stokes to Robert E. Park, July 5, 1936, DBP.

41. Stokes to Park, July 5, 1936, DBP.

42. Robert E. Park to Anson Phelps Stokes, August 4, 1936, DBP.

43. Lewis (2000, 442). At the time Guy B. Johnson was chosen to replace Park as Du Bois's deputy editor of the *Encyclopedia* he was a sociology professor at the University of North Carolina. He was a moderate regarding racial matters who believed that only judicial action could change Jim Crow. In an interview in 1990 Guy recalled that racial segregation "was not going to be solved by political action in the South because they were not ready for it. . . . You can get out there and talk and shout your head off about getting rid of segregation, but that's not going to get rid of it. You're going to get rid of it through judicial action" (G. Johnson 1990). Thus Professor Guy was acceptable to white elite funders and scholars because his background suggested that his views would dampen Du Bois's radical tendencies. Despite Johnson's involvement, the encyclopedia project could not be saved. The two editors did manage to publish an insignificant preparatory volume. See Du Bois and Johnson (1945).

44. Du Bois to J. H. Dillard, November 30, 1931, DBP.

45. Shari Cohen (2004, 9).

46. Lewis (2000, 451).

47. Lewis (1995, 8).

48. Keppel (1944); Myrdal (1944, vii).

49. Myrdal (1944, xvii).

50. Gates (2000, 214).

51. Spark (2001, 477, 476).

52. Myrdal (1944, xvii).

53. Keppel (1944, vii).

54. Myrdal (1944, xlvii).

55. Myrdal (1944, lxix).

56. Myrdal (1944, li).

57. Myrdal (1944, 928).

58. Myrdal (1944, 929).

59. Myrdal (1944, 929).

60. Myrdal (1944, 75).

61. Dutt (2008, 1).

62. Dutt (2008, 1).

63. Roberts and Klibanoff (2006, 4).

64. Myrdal (1944, lxix).

65. Myrdal (1944, 998).

66. Myrdal (1944, lxix).

67. I owe this saying to the major civil rights leader Fred Shuttlesworth, whom I interviewed on September 12, 1978, in Cincinnati.

68. Du Bois (1935).

69. Du Bois ([1924] 1970, [1903b] 2007).

70. David Levering Lewis, e-mail to author, January 27, 2014.

71. Ellison (1964, 315–16).

72. Morris (2000).

73. Du Bois to Gunnar Myrdal, memo, April 13, 1939, DBP.

74. Du Bois to Myrdal, memo, April 13, 1939, DBP.

75. Du Bois to Myrdal, memo, April 13, 1939, DBP.

76. Myrdal (1944, 1132).

77. Wilson (2006, 57).

78. Gershenhorn (2004, 99–100).

79. Du Bois (1940b, 212).

80. Rabaka (2010).

81. Gilkes (2012).

82. C. Young (2009).

83. L. Baker (1998, 113).

84. L. Baker (1998, 107).

85. Bobo (2000, 196).

86. For examples of Bobo and his colleagues' work on racial attitudes, see also Schuman et al. (1997).

87. Bobo (2000, 196).

88. Du Bois (1935).

89. Lewis (2000, 349–87).

90. Du Bois ([1920] 2007, 15).

91. Du Bois ([1920] 2007, 16).

92. Du Bois (1935, 700).

93. Roediger (1991); Allen (1994).

94. Decker (2013, 2).

95. Du Bois ([1920] 2007, 87).

96. Hancock (2005, 79).

97. Gilkes (1996, 112).

98. Some scholars argue that although Du Bois's stance on women was pro-feminist, his actual treatment of women exemplified a promasculinist point of view. For examples of these criticisms, see James (1996); P. Giddings (2001).

99. Gabbidon (2007, 65).

100. For discussions of Du Bois's influence on black studies, see Grossman (1974); Warren (2011); Stewart (1984). For discussions of black studies and the civil rights and Black Power movements, see Biondi (2012); I. Rogers (2012). For a discussion of Du Bois's pioneering role in criminology, see Gabbidon (2007).

101. Quoted in P. Baker (1973, 258).

102. Robert E. Park to Booker T. Washington, n.d. [ca. 1914], in Raushen-bush (1979, 63).

103. Magubane (2014, 12).
104. Go (2013).
105. Go (2013, 49–50).
106. Quoted in King (1957, 29).
107. Lengermann (1979).
108. See Lengermann and Niebrugge-Brantley (1998).

References

Abbott, Andrew. 1999. *Department and Discipline: Chicago Sociology at One Hundred*. Chicago: University of Chicago Press.

Abbott, Andrew, and Rainer Egloff. 2008. "The Polish Peasant in Oberlin and Chicago: The Intellectual Trajectory of W.I. Thomas." *American Sociologist* 39 (4): 217–58.

Abraham, Gary A. 1991. "Max Weber: Modernist Anti-pluralism and the Polish Question." *New German Critique* 53:33–66.

Addams, Jane. 1908. "Address of Miss Jane Addams: Advantages and Disadvantages of a Broken Inheritance." *Atlanta University Bulletin*, no. 183 (June): 1–2.

———. 1910. *Twenty Years at Hull House*. Urbana: University of Illinois Press.

Alderman, Edwin. 1901. "Northern Aid to Southern Education." *Independent*, September 5, 2411–13.

Aldrich, Mark. 1979. "Progressive Economists and Scientific Racism: Walter Willcox and Black Americans, 1895–1910." *Phylon Quarterly* 40 (1): 1–14.

Allen, Theodore W. 1994. *The Invention of the White Race*. Vol. 1. *Racial Oppression and Social Control*. New York: Verso.

Amsterdamska, Olga. 1985. "Institutions and Schools of Thought: The Neogrammarians." *American Journal of Sociology* 92 (2): 332–58.

Anderson, James D. 1988. *The Education of Blacks in the South, 1860–1935*. Chapel Hill: University of North Carolina Press.

Appiah, Anthony. 1985. "The Uncompleted Argument: Du Bois and the Illusion of Race." *Critical Inquiry* 12 (1): 21–37.

Bacote, Clarence A. 1969. *The Story of Atlanta University: A Century of Service, 1865–1965*. Atlanta, GA: Atlanta University Press.

Baker, Lee D. 1998. *From Savage to Negro: Anthropology and the Construction of Race, 1896–1954*. Berkeley: University of California Press.

Baker, Paul J. 1973. "The Life Histories of W.I. Thomas and Robert E. Park." *American Journal of Sociology* 79 (2): 243–60.

Baker, Ray Stannard. 1908a. *Following the Color Line*. New York: Doubleday, Page.

———. [1908b] 2007. "An Ostracized Race in Ferment." *The New Negro: Readings on Race, Representation, and African American Culture, 1892–1938*, edited by Henry Louis Gates Jr. and Gene Andrew Jarrett, 69–78. Princeton, NJ: Princeton University Press.

Baldwin, James. 1984. "On Being White . . . and Other Lies." *Essence*, April.

Bay, Mia. 1998. "'The World Was Thinking Wrong about Race': *The Philadelphia Negro* and Nineteenth-Century Science." In Katz and Sugrue, 41–60.

Bell, Bernard, W., Emily R. Grosholz, and James B. Stewart, eds. 1996. *W.E.B. Du Bois on Race and Culture: Philosophy, Politics, and Poetics*. New York: Routledge.

Bendix, Reinhard. 1962. *Max Weber: An Intellectual Portrait*. Garden City, NY: Doubleday.

Bernard, Luther L. 1948. "Sociological Trends in the South." *Social Forces* 27 (1): 12–19.

Bernard, Luther L., and Jessie Bernard. 1943. *Origins of American Sociology; The Social Science Movement in the United States*. New York: Russell and Russell.

Biondi, Martha. 2012. *The Black Revolution on Campus*. Berkeley: University of California Press.

Blackwell, James E., and Morris Janowitz. 1974. *Black Sociologists: Historical and Contemporary Perspectives*. Chicago: University of Chicago Press.

Blassingame, John W. 1972. *The Slave Community: Plantation Life in the Antebellum South*. New York: Oxford University Press.

Boas, Franz. [1894] 1974. "Human Faculty as Determined by Race." In *A Franz Boas Reader: The Shaping of American Anthropology, 1883–1911*, edited by George W. Stocking Jr., 223–27. Chicago: University of Chicago Press.

———. 1911. *The Mind of Primitive Man*. New York: Macmillan.

———. 1916. "Old African Civilizations: Commencement Address, Atlanta University, May 31, 1906." In *Select Discussions of Race Problems*, edited by J.A. Bigham, 83–85. Atlanta University Publications No. 20. Atlanta, GA: Atlanta University Press.

Bobo, Lawrence. 2000. "Reclaiming a Du Boisian Perspective on Racial Attitudes." *Annals of the American Academy of Political and Social Science* 568 (1): 186–202.

Booth, Charles. 1892–97. *Life and Labour of the People in London*. London: Macmillan.

Bourdieu, Pierre. 2004. *Science of Science and Reflexivity*. Chicago: University of Chicago Press.

Bracey, John H., August Meier, and Elliott Rudwick. 1971. *The Black Sociologists: The First Half Century*. Belmont, CA: Wadsworth.

Braude, Lee. 1970. "'Park and Burgess': An Appreciation." *American Journal of Sociology* 76 (1): 1–10.

Breslau, Daniel. 2007. "The American Spencerians: Theorizing a New Science." In *Sociology in America: A History,* edited by Craig Calhoun, 39–62. Chicago: University of Chicago Press.

Brewer, William M. 1958. Review of *Southern Race Progress, The Wavering Color Line,* by Thomas J. Woofter. *Journal of Negro History* 43 (2): 161–63.

Brigg, Charles. 2005. "Genealogies of Race and Culture and the Failure of Vernacular Cosmopolitanisms: Rereading Franz Boas and W.E.B. Du Bois." *Public Culture* 17 (1): 75–100.

Broderick, Frances L. 1958. "German Influence on the Scholarship of W.E.B. DuBois." *Phylon Quarterly* 19 (4): 367–71.

———. 1974. "W.E.B. Du Bois: History of an Intellectual." In *Black Sociologists: Historical and Contemporary Perspectives,* edited by James E. Blackwell and Morris Janowitz, 3–24. Chicago: University of Chicago Press.

Bulmer, Martin. 1984. *The Chicago School of Sociology: Institutionalization, Diversity and the Rise of Sociological Research.* Chicago: University of Chicago Press.

———. 1985. "The Chicago School of Sociology: What Made It a 'School'?" *History of Sociology* 5 (2): 61–77.

———. 1991. "The Decline of the Social Survey Movement and the Rise of American Empirical Sociology." In Bulmer, Bales, and Sklar, 291–315.

Burawoy, Michael. 2004. "Public Sociologies: Contradictions, Dilemmas, and Possibilities." *Social Forces* 82 (4): 1–16.

Burawoy, Michael, William Gamson, Charlotte Ryan, Stephen Pfohl, Diane Vaughan, Charles Derber, and Juliet Schor. 2004. "Public Sociologies: A Symposium from Boston College." *Social Problems* 51 (1): 103–30.

Burgess, Ernest W. 1961. "Social Planning and Race Relations." In *Race Relations Problems and Theory: Essays in Honor of Robert E. Park,* edited by Jitsuichi Masuoka and Preston Valien, 13–25. Freeport, NY: Libraries Press.

Butler, John S. 2007. *Entrepreneurship and Self-Help among Black-Americans: A Reconsideration of Race and Economics.* Albany: State University of New York Press.

Camic, Charles, and Yu Xie. 1994. "The Statistical Turn in American Social Science: Columbia University, 1890 to 1915." *American Sociological Review* 59 (5): 773–805.

Chandler, Nahum D. 2007. "The Possible Form of an Interlocution: W.E.B. DuBois and Max Weber in Correspondence, 1904–1905." *New Centennial Review* 6 (3): 193–239.

Chicago Commission on Race Relations. 1922. *The Negro in Chicago: A Study of Race Relations and a Race Riot.* Chicago: University of Chicago Press.

Cohen, Shari. 2004. "The Lasting Legacy of *An American Dilemma*." *Carnegie Results* [Carnegie Corporation of New York], Fall, 9.

Cohen, Steven R. 1991. "The Pittsburgh Survey and the Social Survey Movement: A Sociological Road Not Taken." In Bulmer, Bales, and Sklar, 245–68.

Cole, Stephen, and Jonathan Cole. 1967. "Scientific Output and Recognition: A Study in the Operation of the Reward System in Science." *American Sociological Review* 32 (3): 377–90.

Collins, Randall. 1998. *The Sociology of Philosophies: A Global Theory of Intellectual Change*. Cambridge, MA: Harvard University Press.

Connell, R.W. 1997. "Why Is Classical Theory Classical?" *American Journal of Sociology* 102 (6): 1511–57.

Coser, Lewis A. 1971. *Masters of Sociological Thought*. New York: Harcourt Brace Jovanovich.

———. 1972. *Sociology through Literature*. 2nd ed. Englewood Cliffs, NJ: Prentice-Hall.

———. 1978. "American Trends." In *A History of Sociological Analysis*, edited by Tom Bottomore and Robert Nisbet, 283–321. New York: Basic Books.

Coulborn, Rushton, and W.E.B. Du Bois. 1942. "Mr. Sorokin's Systems." *Journal of Modern History* 14 (4): 500–521.

Crummell, Alexander. 1898. *The Attitude of the American Mind toward the Negro Intellect*. American Negro Academy, Occasional Papers, No. 3. Washington, DC: American Negro Academy.

Darity, William A., Jr. 1994. "Many Roads to Extinction: Early AEA Economists and the Black Disappearance Hypothesis." *History of Economics Review* 21 (Winter): 47–64.

Decker, Robert Julio. 2013. "The Visibility of Whiteness and Immigration Restriction in the United States, 1880–1930." *Critical Race and Whiteness Studies* 9 (1): 1–20.

Deegan, M.J. 1988. "W.E.B. Du Bois and the Women of Hull-House, 1895–1899." *American Sociologist* 19 (4): 301–11.

———. 1990. *Jane Addams and the Men of the Chicago School, 1892–1918*. New Brunswick, NJ: Transaction Books.

———. 2001. "The Chicago School of Ethnography." In *Handbook of Ethnography*, edited by P.A. Atkinson, A.J. Coffey, S. Delamont, J. Lofland, and L. Lofland, 11–25. London: Sage Publications.

———. 2006. "The Human Drama behind the Study of People as Potato Bugs: The Curious Marriage of Robert E. Park and Clara Cahill Park." *Journal of Classical Sociology* 6 (1): 101–22.

Dill, Augustus Granville. 1914. Autobiographical postgraduation entry in "Records of the Class." In *Secretary's Second Report: Harvard College, Class of 1908, Sexennial Celebration, June*, edited by Guy Emerson, 92–94. Cambridge, MA: Harvard University Printing Office.

Drake, St. Clair. 1983. "The Tuskegee Connection: Booker T. Washington and Robert E. Park." *Society* 20 (4): 82–92.

Drake, St. Clair, and Horace A. Cayton. [1945] 1993. *Black Metropolis: A Study of Negro Life in a Northern City*. Chicago: University of Chicago Press.

Du Bois, W.E.B. Papers. Department of Special Collections and University Archives, University of Massachusetts Amherst Libraries.

———. 1896. *The Suppression of the African Slave-Trade to the United States of America, 1638–1870*. New York: Longmans, Green.

———, ed. 1897–1914. Atlanta University Studies of the Negro Problem. Annual Conferences. Atlanta, GA: Atlanta University Press.

———. 1897a. *The Conservation of Races*. American Negro Academy, Occasional Papers, No. 2. Washington, DC: American Negro Academy.

———. 1897b. Review of *Race Traits and Tendencies of the American Negro* by Frederick L. Hoffman. *Annals of the American Academy of Political and Social Science* 9 (January): 127–33.

———. 1897c. "Strivings of the Negro People." *Atlantic Monthly*, August, 194–97.

———. 1898a. "The Negroes of Farmville, Virginia: A Social Study." *Bulletin of the Department of Labor*, no. 14 (January): 1–38.

———. 1898b. "The Study of the Negro Problems." *Annals of the American Academy of Political and Social Science* 2 (January): 1–23.

———. 1899a. "The Negro in the Black Belt: Some Social Sketches." *Bulletin of the Department of Labor* no. 22 (May): 401–17.

———. [1899b] 1973. *The Philadelphia Negro*. Millwood, NY: Kraus-Thomson.

———. 1900. "The American Negro at Paris." *American Monthly Review of Reviews* 22, no. 5 (November): 575–77.

———. [1901a] 1969. *The Black North in 1901: A Social Study*. New York: Arno Press and New York Times.

———. 1901b. "The Relation of the Negroes to the Whites in the South." *Annals of the American Academy of Political and Social Science* 18: 121–40.

———, ed. 1902. *The Negro Artisan: Report of a Social Study Made under the Direction of Atlanta University; Together with the Proceedings of the Seventh Conference for the Study of the Negro Problems, Held at Atlanta University, on May 27th, 1902*. Atlanta University Publications 7. Atlanta, GA: Atlanta University Press.

———, ed. 1903a. *The Negro Church: Report of a Social Study Made under the Direction of Atlanta University; Together with the Proceedings of the Eighth Conference for the Study of the Negro Problems*. Atlanta University Publications 8. Atlanta, GA: Atlanta University Press.

———. [1903b] 2007. *The Souls of Black Folk*. Edited by Henry Louis Gates. Oxford: Oxford University Press.

———. 1903c. "The Talented Tenth." In *The Negro Problem: A Series of Articles by Representative American Negroes of Today*, edited by Booker T. Washington, 31–76. New York: James Pott.

———. 1904a. "The Development of a People." *International Journal of Ethics* 14 (3): 292–311.

———. [1904b] 2002. "Heredity in Public Schools." In *Du Bois on Education*, edited by Eugene F. Provenzo Jr. Walnut Creek, CA: Altamira Press.

———, ed. 1904c. *Some Notes on Negro Crime Particularly in Georgia. Report of a Social Study Made under the Direction of Atlanta University; Together with the Proceedings of the Ninth Conference for the Study of the Negro Problems, Held at Atlanta University, May 24, 1904*. Atlanta University Publications 9. Atlanta, GA: Atlanta University Press.

———, ed. 1906a. *The Health and Physique of the Negro American: Report of a Social Study Made under the Direction of Atlanta University, Together with the Proceedings of the Eleventh Conference for the Study of the Negro*

Problems, Held at Atlanta University, on May the 29th, 1906. Atlanta University Publications 11. Atlanta, GA: Atlanta University Press.

———. 1906b. "A Litany of Atlanta." *Independent*, October 11, 856–58.

———. [1906c] 2006. "Die Negerfrage in den Vereinigten Staaten." Translated by Joseph G. Fracchia as "The Negro Question in the United States." *New Centennial Review* 6 (3): 241–90.

———. 1907. "Religion in the South." In *The Negro in the South: His Economic Progress in Relation to His Moral and Religious Development*, by Booker T. Washington and W. E. Burghardt Du Bois, 123–91. Philadelphia: George W. Jacobs.

———, ed. 1908. *The Negro American Family: Report of a Social Study Made Principally by the College Classes of 1909 and 1910 of Atlanta University, under the Patronage of the Trustees of the John F. Slater Fund, Together with the Proceedings of the 13th Annual Conference for the Study of the Negro Problems, Held at Atlanta University on Tuesday, May the 26th, 1908.* Atlanta University Publications 13. Atlanta, GA: Atlanta University Press.

———. 1909a. *Efforts for Social Betterment among Negro Americans.* Atlanta, GA: Atlanta University Press.

———. 1909b. "The Evolution of the Race Problem." In *Proceedings of the National Negro Conference, 1909, New York, May 31 and June 1*, 142–58. New York: n.p.

———. 1909c. *John Brown.* Philadelphia: George W. Jacobs.

———. 1910. "Reconstruction and Its Benefits." *American Historical Review* 15 (4): 781–99.

———. 1913. "The Negro in Literature and Art." *Annals of the American Academy of Political and Social Science* 49 (September): 862–67.

———. 1915a. "African Roots of War." *Atlantic Monthly*, May, 707–14.

———. 1915b. *The Negro.* New York: Henry Holt.

———. 1915c. "Woman Suffrage." *Crisis*, April, 29–30.

———. 1918. "Negro Education." *Crisis*, February, 173–78.

———. [1920] 2007. *Darkwater: Voices from within the Veil.* Edited by Henry Louis Gates. Oxford: Oxford University Press.

———. [1921] 1996. "Manifesto of the Second Pan-African Congress." In *The Oxford W. E. B. Du Bois Reader*, edited by Eric J. Sundquist, 640–43. New York: Oxford University Press.

———. [1924] 1970. *The Gift of Black Folk.* New York: Washington Square Press.

———. 1935. *Black Reconstruction in America, 1860–1880: An Essay toward a History of the Part Which Black Folk Played in the Attempt to Reconstruct Democracy in America.* New York: Henry Holt.

———. 1939. *Black Folk Then and Now: An Essay in the History and Sociology of the Negro Race.* New York: Henry Holt.

———. [1940a] 2007. *Dusk of Dawn: An Essay towards an Autobiography of a Race Concept.* Edited by Henry Louis Gates. Oxford: Oxford University Press.

———. 1940b. "Social Development of the American Negro." Review of *The Negro Family in the United States*, by E. Franklin Frazier. *Journal of Negro Education* 9 (2): 212–13.

———. 1944. "Prospect of a World without Race Conflict." *American Journal of Sociology* 49 (5): 450–56.

———. 1968. *The Autobiography of W.E.B. DuBois: A Soliloquy on Viewing My Life from the Last Decade of Its First Century.* New York: International Publishers.

———. 1973. *The Correspondence of W.E.B. DuBois.* Vol. 1. *Selections, 1877–1934.* Edited by Herbert Aptheker. Amherst: University of Massachusetts Press.

———. 1997. *The Correspondence of W.E.B. Du Bois.* Vol. 3. *Selections, 1944–1963.* Edited by Herbert Aptheker. Amherst: University of Massachusetts Press.

———. 2000. "Sociology Hesitant: Thinking with W.E.B. Du Bois." *Boundary 2* 27 (3): 37–44.

Du Bois, W.E.B., and Augustus Granville Dill, eds. 1910. *The College-Bred Negro: Report of a Social Study Made by Atlanta University under the Patronage of the John F. Slater Fund; Together with the Proceedings of the 15th Annual Conference for the Study of the Negro Problems, Atlanta University, May 24, 1910.* Atlanta University Publications 15. Atlanta, GA: Atlanta University Press.

———, eds. 1911. *The Common School and the Negro American: Report of a Social Study Made by Atlanta University under the Patronage of the Trustees of the John F. Slater Fund; with the Proceedings of the 16th Annual Conference for the Study of the Negro Problems, Atlanta University, May 30, 1911.* Atlanta University Publications 16. Atlanta, GA: Atlanta University Press.

———, eds. 1912. *The Negro American Artisan: Report of a Social Study Made by Atlanta University under the Patronage of the Trustees of the John F. Slater Fund; with the Proceedings of the 17th Annual Conference for the Study of the Negro Problems, Atlanta University, May 27, 1912.* Atlanta University Publications 17. Atlanta, GA: Atlanta University Press.

———, eds. 1914. *Morals and Manners among Negro Americans: Report of a Social Study Made by Atlanta University under the Patronage of the Trustees of the John F. Slater Fund; with the Proceedings of the 18th Annual Conference for the Study of the Negro Problems, Atlanta University, May 26, 1914.* Atlanta University Publications 18. Atlanta, GA: Atlanta University Press.

Du Bois, W.E.B., and Guy Johnson. *Encyclopedia of the Negro: Preparatory Volume with Reference Lists and Reports.* New York: Phelps-Stokes Fund, 1945.

Dutt, Amitava Krishna. 2008. "Myrdal, Gunnar, 1898–1987." In *International Encyclopedia of the Social Sciences.* www.encyclopedia.com/topic/Gunnar_Myrdal.aspx.

Eaton, Isabel. [1899] 1973. "Special Report on Negro Domestic Service In the Seventh Ward Philadelphia." In *The Philadelphia Negro*, by W.E.B. Du Bois, 427–520. Millwood, NY: Kraus-Thomson.

Ellison, Ralph. [1952] 1995. *The Invisible Man.* New York: Vintage International.

———. 1964. "The American Dilemma: A Review." In *Shadow and Act*, 303–17. New York: Random House.

England, Lynn, and Keith W. Warner. 2013. "W.E.B. Du Bois: Reform, Will, and the Veil." *Social Forces* 91 (3): 955–73.

Faris, Robert E.L. 1967. *Chicago Sociology, 1920–1932*. Chicago: University of Chicago Press.

Farrell, Michael P. 2001. *Collaborative Circles: Friendship Dynamics and Creative Work*. Chicago: University of Chicago Press.

Feagin, Joe, and Clairece Booher Feagin. 2007. *Race and Ethnic Relations*. Upper Saddle River, NJ: Prentice Hall.

Fine, Gary A., ed. 1995. *A Second Chicago School?* Chicago: University of Chicago.

Franklin, John Hope. 1968. *From Slavery to Freedom: A History of African Americans*. New York: Alfred A. Knopf.

Frazier, E. Franklin. 1935. *The Negro in Harlem: A Report on Social and Economic Conditions Responsible for the Outbreak of March 19, 1935*. Mayor's Commission on Conditions in Harlem. New York: n.p.

Gabbidon, Shaun L. 2007. *W.E.B. Du Bois on Crime and Justice: Laying the Foundations of Sociological Criminology*. Aldershot: Ashgate.

Galton, Francis. 1904. "Eugenics: Its Definition, Scope, and Aims." *American Journal of Sociology* 10 (1): 1–25.

Gates, Henry Louis, Jr. 2000. "W.E.B. Du Bois and the Encyclopedia Africana." *Annals of the American Academy of Political and Social Science* 568 (March): 203–17.

Gershenhorn, Jerry. 2004. *Melville J. Herskovits and the Racial Politics of Knowledge*. Lincoln: University of Nebraska Press.

Giddings, Franklin H. 1896. *Principles of Sociology*. New York: Macmillan.

Giddings, Paula. 2001. "Missing in Action: Ida B. Wells, the NAACP, and the Historical Record." *Meridians* 1 (2): 1–17.

Gilkes, Cheryl Townsend. 1996. "The Margin as the Center of a Theory of History." In Bell, Grosholz, and Stewart, 111–39.

———. 2012. Critic at the "Author Meets Critic" session on *Blacks and Whites in Christian America: How Racial Discrimination Shapes Religious Convictions*, by Jason E. Shelton and Michael O. Emerson. Annual meeting of the Association of Black Sociologists, Denver, CO, August 18.

Go, Julian. 2013. "For a Postcolonial Sociology." *Theory and Society* 42 (January): 25–55.

Goggin, Jacqueline. 1993. *Carter G. Woodson: A Life in Black History*. Baton Rouge: Louisiana State University Press.

Goldberg, Chad A. 2012. "Robert Park's Marginal Man: The Career of a Concept in American Sociology." *Laboratorium: Russian Review of Social Research* 4 (2): 199–217.

Gooding-Williams, Robert. 2011. *In the Shadow of Du Bois: Afro-Modern Political Thought in America*. Cambridge, MA: Harvard University Press.

Gramsci, Antonio. 1971. *Selections from the Prison Notebooks*. New York: International Publishers.

Green, Dan S., and Edwin Driver, eds. 1978. *W.E.B. DuBois on Sociology and the Black Community*. Chicago: University of Chicago Press.

Grossman, Jonathan. 1974. "Black Studies in the Department of Labor, 1897–1907." *Monthly Labor Review* 97:17–27.

Guglielmo, Jennifer, and Salvatore Salerno, eds. 2003. *Are Italians White? How Race Is Made in America*. New York: Routledge.

Hancock, Angie-Marie. 2005. "W.E.B. Du Bois: Intellectual Father of Intersectionality?" *Souls* 7 (3): 74–84.

Harlan, Louis R. 1972. *Booker T. Washington: The Making of a Black Leader, 1856–1901*. Oxford: Oxford University Press.

———. 1983. *Booker T. Washington: The Wizard of Tuskegee, 1901–1915*. New York: Oxford University Press.

Haynes, George Edmund. 1912. *The Negro at Work In New York City: A Study in Economic Progress*. New York: Columbia University Press.

Herskovits, Melville J. 1941. *The Myth of the Negro Past*. New York: Harper Brothers.

Hine, Darlene Clark, ed. 1993. *Black Women in America: An Historical Encyclopedia*. Vol. 1. Brooklyn, NY: Carlson.

Hoffman, Frederick L. 1896. *Race Traits and Tendencies of the American Negro*. Publications of the American Economic Association 11/1–3. New York: Macmillan.

Hofstadter, Richard. 1944. "U.B. Phillips and the Plantation Legend." *Journal of Negro History* 29 (2): 109–24.

Holt, Thomas. 1998. "W.E.B. DuBois's Archaeology of Race: Rereading 'The Conservation of Races.'" In Katz and Sugrue, 61–76.

Honigsheim, Paul. 2000. *The Unknown Max Weber*. Edited by Alan Sica. New Brunswick, NJ: Transaction.

Horne, Gerald, and Mary Young, eds. 2001. *W.E.B. Du Bois: An Encyclopedia*. Westport, CT: Greenwood Press.

Hunter, Albert. 1980. "Why Chicago? The Rise of the Chicago School of Urban Social Science." *American Behavioral Scientist* 24 (2): 215–27.

Hunter, Marcus Anthony. 2013a. *Black City Makers: How the Philadelphia Negro Changed Urban America*. Oxford: Oxford University Press.

———. 2013b. "A Bridge over Troubled Urban Waters: W.E.B. Du Bois's *The Philadelphia Negro* and the Ecological Conundrum." *Du Bois Review* 10 (1): 1–25.

James, Joy. 1996. "The Profeminist Politics of W.E.B. Du Bois with Respects to Anna Julia Cooper and Ida B. Wells." In Bell, Grosholz, and Stewart, 142–60.

Jazbinsek, Dietmar, Bernwald Joerges, and Ralf Thies. 2001. "The Berlin 'Großstadt-Dokumente': A Forgotten Precursor of the Chicago School of Sociology." Social Science Research Center, Berlin, WZB Discussion Paper, No. FS II 01–502. http://bibliothek.wzb.eu/pdf/2001/ii01-502.pdf.

Johnson, Brian Lamont. 2003. "William Edward Burghardt Du Bois (1883–1934): Authorship, Reform Writing and Periodical-Based Leadership." PhD diss., University of South Carolina.

Johnson, Donald. 2000. "W. E. B. Du Bois, Thomas Jesse Jones and the Struggle for Social Education, 1900–1939." *Journal of Negro History* 85 (3): 71–95.

Johnson, Guy. 1990. Interview A-0345. July 22. By John Egerton. Southern Oral History Program Collection, Louis Round Wilson Special Collections Library, University of North Carolina, Chapel Hill. http://dc.lib.unc.edu/cdm/compoundobject/collection/sohp/id/8675/rec/1.

Jones, Thomas Jesse. 1906. *Social Studies in the Hampton Curriculum*. Hampton, VA: Hampton Institute Press.

———. 1917. *Negro Education: A Study of the Private and Higher United States Schools for Colored People in the United States*. Washington, DC: Government Printing Office.

Katz, Michael B., and Thomas J. Sugrue, eds. 1998. *W. E. B. DuBois, Race, and the City: "The Philadelphia Negro" and Its Legacy*. Philadelphia: University of Pennsylvania Press.

Keppel, F. P. 1944. Foreword to *An American Dilemma*, by Gunnar Myrdal. New York: Harper and Brothers.

King, Martin Luther. 1957. "Facing the Challenge of a New Age." *Phylon Quarterly* 1 (1): 25–34.

Knight, Louise, W. 2005. *Citizen: Jane Addams and the Struggle for Democracy*. Chicago University of Chicago Press.

Kuhn, Thomas. 1962. *The Structure of Scientific Revolutions*. Chicago: University of Chicago Press.

Lengermann, Patricia Madoo. 1979. "The Founding of the *American Sociological Review*: The Anatomy of a Rebellion." *American Sociological Review* 44 (2): 185–98.

Lengermann, Patricia Madoo, and Jill Niebrugge-Brantley, eds. 1998. *The Women Founders: Sociology and Social Theory, 1830–1930*. Boston: McGraw-Hill.

Lewis, David Levering. 1993. *W. E. B. DuBois: Biography of a Race*. New York: Henry Holt.

———. 1995. Introduction to *W. E. B. DuBois: A Reader*, edited by David Levering Lewis, 1–15. New York: Henry Holt.

———. 2000. *W. E. B. DuBois: The Fight for Equality and the American Century, 1919–1963*. New York: Henry Holt.

Liberson, Stanley. 1980. *A Piece of the Pie: Blacks and White Immigrants since 1880*. Berkeley: University of California Press.

Lindsay, Samuel McCune. 1898. "The Unit of Investigation or of Consideration in Sociology." *Annals of the American Academy of Political and Social Science* 12 (September): 42–56.

Lyman, Stanford, M. 1972. *The Black American in Sociological Thought*. New York: G. P. Putnam's Sons.

Madge, John. 1962. *The Origins of Scientific Sociology*. New York: Free Press of Glencoe.

Magubane, Zine. 2014. "Science, Reform, and the 'Science of Reform': Booker T. Washington, Robert Park, and the Making of a 'Science of Society.'" *Current Sociology* 62 (March): 1–16.

Marable, Manning. 1986. *W. E. B. Du Bois: Black Radical Democrat*. Boulder, CO: Paradigm.

Marvick, Elizabeth Wirth. 1964. "Louis Wirth: A Biographical Memorandum." In *Louis Wirth on Cities and Social Life: Selected Papers*, edited by Albert I. Reiss Jr., 333–40. Chicago: University of Chicago Press.

Massey, Douglas S., and Nancy Denton. 1993. *American Apartheid: Segregation and the Making of the Underclass*. Cambridge, MA: Harvard University Press.

Matthews, Fred H. 1977. *Quest for an American Sociology: Robert E. Park and the Chicago School*. Montreal: McGill-Queen's University Press.

McKee, James B. 1993. *Sociology and the Race Problem: The Failure of a Perspective*. Urbana: University of Illinois Press.

McMurry, Linda O. 1985. *Recorder of the Black Experience: A Biography of Monroe Nathan Work*. Baton Rouge: Louisiana State University Press.

Meier, August, and Elliot Rudwick. 1966. *From Plantation to Ghetto*. New York: Hill and Wang.

Merton, Robert. [1948] 1968. *Social Theory and Social Structure*. Enl. ed. New York: Free Press.

———. 1957. "Priorities in Scientific Discovery: A Chapter in the Sociology of Science." *American Sociological Review* 22 (5): 635–59.

Miller, Kelly. 1897. *Review of "Race Traits and Tendencies of the American Negro," by Frederick Ludwig Hoffman*. American Negro Academy, Occasional Papers, No. 1. Washington, DC: American Negro Academy.

Mills, Charles W. 1997. *The Racial Contract*. Ithaca, NY: Cornell University Press.

Mommsen, Wolfgang J. 1984. *Max Weber and German Politics, 1890–1920*. Translated by Michael Steinberg. Chicago: University of Chicago Press.

———. 2000. "Max Weber's 'Grand Sociology': The Origins and Composition of *Wirtschaft und Gesellschaft: Soziologie*." *History and Theory* 39 (3): 364–83.

Morris, Aldon D. 1984. *The Origins of the Civil Rights Movement: Black Communities Organizing for Change*. New York: Free Press.

———. 2000. "Reflections on Social Movement Theory: Criticisms and Proposals." *Contemporary Sociology* 29 (May): 445–54.

———. 2007. "Sociology of Race and W. E. B. DuBois: The Path Not Taken." In *Sociology in America: A History*, edited by Craig Calhoun, 503–34. Chicago: University of Chicago Press.

Morris, Aldon D., and Naomi Braine. 2001. "Social Movements and Oppositional Consciousness." In *Oppositional Consciousness: The Subjective Roots of Social Protest*, edited by Jane Mansbridge and Aldon Morris, 20–37. Chicago: University of Chicago Press.

Morris, Aldon D., and Amin Ghaziani. 2005. "DuBoisian Sociology: A Watershed of Professional and Public Sociology." *Souls: A Critical Journal of Black Politics, Culture, and Society* 7 (3–4): 47–54.

Muhammad, Khalil Gibran. 2010. *The Condemnation of Blackness: Race, Crime, and the Making of Modern Urban America*. Cambridge, MA: Harvard University Press.

Munters, Q.J. 1972. "Max Weber as Rural Sociologist." *Sociologia Ruralis* 12 (2): 129–45.

Myrdal, Gunnar. 1944. *An American Dilemma: The Negro Problem and Modern Democracy.* New York: Harper and Brothers.

Oberschall, Anthony. 1972. "The Institutionalization of American Sociology." In *The Establishment of Empirical Sociology: Studies in Continuity, Discontinuity, and Institutionalization,* edited by Anthony Oberschall, 187–51. New York: Harper and Row.

Odum, Howard W. 1910. *Social and Mental Traits of the Negro: Research into the Conditions of the Negro Race in Southern Towns, A Study in Race Traits, Tendencies and Prospects.* New York: Columbia University Press.

———. 1951. *American Sociology: The Story of Sociology in the United States through 1950.* New York: Longmans, Green.

Omi, Michael, and Howard Winant. 1994. *Racial Formation in the United States: From the 1960s to the 1990s.* New York: Routledge Press.

Ordover, Nancy. 2003. *American Eugenics: Race, Queer Anatomy, and the Science of Nationalism.* Minneapolis: University of Minnesota Press.

Outlaw, Lucius. 1996. "'Conserve' Races? In Defense of W.E.B. Du Bois." In Bell, Grosholz, and Stewart, 1–37.

Ovington, Mary W. 1911. *Half a Man: The Status of the Negro in New York.* New York: Longmans, Green.

———. 1947. *The Walls Came Tumbling Down.* New York: Schocken Books.

Park, Robert E. 1913a. "Negro Home Life and Standards of Living." *Annals of the American Academy of Political and Social Science* 49 (September): 147–63.

———. [1913b] 1950. "Racial Assimilation in Secondary Groups: With Special Reference to the Negro." In Park 1950c, 204–20.

———. 1915. "The City: Suggestions for the Investigation of Human Behavior in the City Environment." *American Journal of Sociology* 20 (5): 577–612.

———. [1918] 1950. "Education in Its Relation to the Conflict and Fusion of Cultures." In Park 1950c, 261–83.

———. [1923] 1950. "Negro Race Consciousness as Reflected in Race Literature." In Park 1950c, 284–300.

———. [1925a] 1950. "Culture and Cultural Trends." In Park 1950c, 24–35.

———. [1925b] 1967. "The City: Suggestions for the Investigation of Human Behavior in the Urban Environment." In *The City,* edited by Robert E. Park, Ernest W. Burgess, and Roderick D. McKenzie, 1–46. Chicago: University of Chicago Press.

———. [1926a] 1950. "Our Racial Frontier on the Pacific." In Park 1950c, 138–51.

———. 1926b. Review of *The Melting-Pot Mistake,* by Henry Pratt Fairchild; *Eugenics and Politics,* by Ferdinand Canning Scott Schiller; *Temperament and Race,* by S.D. Porteus and Marjorie E. Babcock; *Intelligence and Immigration,* by Clifford Kilpatrick; and *The Immigration Problem: A Study of American Immigration Conditions and Needs,* by Jeremiah W. Jenks, W. Jett Lauck, and Rufus D. Smith. *American Journal of Sociology* 32 (2): 300–303.

———. [1928a] 1950. "The Bases of Race Prejudice." In Park 1950c, 230–43.

———. 1928b. "Human Migration and the Marginal Man." *American Journal of Sociology* 33 (6): 881–93.

———. [1931] 1950. "Mentality of Racial Hybrids." In Park 1950c, 377–92.

———. [1937a] 1950. "The Etiquette of Race Relations in the South." In Park 1950c, 177–88.

———. 1937b. Review of *Primitive Behavior*, by W. I. Thomas. *American Sociological Review* 2:286–90.

———. 1941. "Methods of Teaching: Impression and a Verdict." *Social Forces* 20 (1): 36–46.

———. [1943] 1950. "Education and the Cultural Crisis." In Park 1950c, 316–30.

———. 1950a. "Autobiographical Note." In Park 1950c, v–ix.

———. 1950b. "Culture and Civilization." In Park 1950c, 15–23.

———. 1950c. *Race and Culture*. Glencoe, IL: Free Press.

Park, Robert E., and Ernest W. Burgess. 1921. *Introduction to the Science of Sociology*. Chicago: University of Chicago Press.

Park, Robert E., and Herbert Adolphus Miller. 1921. *Old World Traits Transplanted*. New York: Harper and Brothers.

Patillo, Mary. 2012. Critic at the "Author Meets Critic" session on *Against Epistemic Apartheid: W. E. B. Du Bois and the Disciplinary Decadence of Sociology*, by Reiland Rabaka. Annual meeting of the Association of Black Sociologists, Denver, CO, August 18.

Phillips, U. B. 1918. *American Negro Slavery*. New York: D. Appleton.

———. 1929. *Life and Labor in the Old South*. Boston: Little, Brown.

Platt, Anthony M. 2001. Introduction to *The Negro Family in the United States*, by E. Franklin Frazier. Notre Dame, IN: University of Notre Dame Press.

Portes, Alejandro, and Ruben G. Rumbaut. 1990. *Immigrant America: A Portrait*. Berkeley: University of California Press.

Rabaka, Reiland. 2010. *Against Epistemic Apartheid: W. E. B. Du Bois and the Disciplinary Decadence of Sociology*. Lanham, MD: Rowman and Littlefield.

Raushenbush, Winifred. 1979. *Robert E. Park: Biography of a Sociologist*. Durham, NC: Duke University Press.

Reed, Adolph L., Jr. 1992. "DuBois's 'Double Consciousness': Race and Gender in Progressive Era American Thought." *Studies in American Political Development* 6 (1): 93–139.

———. 1997. *W. E. B. Du Bois and American Political Thought: Fabianism and the Color Line*. New York: Oxford University Press.

Roberts, Gene, and Hank Klibanoff. 2006. *The Race Beat: The Press, the Civil Rights Struggle, and the Awakening of a Nation*. New York: Alfred A. Knopf.

Roediger, David, R. 1991. *The Wages of Whiteness: Race and the Making of the American Working Class*. New York: Verso.

———. 2005. *Working toward Whiteness: How America's Immigrants Became White. The Strange Journey from Ellis Island to the Suburbs*. New York: Basic Books.

Rogers, Howard J., ed. 1904. *Congress of Arts and Science: Universal Exposition, St. Louis, 1904*. Vol. 1. Boston: Houghton Mifflin.

Rogers, Ibram H. 2012. *The Black Campus Movement: Black Students and the Racial Reconstruction of Higher Education, 1965–1972*. New York: Palgrave Macmillan.

Roth, Guenther, and Claus Wittich, eds. 1978. *Max Weber: Economy and Society*. Berkeley: University of California Press.

Rudwick, Elliott. 1957. "W. E. B. Du Bois and the Atlanta University Studies on the Negro." *Journal of Negro Education* 26:466–76.

———. 1969. "Note on a Forgotten Black Sociologist: W. E. B. Du Bois and the Sociological Profession." *American Sociologist* 4 (4): 303–6.

———. 1972. *W. E. B. Du Bois: Propagandist of the Negro Protest*. New York: Doubleday, Page.

Saint-Arnaud, Pierre. 2009. *African American Pioneers of Sociology: A Critical History*. Translated by Peter Feldstein. Toronto: University of Toronto Press.

Sanborn, Frank R., ed. 1905. "Proceedings of the American Association." *Journal of Social Science, Containing the Proceedings of the American Association*, no. 43.

Sanders, Frederic W. 1896. Review of *Hull House Maps and Papers*, by Jane Addams. *Political Science Quarterly* 11:340–42.

Scaff, Lawrence. 2011. *Max Weber in America*. Princeton, NJ: Princeton University Press.

Schafer, Axel R. 2000. *American Progressives and German Social Reform, 1875–1920*. USA-Studien 12. Stuttgart: Steiner.

———. 2001. "W. E. B. Du Bois, German Social Thought, and the Racial Divide in American Progressivism, 1892–1909." *Journal of American History* 88 (3): 925–49.

Schuler, Anja. 2004. *Frauenbewegung und soziale Reform: Jane Addams und Alice Salomon im transatlantischen Dialog, 1889–1933*. Stuttgart: Franz Steiner.

Schuman, Howard, Charlotte Steeh, Lawrence Bobo, and Maria Krysan. 1997. *Racial Attitudes in America: Trends and Interpretations*. Rev. ed. Cambridge, MA: Harvard University Press.

Schwendinger, Herman, and Julia Schwendinger. 1974. *The Sociologists of the Chair: A Radical Analysis of the Formative Years of North American Sociology (1883–1922)*. New York: Basic Books.

Scott, Emmett J., and Lyman Beecher Stowe. 1916. *Booker T. Washington, Builder of a Civilization*. Garden City, NY: Doubleday Page.

Seligman, E. R. 1924. "Biographical Memoir, Richmond Mayo-Smith, 1854–1901." *Memoirs of the National Academy of Sciences* 17:71–77.

Sica, Alan. "A Century of Sociology at Kansas." *Footnotes* [American Sociological Association], March 8, 1991.

Sklar, Kathryn Kish. 1991. "Hull-House Maps and Papers: Social Science as Women's Work in the 1890s." In Bulmer, Bales, and Sklar, 111–47.

Small, Albion W. 1905. "Interests." In *General Sociology*, 425–42. Chicago: University of Chicago Press.

———. 1916. "Fifty Years of Sociology in the United States (1865–1915)." *American Journal of Sociology* 21 (6): 721–864.

Spark, Clare I. 2001. "Race, Caste, or Class? The Bunche-Myrdal Dispute over 'An American Dilemma.'" *International Journal of Politics, Culture, and Society* 14 (3): 465–511.

Spencer, Herbert. 1851. *Social Statics: The Conditions Essential to Human Happiness.* London: John Chapman.

Stanfield, John H. 1985. *Philanthropy and Jim Crow in American Social Science.* Westport, CT: Greenwood Press.

Steinberg, Stephen. 2007. *Race Relations: A Critique.* Stanford, CA: Stanford University Press.

———. 2010. "Civilizing the Primitive: From Robert Ezra Park to William Julius Wilson, from Tuskegee to the Harlem Children's Zone." Paper presented at the Workshop on Race and Racial Ideologies, University of Chicago, October 7.

Steward, Theophilus Bolden. 1903. Review of *The Souls of Black Folks: Essay and Sketches,* by W. E. B. Du Bois. *American Journal of Sociology* 9:136–37.

Stewart, James B. 1984. "The Legacy of W. E. B. Du Bois for Contemporary Black Studies." *Journal of Negro Education* 53 (3): 296–311.

Stocking, George W., Jr. 1966. "Franz Boas and the Culture Concept in Historical Perspective." *American Anthropologist* 68 (4): 867–82.

Stonequist, Everett V. 1935. "The Problem of the Marginal Man." *American Journal of Sociology* 41 (1): 1–12.

———. 1937. *The Marginal Man: A Study in Personality and Culture Conflict.* New York: Charles Scribner's and Sons.

Strickland, William. 2011. "W. E. B. Du Bois: The Prime Minister of the State We Never Had." In *Black Politics in a Time of Transition,* edited by Michael Mitchell and David Covin, 91–102. New Brunswick, NJ: Transaction.

Sudarkasa, Niara. 2007. "Interpreting the African Heritage in African American Family Organization." In *Black Families,* 4th ed., edited by Harriette Pipes McAdoo, 29–47. Thousand Oaks, CA: Sage Publications.

Sugrue, Thomas J. 2010. *Sweet Land of Liberty: The Forgotten Struggle for Civil Rights in the North.* New York: Random House.

Sullivan, Teresa. 1982. "Introductory Sociology through Literature." *Teaching Sociology* 10 (1): 109–16.

Sumner, William Graham. 1906. *Folkways.* New York: Dover.

Sundquist, Eric J. 1996. *The Oxford W. E. B. Du Bois Reader.* New York: Oxford University Press.

Tarde, Gabriel. 1903. *The Laws of Imitation.* New York: Henry Holt.

Taylor, Howard. 1973. "Playing the Dozens with Path Analysis: Methodological Pitfalls in Jencks et al., *Inequality.*" *Sociology of Education* 46 (4): 433–50.

Thom, William Taylor. 1901a. "The Negroes of Litwalton, Virginia: A Social Study of the 'Oyster Negro.'" *Bulletin of the Department of Labor* 37 (November): 1115–70.

———. 1901b. "The Negroes of Sandy Spring, Maryland: A Social Study." *Bulletin of the Department of Labor* 32 (January): 43–102.

———. 1902. "The True Reformers." *Bulletin of the Department of Labor* 41 (July): 807–14.

Thomas, W.I. 1912. "Race Psychology: Standpoint and *Questionnaire,* with Particular Reference to the Immigrant and the Negro." *American Journal of Sociology* 17 (May): 725–75.

Thomas, W.I., and Dorothy Thomas. 1928. *The Child in America: Behavior Problems and Programs.* New York: Knopf.

Thomas, W.I., and Florian Znaniecki. 1918–20. *The Polish Peasant in Europe and America.* Boston: Gorham Press.

Tolman, Frank, L. 1902. "The Study of Sociology in Institutions of Learning in the United States." *American Journal of Sociology* 8 (1): 251–72.

Treitler, Bashi Vilna. 2013. *The Ethnic Project: Transforming Racial Fiction into Ethnic Factions.* Stanford, CA: Stanford University Press.

Tribe, Keith. 1989. "Prussian Agriculture-German Politics: Max Weber 1892–97." In *Reading Weber,* 85–120. London: Routledge.

Turner, Stephen P., and Jonathan H. Turner. 1990. *The Impossible Science: An Institutional Analysis of American Sociology.* Beverly Hills, CA: Sage Publications.

Wallace, Robert. 1989. "The Institutionalization of a New Discipline: The Case of Sociology at Columbia University, 1891–1931." PhD diss., Columbia University.

Ward, Lester. 1906. "Address of the President of the American Sociological Society." Presented at the annual meeting of the American Sociological Society, Providence, RI, December.

Warner, W. Lloyd. 1936. "American Caste and Class." *American Journal of Sociology* 42 (2): 234–37.

Warren, Nagueyalti. 2011. *Grandfather of Black Studies: W.E.B. Du Bois.* Trenton, NJ: Africa World Press.

Washington, Booker T. [1895] 1974. "Atlanta Compromise Speech." In *The Booker T. Washington Papers,* vol. 3, *1889–95,* edited by Louis R. Harlan and Raymond W. Smock, 583–87. Urbana: University of Illinois Press.

———. 1901a. "The Negro in Business." *Gunton's Magazine* 20:215–17.

———. 1901b. *Up from Slavery.* Garden City, NY: Doubleday.

———. 1902. Address, "The Negro Artisan." In *The Negro Artisan: Report of a Social Study Made under the Direction of Atlanta University; Together with the Proceedings of the Seventh Conference for the Study of the Negro Problems, Held at Atlanta University, on May 27th, 1902,* edited by W.E.B. Du Bois, Atlanta University Publications 7. Atlanta, GA: Atlanta University Press.

———. [1904] 1977. "Statement before the Washington Conference on the Race Problem in the United States." In *The Booker T. Washington Papers,* vol. 7, *1903–4,* edited by Louis R. Harlan and Raymond W. Smock, 340–42. Urbana: University of Illinois Press.

———. 1907. "The Economic Development of the Negro Race since Its Emancipation." In *The Negro in the South: His Economic Progress in Relation to His Moral and Religious Development,* by Booker T. Washington and W.E.B. Du Bois. Philadelphia: George W. Jacobs.

———. 1911. *My Larger Education.* Garden City: NY, Doubleday, Page.

———. 1974. *The Booker T. Washington Papers.* Vol. 3. *1889–95.* Edited by Louis R. Harlan and Raymond W. Smock. Urbana: University of Illinois Press.

———. 1979. *The Booker T. Washington Papers*. Vol. 8. *1904–6*. Edited by Louis R. Harlan and Raymond W. Smock. Urbana: University of Illinois Press.

———. 1980. *The Booker T. Washington Papers*. Vol. 9. *1906–8*. Edited by Louis R. Harlan and Raymond W. Smock. Urbana: University of Illinois Press.

———. 1981. *The Booker T. Washington Papers*. Vol. 10. *1909–11*. Edited by Louis R. Harlan and Raymond W. Smock. Urbana: University of Illinois Press.

———. 1982. *The Booker T. Washington Papers*. Vol. 12. *1912–14*. Edited by Louis R. Harlan and Raymond W. Smock. Urbana: University of Illinois Press.

Watkins, William H. 1996. "Jones, Thomas Jesse." In *Encyclopedia of African American Education*, edited by Faustine Jones-Williams et al. Westport, CT: Greenwood Press.

Watts, Jerry, G. 2006. "The Souls of Black Folk and Afro-American Intellectual Life." In *The Souls of W. E. B. Du Bois*, edited by Alford A. Young Jr., Jerry G. Watts, Manning Marable, Charles Lemert, Elizabeth Higginbotham, and Jerry C. Watts. Boulder, CO: Paradigm.

Weber, Max. [1910] 1973. "Max Weber, Dr. Alfred Ploetz and W. E. B. Du Bois (Max Weber on Race and Society II)." Panel discussion. Translated by Benjamin Nelson and Jerome Gittleman. *Sociological Analysis* 34 (4): 308–12.

———. [1922] 1978. *Economy and Society*. Edited by Guenther Roth and Claus Wittich, eds. Berkeley: University of California Press.

———. 1958. *The Protestant Ethic and the Spirit of Capitalism*. Translated by Talcott Parsons. New York: Charles Scribner's Sons.

———. 1971. "Max Weber on Race and Society." Translated by Jerome Gittleman. *Social Research* 38 (1): 30–41.

———. 1989. "Developmental Tendencies in the Situation of East Elbian Rural Laborers." Translated by Keith Tribe. In *Reading Weber*, 158–87. London: Routledge.

White, Harrison C. 1993. *Careers and Creativity: Social Forces in the Arts*. Boulder, CO: Westview Press.

Williams, Vernon J., Jr. 2006. *The Social Sciences and Theories of Races*. Urbana: University of Chicago Press.

Wilson, Francille Rusan. 2006. *The Segregated Scholars: Black Social Scientists and the Creation of Black Labor Studies, 1890–1950*. Charlottesville: University of Virginia Press.

Woodson, Carter G. 1933. *The Mis-Education of the Negro*. Washington, DC: Associated Publishers.

———. 1936. *The African Background Outlined*. New York: Negro Universities Press.

Work, Monroe Nathan. 1900. "Crime among Negroes of Chicago: A Social Study." *American Journal of Sociology* 6 (2): 204–23.

Wortham, Robert A. 2009. *W. E. B. Du Bois and the Sociological Imagination: A Reader, 1897–1914*. Waco, TX: Baylor University Press.

Wright, Earl, II. 2000. "Atlanta University and American Sociology, 1896–1917: An Earnest Desire for the Truth Despite Its Possible Unpleasantness." PhD diss., University of Nebraska, Lincoln.

———. 2002a. "The Atlanta Sociological Laboratory, 1896–1924: A Historical Account of the First American School of Sociology." *Western Journal of Black Studies* 26 (3): 165–74.

———. 2002b. "Using The Master's Tools: Atlanta University and American Sociology, 1896–1924." *Sociological Spectrum* 22 (1): 15–39.

———. 2002c. "Why Black People Tend to Shout! An Earnest Attempt to Explain the Sociological Negation of the Atlanta Sociological Laboratory Despite Its Possible Unpleasantness." *Sociological Spectrum* 22 (3): 325–61.

———. 2006. "W.E.B. Du Bois and the Atlanta University Studies on the Negro, Revisited." *Journal of African American Studies* 9 (4): 3–17.

———. 2008. "Deferred Legacy! The Continued Marginalization of the Atlanta Sociological Laboratory." *Sociology Compass* 2 (1).

———. 2009. "Beyond W.E.B. Du Bois: A Note on Some of the Lesser Known Members of the Atlanta Sociological Laboratory." *Sociological Spectrum* 29 (6): 700–717.

———. 2010. "The Tradition of Sociology at Fisk University." *Journal of African American Studies* 14 (1): 44–60.

Wright, Richard R., Jr. 1903. "The Negroes of Xenia, Ohio: A Social Study." *Bulletin of the US Bureau of Labor*, no. 48 (September): 1006–44.

———. [1912] 1969. *The Negro in Pennsylvania: A Study in Economic History*. New York: Arno Press.

———. 1965. *87 Years behind the Black Curtain*. Philadelphia: Rare Book Company.

Yancy, Dorothy C. 1978. "William Edward Burghardt Du Bois' Atlanta Years: The Human Side—Study Based upon Oral Sources." *Journal of Negro History* 63:59–67.

Young, Alford A., Jr., Manning Marable, Elizabeth Higginbotham, Charles Lemert, and Jerry G. Watts. 2006. *The Souls of W.E.B. Du Bois*. Boulder, CO: Paradigm.

Young, Cristobal. 2009. "The Emergence of Sociology from Political Economy in the United States: 1890 to 1940." *Journal of the History of the Behavioral Sciences* 45 (2): 91–116.

Zimmerman, Andrew. 2006. "Decolonizing Weber." *Postcolonial Studies* 9 (1): 53–79.

Zuckerman, Phil, ed. 2004. *The Social Theory of W.E.B. Du Bois*. Thousand Oaks, CA: Pine Forge Press.

Zumwalt, Rosemary, L., and William S. Willis. 2008. *Franz Boas and W.E.B. Du Bois at Atlanta University, 1906*. Philadelphia: American Philosophical Society.

Illustration Credits

Du Bois at his Harvard graduation, 1890: Special Collections and University Archives, W. E. B. Du Bois Library, University of Massachusetts, Amherst.

Du Bois as a graduate student at the University of Berlin, 1894: Special Collections and University Archives, W. E. B. Du Bois Library, University of Massachusetts, Amherst.

Du Bois at Atlanta University, 1909: Special Collections and University Archives, W. E. B. Du Bois Library, University of Massachusetts, Amherst.

Robert E. Park: University of Chicago Library, Special Collections Research Center.

Richard R. Wright Sr. and Richard R. Wright Jr.: Special Collections and University Archives, W. E. B. Du Bois Library, University of Massachusetts, Amherst.

Monroe Work: Tuskegee University Archives, Tuskegee, Alabama.

Richard R. Wright Jr.: Special Collections and University Archives, W. E. B. Du Bois Library, University of Massachusetts, Amherst.

George Edmund Haynes: Photo courtesy of Bruce D. Haynes, grandson.

John Hope: Special Collections and University Archives, W. E. B. Du Bois Library, University of Massachusetts, Amherst.

Mary White Ovington: Special Collections and University Archives, W. E. B. Du Bois Library, University of Massachusetts, Amherst.

Jane Addams: Photographed by Fred Hollyer, ca. 1883–96. Jane Addams Hull-House Photographic Collection, University of Illinois at Chicago Library, Special Collections.

Max Weber: Special Collections and University Archives, W. E. B. Du Bois Library, University of Massachusetts, Amherst.

Board of directors of the *Encyclopedia of the Negro*, 1936: Special Collections and University Archives, W. E. B. Du Bois Library, University of Massachusetts, Amherst.

Index